Desire and Fictional Narrative in Late Imperial China

Harvard East Asian Monographs 202

Desire and Fictional Narrative in Late Imperial China

Martin W. Huang

Published by the Harvard University Asia Center
and distributed by Harvard University Press
Cambridge (Massachusetts) and London 2001

Printed in the United States of America

The Harvard University Asia Center publishes a monograph series and, in coordination with the Fairbank Center for East Asian Research, the Korea Institute, the Reischauer Institute of Japanese Studies, and other faculties and institutes, administers research projects designed to further scholarly understanding of China, Japan, Vietnam, Korea, and other Asian countries. The Center also sponsors projects addressing multidisciplinary and regional issues in Asia.

Library of Congress Cataloging-in-Publication Data

Huang, Martin W., 1960–

Desire and fictional narrative in late imperial China / Martin W. Huang.

p. cm. – (Harvard East Asian monographs ; 202)

Includes bibliographical references and index.

ISBN 0-674-00513-9 (alk. paper)

1. Chinese fiction--Ming dynasty, 1368–1644--History and criticism. 2. Chinese fiction--Qing dynasty, 1644–1912--History and criticism. 3. Sex in literature. I. Series.

PL2437.H828 2001

895.1'3093538--dc21

2001016785

Index by the author

♾ Printed on acid-free paper

Last figure below indicates year of this printing

11 10 09 08 07 06 05 04 03 02 01

To Yang Yi and Yiqin

Acknowledgments

The research for this project started during a one-year sabbatical leave (1994–95) made possible by a University of California President Fellowship in Humanities. The research was also aided by a summer research stipend from the National Endowment of Humanities that I was awarded during 1995. The Research and Travel Committee and the Council on Collaborative Research in the School of Humanities and the Committee on Research at University of California, Irvine, have also provided crucial support to my research in the form of various grants.

Many individuals have helped me at the different stages of the research and writing of this book. They include Guan Daoxiong, Patrick Hanan, Huang Ziming, David Rolston, Charles Stone, Sun Xun, Richard Wang (Wang Gang), and Xia Xianchun. I have benefited from many interesting conversations with Michael Fuller, my colleague at University of California, Irvine, and his comments on the manuscript. His computer expertise has made my computers much friendlier to me. Robert Hegel, teacher and friend, was the first reader of the entire manuscript, while he had patiently read the drafts of several chapters more than once as this project evolved through different earlier stages. His encouragement and guidance are deeply appreciated.

I am indebted to several individuals at different libraries for their assistance in giving me access to various research materials: William Wong, the East Asian librarian, and the interlibrary-loan staff at the Main Library,

University of California, Irvine; Wu Ge, the Curator of the Rare Book Collection at Fudan University; and Shen Jin, the Curator of the Rare Book Collection at the Harvard-Yenching Library.

I am grateful to the two anonymous readers for the Harvard Asia Center Publications for their careful reading. Their comments have compelled me to rethink and clarify several important issues. My thanks also go to John Ziemer, my editor, for his interest in my work, his critical insights, and his careful editing, which have improved this book in a variety of ways. Needless to say, I am solely responsible for all the errors and inaccuracies that remain.

I wish to thank Yang Yi for her encouragement and support and our daughter, Yiqin, for the joy she has brought into our lives and for all the necessary distractions. To them this book is affectionately dedicated.

Portions of Chapters 2 and 6 have previously appeared in the form of journal articles, "Karmic Retribution and the Didactic Dilemma in the *Xingshi yinyuan zhuan*," *Chinese Studies* (*Hanxue yanjiu*), 15, no. 1 (1997), and "Sentiments of Desire: Thoughts on the Cult of *Qing* in Ming-Qing Literature," *Chinese Literature: Essays, Articles, Reviews* 20 (1998). I am grateful to the editors of the two journals for permission to incorporate parts of the articles into this book.

M.W.H.

Contents

Note on Romanization

For the sake of consistency, throughout this study the romanizations of Chinese names or terms given in the Wade-Giles system in quoted translations have been converted to *pinyin*.

Desire and Fictional Narrative in Late Imperial China

Introduction

Any attempt to discuss in English how "desire" is conceived in Chinese culture faces the inescapable dilemma of dealing with all the baggage (classic, modern, and postmodern) associated with this loaded English term. In contemporary Western discourses, the question "What constitutes desire?" has as many answers as there are serious attempts to answer this question. "Desire," Judith Butler warns us in typical postmodern fashion, "will be that which guarantees a certain opacity in language, an opacity that language can enact and display, but without which it cannot operate."[1] If she is right, then the "opacity" will only get thicker when we try to appropriate this concept to interpret a culture such as that of pre-twentieth-century China.

Michel Foucault has argued that in the West desire became a preoccupation of discourse only in modern times.[2] In ancient Greece, desire appeared as Eros in Plato, but it was reduced in importance by later philosophers. As a focus of serious philosophical speculation, the term did not resurface until Immanuel Kant made it central to his *Critique of Practical Reason*, where it was treated mainly as a psychic motive within the moral sphere. Hegel was probably the first thinker to emphasize the power of the "negative" and the significance of "absence" in the concept of desire, and his views would

1. Butler, "Desire" p. 369.

2. Ibid.; and Foucault, *History of Sexuality*, 1: 20, 23–25. Foucault more often uses the word "sex," although sex and desire are almost interchangeable concepts here in his writing.

influence many later theories of desire.[3] Because of the influence of Freudian psychoanalytic theory, desire became an extremely popular term in the twentieth-century West. The contemporary French theoretician Jacques Lacan has tried, however, to rehabilitate desire by emptying it of much of its biological and institutional content. For Lacan, desire "appears in the rift which separates need and demand; it cannot be reduced to need, since, by definition, it is not a relation to a real object independent of the subject but a relation to phantasy."[4] In literary studies, desire "has been employed primarily in correlation with the Hegelian notion of representation. . . . Representation signifies the absence of the object," and desire "constitutes a continuous, driving force which can never attain its (phantasized) object."[5] Despite the controversies surrounding desire, this emphasis on absence and representation seems to be shared by almost all the major contemporary theories of desire in the West.[6]

Despite all the baggage, there are distinct advantages associated with the use of the English term "desire" as a central concept in this study, since one of my goals is to provide different perspectives for examining issues that were the subject of frequent debate in late imperial China. Indigenous concepts such as *yu* 欲 and *qing* 情 were never any more transparent in late imperial China than desire has been in the West, and throughout Chinese history people seemed never to have tired of redefining or reinterpreting them. Although these terms were never clearly defined, everyone in late imperial China appears to have had a sense of what these terms meant in daily discourse, just as everyone in the West seems to know what "desire" is despite all the scholarly disputes over its meaning. Furthermore, in discussions of the implications of desire in works such as the late Ming (1368–1644) drama *Mudan ting* 牡丹亭 (The peony pavilion) and the eighteenth-century

3. For a study of this Hegelian influence on French theories of desire, see Butler, *Subjects of Desire*. See, e.g., Butler's reading of Sartre (ibid., p. 117): "Desire does not attend to what is given in perception, but, rather what is hidden in perception; it is, in a sense, an investigation into the significant dimension of absence. It thematizes absence and thereby makes it present to itself." She further observes (p. 147) that for Sartre "desire must subject the body to the imaginary; it must create anew its object and itself in order to be satisfied."

4. Laplanche and Pontalis, *The Language of Psycho-analysis*, p. 483.

5. Oxenhandler, "The Changing Concept of Literary Emotions," p. 115. My brief account of the "history" of desire in the West is much indebted to this essay.

6. For a discussion of some major postmodern theories of desire in the West, see Fuery, *Theories of Desire*.

novel *Honglou meng* 紅樓夢 ("The dream of the red chamber" or "The story of the stone"), the emphasis on "absence" and "negativity" in contemporary Western theories might not be entirely irrelevant. Even so, I stress that I employ "desire" as a central term in this study with full awareness of its provisionality. However, it is my hope that its deployment through negotiations with several related indigenous concepts in this study will yield new insights into the cultural and historical specificity of various issues associated with desire in late imperial China.

The interest in desire was relatively more consistent in traditional China than it was in the West. Xunzi 荀子 (ca. 312–230 B.C.) was perhaps the first important thinker to offer a detailed discussion of desire and treated it as a concept central to his elaborate theory of ritual. One historian of Chinese thought has argued that "the notion of desire is at the heart of most Chinese thought."[7] The status of desire became more complicated during the late Ming (approximately from the late sixteenth century to the mid-seventeenth century) when more diverse and often more radical views of desire were being proposed. As was generally true of philosophical discourses in pre-twentieth-century China, the late Ming debates on desire were almost always framed in ethical terms. During the same period, literature, especially drama and prose fiction, was becoming increasingly preoccupied with desire, but its explorations certainly went well beyond the ethical implications of the phenomenon.

A main argument of this study is that the development of traditional Chinese fiction as a narrative genre was closely related to the changing views of desire in late imperial China. Specifically, the rise of vernacular fiction during the late Ming has to be studied in the contexts of the contemporary debates on desire in the cultural and intellectual arenas and of the new and more complex views that emerged from these debates. I will attempt to show that the obsession with individual desire is an essential quality that defines traditional Chinese fiction as a narrative genre. In fact, the maturing of this genre can best be appreciated in terms of the sophistication with which the phenomenon of desire is explored in many works of vernacular fiction.

The first part of the study (Chapters 1–3) is designed to provide a broad historical context for the readings of specific fictional texts in the rest of the study. The second part (Chapters 4–6) focuses on those works in which the

7. Lau, "The Doctrine of Kuei Sheng," p. 59.

issue of physical aspects of desire (*yu* defined in a narrower sense) receives more attention. The third part (Chapters 7–10) deals with texts that tend to explore the complex phenomenon known as *qing* (usually understood in a narrow sense as romantic sentiments) and its subtle relationship to various forms of physical desires. I try to demonstrate in this part how the dichotomy between *qing* and *yu*, which served as the basic framing rationale for most debates on desire in traditional literature, was being rethought and how the problem of desire was being formulated on a new level of sophistication in these fictional texts of late imperial China.

This study is not meant to be a historical survey of representative views of desire or the fictional representation of such views in late imperial China. Rather, it is a series of readings of specific *xiaoshuo* 小說 (fictional) texts produced in late imperial China that seem to have been shaped by a profound concern with the complicated ramifications of desire. One issue I seek to explore is how *xiaoshuo* fashions particular views of desire and how it writes or rewrites various "boundaries," which are crossed or simply ignored in the busy traffic of desires. Most of the works examined in detail in this study can roughly be characterized as "domestic novels," and the focus of my discussions is sexual desire (broadly defined), although other kinds of desire are also explored. This explains in part why some important works such as the eighteenth-century *Rulin waishi* 儒林外史 (The scholars) are not analyzed in detail in this study, despite the fact that desires, especially those associated with worldly fame and career successes, are the main topics in *Rulin waishi*. Another important issue not explored in depth in this study is the question of the possible "solutions" (religious or otherwise) to desire proposed in some fictional works. My hesitation in tackling this important topic is due in part to the simple fact that I have not done enough research on this question and in part to the conviction that this topic is complicated and important enough to merit a separate study.[8]

8. Both Wai-yee Li in *Enchantment and Disenchantment* and Anthony Yu in *Rereading the Stone* have touched on this topic. For other discussions of this issue, see Li Qiancheng, "Fictions of Enlightenment"; and Xiao Chi, *The Chinese Garden as a Lyrical Enclave*.

CHAPTER ONE
Desire, Anxiety, and Ambivalence During the Late Ming

In the thirty-third year of the Wanli 萬歷 reign period (1605), the sixty-three-*sui*-old writer Tu Long 屠龍 (1543–1605) fell seriously ill. A friend, the famous dramatist Tang Xianzu 湯顯祖 (1550–1616), wrote him a set of ten poems under the lengthy title: "Changqing [Tu Long] has been suffering from the 'sores of love' (*qingji zhiyang* 情寄之瘍), which have caused infections over his body; the pain forces him to cry aloud; it becomes easier to endure, however, whenever he asks his family to recite the name of Bodhisattva Guanshiyin [Avalokiteśvara]. I have playfully composed these poems and am sending them to him." A couplet in one of the poems reads: "What are the causes for this strange disease? / You should regret having allowed your heart to float in clouds and rain" (雌風病骨因何起，懺悔心隨雲雨飛).[1] According to Tang Xianzu, Tu Long's illness, which probably led to his death soon afterward, was a result of his promiscuous life-style. Based on various accounts of Tu Long's lifelong pursuit of sensual pleasures, some modern scholars believe that the "sores of love" were a kind of venereal disease.[2] What is of interest here, however, is not that Tu Long probably died

1. Tang Xianzu, *Shiwenji*, *juan* 15, pp. 601–2. "Float in clouds and rain" is a euphemism for overindulgence in sex.

2. Xu Shuofang, "Tu Long nianpu," pp. 392–93; for accounts of Tu Long's life of sensuality, see Zheng Run, *"Jin Ping Mei" he Tu Long*, pp. 160–65.

of this disease but that Tang Xianzu wrote about his friend's promiscuity and its consequences in such a playful way. Although Tang insisted on Tu Long's responsibility for his own sufferings, the frolicsome tone of these poems compels the reader not to take this insistence too seriously.

Li Kaixian 李開先 (1502–68), a writer of an earlier generation, must have been bothered by the same disease. In a biography of his deceased wife, Li mentioned as a proof of her wifely virtue the fact that she did not complain after she contracted a skin disease (*jiedu* 疥毒) from him. Li apparently felt no need to shy away from the fact that he himself had got this disease from sleeping with a prostitute.[3] Perhaps suffering from venereal disease was not considered such a shameful thing among the "romantic" literati of that time. Otherwise, Tang Xianzu would not have mocked Tu Long's illness so openly, especially since the two were good friends.[4] After all, the term *lin* 淋, or syphilis, was common enough to have become a cussword, uttered, for example, by a character in Tang Xianzu's famous play *The Peony Pavilion*.[5]

Some scholars have cited these poems by Tang Xianzu as evidence of a more "relaxed" attitude toward desire during the late Ming, attitudes believed to have contributed to the particular cultural milieu that helped to produce literary works such as the classic novel *Jin Ping Mei* 金瓶梅 ("The plum in the golden vase" or "The golden lotus"), which is known for its explicit descriptions of sex.[6] All this has been considered part of what some scholars have called the "revalorization of desire" during the late Ming.[7]

One argument of this study is that the late Ming revalorization of desire was much more than an attempt to assert the priority of desire during an age known for its cultural pluralism. It is probably true that never before in Chinese history were people so openly fascinated with desire and so eager to experience it in different forms and so anxious to discuss these experiences. And yet it is even truer that never before were people so acutely aware of the

3. Li Kaixian, "Wangqi Zhang yiren sanzhuan" 亡妻張宜人散傳, in idem, *Xianju ji* 閒居集, reprinted in *Li Kaixian ji*, *juan* 9, p. 551.

4. Elsewhere, Tang Xianzu even expressed his admiration for Tu's romantic life-style; see his poem "Huai Tai Siming xiansheng bingwen Tu Changqing" 懷戴四明先生並問屠長卿, in Tang Xianzu, *Shiwen ji*, *juan* 7, pp. 202–3.

5. Scene no. 7, "Guishu" 閨塾, in Tang Xianzu, *Mudan ting*, p. 34.

6. See, e.g., Liu Hui and Yang Yang, *"Jin Ping Mei" zhi mi*, pp. 220–22.

7. Plaks, *The Four Masterworks of the Ming Novel*, p. 20.

complex implications of desire. The so-called late Ming liberation of desire,[8] if there was indeed such a liberation, was almost always accompanied by a profound anxiety over the different ramifications of desire. Desire as a human phenomenon probably had never appeared to be so complex as well as so perplexing as it did to the people of the late Ming precisely because they were so eager to experience it and so anxious to talk about their experiences. In this regard, Tu Long is representative.

Tu Long was preoccupied with the pursuit of sensual pleasures, but he was also prone to agonize over the consequences of such pursuits. He was one of those who explicitly asserted that people had sex for the sake of pleasure rather than procreation, a simple fact few orthodox Confucian thinkers were ready to acknowledge openly:

> You may ask: "Why is it so hard to eradicate the desire between man and woman (*nannü zhiyu* 男女之慾)?"
>
> My answer is that according to Taoism, the reason why parents give birth to a child is due to this [desire]. This is why this root is so difficult to eradicate. Those in ancient India claimed they were without desire by emphasizing the emptiness of everything. Although God rules, there is still the realm of desire. Those as high as immortals will come down to the world of sentient beings whenever they are struck by longing, while those ancient emperors kept so many women as their wives. The Confucian scholars claim that they do it for the purpose of having many descendants rather than that of gratifying their sexual desire. This is only an excuse invented to maintain moral order and avoid debauchery, given the fact that sexual desire was something that could not be eradicated. . . . Confucius said, "I haven't seen anyone who likes virtue as much as he likes pretty women." These are indeed bitter words of sadness. It is extremely difficult to go deep to where the roots are for eradication. Even a sage could not stay away from desire (*liyu* 離慾). What he could do is to merely alleviate it. Staying away from desire is something only the Buddha is capable of, whereas the sage is capable only of reducing his desires; a wise man is able to keep his desires at minimum, but an ordinary man indulges his desires.[9]

According to Tu Long, the claim that people have sex solely for procreation is in most cases a "prescriptive" statement of moral ideals rather than a "descriptive" statement of facts. Confucius' famous remark on virtue and sexual attraction is reinterpreted here to underscore the fact that there are

8. This is a view shared by many scholars in Mainland China. See, e.g., Chen Dongyou, *Reyu de jiefang*.

9. Tu Long, "Yu Li Guancha" 與李觀察, *Baiyu ji*, 9.31a–b (pp. 511–12).

far more people attracted to sex for pleasure than those attracted to virtue for the sake of morality. Of course, Tu Long himself was notorious for indulging in various sensual pleasures. In fact, his "liberal" views on sex as well as his own uninhibited behavior contributed directly to the abrupt end of his otherwise promising official career. In 1583 Tu was accused of sexual misconduct and was impeached just a year after he had been promoted to the position of secretary in the Ministry of Rites in Beijing.[10]

Tu Long's views on sexual desire were shared by many of his contemporaries, including the famous writer Yuan Hongdao 袁宏道 (1568–1610). Yuan Hongdao expressed a similar disbelief that there had ever been a man who was not attracted to pretty women (or sex), and he insisted that if this had been the case Confucius would not have made the comparison between one's love for virtue and one's attraction to pretty women.[11] In fact, Yuan Hongdao's observations on what he called "five true happinesses" (*zhenle* 眞樂) have often been quoted by historians as an example of the typical late Ming hedonism:

One should experience all colors with one's eyes, all sounds with one's ears, all delicacies with one's body, and interesting conversations with one's mouth. This is the first happiness. In front of the hall, there are cauldrons; in the back, music. The hall is full of guests, men and women mingling with the smell of candles, with jewelry scattered everywhere. When the money has run out, one should sell off lands to continue this gathering. This is the second happiness. The bookcases are filled with tens of thousands of books, all of which are rare editions. In the studio next to the house gather a dozen good friends, among whom stands a man of great insight like Sima Qian 司馬遷 [b. 145 B.C.], Luo Guanzhong 羅貫中 [ca. 1300–1400] or Guan Hanqing 關漢卿 [d. 1279] acting as a leader. They will be divided into several groups to write books criticizing the pedantic Confucian scholars of the Tang and Song dynasties or finish a great work of the present era. This is the third happiness. Spend a thousand taels of gold to purchase a boat. In the boat, there will be a music band, several prostitutes and concubines, and some idlers. Living in such a floating

10. See Goodrich and Fang, *Dictionary of Ming Biographies*, p. 1325; and Xu Shuofang, "Tu Long nianpu," pp. 341–48; According to Shen Defu 沈德符 (1578–1642), Tu Long's later *chuanqi* play *Tanhua ji* 曇花記 is an apology for this incident; see Shen Defu, *Wanli yehuo bian*, *juan* 25, "Ciqu" 詞曲, pp. 644–45. Another famous Ming literati dramatist Zang Maoxun 臧懋循 (1550–1620) also lost his prestigious job as professor in the imperial academy in Nanjing thanks to his romantic involvement with another young man; see Shen Defu, *Wanli yehuo bian*, *juan* 26, "Chibi" 嗤鄙, p. 676.

11. Yuan Hongdao, "Lanting ji" 蘭亭記, *Ji*, *juan* 10, p. 444.

house, one won't realize that one is getting old. This is the fourth happiness. Enjoying life in such a fashion, one is likely to exhaust one's fortunes within less than ten years. Although living from hand to mouth and disgraced, one can beg for food in the pleasure quarters and share food with the lonely and the old. Seeking help among relatives, one does not need to feel ashamed. This is the fifth happiness. If a literatus is able to enjoy only one of the five happinesses mentioned above, he should have no regrets when alive, and his name will endure after death.[12]

The first and most important happiness listed here is sensual pleasure. Elsewhere, Yuan Hongdao went so far as to claim that one should feel ashamed, if, by the age of thirty, one was still unable to enjoy material comforts and sensual pleasures.[13] The audacity with which Yuan Hongdao asserted the right of an individual to do almost whatever he liked to fulfill his own desires in disregard of social conventions and his emphasis on sensual enjoyment are indeed indicative of an unprecedented hedonistic attitude toward desire.

However, by the late sixteenth century, the pursuit of "true happiness" had reached such a feverish scale that it became almost a fashion among some high-minded literati to complain that their contemporaries were being overwhelmed by "the overflow of human desires" (*renyu hengliu* 人欲橫流) and that the pursuit of material pleasures had corrupted social morality.[14] These complaints were more than routine moralizing by puritanical orthodox Confucians. They pointed to a widespread anxiety as well as a deep sense of loss of control, an important aspect of the implications of desire as it was being experienced during the late Ming.

What is perhaps even more interesting here is the seemingly paradoxical fact that those most enthusiastic and articulate in promoting the cause of desire were often the same people who were most conscious of, as well as vocal about, the fear of the inevitable perils of desire. For example, Yuan Hong-

12. Yuan Hong dao, "Gong Weichang xiansheng" 龔惟長先生, *Ji*, *juan* 5, pp. 205–6. Translation (modified) from Chou, *Yüan Hung-tao and the Kung-an School*, pp. 98–99.

13. Yuan Hongdao, "Mao Taichu" 毛太初, *Ji*, *juan* 5, p. 209.

14. See, e.g., Zhang Han's 張瀚 (1511–93) often-quoted complaint that "people's behaviors have turned increasingly dissolute while waste and extravagance are becoming the norm in society" (Zhang Han, "Fengsu ji" 風俗記, *Songchuang mengyu*, p. 123). See also Fan Lian (b. 1540), *Yunjian jumu chao* 雲間據目抄, 2.8, reprinted in *Biji xiaoshuo daquan*, vol. 13, p. 114; and Gu Qiyuan (1565–1628), "Jianye fengsu ji" 建業風俗記, *Kezuo zhuiyu*, 5.30b–32a. For a discussion of the anxiety caused by "overconsumption" during the late Ming, see Clunas, *Superfluous Things*, pp. 141–65.

dao, despite his openly hedonistic views, constantly voiced regret over his own obsession with sex (*qing'e zhi pi* 青娥之癖) and tried hard, but apparently failed repeatedly, to distance himself from the temptations of sensual pleasures (*li shengse zhi le* 離聲色之樂).[15] Nor was it unusual that Yuan Hongdao, at an older age, began to regret his earlier behavior.[16] However, what merits special attention is that despite his constant regrets and full awareness of the dangers of sensual pleasures, he never succeeded in becoming less vulnerable to the temptations of such pleasures. His love for the art of the bedchamber (*fangzhong shu* 房中術) remained unchanged during his later years (he died at the relatively young age of 42). In a poem written when he was thirty-eight, Yuan Hongdao expressed his envy that a friend was still able to have a son by a young woman when he was over seventy; he suspected that this must have been due to that friend's mastering of the secrets of the art of the bedchamber.[17] In fact, some of his contemporaries believed that Yuan Hongdao died an early death largely as a result of his overindulgence in sensual pleasures.[18] This simultaneous obsession and apprehension were important aspects of the late Ming attitude toward desire.

The case of Yuan Hongdao's younger brother, Yuan Zhongdao 袁中道 (1570–1624), is even more illuminating of this paradoxical aspect of the late Ming effort to come to terms with desires. Although generally thought to be more conservative than his elder brother, Yuan Zhongdao was also quite given to sensual pleasures. He repeatedly expressed regret over his promiscuity and his failure to reform. The most revealing confession is found in his long essay "Xinlü" 心律 (The regulation of the heart/mind):

15. Yuan Hongdao, "Li Xiangzhou bianxiu" 李湘洲編修, *Ji*, *juan* 42, p. 1233.

16. Yuan Hongdao made this remark when he was thirty-two. Many, including his own younger brother, Yuan Zhongdao 袁中道, called attention to Yuan Hongdao's increasing conservatism during the last decade of his life; see Chen Wanyi, "WanMing xingling wenxue sixiang yanjiu," pp. 128–29.

17. Yuan Hongdao, "Yu Wang Baigu" 與王百穀, *Ji*, *juan* 43, pp. 1270–71.

18. The diaries of his younger brother, Yuan Zhongdao, contain references to Yuan Hongdao's almost-too-late realization that overindulgence in sex after the age of forty would lead to early death, a realization Yuan Hongdao reached only a few days prior to his own sudden but painful death. According to Yuan Zhongdao (*Youjue feilu* 遊居杮錄, *juan* 5, *Kexue zhai ji*, p. 1210; see also pp. 1207–9), his brother died of too much blood loss through urination and bowel movements (大小便血不止). Yuan Zhongdao's descriptions of Yuan Hongdao's death and of the disease he himself was suffering as a result of overindulgence (quoted below) are reminiscent of Ximen Qing's gruesome death after a series of sexual escapades in Chapter 79 of *Jin Ping Mei*.

I have never had any adulterous affairs in my life, although I could not completely shun brothels. Licensed quarters became a source of consolation when I was young and frustrated in my career. Following the examples of Bai Letian [Bai Juyi 白居易; 772–846] and Su Zichan [Su Shi 蘇軾; 1037–1101], I tried to seek emotional refuge there. Besides, I was often away from my family. I occasionally did this when I could not control my desire (*qingyu weiduan* 情慾未斷). . . . As for relationships with other men, this was something difficult to avoid. I regret that I got involved in these kinds of relationship when I traveled to those distant places. However, it is really shameful for those people in the areas of Wu, Yue, and Jiangnan to treat their male partners as spouses.

Thinking about these things now, I find them absolutely against reason and myself deserving of severe punishment. If a widow is able to endure the hardships of the single life under social pressures, why should not a man be able to control himself if he has seen through this world, if he has any hope of gaining serene joy through perseverance, and if he is constantly reminded of the punishments he is to receive for his sins? Why is it so difficult for a man to control himself if his sexual desire (*qingyu* 情慾) is still given some chance of fulfillment since he at least has concubines and maids? I am suffering from a blood disease as a result of my promiscuous life in my youth. Whenever the disease begins to strike, I have problems breathing, and my stomach aches as if there were pieces of stone inside me; I cannot sleep; I am frightened out of my wits when I find myself spitting blood, believing that I am about to die. Repentance sometimes makes me wish that I could completely reform myself. However, I gradually forget about this once the symptoms of the disease begin to recede. I soon again start to indulge myself in sexual pleasures as before (*zongqing siyi* 縱情肆意).[19]

This is a graphic and surprisingly candid confession of Yuan Zhongdao's repeated failures to control his desires and the dire consequences he had suffered. There is an overwhelming sense of despair. The image conjured up here is that of a hopeless "addict" who, although fully aware of the dangers of sex, can do nothing about this addiction. He seems to tell us that any attempt to fight an addiction to sex is doomed from the start. Yuan Zhongdao was certainly not alone among his contemporaries in venting his despair in such candid fashion. Tu Long, a more enthusiastic advocate of the cause of desire, was equally forthright in his own confession:

I have no special penchant for any particular thing under Heaven. But as for the desire between man and woman, [I certainly have it] just like an ordinary person. This

19. Yuan Zhongdao, "Xinlü," *Kexue zhai ji, juan* 22, pp. 954–55.

should keep me further away from the Way since I am already bothered by worries about fame. [Trying to rid myself of desire,] I wrote words of warning on my waist belt, swore to the gods, attempted corporeal self-punishment, and constantly scrutinized myself. I was restless all the time as if I was struggling with an almighty enemy and desperately trying to contain a poisonous dragon. All these efforts, however, have had very little effect.[20]

Elsewhere in the same letter Tu Long wrote even more vividly about his doomed attempts to control his desire:

I have been trying to rid myself of desire (*zhiyu* 治慾) for three years. [The result is like] using large numbers of troops to attack a well-defended city. Every means of attack, such as trying to climb the city wall by setting up cloud ladders or digging tunnels, has been tried but failed to bring about a victory. It is also like using a huge piece of rock to stamp down grass: once the rock runs over the grass, it will start to grow again. Or it is like using cold spring water to quench one's thirst. One feels cool when drinking it, but the heat will come back nevertheless. There is really nothing one can do about it![21]

Another late Ming writer, Song Maocheng 宋懋澄 (ca. 1569–1620), pushed this rhetoric of despair even further by asserting that, short of death, only illness could help one minimize one's desire (惟病可以寡欲). Illness, for this reason, became something one should celebrate rather than complain about. He worried only that he could not get ill more often (惟恐病不常來).[22] Here by a strange twist of logic, illness, which, as Yuan Zhongdao complained, might be a direct result of a failure to control the desires, now counted as a blessing precisely because it might reduce one's capacity to indulge in desire. One might take one step further and argue that one should indulge in desire as much as possible, since indulgence will lead to illness, which, in turn, will reduce one's capacity for further indulgence. Consequently, one does not have to worry about self-control at all since the consequence of desire is illness that limits desire. There was almost an assumption of a self-protecting mechanism in desire. The resort to such a logic for coping with desire reveals how desperate people had become.

20. Tu Long, "Yu Li guanzha," *Baiyu ji*, 9.30b–31a (pp. 510–11); for an expression of similar frustrations in another of his letters, see "Yu Wang Yuanmei xiansheng" 與王元美先生, 7.21b (p. 348) and 7.22a (p. 351).

21. Tu Long, "Yu Li guanzha," *Baiyu ji*, 9. 28b–29a (pp. 506–7).

22. Song Maocheng, "Yu Chen Er" 與陳二, *Jiuyue bijie* 九籥別集, *juan* 1, *Jiuyue ji*, p. 250.

If a frontal assault on desire proved to be futile, flanking approaches had to be sought or invented. Another desperate strategy suggested by Yuan Zhongdao in face of the almost irresistible temptation of sex was to "seek pleasures beyond this world if one is not supposed to enjoy worldly pleasures" (世樂必不可得, 因尋世外之樂).[23] Here "pleasures beyond this world" refers to the enjoyment of "mountains and rivers" (*shanshui* 山水), or nature, and "worldly pleasures" refers mainly to sensual delights such as sex. Yuan Zhongdao believed that a man's desire for women (sex) could be replaced or at least alleviated by a longing for nature (山水可以代粉黛).[24] In other words, if the pleasures of sex were too costly to enjoy (one, he believed, would eventually have to pay with one's own health), then one should instead turn to the pleasures of the natural landscape, which were supposed to be good for one's health. Yuan Zhongdao confessed:

> Alas! I have not forgotten about the sensual pleasures of this world (*shijian zhi shengse* 世間之聲色). Once I get involved in this mundane world, I cannot avoid them. Since I contracted various diseases, I have come to understand the subtle relationship between the control of temperature and the time the maturing of a silkworm will take [thus the need to nourish life or *yangsheng*]. I tried to avoid [the sensual pleasures of this world] as much as I could. But my illness did not recede. I have to fight it by turning to the "sensual pleasures" beyond this world (*shiwai zhi shengse* 世外之聲色), in the hope of a victory during this fight.[25]

He tried to turn away from pretty women and sex, we are told, not because they no longer appealed to him or he feared moral condemnation but because his own declining health and advanced age simply did not permit him further indulgence.[26] Yuan Zhongdao vehemently defended this alternative,

23. Yuan Zhongdao, "Da Qian Shouzhi" 答錢受之, *Kexue zhai ji, juan* 24, p. 1025.

24. Ibid., p. 1025. This view is certainly shared by Yuan Zhongdao's elder brother, Yuan Hongdao; cf. the latter's observation: "Those eremitic gentlemen of peaceful minds have to like nature (*shanshui huazhu* 山水花竹) if they have decided to give up seeking sensual pleasures (聲色)." (Yuan Hongdao, "*Pingshi yin*" 瓶史引, *Ji, juan* 24, p. 817).

25. Yuan Zhongdao, "Yuquan shiyi ji" 玉泉拾遺記, *Kexue zhai ji, juan* 15, pp. 656–57. Yuan Zhongdao's reference to the silkworm may be an allusion to Ji Kang's 嵇康 (223–62) "Da nan yangsheng lun" 答難養生論 (An answer to the refutation of [my essay on] nourishing life), in which Ji Kang referred to the relationship between temperature and the maturing of silkworms apparently to emphasize the importance of nourishing one's life or *yangsheng* (Ji Kang, *Ji*, pp. 179–80).

26. For this reason, Yuan Zhongdao ("Xinlü," *Kexue zhai ji, juan* 22, pp. 955–56) agreed with Yuan Hongdao that a man should not take concubines after the age of forty.

which, in the eyes of the more orthodox, might have devalued the sacred "mountains and rivers" celebrated in traditional literati culture:

> You asserted that those who turn to mountains and rivers do so only because they are trying to escape from the pleasures of sex after they have failed to get them and that they are not true men of the Way. You have really seen through these people's tricks. But I also happen to believe that they are nevertheless worth admiration if they are able to seek refuge in nature and then later become adapted [even though he makes this choice] only after the pleasure of sex and other worldly pleasures become unavailable.[27]

The tactic is to substitute one pleasure for another. Both, nevertheless, are pleasures, and both are supposed to appeal to the senses.

However, Tu Long, for one, was not persuaded that this was an effective strategy. He came to the painful conclusion that hobbies such as collecting antiques and enjoying "mountains and rivers" are desires just as dangerous as the lust for sex and money. The deluded (*hunyong zhiren* 昏庸之人) indulge in the crude lust for sex and wealth, whereas self-proclaimed recluses (*qingshi* 清士) take to poetry, mountains and rivers, books, and antiques. But both are obsessed with desire. He then went on to observe: "When standing on top of a mountain or beside a stream, one inevitably thinks about beautiful women; thinking about beautiful women inevitably leads to going to brothels; going to brothels inevitably leads to seeking sensual pleasures."[28] Indeed, in the minds of many late Ming literati the association between the appeal of the natural landscape and that of a sensuous woman was simply too obvious to suppress. For Tu Long at least, the association was simply unequivocal. At moments of self-scrutiny, he considered even the urge to write an essay or a poem a form of deeply rooted desire (*wenzi yi yu ye* 文字亦慾也) that one should get rid of for the sake of total salvation.[29] Tu Long's view of writing as a form of desire was also affirmed by the writer Zhong Xing 鍾惺 (1574–1625):

27. Yuan Zhongdao, "Da Qian Shouzhi," *Kexue zhai ji*, *juan* 24, p. 1026.

28. Tu Long, "Yu qingzhuo" 慾清濁, *Hongbao ji*, 38.6a; see also his comments on the literati passion for antiques, gardens, landscapes, and books in his essay "Xiaoyao" 消搖, ibid., 35.9a.

29. Tu Long, "Yu Wang Taichu Tianshu er daoyou" 與王太初田叔二道友, *Hongbao ji*, 40.6b.

Yuan Shigong [Yuan Hongdao] once said: "People like us could not live without writing poetry and prose." I quite agree with him. Once there was someone asking about the secret of longevity. He was told the secret was nothing but extinguishing desire (*duanyu* 斷欲). Shaking his head, he said: "If this should be the case, then what would be the benefit even if one could indeed live one thousand years?" If people like us could not write poetry and prose, what would be the fun of being alive?[30]

This helps explain a curious phenomenon in late Ming literature: the vocabulary traditionally used to describe a sensuous woman was more frequently employed to depict the appeal of a natural scene in prose and verse on nature during an age when the genre of *youji* 遊記 (travel essays) flourished. Yuan Hongdao, again, is a good example:

On the mountain there used to be a place called the Verandah of Noisy Steps. There were many pine trees growing in the valley, and those below the verandah were especially luxuriant. Whenever there was strong wind, the trees made loud noises that sounded like sea waves. I once joked to a monk: "This is the sound coming from the bracelets and earrings of a strolling beauty. You'd better excuse yourself if you have to follow the Buddhist clerical rules." Staring at me, the monk was at a loss. There were traces of the footprints left by Xishi (西施) on the rock, and I asked the servant to wipe it with his sleeves. The servant hesitated and seemed to be perturbed (*sedong* 色動). On the rock that reminded one of [this famous beauty's] pretty hair, people felt that they could still discern the green silk ribbon and yellow pins. One is bound to be intoxicated by this scene even if his heart is made of stone and iron. This is the power of female beauty (*se* 色). . . . Alas! the mountain and river in distance look like a refreshed beauty (*fendai* 粉黛).[31]

30. Zhong Xing, "Ziti shihou" 自題詩後, *Yingxiu xuan ji, juan* 35, p. 561. Zhong Xing's friend Tan Yuanchun 譚元春 (1585–1637) posed the rhetorical question whether studying to pass the civil-service examinations differed from various "vulgar forms of desire indulged in by common people" (*renshi shiyu* 人世嗜欲) even though only the former could win a good reputation (Tan Yuanchu, "*Jin Zhengxi wengao xu*" 金正希文稿序, *Ji, juan* 23, p. 630).

31. Yuan Hongdao, "Lingyan" 靈巖, *Ji, juan* 4, p. 165. For examples of Yuan Hongdao's many similar descriptions of natural landscape that emphasize sensuality or *se*, see "Shangfang" 上方, *juan* 4, p. 160; "Xihu yi" 西湖一, *juan* 10, p. 422; "Feilai feng" 飛來峰, *juan* 10, p. 428; "Manjing youji" 滿井遊記, *juan* 17, p. 681. Similar descriptions by Yuan Zhongdao can be found in *Kexue zhai ji*: see, e.g., "You Qingxi ji" 遊青溪記, *juan* 15, p. 639; and "You Luyuan shan ji" 遊鹿苑山記, *juan* 15, p. 649. Even in an essay advocating the benefits of seeking refuge in the "pleasures beyond this world," Yuan Zhongdao could not help describing the appeal of nature by comparing it to the image of beautiful women. See, e.g., "Yuquan shiyi ji," *Kexue zhai ji, juan* 15, p. 657. For a brief discussion of this tendency to sensualize nature in late Ming literature, see Xia Xianchun, *WanMing shiwen yu wenxue*, pp. 101–2.

Nature is appreciated as a sensuous woman, and it can be fully experienced only through one's senses. The implications of *se* are everywhere. The term Yuan Hongdao here chose to describe nature, which is supposed to give people "the pleasures beyond this world," is "female beauty" (*fendai*), the exact term employed by Zhongdao to refer to "worldly pleasures" (*zhijian zhile* 世間之樂), the very thing one was supposed to avoid by seeking refuge in nature. Consequently, the distinctions between these two kinds of pleasure (one in this world and the other beyond this world) became extremely problematic, and often in writings as well as in life the two worlds simply merged into one, as exemplified in a poem by Tao Wangling 陶望齡 (b. 1562; *jinshi* 1589):

> Serving as an official in a city of courtesans charmingly dressed,
> Sojourning in a village full of pretty women;
> Spending a few nights in a mountain of tender songs and sensual dance,
> Traveling a few times on the water in the company of the plainly dressed with faces heavily made up;
> Drinking wine and patronizing prostitutes are sensual pleasures outside the realm of sensuality,
> The soul is awakened with the heart dying in an unfeeling state of feelings;
> Seeking instructions from the Chan master in the temple of mandarin ducks,
> Praying for a son by rapping utensils in the pleasure quarters.[32]

> 作吏於館娃脂粉之城,爲客於浣紗娥眉之里;
> 宿幾夜嬌歌艷舞之山,走三回濃抹淡妝之水;
> 色非色界酒肆與淫坊,情無情間魂惺而心死;
> 鴛鴦寺傳法秉教禪師,歌姬院瓦罐爻槌乞子.

Here, metaphorically as well as literally, these two kinds of pleasure become one. Tao Wangling's clever oxymoron—*se fei sejia* or "sensual pleasures outside the realm of sensuality" captures this sense of the happy though awkward "union" of the two realms—*shiwai* 世外 (the realm beyond this world) and *shijian* 世間 (the realm of this world). Paradoxically, it was ultimately one's desire for sensual pleasures that helped to erase the boundaries that were supposed to separate the two realms. Nature, which was traditionally

32. Tao Wangling, "Youxi xiaolaipian jiuyan sanyan" 又戲效來篇九言三言, *Xie'an ji*, 2.5b–6a (pp. 170–71).

thought to cleanse a man of his desires, was now instead valued for its appeal to one's senses. In the end, the alternative of turning to mountains and rivers to seek freedom from one's desire turned out to be a completely ineffective solution.[33]

Of course, not everyone's liking for mountains and rivers was due to a desire for sensual pleasures or even a result of an attempt to divert himself from such pleasures. Some people may have wanted to pursue a life-style that was supposed to elevate their status in the eyes of others. It was nevertheless a form of desire, desire for fame. According to Tu Long, for the well educated, such as himself (*wubei* 吾輩), the desire for fame (*mingzhang* 名障) is a much more fatal attraction than that of carnal pleasures (a kind of *yugen* 慾根, which were supposed to be a more serious problem for the common folks or *zhongren* 衆人), although both desires are difficult to get rid of.[34]

A more radical approach had to be found. For many, religion was the answer. Conceding that it was not easy to define the boundaries of the appropriateness of a desire but very easy to lose control once in the clutches of a desire, some suggested that one would be better off by having as little desire as possible. This sense of despair is quite obvious in the works of He Liangjun 何良俊 (1506–73), a writer of an earlier generation:

> Desire [*yu*] has a special power to seduce people; once entrapped, one won't be able to get free again. How many even among those morally above the average could free themselves once they get entangled? This is why Mencius proposed that the best way to nurture one's heart/mind was to keep one's desire at minimum, and Laozi suggested that one should pursue the Way by gradually taking less and less action.[35]

33. In *Rou putuan* 肉蒲團 (Carnal prayer mat), attributed to Li Yu 李漁 (1611–80), the Buddhist monk Lone Peak 孤峰, contrary to the popular practice at that time, purposely chooses to build his temple in a rather unscenic spot because he believes that the beauty of nature will give rise to desire in man (Li Yu, *Rou putuan*, 2.147). Here the famous observation by Confucius that "the wise find joy in water; the benevolent find joy in mountains" (知者樂水，仁者樂山) becomes problematic (Liu Baonan, *Lunyu zhengyi*, p. 127; and Lau, *The Analects*, 6.23 [p. 84]).

34. Tu Long, "Yu Wang Yuanmei xiansheng," *Baiyu ji*, 7.4a (p. 351).

35. He Liangjun, "Huoni" 惑溺 in "Heshi yulin xulun" 何氏語林序論, *Ji*, 14.9a (p. 485). It is worth pointing out here that He Liangjun was another late Ming figure who sometimes led a very "free" life despite his frequent cautions (to others as well as to himself) against loose behavior. His warning here must have been a result of his own personal experiences. According to Shen Defu, He Liangjun's life was once extremely romantic. The famous official and writer Wang Shizhen 王世貞 (1526–90) once wrote a long poem on He's having his

It is partly due to this desperate sense of "no return" that many began to accept the radical theories of "no-desire" elaborated in Taoism and Buddhism. Yuan Hongdao, Yuan Zhongdao, and Tu Long were all involved in the so-called lay Buddhism movement during the late Ming.[36] The fact that Tu Long ordered his family members to recite the name of the bodhisattva Guanyin to help alleviate his pain was not accidental. Tu Long's many didactic works advising people against sensual pleasures were couched in religious terms. In his essay "On Awakening from Delusions" ("Xingmi lun" 醒迷論), for example, Tu Long argued that retribution was the most effective means of discouraging people from committing the sins caused by greed.[37] In an essay entitled "Ten Delusions" ("Shimi" 十迷), Tu Long meticulously listed different desires and their respective delusory nature.[38] Such cautionary remarks filled Tu Long's writings. Probably no one was so conscious of, as well as so vocal about, the danger of desire as Tu Long. But curiously enough, these didactic works did not necessarily have their intended effect on their author himself. Despite his repeated expression of remorse and his cautions to others, Tu Long continued his promiscuous life-style at a quite advanced age. At the age of fifty-one, Tu Long, we are told, was still boasting of his sexual potency, which enabled him to "conquer" ten girls and boys during a single night.[39] Consequently, it should come as no surprise that he died of venereal disease, as some suspect. Tu Long's life was full of

guests drink wine out of the shoes of a courtesan (*jixie xingjiu* 妓鞋行酒; see Shen Defu, *Wanli yehuo bian*, *juan* 23, p. 600), a "romantic" behavior sometimes described in Ming erotic fiction (see, e.g., *Jin Ping Mei cihua*, 6.58; and Roy, trans., *Plum in the Golden Vase*, vol. 1, pp. 123, 490–91*n*19). However, He Liangjun also complained repeatedly about the moral decline of contemporary society in his famous *Siyou zhai congshuo* (*juan* 34, p. 311–15). Indeed, He Liangjun, like Tu Long and the Yuan brothers, was a typical late Ming man of "contradictions."

36. For lay Buddhism during the late Ming, see Brook, *Praying for Power*; and Chün-fang Yü, *The Renewal of Buddhism in China*.

37. This essay was attributed to Yi'na daoren 一衲道人 and included in Li Zhi, *Shanzhong yixi hua*, 4.35a–37a. Yi'na daoren is believed to be Tu Long's studio name.

38. Tu Long, "Shimi," *Hongbao ji*, 42.1a–8b; For a satirical reference to Tu Long's religious faith, see his contemporary Xie Zhaozhi's (*jinshi* 1602) essay "Shibu san" 事部三, *Wuzazu*, *juan* 15, vol. 2, pp. 296–97.

39. According to Tu Long's friend Feng Mengzhen 馮夢禎 (1546–1605), "Although Changqing [Tu Long] claims himself to be a man who has already entered the Way, he is not a vegetarian and is obsessed with young boys. . . . He once boasted that he could conquer ten women or young boys during one night" (Feng Mengzhen, "Kuaixue tang riji" 快雪堂日記, *Kuaixue tang ji*, 57. 22a–b; see also Xu Shuofang, "Tu Long nianpu," p. 381).

apparent contradictions, the essence of which was best captured in his own words:

I once said there were only two important things in this world: the first is learning the Way and cultivating oneself (*xiushen xuedao* 修身學道) by preserving energy and resting one's spirit; the second is seeking as much pleasure as one can at the present moment (*jishi xingle* 及時行樂) and not paying any attention to one's posthumous reputation.[40]

Obviously, according to Tu Long, learning the Way need not be in conflict with enjoying life and various sensual pleasures, a view apparently shared by Yuan Hongdao. He insisted that he would not object to becoming an official only if it did not interfere with his enjoyment of wine and women and his practice of Chan Buddhism.[41] Yuan Zhongdao once expressed the wish to build a three-story house. His plan was to do meditation on the top level, read Buddhist sutras and Taoist texts on the second, and enjoy the company of prostitutes on the ground floor.[42] In fact, for many late Ming literati, the distinctions between learning the Way and gratifying one's desires were never clear, as satirized in the following poignant remark made by Tan Yuanchun 譚元春 (1585–1637):

The reason why I could not learn the Way is due to my weak will and my love for beautiful things; although old, I am full of energy; throughout my life, I have adored nature, and I could not tear myself away from it even though its appearance changes day and night. Look at those who claim to have learned the Way: they desire official position as much as I do; they desire wealth as much as I do; they love women as much as I do. . . . I really don't understand why I should be considered blameworthy if I don't try to learn the Way. Feeling wronged, I put this question to those [who claim to have learned the Way]. They replied, "How could these desires be in conflict with the Way? You really know nothing about the Way."[43]

Indeed, the various practices for achieving religious transcendence, such as that of Chan Buddhism, had been "secularized" to such a degree by the late Ming that they had lost much of their persuasiveness as a religion that was capable of helping people to achieve ultimate transcendence. This was

40. Tu Long, "Yu Lü Wenxin" 與呂文心, *Baiyu ji*, 9.1b–2a (pp. 452–53).

41. Yuan Hongdao, "Mei Kesheng" 梅客生, *Ji*, *juan* 11, p. 484.

42. See the tenth poem in Yuan Zhongdao, "Ganhuai shi wushi ba shou" 感懷詩五十八首, *Kexue zhai ji*, *juan* 5, p. 192.

43. Tan Yuanchu, "Da Jin Zhengxi" 答金正希, *Ji*, *juan* 28, p. 783.

probably one of the reasons that people like Yuan Hongdao gradually turned away from Chan Buddhism to practicing Pure Land (Jingtu 淨土) Buddhism, which emphasized much more the "otherworldliness" of Buddhahood, especially when they became more serious about redemption and salvation beyond this life.[44]

However, examined more carefully, this perceived cozy relationship between "learning the Way" and "desiring beautiful things and pretty women" may be much more than a result of the secularization of the former or a desperate act of hypocrisy. More subtly, this awkward ambivalence betrayed a genuine psychological as well as practical need for "religious transcendence" on the part of those seeking the maximum gratification of worldly desires. In other words, people may have had many different needs, some of which could appear to contradict others—they wanted to enjoy worldly pleasures, but they also wanted to be assured of religious salvation. The ambivalence or contradiction was at least partially expected and even intended. The more a person indulged in sensual pleasures, the more that person might feel the need for spiritual redemption, especially if he believed that his pleasure-seeking was doing serious harm to his physical health and to his chance of ascending to heaven after this life. This clinging to the possibilities of redemption or transcendence testifies to the presence of a profound fear of the destructiveness of desire, a fear made all the more disturbing due to the realization of one's sheer inability to contain such desire. The wish to achieve religious transcendence became all the more genuine as well as more desperate only after one had experienced all the contours of desire, especially its dark side.

The acute awareness of the perils of desire is by no means a phenomenon unique to late Ming culture. What is unique about late Ming attitudes toward desire, however, is their ambivalence and the profound sense of despair over what one should do about desires that refused to be tamed. This pessimism, paradoxically, can be regarded as an unexpected result of the unprecedented faith in man's "innate goodness" or *liangzhi* 良知, so much celebrated by the *xinxue* 心學 school of Neo-Confucianism that dominated the intellectual scene of sixteenth-century China. If the emphasis on the auton-

44. For a study of Yuan Hongdao's religious beliefs and practices, see Qiu Minjie, *Canchan yu nianfo.*

omy of human subjectivity or moral autonomy, directly or indirectly, contributed to the valorization of private desire, it also compelled people to confront the ultimate fallibility of man and his proclivity to evil. This is especially true of those who realized how frail the human mind could be in face of temptations without the support of an "outside" moral authority (when a person was left alone to deal with his own conscience without the usual support of the moral teachings of the ancient sages).[45] For some late Ming literati, desire, when it became uncontrollable, came to mean "death," the perishing of that person who desired.[46] This enhanced sense of human fallibility helps, at least in part, to explain these late Ming writers' eagerness to discourse on their own moral failures. Tan Yuanchun even proposed that the capacity for repentance (*hui* 悔) be used as a yardstick to judge if one could be considered a genuine literatus (*zhen wenren* 眞文人). According to Tan, only people such as Yuan Hongdao, by virtue of their capacity for repentance, were worthy to be honored with the title "genuine literatus."[47]

Many late Ming literati were eager to talk about desire, not in general or in the abstract, but in terms of their personal and private experiences.[48] The proliferation of discourses on desire during that period is unprecedented in Chinese history. It is probably no exaggeration to say that there was an explosion of discourses on desire during the late Ming; among these, *xiaoshuo*, or fiction, was obviously one of the most important. With its unique narrative capacity and representational power, fiction seems to have offered itself as the best medium to explore in depth the complexities, ambivalences, and contradictions associated with desire in contemporary discourses. It is no coincidence that many literati figures who personified so well the late Ming ambivalence toward desire were also in one way or another closely associated with the late Ming boom in vernacular literature. Among those whose views on desire have been discussed, Tu Long, Tang Xianzu, and Li Kaixian have

45. For the "crushing responsibility" that resulted from this unprecedented faith in one's own moral initiatives, see Brokaw, *Ledgers of Merit and Demerit*, pp. 119–20.

46. The close association between desire and death experienced by these late Ming literati will find echoes in Ximen Qing and Jia Baoyu, respectively the male protagonist in the sixteenth-century *Jin Ping Mei* and the eighteenth-century *Honglou meng*, as we will see in Chapters 4 and 10.

47. Tan Yuanchun, "*Yuan Zhonglang xiansheng xuji* xu" 袁中郎先生續集序, *Ji*, *juan* 22, pp. 599–60.

48. For discussions of the unprecedented confessional tendency exhibited in the autobiographical writings of the late Ming, see Pei-yi Wu, *The Confucian's Progress*, pp. 209–34.

even been proposed as candidates for the authorship of the famous *Jin Ping Mei* (in part because of the similarities between their views on desire and those of the novel's author). Yuan Hongdao and many of his peers in the famous literati club, the Putao she 葡萄社 (Grape Club), were avid readers of this novel.[49] All this suggests that the rise and maturation of Chinese vernacular fiction as a narrative genre have to be studied in the context of the complicated status of desire in late Ming culture, a topic explored in more detail in the next two chapters. In this chapter, I have focused on the ambivalence found in late Ming literati's personal observations on desire. In Chapter 2, I will examine how the issue of desire was debated in the more formal intellectual discourses of that period.

49. Both Li Zhi and Yuan Hongdao were champions of vernacular literature. For discussion of Yuan Hongdao's relationship with popular literature, including vernacular literature, see Chou, *Yüan Hung-tao*, pp. 54–60. Some scholars have suggested Tu Long, himself a dramatist, as a possible author of *Jin Ping Mei.* Although the available evidence is far from conclusive, many of Tu Long's views do find their echoes in this novel. See Huang Lin, "*Jin Ping Mei* zuozhe Tu Long kao"; idem, "*Jin Ping Mei* zuozhe Tu Long xukao"; and Zheng Run, *Jin Ping Mei he Tu Long*, pp. 125–32. For an attribution of the authorship of *Jin Ping Mei* to Tang Xianzu, see Roy, "The Case for T'ang Hsien-tzu's Authorship of the *Jin Ping Mei*"; for an attempt to attribute the authorship to Li Kaixian, see Bu Jian, *"Jin Ping Mei" zuozhe Li Kaixian kao.*

CHAPTER TWO
The Debates on Qing in Late Imperial China

Yu 欲 (often written as 慾),[1] a term that appears frequently in the discussion in Chapter 1, is usually the first word that comes to mind as the Chinese equivalent of the English word "desire." The definition of *yu* in Xu Shen's 許慎 (58–147) *Shuowen jiezi* 說文解字 dictionary is somewhat redundant and even circular. Xu glossed *yu* as "the covetous *yu*" (*yu tanyu ye* 欲貪欲也) and used the character *yu* in the form of the compound *yuwu* 欲物 (desiring things) to define the meaning of *tan* 貪.[2] This is probably what led the Qing philologist Duan Yucai 段玉裁 (1735–1815) to label *yu* an erroneous character resulting from miswriting (*yanzi* 衍字) and a case of "incompetent people trying to invent characters" (*qianren zengzi* 淺人增字). The character *yu* is composed of two radicals: *qian* 欠 and *gu* 谷. The former, Duan

1. Duan Yucai 段玉裁 (1735–1815), in his annotations to the entry on *yu* in the *Shuowen jiezi*, asserts that the character *yu* with the heart radical was fabricated (*zhi* 製) by people of later ages (see Xu Shen, *Shuowen jiezi zhu*, 10B.24b [p. 411]). When asked about the differences between the two *yu*, Zhu Xi 朱熹 (1130–1200; *Zhuzi yulei*, *juan* 87, p. 2242) explained that the *yu* without the heart radical tended to be "more general" (*xu* 虛), and the *yu* with the heart radical more specific (*shi* 實). The former was more common, and the latter was largely used for emphatic (*zhong* 重) purpose, although the two were basically interchangeable. Throughout this study, I distinguish the two *yu* whenever the distinction is significant in the original text under discussion.

2. Xu Shen, *Shuowen jiezi zhu*, 8B.20b (p. 411), 6B.20b (p. 282).

explained, refers to one's mouth watering because of envy (*muye* 慕液), and the latter to the state of being empty and ready to receive (*xushou* 虛收).[3] Consequently, in this Eastern Han (25–220) dictionary, *yu* is defined as "being covetous." This apparently does not cover all pre-Han (before 206 B.C.) usages; in many early texts *yu* denotes desires that can be either legitimate or excessive. For example, in *Lunyu* 論語 (The analects), we find the following passage: "Standing firm against the temptation to press one's advantage, to brag about oneself, to harbor grudges, or to be covetous [*yu*] may be called 'benevolent'" (克伐怨欲不行焉, 可以爲仁矣).[4] Here *yu* denotes a tendency to be overcome. Elsewhere in *Lunyu*, however, the character *yu* is used to refer to morally appropriate desires: "[one] desires without being greedy" (*yu er butan* 欲而不貪).[5] This example suggests that the referent of *yu* is quite different from what is defined as *tan* in *Shuowen jiezi*. *Yu*, however, is used more often as a transitive verb, "to want," and followed by a specific object; much less frequently it is used as a noun denoting a general state of mind of wanting or desiring. Of the forty-three occurrences of *yu* in *Lunyu*, in only three is it used as a noun referring to a state of mind.[6] In *Mengzi* 孟子 (Mencius), the nominal usage is even rarer (four out of ninety-nine occurrences).[7]

Another conceptual term similar to "desire" in English is *qing* 情, a much broader as well as a much more ambiguous word. *Qing* and *yu* are closely related concepts and sometimes interchangeable. In *Shuowen jiezi*, *qing* is defined as "that which in a human being's *yin* ether has wants" (人之陰氣有欲者).[8] Xunzi 荀子 was one of the first to discuss the relationship between *qing* and *yu* in terms of *xing* 性 (one's inborn nature): "One's inborn nature is the consequence of Heaven; *qing* is the substance of nature; *yu* is the response of *qing*. To seek what *yu* regards as attainable is that which *qing* cannot avoid" (性者,天之就也,情者,性之質也;欲者,情之應也.以所欲爲可得而求之,情之所必不免也).[9] In *Liji* 禮記 (Book of rites), we read:

3. Ibid., 8B.20b (p. 411).
4. Liu Baonan, *Lunyu zhengyi*, p. 300; Lau, trans., *The Analects*, 14.1, p. 124.
5. Liu Baonan, *Lunyu zhengyi*, p. 417. Lau, trans., *The Analects*, 20.2, p. 159.
6. Yang Bojun, "*Lunyu* cidian" 論語詞典, in idem, *Lunyu yizhu*, pp. 276, 301.
7. Yang Bojun, "*Mengzi* cidian" 孟子詞典, in idem, *Mengzi yizhu*, p. 425.
8. Xu Shen, *Shuowen jiezi zhu*, 10B.24a (p. 502).
9. "Zhengming" 正名, in Wang Xianqian, *Xunzi jijie*, p. 284; cf. John Knoblock's translation, *Xunzi*, vol. 3, p. 136.

"What is meant by human *qing*? Pleasure, anger, sadness, fear, love, hate, and *yu*. These seven, men are capable of without having learned them."[10] Here Xunzi defined *yu* as something arising from *qing*, and, in the broad definition of *Liji*, *qing* comprises *yu* and six other emotions.

It is probably accurate to say that in pre-Han texts, *qing* and *xing* often overlap in meaning, although they are not synonymous with each other. This is why Mencius (ca. 372–289 B.C.) said: "If you allow people to follow their *qing*, they will be able to do good" (乃若其情，則可以爲善矣).[11] Here *qing* is understood as something basically similar to one's nature (*xing*) in the sense that it is the spontaneous manifestation of *xing*. However, by the Western Han dynasty (206 B.C.–A.D. 8), the differences between these two concepts began to receive more attention, and they were increasingly treated antithetically. Significantly, *xing* was considered to be morally good, whereas *qing* increasingly had negative connotations.[12] Dong Zhongshu 董仲舒 (ca. 179–104 B.C.) was one of the first to suggest this antithesis.[13] This dualistic view later became much more explicit and categorical in Li Ao's 李翺 (ca. 772–841) *Fuxing shu* 復性書 (The book on restoring nature):

That whereby a man may be a sage is his true nature; that whereby he may be deluded as to this nature is *qing*. Joy, anger, sorrow, fear, love, hate, and desire [*yu*]—these seven are the workings of *qing*. When *qing* has become darkened, the nature is

10. "Liyun" 禮運, in Sun Xidan, *Liji jijie*, p. 606; English trans. based on Legge, *Li Chi*, vol. 1, p. 379.

11. Jiao Xun, *Mengzi zhenyi*, p. 443; English trans. (modified) from Chan, *Source Book*, 6a.6, p. 54. Cf., e.g., the late Qing philologist Yu Yue's 俞樾 (1822–1906; "*Mengzi* pingyi" 孟子平議, *Qunjing pingyi*, 2.21b [p. 2162]) comment that "people of recent times make distinctions between *xing* and *qing* while people of ancient times considered *qing* to be nothing else but *xing*."

12. See He Qimin, *Zhulin qixian yanjiu*, pp. 92–94; and Mori, *Jōko yori Kandai ni itaru seimeikan no tenkai*, pp. 63, 209–12, 226, 234–36.

13. Dong Zhongshu was quoted by Wang Chong 王充 (ca. 27–ca. A.D. 100) as saying that "*xing* [nature] is born of yang and *qing* is born of yin. The force of yin results in covetousness and that of yang results in benevolence. Those who say *xing* is good have insight about yang and those who say that *xing* is evil have insight about yin" ("Benxing pian" 本性篇 [On original nature], *Lunheng*, p. 30; English trans. [modified] from Chan, *Source Book*, p. 295. See also discussions in Fung, *A History of Chinese Philosophy*, vol. 1, pp. 32–37.

hidden, but this is through no shortcoming of the nature: these seven follow one another in constant succession, so that nature cannot achieve its fullness.[14]

In Song Neo-Confucianism *qing* was conceived mainly in terms of the concepts of *weifa* 未發 (the state before being aroused) and *yifa* 已發 (the state after being aroused) found in *Zhongyong* 中庸 (Doctrine of the mean). This work was originally a chapter in *Liji*; due largely to Zhu Xi's 朱熹 (1130–1200) efforts, it has been known as one of the Confucian *Sishu* 四書 (Four books) since the Southern Song dynasty (1127–1279).

Before pleasure, anger, sorrow, and joy are aroused (*weifa*), it is called equilibrium (*zhong* 中). When they [these *qing*] are aroused (*yifa*), and each and all attain due measure and degree (*zhongjie* 中節), it is called harmony (*he* 和). Equilibrium is the great foundation of the world, and harmony its universal path. When equilibrium and harmony are realized to the highest degree, Heaven and earth will attain their proper order, and all things will flourish.[15]

Based on this idea in *Zhongyong*, Zhu Xi offered a more elaborate view of *qing*:

Xing is the state before activity begins, *qing* is the state when activity has started, and the mind includes both of these states. For *xing* is the mind before it is aroused, while *qing* is the mind after it is aroused, as is expressed in [Zhang Zai's 張載 (1020–77)] saying, "The mind commands man's *xing* and *qing*." *Yu* emanates from *qing*. The mind is comparable to water, *xing* is comparable to the tranquillity of still water, *qing* is comparable to the flow of the water, and *yu* [desire] is comparable to its waves. Just as there are good and bad waves, so there are good *yu*, such as when "I want humanity," and bad *yu*, which rush out like wild and violent waves. When bad *yu* is substantial, it will destroy the Principle of Heaven, as water bursts a dam and damages everything. When Mencius said that "*qing* enables people to do good," he meant that the correct *qing* flowing from our nature is originally all good.[16]

14. Li Ao, *Li Wengong ji*, 1.1; English trans. (modified) from Barrett, *Li Ao*, p. 88. The traditional view is that Li Ao's dualistic theory was a result of Buddhist influence, a view Barrett tries to refute in his book. However, in more general terms, that the rise of Buddhism from the Han to the Tang (618–907) contributed to the formation of this negative attitude toward *qing* seems beyond doubt.

15. Zhu Xi, *Zhongyong zhangju* 中庸章句, in idem, *Sishu zhangju jizhu*, p. 18; English trans. (modified) from Chan, *Source Book*, p. 98.

16. Zhu Xi, *Zhuzi quanshu*, 45.4; English trans. from Wing-tsit Chan, *Source Book*, p. 631; see also Zhu Xi, *Zhuzi yulei*, *juan* 5, pp. 93–94. Zhu Xi's view must have been inspired by

Nature (*xing*) is the state before being aroused (*weifa*), or tranquillity (*jing* 靜); for Zhu Xi, this is the pure state of principle (*li* 理). The problem is how to achieve due measure (*zhongjie*) in the state after being aroused (*yifa*) or the state of movement (*dong* 動). Thomas Metzger has called attention to the relationship between these states and the Neo-Confucian conceptions of the two realms: the "metaphysical" (*xing er shang* 形而上) and the "experiential" (*xing er xia* 形而下). *Xing* (nature), *li* (principle), *tian* 天 (Heaven), and *jing* (tranquillity) belong to the metaphysical realm; *qi* 氣 (ether), *dong* (activity), and *qing* belong to the experiential realm.[17] Although Zhu Xi and probably many other Neo-Confucian thinkers never intended the distinction between the two realms to be rigorously dualistic, the implied view that evil becomes possible only in the experiential realm is unmistakable and suggests a dyadic pattern of moral valorization (the metaphysical realm is absolutely good, whereas evil often arises in the experiential realm). Compared with that of Mencius, Zhu Xi's view of *qing* was substantially more pessimistic, a fact well attested by their different uses of the image of water. Whereas Mencius asserted that "man's nature is naturally good, just as water naturally flows downward," Zhu Xi often used the image of water to emphasize the possibility of *qing* overflowing (becoming excessive): flowing water (*qing*) could become turbulent waves (*yu* or excessive desires) and result in damage.[18] In other words, the possibilities of evil arise as soon as there is *qing* (*yifa*). In the Neo-Confucian scheme, *qing* is morally suspect. Consequently, the dichotomy between *xing* and *qing* (*xingshan qing'e* 性善情惡) established in the Han was largely maintained in Song-Ming Neo-Confucianism and became even more sophisticated.[19]

Cheng Yi 程頤 (1033–77). For Cheng Yi's views on *qing*, see *Yichuan wenji*, 4.1a; English trans. in Wing-tsit Chan, *Source Book*, pp. 547–48.

17. Metzger, *Escape from Predicament*, pp. 82–85.

18. Cf. ibid., p. 114. My discussion here is indebted to Metzger's analysis (pp. 49–165) of what he has called "the Neo-Confucian sense of predicament"—an almost unshakable faith in "metaphysical" goodness and a constant anxiety over the potential for evil in the experiential realm.

19. For Wang Yangming's 王陽明 (1472–1529) cautious and equally negative view of *qing*, see *Chuanxi lu* 傳習錄, pp. 17, 65, 111; and Chan, trans., *Instructions for Practical Living*, pp. 38–39, 138–39, 228–29. What I have been trying to do in the preceding is to establish a minimum context for discussing some of the new attitudes toward *qing* that appeared during the late Ming. A full survey of the development of the concept of *qing* in the history of traditional Chinese philosophy is obviously beyond the scope of this study. For other accounts of the

As for the relationship between *qing* and *yu* in this antithetical scheme, the latter tends to be viewed with even stronger suspicion, and there is often a subtle hierarchical pattern of moral valorization implied when these two concepts are juxtaposed. In a favorite metaphorical comparison, Zhu Xi compared nature to the tranquillity of still water, *qing* to the flow of the water, and *yu* to the waves. "Violent" waves (*yu* or excessive desires) will cause the water to overflow (to burst the dam and damage everything, to use Zhu Xi's words). He used the image of flooding to drive home this point: "The mind is water; *xing* is the principle of the water. *Xing* is maintained because the water is still; *qing* begins to flow due to the movement of the water; *yu* is the flow of the water that begins to flood (*lan* 濫)."[20] Compared with *qing*, *yu* is even more "active," even further "removed" from *xing* (which is supposed to be absolutely tranquil and good), and therefore more dangerous.

Even though Zhu Xi and others never explicitly condemned *yu*, or desire, per se as evil, the absolute incompatibility between Heavenly Principle (*tianli* 天理) and human desire (*renyu* 人欲) so emphasized by many Neo-Confucian thinkers did add to the perception of desire as morally suspect.[21] This antithetical treatment of *tianli* and *renyu* received even more emphasis in the writings of some Ming Neo-Confucian thinkers, including Wang Yangming 王陽明 (1472–1529), even though Wang's unprecedented emphasis on human subjectivity played an important role in the subsequent rise of

---

concept of *qing* in Chinese intellectual history, see Zhang Dainian, *Zhongguo zhexue dagang*, pp. 467–79; Wong, "*Ch'ing* in Chinese Literary Criticism," pp. 288–308; and Zhang Liwen, "Xingqing lun" 性情論, in idem, *Zhongguo zhexue fanchou fazhan shi*, pp. 470–522. Anthony Yu's *Rereading the Stone* (pp. 53–109) contains the most thoroughgoing discussion in English of the early history of *qing*.

20. Zhu Xi, *Zhuzi yulei*, vol. 1, *juan* 5, p. 97.

21. Zhu Xi's concept of "human desire," as many have pointed out, refers only to "selfish desires," which need to be exterminated, rather than desire per se, and implies that there are "desires" that are in accordance with Heavenly Principle. See, e.g., Qian Mu, *Zhuzi xin xue'an*, 2.10, pp. 280–88; and Wang Yuji, *Tianli yu renyu*, pp. 135–39. However, the specific choice of the word "human desire" (to pair with "Heavenly Principle") might be misleading to many and leave the impression that Zhu Xi was condemning desire absolutely. This impression was probably one reason behind the repressive attitude toward desire that became dominant during many periods in post-Song China, when the Song Neo-Confucian ideology received rigid interpretations under the sponsorship of the imperial government.

the cult of *qing*.[22] The early Ming Neo-Confucian thinker Liu Ji's 劉基 (1311–75) fear of *yu* and *qing* almost reached the level of despair:

> *Qi* [ether] is the poison of the *Dao*, and *qing* is the knife blade of *xing*. What makes them become poison and knife blade is *yu* [desire]. Alas! Heaven and man are the essence of the universe, but they have to be under the control of *yu* so that *qi* and *qing* can have their way and *xing* and the *Dao* have to follow them. There is nothing one can do about this fact since this is the intention of the Creator.[23]

Consequently, by the Ming, *yu* or *renyu* had been used so frequently in disparaging contexts that their rehabilitation became difficult even when some began to feel the need to revalorize the phenomenon of desire.

Whatever rehabilitation there was, was limited and appeared to have been confined largely to abstract philosophical discourses. Luo Qinshun 羅欽順 (1465–1547) was probably one of the first Ming Confucian thinkers who found the Song Neo-Confucian dualistic approach to *li* and *yu* problematic enough to warrant rediscussion:

> The fact that people have desires definitely derives from Heaven. Some are necessary and are what one cannot help (*burongyi* 不容已); some are appropriate and cannot be changed. If these are what one cannot help and all of them conform to the principle of what is appropriate, how can they not be good? It is only heedlessly giving way to passions, indulging the desires, and not knowing how to turn back that is evil. Confucians of the past often spoke about eliminating or restraining human desires and thought it necessary to resort to severe means in order to repress them. But their mode of expression seems one-sided and exaggerated. The desires, together with pleasure, anger, sorrow, and joy, are qualities of nature. Can pleasure, sorrow, anger, and joy also be eliminated?[24]

22. Despite his many differences from Zhu Xi, Wang Yangming's view on the relationship between *tianli* and *renyu* was surprisingly similar to that of Zhu (see Wang Yuji, *Tianli yu renyu*, pp. 182–93). Wang Yuji's study provides a convenient but relatively detailed survey of the development of the concept of *yu* in Chinese intellectual history, although his indiscriminate treatment of the different uses of the concept of *li* before and after Song Neo-Confucianism may be a cause for concern.

23. This remark is presented through the voice of the persona Yulizi 郁離子 in Liu Ji's fictional allegory of the same name; see "Tiandao" 天道, *Yulizi* 郁離子, in *Chengyi bo wenji*, 18.42.

24. Luo Qinshun, *Kunzhi ji*, *juan xia* 卷下, item 14, p. 28. English trans. (modified) from Bloom, *Knowledge Painfully Acquired*, p. 121. Cf. Bloom's (p. 20) observation: "One of the corollaries of Luo's denial of the notion of two natures, an original nature and a physical nature,

Burongyi is a favorite term of many late Ming writers to refer to the primordial, intuitive, almost pre-conscious state of the human mind.[25] Here Luo tries to defend desire by emphasizing that it is completely "natural" and therefore ethically good.

The most eloquent advocate for re-evaluating the status of desire was the late Ming–early Qing literati thinker Chen Que 陳確 (1604–77). Chen worried that "if the distinctions between Heavenly Principle and human desire are stressed too much, the latter will have no place to hide. This will do harm to one's mind and body."[26]

> All desires for food and sex originate from righteousness and principle, whereas longings for examination success, fame, wealth, and rank are motivated by one's moral virtue. As I said before, originally there was no Heavenly Principle in one's mind; Heavenly Principle is perceivable only through human desires (人心本無天理，天理正從人欲中見). Human desires, when proper, become Heavenly Principle. Without human desires, there would be no Heavenly Principle to talk about. . . . Desires are the intent arising from one's mind. They are the origins of all virtue. When talking about desires, one can ask only whether they are excessive, but one should never ask whether they are something that one should have or something that one should not have.[27]

Given the Neo-Confucian propensity to distrust anything that occurred in the state after being aroused (*yifa*), Chen Que had perhaps reached the limits within which he could justify human desires. However, even Chen Que had to admit that the difference between an ordinary person and a sage was

---

was his rejection of the idea, basic to the psychological thought of most of the Song Neo-Confucians, that there was a fundamental antagonism between the Principle of Nature (*tianli*) and the human desires (*renyu*). . . . Human desires, in Luo's view, are, like the emotions, signs and expressions of human nature. They are natural and in conformity with principle. What requires control and regulation is the extremity of 'selfishness' per se, the lack of awareness that one is fundamentally like others and has the same disposition and needs." For Luo's contemporary, Wu Tinghan's 吳廷翰 (ca. 1470–1559) similar view, see his *Jizhai manlu* 吉齊漫錄, in idem, *Ji*, p. 66.

25. For a discussion of this important concept of *burongji* in late Ming philosophical discourses, see Mizoguchi, *Zhongguo qian jindai sixiang*, pp. 69–90. Mizoguchi's study is one of the best studies of late Ming, early Qing intellectual history that I have ever read.

26. Chen Que, "Guyan yi" 瞽言一, in idem, *Ji*, p. 424.

27. Chen Que, "Wuyu zuo sheng bian" 無欲作聖辨, in idem, *Ji*, p. 461.

that the sage did not indulge in desire, which was still something one should be vigilant against.[28]

However, despite their best efforts, the words *yu* and *renyu* had been used derogatorily for so long that an effective rehabilitation was virtually impossible. On the other hand, *qing*, as a broader as well as a more ambiguous concept, offered itself as a convenient alternative for those literati writers who were seriously re-examining the implications of desire (including its more "physical" aspects). An important strategy was to *sentimentalize* desires and emphasize what they conceived to be the *qing* elements in *yu*. The preference for the word *qing* was not entirely a matter of default or a wish to avoid the bad associations of *yu*. The choice was much more than a rhetorical tactic. With all its close associations with *xing* (especially as conceived in various pre-Han texts), *qing* could always be presented, if necessary, as something worthy of celebration; unlike *yu*, *qing* did not require constant apology. The popularity of the term *qing* among late Ming writers was undoubtedly related to its ambiguity as a concept in traditional Chinese philosophical discourses, an ambiguity well attested by the debate over its meaning among some China scholars in the West.

A. C. Graham has argued that the Song Neo-Confucian contrast between *qing* "passions" and *xing* "nature" is not found in pre-Han texts. In these early writings, *qing* as a noun means "facts," and as an adjective, "genuine" or "essential." He also relates it to naming: "The *qing* of X is what X cannot lack if it is to be called 'X.'"[29] Although agreeing with Graham's "baseline insight" that *qing* is "connected with reality, and it does have to do with naming," Chad Hansen faults Graham for failing to explain the drastic change in meaning from "facts" to "passions":

> Graham's account relies on his theory of the relation of *qing* to naming and goes as follows: That without which *ren* [human] could not be called *ren* is passions. Therefore, the *qing* [essence] of human nature is passion. Therefore, *qing* [feeling] comes to mean passions. Graham traces a number of different examples and postulates that the meaning changes occur gradually. He suggests that in the *Xunzi*, *qing* [feeling] refers to the passions but does not yet mean *passions*. The trouble, of

28. Ibid. For discussions of the Ming-Qing trend to revalorize desire, see Wang Yuji, *Tianli yu renyu*, pp. 194–431; and Chung-ying Cheng, "Reason, Substance, and Human Desires in Seventeenth-Century Neo-Confucianism"; and Mizoguchi, *Zhongguo qian jindai sixiang*.

29. Graham, "The Meaning of *Ch'ing*," pp. 59, 63.

course, is that if Graham is right, Xunzi would have no way to express the internal conclusion. All he could say is that the *qing* [essence] of human nature is *qing* [essence]. This requires that the meaning of *qing* [essence] be suddenly and inexplicably relativized to humans. So Graham's explanation still presupposes an unexplained change in meaning.[30]

Hansen offers his own definition of *qing* as "reality feedback" or "reality input." He further explains that *qing* "are all reality-induced discrimination [*sic*] or distinction-making reactions in *dao* executors."[31] Thus *qing* is presented as a concept in which "external reality" and "internal response" converge, and this explains why *qing* can contain such antitheses as "facts" and "passions." However, Anthony Yu finds Hansen's revision of Graham not completely satisfactory: "Hansen's consistent emphasis on the external, social ordering of all human reality finally, I think, leaves the Chinese subject virtually bereft of all capacity for subjectivity."[32] Yu then cites Xunzi's definition of *qing* (quoted above) in which "the three aspects of human subject [*xing*, *qing*, and *yu*] are categorically placed on one continuum" to argue for the "subjective" implications of *qing*. He translates *qing* here as "disposition" or "affective disposition" and emphasizes the action of "seeking" (*qiu* 求) in Xunzi's definition.

In fact, under the influence of Buddhism, some thinkers began to emphasize the subjective nature of *qing*, although such emphases were almost always made to call attention to the potential dangers of *qing*. The Song thinker Shao Yong's 邵雍 (1011–77) views are representative: "To observe things in terms of those things: this is to follow one's nature [*xing*]. But to observe things in terms of the self: this is to follow one's feelings [*qing*]. The nature is impartial and enlightened; the feelings are partial and blind" (以物觀物, 性也. 以我觀物, 情也. 性公而明, 情偏而暗).[33] But the fact that

30. Hansen, "*Qing* (Emotions) in Pre-Buddhist Chinese Thought," 207*n*24; see also his critique of Graham on p. 201.

31. Ibid., p. 196.

32. Anthony Yu, *Rereading the Stone*, p. 57.

33. Shao Yong, "Guanwu waipian" 觀物外篇, in idem, *Huangji jingshishu jie*, 14.38b. English trans. from Fung Yu-lan, *History of Chinese Philosophy*, vol. 2, p. 467. Cf. the translation of this same passage in Birdwhistell, *Transition to Neo-Confucianism*, p. 186: "If one perceives things from the viewpoint of things, it is their nature [that one perceives]. If one perceives things from the viewpoint of one's self, it is a matter of one's feelings. The nature is public and clear. The feelings are private and obscured." It seems to me that in the original passage *xing* refers to the observer's own nature rather than the nature of the things being observed (as

the term *qing* could be employed to refer to both "reality" and "subjective feelings" points to its wide range of meanings. This in part explains why it became such a popular term with those during the late Ming who were trying to find justifications for "desire."

A related explanation for the valorization of *qing* is that despite the strong suspicions directed toward *qing* in philosophical discourse ever since the Han dynasty, the use of the term in the domain of literature, especially in poetry and poetry criticism, was rather different. Ever since Lu Ji's 陸機 (261–303) pathbreaking redefinition of *shi* 詩 (poetry) as *shi yuanqing* 詩緣情 (poems follow from *qing*),[34] *qing* was almost always considered an important and positive element in writing and reading poetry despite controversies over its specific implications.[35] What some late Ming writers did was to make *qing*

---

translated by Birdwhistell), and this reading is confirmed by the second sentence regarding *qing*, which is supposed to parallel the first one. For brief discussions of possible Buddhist influence on Shao Yong, see Birdwhistell, pp. 128–32 *passim*.

34. Lu Ji's use of *qing* to substitute for *zhi* 志 (intention) in the canonical definition of poetry—*shi yan zhi* 詩言志 (the poem expresses what is intended in the mind) as formulated in *Shujing* 書經 and in the "Great Preface" to *Shijing* 詩經 has been considered to be a watershed in the history of the development of Chinese poetry criticism. For a detailed discussion and English translation of Lu Ji's *Wenfu* 文賦 (The poetic exposition on literature), see Owen, *Readings in Chinese Literary Thought*, pp. 73–181, esp. 130–31. Cf. Siu-kit Wong's observation ("*Ch'ing* in Chinese Literary Criticism," p. 29): "It is in this period that the meaning of the word [*qing*] first becomes more or less clearly defined and can be fairly safely translated as 'emotion.' . . . There was also a narrowing down of the range of *qing* to the more private kind of emotion." The concept of *qing* also figures prominently in Liu Xie's 劉勰 (ca. 465–520) *Wenxin diaolong* 文心雕龍 (The Literary mind and the craft of carving dragons), although, for Liu Xie, *qing* is still a very broad concept (see Wong's discussion, in ibid., pp. 32–43). The different valorizations of *qing* in philosophy and literature are perhaps best attested by Liu Xie, who, according to some scholars, was also the author of *Liuzi* 劉子. In that text Liu Xie is surprisingly negative about *qing*: "*Xing* and *qing* are integral to man, who is endowed with ether (*qi* 氣). What *xing* responds to is *qing*; what *qing* tries to satisfy is *yu*. *Qing* originates from *xing* and yet *qing* also runs *xing*; *yu* originates from *qing* and yet *yu* also harms *qing*" (see Liuzi, "Fangyu di'er" 防欲第二, *Liuzi jijiao*, p. 6). The editors of the *Liuzi*, Lin Qitan and Chen Fengjin (ibid., p. 1–23), argue for the attribution of this text to Liu Xie. For a view that disputes this attribution, see Yang Mingzhao's editorial comments in Liuzi, *Liuzi jiaozhu*, pp. 1–25. Siu-kit Wong ("*Ch'ing* in Chinese Literary Criticism," pp. 119–220) notes a somewhat similar, though less extreme, case of ambivalence toward *qing* in Wang Fuzhi 王夫之 (1619–92).

35. Siu-kit Wong ("*Ch'ing* in Chinese Literary Criticism," pp. 77–80) characterizes the status of *qing* in the Song-Yuan period (from the tenth to the fourteenth century) as one of "survival": although still in circulation, *qing* as a critical term was often replaced by the word *yi* 意, and *qing* "occupied a less important place in Sung criticism than in that of either the pre-

into a central issue in fiction and drama by promoting it as a supreme human value and worthy of celebration. By virtue of their unique mimetic capacity, fiction and drama, as literary genres that catered to the tastes of a much wider social spectrum than did poetry, seemed to have compelled representations of *qing* to become more sensuous as well as more earthly.

This prosaic approach appears to have sensualized (*yuhua* 欲化) as well as secularized *qing*. For instance, in late Ming writings, *qing* was often presented as sexual love between man and woman, instead of, say, a literati poet's aesthetic response to a magnificent landscape as in a lyrical poem.[36] One result was to make it more vulnerable to censure by conservative moralists. An interesting corollary during this period was the blurring of the distinctions between *qing* and *yu*: as physical desire was being sentimentalized, romantic sentiments were becoming sensualized. Witness the predilection in late Ming literature to celebrate the beauty of the natural landscape in terms of the sensual appeal of a pretty woman and Tu Long's assertion of the close association between the attractions of landscape and the pleasures of the brothel discussed in Chapter 1. For people like the Yuan brothers and Tu Long, the distinctions between *qing* and *yu* were becoming more difficult to maintain. Such confusion was in turn fueled by the increasing popularity of *qing* as a new or reinvented concept and by its wide currency in late Ming discourse.

Philosophically, Yang Shen 楊慎 (1488–1559) was probably one of the first in the mid-Ming to have felt the need to re-examine the status of *qing*. He complained that historically, with a few exceptions, little attention had been paid to *qing*. He tried to come up with a more balanced view of *xing* and *qing*: "What would happen if one promoted *xing* but neglected *qing*? He would become dead ashes. What would happen if one were moved by *qing*

---

ceding periods or that of Ming and Ch'ing." Wong seems to attribute this at least partly to the influence of the Song Neo-Confucian philosophers. For discussions of the status of *qing* in Ming poetry criticism and especially the relevant views of the so-called "Former Seven Masters," see Wong, ibid., pp. 136–94 (esp. 144–62). His discussion shows that well before the rise of the cult of *qing* in the late Ming, *qing* as a critical concept had already received ample attention in mid-Ming poetry criticism; see also Liao Kebin's discussions in his recent *Mingdai wenxue fugu yundong yanjiu*, pp. 90–105, 247–50.

36. Weary of what he perceived to be the "confusion" of *yu* with *qing* in poetic discourse, Wang Fuzhi insisted that "poetry should express *qing* (feelings) but not *yu* (desires)"; see his "Lun Beimen" 論北門, in "Beifeng" 邶風, *Shi guangzhuan* 詩廣傳, *juan* 1, in idem, *Chuanshan quanshu*, vol. 3, p. 325.

but forgot about *xing*? He would become an animal."[37] Yan Jun 顏鈞 (1504–96), who was a member of the Taizhou school (the more radical wing of the Neo-Confucian School of the Mind founded by Wang Yangming), reportedly also lectured on *qing*.[38] What makes this significant is the fact that Luo Rufang 羅汝芳 (1515–88), another member of the Taizhou school, was Yan Jun's disciple, and Tang Xianzu, the central figure in the cult of *qing* of the late Ming, was Luo's student. Tang Xianzu reportedly claimed that he wanted to talk about *qing* rather than *xing* when asked why a man with talents such as his had become involved in theater instead of becoming a philosopher/teacher.[39]

With more and more writers claiming allegiance to the concept of *qing*, many "moralists" felt compelled to attack *qing* because of its increased visibility. To counter the pressure of criticism, some serious advocates of *qing* had to be more emphatic as well as more articulate in espousing the values of *qing*. Such self-conscious and emphatic efforts, in turn, helped to raise the status of *qing* further among a fairly large group of literati during the late Ming.

Literati and the Strategies of *Qing*

Beginning in the mid-Ming, increasing numbers of literati found themselves "disenfranchised." The low quotas for successful candidates in the examination system and the small number of bureaucratic posts in relation to the growing cadre of qualified educated men left many without access to that traditional means of gaining elite status. The relationship between the experiences of some members of this group and their unprecedented enthusiasm for *qing* is worth a close look since it was those literati who played an essential role in inventing as well as defining the specific content of *qing* (a point I

37. Yang Shen, "Xing qing lun," in idem, *Sheng'an ji*, 5.13. Yang Shen has been appreciated mainly as a writer. However, his achievements as a thinker are also beginning to attract attention; see, e.g., Lu Fuchu, *Bei lishi yiwang de yidai zheren*. For a brief discussion of Yang Shen's view of *qing* in poetry criticism, see Siu-kit Wong, "*Ch'ing* in Chinese Literary Criticism," pp. 159–62.

38. Huang Zongxi, "Taizhou xue'an" 泰州學案, in idem, *Mingru xue'an*, *juan* 32, vol. 7, p. 822.

39. As quoted in Chen Jiru 陳繼儒 (1558–1639), "*Mudan ting* tici" 牡丹亭題詞, in Mao Xiaotong, *Tang Xianzu yanjiu ziliao huibian*, vol. 2, p. 855. This remark seems to have caught the attention of many Ming-Qing writers such as Huang Zongxi and Zhou Lianggong 周亮工 (1612–72); see ibid., vol. 2, pp. 676, 875.

discuss further in Chapter 3). Some of them worshipped *qing* with a fervor that was almost religious. Feng Menglong 馮夢龍 (1574–1646) is a case in point. In a preface to his *Qingshi* 情史 (A history of *qing*), a large collection of stories about *qing*, Feng wrote:

> It has always been my ambition to write a history of *qing*, and ever since I was a young man, I have prided myself on being a *qing* fanatic. I always bare my soul among my friends, sharing with them in times both good and bad. . . . Whenever I meet a person rich in *qing* (*youqing ren* 有情人), I always want to show my respect to him, and whenever I see a person who lacks *qing* (*wuqing ren* 無情人) and whose views do not agree with mine, I always try to guide him patiently with *qing*. I give up only when that person absolutely refuses to listen. I have said in jest before that I would become a Buddha to save the world after I die because I cannot forget my *qing* for the people of this world (*buneng wangqing shiren* 不能忘情世人). And I would come to this world under the title "Buddha of Boundless Love and Joy."[40]

The intensely personal tone of this passage reveals Feng's interest in this project, which was supposedly about other people's *qing*. Indeed, this book may have been much more to its author than a collection of anecdotes about love. That Feng Menglong was himself a man of *qing* (*youqing ren*) can best be seen in his outpouring of emotions when his love affair with the courtesan Hou Huiqing 侯慧卿 ended.[41] Although dallying with courtesans was considered part of the life-style of the romantic literati during this period, it probably meant much more for someone like Feng Menglong. Feng Menglong received his licentiate (*xiucai* 秀才) degree in his twenties. Not until several decades later was he, as a fifty-six-year-old stipendiary student (*gongsheng* 貢生), offered the very minor position of assistant county instructor; four years later he was appointed, at the advanced age of sixty, the magistrate of a remote county, an official position of the seventh grade (*qipin* 七品).[42]

40. "*Qingshi* xu" 情史敘 (written under the name of Long Ziyou 龍子猶), in Feng Menglong, *Qingshi* 情史, 1a–2a, in idem, *Quanji*, vol. 37, pp. 1–3. For a complete translation of this preface, see Mowry, *Chinese Love Stories*, pp. 12–14.

41. For a discussion of this romantic affair, see Wang Ling, "Feng Menglong yu Hou Huiqing" 馮夢龍與侯慧卿, in idem, *Qiren, qingzhong, qipin guan*, pp. 23–28. For discussions of the relationship between courtesans and literati in the seventeenth century, see Kang-i Sun Chang, *The Late-Ming Poet Ch'en Tzu-lung*, pp. 9–18; and Wai-yee Li, "The Late-Ming Courtesan." Chang (p. 12) claims that the late Ming "cult of love was largely a product of the courtesan culture."

42. For information on Feng's life, see Wang Ling, "Feng Menglong shengping jianbian" 馮夢龍生平簡編, in idem, *Qiren, qingzhong, qipin guan*, pp. 115–39; Xu Shuofang, "Feng

These facts tell us at least two things: Feng had a very frustrating examination career, and he remained interested in public service (he was still willing to serve as a seventh-grade official at the age of sixty).

It was not unusual for those frustrated in their careers to seek solace in the arms of a courtesan. Some common element shared by courtesans and frustrated literati must have made the former especially appealing to the latter. Here Fu Shan's 傅山 (1607–84) observation is pertinent: "A famous courtesan who has been forced into prostitution is no different from a romantic scholar who has suffered many career frustrations in the sense that both have failed to fulfill their lifelong ambitions."[43] Indeed, after numerous setbacks in his career, Feng must have found appealing the alternative of a career as a writer promoting *qing* as a way to vindicate his own unrecognized talents. In fact, for many frustrated literati, pursuing *qing* in life (that is, romancing courtesans) and, more significant, writing about *qing* became special means of compensation for career setbacks.[44] The late Ming writer Wei Yong 衛泳 (fl. seventeenth century) was straightforward in depicting the therapeutic functions of *qing*:

> *Qing* is that for which the living could die and because of which the dead could be resurrected. This is why filial sons, men of righteousness, and chaste women are all people rich in *qing* (*youqing ren*). When a man can find no one to appreciate his talents and no opportunity to fulfill his genuine desires (*zhenqing* 眞情) to seek glory

---

Menglong nianpu," pp. 393–452; and Mowry, "*Ch'ing-shih* and Feng Meng-lung," pp. 441–48. Xu Shuofang (p. 432) believes that Feng assumed the position of the magistrate of Shouning county at the age of sixty-one rather than sixty.

43. Li Zhongxia, "Liancai haoju" 憐才豪舉, in idem, *Yuan Li erzhai*, vol. 2, p. 7.

44. Interpreted in terms of this relationship between a literatus's obsession with *qing* and his career setbacks, the fact that Tang Xianzu wrote *Mudan ting* just after he was forced to quit the bureaucracy should not be considered a mere coincidence. For an account of Tang's life and the dating of *Mudan ting*, see Xu Shuofang, "Tang Xianzu nianpu"; and idem, "*Yuming tang chuanqi* chuangzuo niandai kao." Many late Ming literati/officials turned to writing plays after being forced to resign from their official posts. Li Kaixian is another example; for a discussion of his life and literary works, see Bu Jian, *Li Kaixian zhuanlüe*. Of course, many seventeenth-century writers of *caizi jiaren xiaoshuo* 才子佳人小說 (scholar-beauty fiction), where *qing* as romantic sentiment was also highly valorized, were often marginalized literati who had suffered career setbacks. See, e.g., Yanshui sanren's 煙水散人 preface to the early Qing collection of short stories *Nücaizi shu* 女才子書 (A book of female talent), and Tianhuazang zhuren's 天花藏主人 preface to the early novel *Pingshan Lengyan* 平山冷燕 (Flat Mountain and Cold Swallow), reprinted in Ding Xigen, *Zhongguo lidai xiaoshuo xuba ji*, pp. 830–32, 1244–45, respectively.

and success in public service, he will seek compensation in love for a pretty woman.[45]

This view is apparent in Feng Menglong's defense of the poet Liu Yong 柳永 (ca. 987–1053), who was known for his romantic involvement with prostitutes. In the twelfth story in Feng Menglong's *Gujin xiaoshuo* 古今小說 (Stories old and new), Liu Yong is presented as a poet of many talents; he loses an opportunity for career success, we are told, only because one of his poems does not happen to please the emperor. In a note, Feng went out of his way to point out that many of the literati who romanced prostitutes have turned out to be great heroes. He emphasizes that a person of *qing* is capable of heroic actions and that *qing* and heroic actions are by no means mutually exclusive.[46] Furthermore, a special term was coined for indulgence in *qing* and *haose* 好色 (love for pretty women) as a deliberate act of "withdrawal from public life": *seyin* 色隱 (withdrawal into the arms of pretty women). Disgusted with the world of men, a real hero turned to a beautiful woman for appreciation (*zhiji* 知己). Thus *seyin* could be a self-conscious act of political protest and as well as of self-vindication on the part of a frustrated literatus, and such an act was often defended or promoted by appealing to the concept of *qing*.[47]

45. Wei Yong, *Yuerong bian*, vol. 4, p. 3301.

46. Feng Menglong, *Gujin xiaoshuo*, in idem, *Quanji*, vol. 12, 12.12b (p. 476); see Hanan's discussion in his *Chinese Vernacular Stories*, pp. 115–16; My discussion of Feng's concept of *qing* here is indebted to Hanan's observations (esp. pp. 75–97). Note also Zhou Quan's 周銓 (ca. 1600) relevant remarks in his "Yingxiong qiduan shuo" 英雄氣短說 (*Bingxue xie*, vol. 2, p. 144) cited by Hanan (ibid., p. 221*n*13): "I think what makes heroes is that they have love in greater measure than others and are capable of greater devotions to something, with their heart and soul in it. . . . When the country called, they responded. There is no mystery about it. They had a big *heart*, and merely transferred that great love from one thing to something else. Therefore, as I say, love is not confined to any one thing. Only those who make some great sacrifice can love truly" (English trans. from Lin Yutang, *The Importance of Understanding*, pp. 117–18). For another interesting discussion of Feng Menglong's personal "investment" in this story about Liu Yong, see Shuhui Yang, *Appropriation and Representation*, pp. 147–52.

47. Wei Yong, "Zhaoyin" 招隱, in idem, *Yuerong bian*, p. 3303. This view was shared by You Tong 尤侗 (1618–1704), who believed that "frustrated men of talent usually seek solace in the pursuits of sensual pleasures" (聲色者才人之寄旅); see his preface to Li Yu's (1611–1680) *Xianqing ouji* 閒情偶記, in Li Yu, *Quanji*, vol. 3, p. 1. Similar views can also be found in some of the late Ming and early Qing erotic novels; see, e.g., the postscript (*ba* 跋) to *Langshi* 浪史 (A history of debauchery) written by the commentator Youxuanzi 又玄子 (p. 271), where the libertine male protagonist is praised as a literati hero (*yingxiong* 英雄) who, how-

Another concept highly valorized by those who advocated *qing* during the late Ming was *zhen* 眞 (the "genuine" or "authentic") as captured in the phrase *zhenqing* (genuine feelings).[48] The most vocal as well as the most eloquent advocate for the *genuine* was the famous radical thinker Li Zhi 李贄 (1527–1602), whose impact on the cult of *qing* was substantial, although Li himself said little about the concept per se.[49] To a large extent, Li Zhi's enthusiastic championing of "genuineness" and "authenticity" seemed to have been a reaction against what he perceived to be a fashion for "falsehood" and "hypocrisy" (*jia* 假) in contemporary literati circles. As a matter of fact, Li Zhi's influential essay "Tongxin shuo" 童心說 (On the childlike mind) was largely an indictment of such falsehood and hypocrisy.[50] What is implied in this critique is that those people like Li Zhi who assumed the task of combating hypocrisy were the "few" still able to retain their genuine, childlike minds. This sense of a "childlike minority" is discernible in Li Zhi's direct praise of the genuine:

> There are "genuine people" (*zhenren* 眞人) because there is a genuine Buddha; the fact that there is a genuine Buddha becomes known because there are genuine people; genuine people are naturally loved because there is a genuine Buddha. Only the genuine can recognize what is genuine, only the genuine will make what is genuine even more genuine, and only the genuine will think of what is genuine.[51]

---

ever, turns away from public service because of the foreign rule by the Mongols, and who, as a great lover (*qiangu qingren* 千古情人), seeks comfort in love and romance. Since many works of Ming-Qing erotic fiction printed in the Siwuxie huibao series published by Taiwan daying baike are carefully collated (with useful information on their textual histories) and are easily available, I refer to the editions from this series whenever possible in my discussions of erotic fiction.

48. For a discussion of the related concept of "spontaneity" in late Ming literature, see Wai-yee Li, "The Rhetoric of Spontaneity in Late Ming Literature."

49. The short essay "Dulü fushuo" 讀律膚說 is probably one of the few places where Li Zhi discoursed on *qing* directly (here he discussed the intimate relationship between *ziran* 自然, or "naturalness," and *xingqing* 性情); see Li Zhi, *Fenshu* 焚書, in *Fenshu, Xu Fenshu*, pp. 132–33.

50. See "Tongxin shuo," in ibid., p. 99; for an English translation, see de Bary, "Individualism and Humanitarianism," p. 195. For excellent discussions of Li Zhi's idea of *tongxin*, see Mizoguchi, *Zhongguo qian jindai sixiang*, pp. 171–88, 195–214; see also Zuo Dongling, *Li Zhi yu WanMing wenxue sixiang*, esp. pp. 160–85.

51. Li Zhi, "San dashi xiang yi" 三大士像議, in idem, *Fenshu, Xu Fenshu*, pp. 146–47.

This calculating, repetitious rhetoric creates an aura of elitism that deliberately excludes—few people are truly "genuine." Ironically enough, this exclusionary agenda of self-vindication was often carried out in the name of "inclusion": the so-called folk song movement of the late Ming, for example, aimed to incorporate folk literature into what could be appreciated and imitated by the literati authors so that their own literature could be revitalized.

Many late Ming literati turned to folk songs or other forms of popular literature as a means to find and preserve the literary works of "genuine feelings." Arguing that the tradition of folk songs could be traced to the Confucian canon—*Shijing* 詩經 (Book of poetry), which was supposed to contain ancient folk songs—Li Kaixian declared that true poetry could be found only among the common people (*zhenshi zai minjian* 眞詩在民間),[52] a view shared by Feng Menglong.[53] By insisting that "genuineness" could be found in literary genres only outside contemporary literati culture and, more important, by suggesting that only people like himself were up to the task of preserving such genuineness, Feng Menglong and his like-minded peers were claiming that they alone were saving the literati culture by ridding it of falsehood. Popular literature, together with concepts such as "genuine feelings," were appropriated by these disenfranchised literati as a means to reassert their elite status as *shi* 士.[54] Indeed, for advocates of *qing* such as Feng Menglong, *qing* could be as valuable as a deed of "cultural immortality," something every aspiring literatus was supposed to pursue. Feng insisted that to the three commonly accepted kinds of cultural immortality (*san buxiu* 三不朽)—namely, achievements in moral self-cultivation, in public service, and in writing (*lide ligong liyan* 立德立功立言)—a fourth should be added: achievement in *qing*.[55]

52. Li Kaixian, "*Shijing yanci* xu" 市井艷詞序, in idem, *Ji*, p. 321.

53. See Feng Menglong, "Xu *Shan'ge*" 敘山歌, *Gua Zhi'er Shan'ge*, in idem, *Quanji*, vol. 42, 1b–2b (pp. 2–4);

54. See Katherine Carlitz's discussions of the relationship between the late Ming cult of *qing* and literati appropriation of vernacular genres in her "Style and Suffering in Two Stories by 'Langxian,'" pp. 211–13, and in her review of Kang-i Sun Chang's book *The Late-Ming Poet Ch'en Tzu-lung*, pp. 226, 228–31. Shuhui Yang (*Appropriation and Representation*, pp. 19–44) also discusses the significance of Feng Menglong and other Ming literati's appropriation of "folk song."

55. Feng Menglong, "Qingxian qu xu" 情仙曲序, *Taixia xinzou* 太霞新奏, in idem, *Quanji*, vol. 15, 1.19a (p. 41).

In fact, the strategy of using the pursuit of *qing* as a means of carving out a relatively advantageous position in a hostile environment can be traced to the Wei-Jin period (220–420) when many literati, persecuted and alienated, turned to various gestures of *qing* and *zhen* for self-vindication (*shuaixing renqing* 率性任情). Here, we need to return briefly to the early history of *qing*. As noted above, the dichotomy between *qing* and *xing* (one's inborn nature) began to appear in Han philosophical discourse. By the Wei-Jin period, this dichotomy was firmly established, and *qing* was more often used as a narrower concept denoting specific "emotions" rather than other general manifestations of inborn nature. *Yu* (desire) began to be perceived as something in opposition to *qing* rather than being included in *qing* as defined in the *Book of Rites*). This tactic of purification stemmed in part from the need of some literati to defend *qing* against the view that *xing* was good and *qing* evil. These literati tried to save *qing* by disassociating it from *yu*. Ji Kang 嵇康 (223–62) wrote, for example:

> When we speak of the "Gentlemen," we mean someone whose mind is unconcerned with right and wrong, whose actions are not opposed to the Way. How can I explain this? One whose breath is tranquil and spirit empty has a mind that does not dwell on arrogance and self-praise; one whose substance is pure and mind penetrating has feelings (*qing*) that are not attached to what he desires (*yu*).[56]

The purification of *qing* by those "romantic" literati during the Wei-Jin period (disassociating it from *yu*, which would later came to mean "excessive desire" or lust) was perhaps one reason why the concept of *qing* could be defended and even cherished by generations of literati writers in face of strong suspicion from conservative moralists. In fact, the kind of romantic life-style pursued by those Wei-Jin literati had little to do with sex. To them, *qing* was "aesthetic" sentiments rather than anything close to "sexual desire," a different phenomenon from the cult of *qing* in the late Ming and early Qing.[57]

For the disenfranchised literati of these two historical periods, the pursuit of *qing* became a desperate gesture of defiance and independence. Yet there

56. Ji Kang, "Shi si lun" 釋私論, in idem, *Ji*, p. 234; English trans. (modified) from Henricks, *Philosophy and Argumentation in Third-Century China*, pp. 107–8 (for another reading of this passage, see Wong, "*Ch'ing* in Chinese Literary Criticism," p. 302).

57. See Fung, *A Short History of Chinese Philosophy*, pp. 231–40. Wai-yee Li (*Enchantment and Disenchantment*, p. 51) considers the Wei-Jin period to be "the age that first discovered the burden of self-conscious passion."

are more differences to be taken into account. During the late Ming, it was no longer possible to maintain the "aesthetic purity" of *qing* as the boundaries of various phenomena became unstable (such as those between romantic sentiments and physical desires, as we shall see in considering erotic novels). For example, the concept of *shuaixing* 率性, which could probably be traced to the phrase "To follow our nature is called the way" (率性謂之道) in *Zhongyong*,[58] was often used during the Wei-Jin period to describe someone who acted "naturally." This term again became popular during the late Ming. Acting naturally now, however, often meant seeking sexual fulfillment unaffectedly. Some of the comments (attributed to Ye Zhou 葉晝 [fl. 1573–1619]) on the famous novel *Shuihu zhuan* 水滸傳 (Water margin) are excellent examples:

Dwarf Wang (王矮虎) is after all a sage, as is dictated by his own *xing* (nature). He loves pretty women (*haose* 好色), and he never tries to pretend otherwise. Even when it comes down to matters of life and death, he still acts according to his own nature (*shuaiqixing* 率其性). If this were to happen to a so-called puritan (*daoxue xiansheng* 道學先生), he would surely try to cover himself up with all kinds of hypocritical deeds.[59]

Despite his "aggressive sexual appetite," Dwarf Wang nevertheless received enthusiastic praise from commentators, presumably because of his unaffected nature. Admiration for "authenticity" and "genuineness" is a familiar theme in various late Ming commentary editions of *Shuihu zhuan*, many of which were published under the name of Li Zhi, whose idea of the childlike mind was extremely influential during that period. In fact, the popularity of this novel among late Ming literati readers had much to do with their fascination with the "genuineness" of some of its characters.[60]

A famous story about the need to express personal feelings from the *Shishuo xinyu* 世說新語 (A new account of tales of the world; attributed to Liu Yiqing 劉義慶 [ca. 403–444]) may help illustrate this difference:

When Wang Rong lost his son, Shan Jian went to visit him. Wang's grief was such that he could not control himself. Jian said, "For a mere babe, why go to such lengths?"

58. Zhu Xi, *Sishu zhangju jizhu*, p. 17; Chan, *Source Book*, p. 98.
59. See the comments at the end of chap. 47, *Shuihu zhuan huiping ben*, vol. 2, p. 897.
60. Cf. Ma Jigao, *Song Ming lixue yu wenxue*, pp. 215–25.

Wang said, "A sage forgets his feelings; the lowest beings aren't even capable of having feelings. But the place where feelings are most concentrated is precisely among people like ourselves (情之所鍾,正在我輩)."[61]

"The place where the feelings are most concentrated is precisely among people like ourselves" would later become a rallying call for many Ming-Qing literati advocates of *qing*. This story is about a father's feelings toward his deceased child (something not even Confucius would frown on). However, when this passage was cited in late Ming literature, the context was often that of sexual love.[62] In fact, the tension between the need to maintain the value of *qing* as a lofty sentiment and the pressures to use this same concept to justify physical desire became a central issue in many late Ming and early Qing works of drama and especially fiction.

Another important difference between late Ming literati and their Wei-Jin predecessors is their respective social status: forced out of governmental office, most Wei-Jin literati could still claim illustrious pedigrees to sustain their sense of belonging to the elite. But because of the much expanded population of the educated and the much more plebeian nature of Ming society, many late Ming literati, especially holders of low-level examination degrees, found themselves in danger of being excluded from the circle of *shidafu* 士大夫 (scholar/official). They had to fight much harder in order to be members of the cultural elite. A related factor is that compared with their Wei-Jin predecessors, the percentage of Ming literati involved in politics was much smaller. Consequently, action such as "withdrawal from public life" was taken much less seriously and therefore became less effective as a means of political protest or self-vindication (this was probably why people such as Wei Yong had to reinvent withdrawal in terms of the ingenious concept of *seyin* to accommodate the new political and social reality of the late Ming). In general, the ma-

61. Liu Yiqing, *Shishuo xinyu xiaojian*, 17.4, p. 349; English trans. from Mather, *A New Account of Tales of the World*, p. 324. Here the sage forgetting feelings is reminiscent of the famous debate between He Yan 何晏 (d. ca. A.D. 249) and Wang Bi 王弼 (ca. 226–49). He Yan, following Zhuangzi 莊子 (bet. 399 and 295 B.C.), maintained that the sage did not have *qing*, whereas Wang Bi argued that although the sage was superior to other men in his intelligence, he was like other men in his having *qing*: "The emotions of the sage are such that though he reacts to things, he is not ensnared by them. It is a great error, consequently, to say that because he is not ensnared by things, he therefore has no (emotional) reactions to them" (Chen Shou, *Sanguo zhi*, vol. 3, p. 795; English trans. from Fung, *A History of Chinese Philosophy*, vol. 2, p. 188).

62. See, e.g., the reference at the beginning of *Jin Ping Mei* 金瓶梅 (*Jin Ping Mei cihua*, , 1.1).

jority of late Ming literati tended to be less political and more pragmatic. All this affected the way *qing* was pursued during the late Ming.

It was probably due to *qing*'s increasingly close association with physical desire or *yu* understood in a narrow sense (the latter, of course, was more susceptible to ethical censorship in traditional China) that prompted some late Ming writers to emphasize *qing* as a mysterious power that could not be judged by the usual ethical standards. The classic example of this defense of *qing* was provided by the famous playwright Tang Xianzu:

> What gives birth to love (*qing*) is unknown, but love runs so deep. The living can die for love, and the dead can also come back to life because of love. That which the living cannot die for and for which the dead cannot be resurrected is not supreme love. . . . Alas, not every event in this world can be fully understood by us. I am not a man of full understanding who can account for everything in terms of reason/principle (*li* 理). You never know when something absolutely impossible according to reason/principle may turn out be something absolutely possible according to love.[63]

First, *qing* is here associated with *sheng* 生 (life) rather than *xing* (nature), as was often the case in philosophical discourse (this should not come as a surprise since Tang Xianzu had indicated that he wanted to talk about *qing* rather than *xing*). The tactic is to relate *qing* to the concept of *shengsheng* 生生 (perpetual renewal of life) from *Yijing* 易經 (Book of changes) in order to authenticate it ontologically.[64] Second, *qing* is described as a power that transcends the boundaries of life and death. Therefore *qing* is something that not only requires no apology but also merits celebration as much as life itself. Third, *qing* is conceived in opposition to *li* (reason or principle; the metaphysical moral concept in Neo-Confucianism).[65] The message is loud and

63. Tang Xianzu, "*Mudan ting tici*" 牡丹亭題詞, in idem, *Shiwenji*, p. 1093.

64. For a discussion of the philosophical background of Tang Xianzu's association of *qing* with the concept of *sheng*, see C. T. Hsia, "Time and the Human Condition in the Plays of T'ang Hsien-tsu," pp. 249–51. See also Wai-yee Li's (*Enchantment and Disenchantment*, pp. 50–77) discussions of Tang's views of *qing* and their relation to his dramatic works.

65. Of course, Tang Xianzu's view on the relationship between *qing* and *li* was complex and changing. Elsewhere, he seemed to be deeply bothered by the insistence of his friend the famous monk Daguan Zhenke 達觀眞可 (1534–1603) on the absolute mutual exclusiveness between *qing* and *li* (here *li* may have Buddhist implications); see his letter to Daguan, in Tang Xianzu, *Shiwenji*, p. 1268; for a discussion of this issue, see Zheng Peikai, "Jiedao duoqing qingjinchu."

clear: many phenomena, such as the heroine Du Liniang's death and then resurrection for the sake of love in the play *Mudan ting*, are beyond the logic of "principle" or "reason." They can be explained only by the power of *qing*. If dying for love is possible, then coming back to life because of love is also possible. This question of whether one has enough faith in *qing* is almost a religious one. Tang Xianzu's eloquent proclamation became the classical statement on the boundless power of *qing* for other late Ming and early Qing promoters of *qing*. Obviously inspired by Tang Xianzu, the late Ming writer Zhang Qi 張琦 (dates unknown) pushed the hyperbolic rhetoric of *qing* even further:

> Man is by nature rich in *qing*; a man without *qing* is not a human being, let alone a supreme man. When it becomes a material force, *qing* can shape what one sees and hears; it can ease one's spirits and facilitate one's reasoning; it can render one oblivious of day and night and unsusceptible to cold and hunger; it enables one to reach every corner of the world and move Heaven and earth; it makes man the leader of all living things; it is the reasons for all the following: the living being alive, the deceased being dead, the living dying, the deceased not having to die, and the living's forgetting about being alive. Its presence and power can be felt everywhere, near and far.[66]

Qing is presented as the defining essence of man, and its transcending power is meticulously categorized in more concrete terms. Many would appeal to the transcendent power of *qing* celebrated here for different purposes. As discussed in Chapter 7, the author of the late Ming collection of homoerotic love—*Bian er chai* 弁而釵 (Hairpins beneath the cap)—through the voice of one of his characters, tries to justify male homosexuality by emphasizing the power of *qing* to transcend conventional gender boundaries.

The Containment of *Qing*

However, to appeal to a wider audience (including less romantic souls), the approach had to be more pragmatic rather than idealistic. The writer and moralist Yuan Huang 袁黃 (1533–1606) offered a carefully reasoned and fairly persuasive defense of *qing*. He tried to call attention to what he consid-

66. Zhang Qi, "Qingzhi wuyan" 情痴寱言, in idem, *Hengqu zhutan*, vol. 4, p. 273. For a similar celebration of the mysterious power of *qing*, see Pan Zhiheng (1556–1622), "Qingchi" 情痴, *Luanxiao xiaopin* 鸞嘯小品, *juan* 3, in idem, *Quhua*, p. 72; Tu Long also associated *qing* with *sheng* in his preface to *Tihong ji* 題紅記 (see Cai Yi, *Zhongguo gudian xiqu xuba huibian*, vol. 2, p. 1294).

ered an important fact—*qing* was much more effective than *li* in motivating people to behave ethically:

In ancient times, the sages kept order under Heaven by setting a good example of self-cultivation. This was nothing more than making full use of the *qing* of an individual. Man is born because of *qing*, and there is *li* [reason/principle)] because of man. *Li* is something not far away from *qing* in the first place. Scholars of later times pursue *li* while neglecting *qing*. They study so much that their minds are blocked. The more they understand *li*, the less they know about how to harmonize their own six pulses [i.e., practical knowledge about their own health]; when given the reins, they do not know how to control a horse. All they should do is to think back about *qing*. . . . Some try to motivate people by punishments and rewards; some try to motivate by predicating judgments from Heaven; some try to motivate by the idea of reputation. All this is relying only on *li*. However, those good at motivating turn to *qing*: when connected to *qing*, people will live in perfect harmony; if *qing* motivates one to go, one will travel a thousand miles as if under strict orders; if *qing* compels one to die, one will go through all kinds of dangers as if death meant nothing; if *qing* makes one feel ashamed, one will refuse bribery and will not be tempted to pick up the things in the street even when called on by others [to do so]. . . . This is why those rich in *qing* are sages; those good at using *qing* are wise men; those who have *qing* but who cannot follow *qing* are men of incompetence; those who use *li* to cover up their own pedantry and idiosyncrasy are ruthless men [men without *qing*]. Those who really understand *li* should not use *li* to separate themselves from people.[67]

Existing before *li*, *qing* is here granted ontological priority, a very bold step on Yuan Huang's part, since this directly contradicts orthodox Neo-Confucianism. But what is more significant for our purposes here is that *qing* is now defended in terms of public morality and the maintenance of social order rather than for the sake of the emotional needs of an individual. This change of perspective from the individual self (as we have witnessed in remarks by people such as Tang Xianzu) to the society becomes more understandable when we learn that Yuan Huang was known as a moralist and started the practice of ledgers of merit and demerit (*gongguo ge* 功過格) during the late Ming.[68] However, Yuan Huang's particular approach is representative of a common tendency among some advocates of *qing* to alleviate the tension among the different implications of *qing* as a broadly defined

67. Yuan Huang, "Qingli lun" 情理論, in idem, *Liangxing zhai ji*, 1.8b–9a.

68. For a study of Yuan Huang and the uses of these ledgers, see Brokaw, *The Ledgers of Merit and Demerit*.

concept. On the one hand, when seen as "personal emotions" or "passions" that defied the logic of reason/principle, *qing* often carried the potential to subvert social order; as Zhu Xi graphically warned, *qing* could become "violent waves" that would damage the dam and cause a flood. On the other hand, when viewed as "reality," "virtue," or as what was in perfect accordance with *xing* (here *xing* is one's moral nature as understood in Neo-Confucianism), *qing* could mean that which would contribute to the maintenance of moral order and social hierarchy or the *raison d'être* of such order or hierarchy, the precise opposite of what this concept seemed to mean in the previous context.

This ambiguity is precisely what some late Ming writers aimed to exploit when they tried to legitimatize *qing*. A consequence of such attempts, however, was often the simultaneous containment of *qing*. Some of Feng Menglong's well-known views on *qing* are a good example:

All the Six Confucian Classics try to instruct through *qing*. For instance, the *Book of Changes* reveres *qing*; the *Book of Poetry* begins with "Guanju" [a love song]; the *Book of Documents* includes an account of Yu's marriage; the *Book of Rites* discourses on the distinction between a woman married with proper betrothal rites and one married without them; and the *Spring and Autumn Annals* quotes in detail a love poem about Ji and Jiang. This is all due to the fact that *qing* begins with what is between man and woman. Since *qing* is something shared by the common people, the sage should give proper guidance in this regard so that they can avoid being misled, and it can be channeled abundantly into the relations between ruler and minister, between father and son, between brothers, and among friends.[69]

Elsewhere Feng Menglong insisted that his *Qingshi* was designed to "transform private *qing* into what is worthy of public sanction" (*siqing huagong* 私情化公).[70]

Qing is valorized here as absolutely essential to the maintenance of the Confucian social order. Consequently, the kind of tension between *qing* and *li* that we have witnessed in Tang Xianzu seems to have lessened considerably in Feng Menglong. What Feng would like to achieve is to make *li* more "humane" (*you renqing wei* 有人情味) by incorporating it into *qing*.

69. "Xu" 敘 (written under the name of Zhanzhan waishi 詹詹外史), *Qingshi*, in Feng Menglong, *Quanji*, vol. 37, 1a–2b (pp. 1–3).

70. Feng Menglong, "*Qingshi* xu," in ibid., 2b (p. 4).

However, this legitimizing strategy was double-edged: on the one hand, it prioritized *qing*; on the other hand, it tended to emphasize the compatibility between *qing* and *li* and diminished the distinctions between the two. Despite all this, *li* was nevertheless presented in a less desirable light in comparison with *qing*, and the emphasis was on the former's "unreasonableness" and "unnaturalness." To highlight its unreasonableness and unnaturalness, *qing* had to be contrasted to *li*, at least rhetorically. The tension between these two poles was still there, although considerably lessened when compared with that in the writings by people like Tang Xianzu. This would change with some early Qing writers whose approach to this problem was substantially different.

Rather than pairing *qing* with *xing* (nature), as was often the case in traditional Chinese philosophical discourse, some preferred to pair it with *li* (principle or reason), probably because *li*, as a Neo-Confucian metaphysical concept, appeared more "impersonal" than *xing* (and therefore there was more reason to underscore the need to accommodate *qing*). In addition, since there was already a long philosophical tradition of emphasizing the compatibility between *xing* and *qing* (no matter how minor this tradition had become after the Han dynasty), it might be seen as preferable to relate *qing* to *li* when the purpose was to prioritize *qing* by focusing on its uniqueness. However, *xing* became a more preferable concept to be paired with *qing*, when containing as well as accommodating was the major concern. This revisionist trend was already visible among some late Ming writers (such as Feng Menglong) when the cult of *qing* was still in full swing. The dramatist Meng Chengshun 孟稱舜 (ca. 1599–1684) offered a typical apology for *qing* by insisting that it was no different from *xing* in terms of moral implications:

Man and woman feel attracted to each other all because of *qing*, although *qing* has the appearance of being morally incorrect. My question is Why are all the faithful women in this world women of *qing*? . . . This play is a story about *qing*, and yet it is also a story about *xing* (nature), just as Mencius said, "If people are allowed to follow their *qing*, they will be able to do good." . . . The temple built in memory of this chaste woman cost plenty of money, which was collected from her admirers everywhere; most of the money used to print the text of this play was donated by people from my native town as well as from Jinling. To praise and promote the act of female virtue and improve social morals are the feelings [*qing*] shared by many people, and this is not something that could be accomplished by one person like me. This is all due to [many people's] moral nature [*xing*], which is absolutely good.[71]

Obviously Meng Chengshun is appealing to the authority of Mencius, who was believed to have said that all *qing* is good. As noted at the beginning of this chapter, *qing* in pre-Han usage was much closer in meaning to *xing*, and the two terms sometimes were interchangeable. Mencius' use of *qing* is certainly the most famous case. Meng Chengshun's tactic is to play *up* the ambiguities of *qing* by referring to a particular use in an ancient text, a use with which many people in the sixteenth and seventeenth centuries were probably no longer that familiar thanks to the long historical evolution of the concept of *qing*.[72]

In a preface to the early Qing novel *Jin Yun Qiao zhuan* 金雲翹傳 (The story of one gentleman and two sisters), the Master of the House of Heavenly Flowers (Tianhuazang zhuren 天花藏主人) also tries to justify *qing* in terms of its close relationship with *xing*. His effort starts with a reference to the Confucian classic *Zhongyong*.

It is said that what Heaven has conferred on us is *xing* (nature; *tianming weixing* 天命爲性), and [an examination of] one's *xing* is supposed to be able to offer a full explanation of why one is faithful or unfaithful in love. [If everyone's nature is the same,] why do different people have different responses to a similar situation? What one's *xing* can fully explain is only something general. Liking, disliking, sorrow, and pleasure, which one's *xing* is capable of, are wonderful *qing*. These wonderful *qing* are what give rise to love and attachment, which, in turn, can become extreme and indulgent. . . . If one is able to keep his *qing* in accordance with *xing* (持情以合性), he can remain shiny even if he has been abraded, he can maintain his true colors even if he has been dyed, and he can keep himself clean even if he has been buried in dirt. . . .

71. Meng Chengshun, "Tici" 題詞, *Yingwu mu zhenwen ji* 鸚鵡墓貞文記, in Cai Yi, *Zhongguo gudian xiqu xuba huibian*, pp. 1353–54; see also Meng's preface to his play *Jiaohong ji* 嬌紅記 (ibid., p. 1354). Here I am adopting the dates of Meng Chengshun given by Xu Shuofang in his "Meng Chengshun xingshi xinian" 孟稱舜行實系年, reprinted in idem, *Ji*, vol. 3, pp. 539–72. However, different dates (1600–1655) are given in his biography in Hu Shihou and Deng Shaoji, *Zhongguo gudai xiqu jia pingzhuan*, p. 469.

72. Wang Hanmin ("Lun Meng Chengshun xiqu de chuanqing yishi," p. 49) argues that Meng Chengshun underwent a "conservative retreat" in terms of the representation of *qing* in his writing career as a dramatist. See also Wang Gang's (Richard G. Wang, *Langman qinggang yu zongjiao jingshen*, pp. 64–113) discussions of the representations of *qing* in Meng's works; and Idema, "Female Talent and Female Virtue."

If our *xing* is only what Heaven can confer on us, then [our] *qing* must be something beyond Heaven's dictate (天但可命性而不可命情).[73]

Taking a cue from *Zhongyong* that our nature (*xing*) is what Heaven has conferred on us, the Master of the House of Heavenly Flowers argues that each individual has his or her own *qing* (because different people have different responses to the same situation). Consequently, without taking into consideration an individual's *qing*, we cannot accurately explain the moral implications of that individual's action. Although judiciously conceding the "supreme" moral status to nature (namely, *qing* should always be harmonized with *xing*), he tries to stress the special functions of *qing* that cannot be fulfilled by one's nature, or *xing*, but are nevertheless crucial to one's moral well-being. *Qing* becomes even more important because it is not something dictated by Heaven, as *xing* apparently is, and is therefore totally dependent on an individual's moral initiative. Paradoxically, his tactic is to promote the importance of *qing* by strictly following the moral logic of the orthodox Neo-Confucian view that *qing* is potentially morally suspect because of its "active" nature (the state after being aroused, or *yifa*). Far more attention needs to be devoted to *qing* precisely because of its "instability"; by the same token, those who are able to stabilize their *qing* merit even more respect. Here *qing* is valorized almost by default: *qing* deserves more attention (even admiration if it is tamed) because of its potential for harming one's moral nature (*luanxing* 亂性).[74] The Neo-Confucian rhetoric here is unmistakable, and the author seems determined to find some maneuvering room for *qing* within the moral world of the orthodox Neo-Confucian ideology. The price of legitimizing *qing* comes at the cost of being incorporated into *xing*, which, in Neo-Confucianism, represents perfect tranquillity (the state of *weifa*) and moral order. Compared with some late Ming writers' more radical views, the posture of retreat is quite visible here, even though *qing* continued to be valorized and cherished. This kind of retreat might be understood, at least in part, as a reaction against what these early Qing writers must have perceived to be an overindulgence in desire during the late Ming, which, they thought, had given *qing* a bad name. In other words, they were trying to rehabilitate *qing*'s reputation by containing its possible radical or transgressive implications.

73. "*Jin Yun Qiao zhuan* xu" 金雲翹傳序, *Jin Yun Qiao zhuan*, pp. 1–2. I discuss this novel at length in Chapter 8.

74. Ibid., p. 2.

The need for containment had already been felt by the participants in the effort to revalorize desire during the late Ming. Geng Dingxiang 耿定向 (1524–96), a figure closely associated with the Taizhou school, repeatedly found himself having to redeem some of his colleagues for their radical views on desire and *shuaixing* (following one's own nature) by reinterpreting some key concepts:

When Zuowu [Li Zhi] asserted that Buddha took sexual desire (*qingyu* 情欲) as one's nature and destiny (*xingming* 性命), he was actually not fabricating. Mencius had already talked about one's mouth desiring good taste and one's eyes desiring beautiful things being one's nature (*xing* 性). But a gentlemen emphasizes destiny (*ming* 命) instead of nature (*xing*). I don't know if Zuowu would agree with me on this. I once said that *Zhongyong* does not say that one's nature is the Way but rather that to fulfill one's nature (*shuaixing* 率性) is the Way. Scholars [nowadays] misunderstand "to fulfill one's nature" simply as "to do whatever one desires" (*renqing* 任情).They do not understand that the character *shuai* 率 in *shuaixing* should be construed as meaning "lead" or "direct," as in a general leading or directing his troops. One's nature is to desire good food and beautiful things. If this nature is given free rein instead of being directed and controlled, [this is just like allowing] the soldiers to loot and plunder the common people [without restraint]. The harmful consequences are beyond words. There is the need to control and direct because one has destiny.[75]

Geng Dingxiang conceded that desire was the essence of human nature, but he ingeniously glossed the character *shuai* in the Confucian classic *Zhongyong* as meaning "direct" and "control" in order to underscore the need to control that nature. Here in the writings of those supposed to be behind the late Ming effort to revalorize desire, we could already discern many signs of the conservative retreat that began to gain momentum during the last few years of the Ming and the early decades of the Qing.

The late Ming thinker and leader of the so-called conservative Donglin literati faction Feng Congwu 馮從吾(1556–1627) is representative in this regard. He was particularly annoyed by the theory advanced by people such as

75. Geng Dingxiang, "Yu Zhou Yatang" 與周柸塘, in idem, *Wenji*, 61b–62a (pp. 366–67); see also "Yunie zhuiyan" 遇聶贅言, 8.37b (ibid., p. 900), and "Qingyu xingming shi" 情欲性命釋, 10.60b (ibid., p. 1114). Geng Dingxiang was closely associated with the Taizhou school although he tended to be more conservative, as can be seen from his strained and complicated relationship with Li Zhi. For a discussion of the famous debate between him and Li Zhi, see Zuo Dongling, *Li Zhi yu WanMing wenxue sichao*, pp. 102–22.

He Xinyin 何心隱 (1517–79) that Confucius' liking for benevolence (*haoren* 好仁) is also *yu* since "desiring benevolence" (欲仁) is nevertheless a desire (thus "being without desire" also means "not practicing benevolence").[76]

> The word *yu* in "desiring to make virtue manifest" or "desiring to become virtuous" (*yu mingming de yu ren* 欲明明德欲仁) actually refers to moral effort (*gongfu* 功夫), and it is used in a semi-metaphoric manner (*banshi banxu* 半實半虛), whereas the word *yu* in "human desire" (*renyu* 人欲) should be understood in the full sense of the word since it refers to the actual state of desiring (*shiti* 實體). These two different kinds of usage of the word should never be confused. Besides, virtue and benevolence are what principle (*li*) is, and "desiring virtue and benevolence" means endeavoring to put principle into practice. How could someone advocate that desire must not be eliminated (*qu* 去) on the pretext of this usage of the word *yu*?[77]

Another conservative late Ming thinker, Zou Yuanbiao 鄒元標 (1551–1624), deplored "the dangerous trends in the present-day learning" of "regarding *yu* as *li* and *qing* as *xing* (以欲爲理, 以情爲性), treating moral prudence as shackles, and treating the proprieties and regulations (*lifa* 禮法) as amusing performances on stage (*xichang* 戲場)."[78] Re-emphasizing the distinctions between *li* and *yu* that seemed to have become blurred during the late Ming, Feng Congwu offered a critique in the form of a dialogue:

> If one were to ask: "Heavenly Principle and human desire cannot be distinguished. When false benevolence and false righteousness are practiced (*jiaren jiayi* 假仁假義), heavenly principle becomes human desire; when one desires money and sex for the sake of the public (*gonghuo gongse* 公貨公色), human desire becomes Heavenly Principle. Is this [observation] correct"?
>
> I would say: "This is not correct. If Heavenly Principle becomes human desire, then it is indeed human desire; if human desire becomes Heavenly Principle, then it is indeed Heavenly Principle. How could one say that the two cannot be distinguished? Besides, benevolence and righteousness are Heavenly Principle in the first place, whereas false benevolence and righteousness are human desire rather than Heavenly Principle. The desire for material goods and sex is human desire in the first place. But when they are desired for the sake of the public, then this is Heavenly Principle rather than human desire. If one insists on distinguishing the two in this manner, it should become clearer. If one instead insists that the two cannot be

76. He Xinyin, "Bian wuyu" 辨無欲, in idem, *Ji*, *juan* 2, p. 42.

77. Feng Congwu, "Bianxue lu" 辨學錄, *You wushi er zhang* 右五十二章, in idem, *Ji*, 1.45b. See also his observation made elsewhere in the same essay (1.46a–b).

78. Zou Yuanbiao, "Wenjiang zhengdao ji" 文江證道記, in idem, *Yuanxue ji*, 5.3b–4a.

distinguished, this is implicitly intended to indulge desire at the expense of principle, an intention everyone should be vigilant against."[79]

What is of special significance is the proposed concept of *gonghuo gongse*, which could be understood as pursuing material goods and sensual pleasures for the sake of, or at least not against, the public interest. That is to say, a particular private desire is permissible as long as it does not conflict with the private desires of others. This idea, which is reminiscent of Xunzi's theory of desire, would be elaborated by many Qing thinkers.[80] The conflict between private desires (*si* 私) and the desires of others (*gong* 公) is here resolved by redefining "public" as the totality of all the private desires of different individuals. Gu Yenwu 顧炎武 (1613–82) is representative of this trend: "When all the private [interests] under Heaven are harmonized, they become the public [interests] under Heaven" (合天下之私，以成天下之公).[81] Wang Fuzhi 王夫之 (1619–92) also insisted that "the public nature of human desire [when enhanced] is the ultimate Heavenly Principle" (人欲之大公即天理之至矣).[82] "Public" is now to be understood as the harmonization of different individuals' private desires rather than something directly antagonistic to the private (*si*).

The eighteenth-century thinker Dai Zhen 戴震 (1723–77) made a deliberate effort to find a justification for private desires and asserted that "one man's desires are the same as the desires of all men under Heaven" (一人之欲，天下人之所同欲也). Precisely because they are universal and shared

79. Feng Congwu, "Bianxue lu," *You wushi san zhang* 右五十三章, in idem, *Ji*, 1.46a–b; see also "Guanzhong shuyuan yulu" 關中書院語錄, in ibid., 12.7a–7b for similar arguments. It is interesting to note that Feng's view on *qing* is surprisingly different and he insists that *qing* and *xing* were originally one thing (*xing qing ben yiwu* 性情本爲一物) ("Fuxing tang ji" 復性堂記, ibid., 15.6b), a view deplored by Zou Yuanbiao, as noted above.

80. Cf. Xunzi's observation: "How did ritual principles arise? I say that men are born with desires which, if not satisfied, cannot but lead men to seek to satisfy them. If in seeking their desires men observe no measure and apportion things without limits, then it would be impossible for them not to contend over the means to satisfy their desires. Such contention leads to disorder. . . . The ancient Kings abhorred such disorder; so they established the regulations contained within ritual and moral principles in order to apportion things, to nurture the desires of men, and to supply the means for their satisfaction" ("Lilun" 禮論, Wang Xianqian, *Xunzi jijie*, p. 231; English trans. from Knoblock, *Xunzi*, vol. 3, p. 55). Of course, Xunzi tended to emphasize more desire's potential for disorder.

81. Gu Yanwu, "Yan siqizong" 言私其豵, in idem, *Rizhi lu jishi*, 3.13b.

82. Wang Fuzhi, *Sishu xunyi* 四書訓義, *juan* 3, in idem, *Chuanshan quanshu*, vol. 7, p. 137.

by all people, "wishing to fulfill one's life and at the same time to fulfill the lives of the others is the spirit of benevolence" (欲遂其生，亦遂人之生，仁也).[83] Dai Zhen shifted his focus to the "sociality" of desire—the mutual dependence of different individuals' private desires for their fulfillment. Such mutual dependence, or "public cooperation," was deemed crucial to, as well as necessitated by, "private desires." Consequently, an individual's desire, while private in nature, is also *inherently* "public." After all, one's desire can achieve adequate fulfillment only in a social context. This is one reason why Dai Zhen often appears paradoxical, if not self-contradictory, when he discusses the relationship between "what is natural" (*ziran* 自然) and "what is necessary" (*biran* 必然):

Desires are the natural tendencies of one's physical nature; loving admirable virtue is the natural tendency of one's knowing mind. . . . When a person has carefully observed what is natural in [the movement of] blood-and-*qi* in order to apprehend what is necessary, what he has gotten is called principle and righteousness. What is the natural and what is the necessary are not two separate things. Thus, when what is natural is completely understood without the slightest mistake, *that* is the necessary. If [a person has approached what is necessary] in this way and there is no regret but only contentment afterward, this means [that he has attained] what is natural in the highest degree. If he allows his natural tendency to lead him into error, then he has lost what is natural. What he has gotten is not what is natural. Therefore, by returning to what is necessary, a person completes what is natural.[84]

83. Dai Zhen, "Li" 理, *Mengzi ziyi shuzheng* 孟子字義疏證, in idem, *Quanshu*, vol. 6, pp. 152, 159; English trans. (modified) from Chin and Freeman, *Tai Chen on Mencius*, pp. 71, 82. My discussions here of this general effort to harmonize the "public" with the "private" are indebted to Mizoguchi's (*Zhongguo qian jindai sixiang*, pp. 195–233 and 253–79) observations on important trends in late imperial Chinese intellectual history, although I have yet to be fully persuaded by his views on the specific "newness" of the thought of many early Qing thinkers. Mizugochi (p. 253) observes that for those late Ming and early Qing revisionists *tianli* accommodates (存人欲的天理) rather than excludes *renyu* (去人欲的天理). Elsewhere he concludes (p. 11) that during the late Ming and early Qing the status of *tianli* was never challenged, although the status of *renyu* changed. The latter, however, never achieved an independent status. The existence of *renyu* was now affirmed because it was accommodated into and contained within *tianli*. It is therefore not accurate to assert that the dominant views on desire were completely changed during that period, although the status of *renyu* indeed changed.

84. Dai Zhen, "Li," *Menzi ziyi shuzheng*, in idem, *Quanshu*, vol. 6, p. 171; Chin and Freeman, *Tai Chen on Mencius*, p. 100.

Despite Dai Zhen's radical rhetoric of anti–Song Neo-Confucianism, even when he was challenging Zhu Xi, he sounded like Zhu Xi, as some have alleged.[85] Here we may recall Feng Menglong's dictum "to transform private *qing* into what is worthy of public sanction" (*siqing huagong*), although what these philosophers were offering was more elaborate as well as more theoretical. The ultimate tension between the private and the public was now "idealized" into a state of perfect harmony by insisting that what is prescriptive is also descriptive.[86]

In the field of literature, Huang Zongxi 黃宗羲 (1610–95) proposed a pair of new concepts, "public *qing*" (*zhongqing* 衆情) and "individual *qing*" (*yiqing* 一情), to define the relationship between the private and the public in literature:

> The frustrations expressed by people such as hermits, abandoned women, and travelers can be quite subtle. However, this kind of individual *qing*, although deep, tends to exclude public *qing* (深一情以拒衆情). As for those gentlemen who have learned the Way, their sorrows must stem from their sufferings for reasons far beyond those of their own individual selves (一身之外). Their frustrations therefore must be much more profound, and their poems must be more forthright as a result.[87]

Here Huang Zongxi was arguing that the *qing* of an individual could achieve its ultimate power only if it is relevant to the public *qing*. Elsewhere, he characterized these two kinds of *qing*, respectively, as "momentary feelings" (一時之性情) and "eternal feelings" (千古之性情).[88] For Huang Zongxi, the best poetry is the product of public *qing* mediated through the individual *qing*.

This attempt to justify private desire by underscoring its "universal nature" would become an important strategy of many Qing dramatists and fic-

85. Chin and Freeman, *Tai Chen on Mencius*, p. 59.

86. Cf. Mizoguchi's (*Zhongguo qian jindai sixiang*, pp., 21–24) discussions of the relationship between the concepts of *ziran* and *benlai* 本來 in Zhu Xi and Lü Kun 呂坤 (1536–1618). A. C. Graham ("What Was New in the Ch'eng-Chu Theory of Human Nature") has touched on this important aspect of traditional Chinese philosophy in terms of what he terms the relationship between "ought" and "is." Elsewhere Graham (*Disputers of the Tao*, p. 251) observes that in Confucian thinking, "the good is what the wisest spontaneously desire."

87. Huang Zongxi, "Zhu Renyuan muzhiming" 朱人遠墓誌銘, in idem, *Nanlei shiwen ji* 南雷詩文集, vol. 10, p. 470.

88. Huang Zongxi, "*Ma Xuehang shi* xu" 馬雪航詩序, in idem, *Nanlei shiwen ji*, vol. 10, p. 91.

tion writers in their exploration of the issue of desire. The early Qing dramatist Hong Sheng 洪昇 (1645–1704) asserted that people became loyal ministers and filial sons because of *qing*.[89] Another dramatist, Jiang Shiquan 蔣士銓 (1725–85), presented an even more elaborate view of *qing* that presented it as being in perfect accord with orthodox Confucian ethical values: "The five cardinal human relationships (*wulun* 五倫) and other relationships all originate from *qing*. Those with *qing* will become loyal ministers and filial sons, men of virtue and righteousness, whereas those without *qing* will become disloyal ministers and bandits, ruthless and wicked men."[90] Here the tension between the public and the private is minimized by emphasizing the universal—what is universal must somehow be publicly sanctioned. Jiang proposed the categories of *zhengqing* 正情 (the proper *qing*) and *bianqing* 變情 (transformed or improper *qing*) to define the ethical meanings of *qing*.[91] This theory of the *causal* relationship between *qing* and one's moral makeup was echoed in many Qing novels, some of which are to be discussed in detail in this study. Jiang explicitly declared that his purpose in writing plays on *qing* was precisely to establish the parameters of what he considered proper *qing* so that future dramatists who wrote on *qing* would know the limits beyond which they were not to step (*siyue* 私越).[92]

The conservative re-examination of the late Ming radicalization of desire also created a significant distance, and this distance made possible the much more subtle as well as the much more sophisticated rethinking of desire seen in works such as the late seventeenth-century drama *Taohua shan* 桃花扇 (The peach blossom fan) and especially the eighteenth-century novel *Honglou meng*. These works, as we shall see in the following chapters, continue to celebrate *qing*, although with a much deeper appreciation of its complexities and ambiguities.

89. Hong Sheng, *Changsheng dian*.

90. Jiang Shiquan, Scene 10, "Lugong" 錄功, *Xiangzu lou* 香祖樓, in idem, *Xiqu ji*, p. 579.

91. Ibid., p. 580.

92. "Zixu" 自序, in ibid., p. 541. For a study of Jiang Shiquan's dramatic works, see Xiong Chenyu, *Jiang Shiquan juzuo yanjiu*, esp. pp. 78–101.

CHAPTER THREE
From Yu *to* Qing: *Desire and Fictional Narrative*

As I hope to show in this chapter, the rise of vernacular fiction in late imperial China was intimately related to the new fascination with desire that began to emerge during the Ming dynasty. Any attempt to explain the maturing of this genre during the late Ming must consider the increasingly complex views of desire taking shape during this period.

Andrew Plaks, in his meticulous analyses of many of the shared features of the four best-known vernacular novels of the Ming dynasty—*Sanguo yanyi* 三國演義 (The romance of the Three Kingdoms), *Shuihou zhuan, Xiyou ji* 西游記 (The journey to the west), and *Jin Ping Mei*—has argued that these works form a special genre of masterworks (*qishu ti* 奇書體). Plaks's search for the "generic" similarities shared by these works, however, obscures an evolutionary process that consideration of the *different* features of these four important novels reveals.[1] I will argue that each of these four works represents a particular stage in the development of the traditional Chinese novel and, when viewed in their temporal sequence, an increasing focus on the individual and the private.

1. See Plaks's *Four Masterworks of the Ming Novel*. Plaks's synchronic approach may have led him to adopt the strategy of reading backwards—his study begins with *Jin Ping Mei*, the latest work, and ends with *Sanguo yanyi*, the earliest work. See also Robert E. Hegel's review of Plaks's book, esp. pp. 349–51.

Although all four novels explore the issue of desire in varying degrees, *Jin Ping Mei* is distinguished by its persistent focus on the minute contours of desire at extremely private and intimate moments. In *Sanguo yanyi*, an individual's desire is presented largely in terms of his "political aspirations" (*zhi* 志) and is noted only so far as it is related to the military and political conflicts among the three warring states. It is the *public* ramifications of desire that matter in this novel. In *Shuihu zhuan*, the private and the individual begin to receive much more attention. The private lives of many characters are important or significant, however, only to the extent that they account for these characters' decision to join the Liangshan rebellion; the narrative itself concentrates on the collective enterprise of the armed rebellion. One of the thematic concerns of *Xiyou ji* is the working of the human mind/heart, or *xin* 心, and the phenomenon of human desire, but the almost total absence of quotidian details makes its representation of desire more "allegorical" than "mimetic." Inevitably, the discourse on desire becomes abstract. It is only in *Jin Ping Mei* that the reader is shown various forms of an individual's private desires in their fullest social context. This novel is especially compelling in demonstrating that no attempt to account for desire as a complicated cultural and social phenomenon can ever be complete without scrutinizing its subtle *private* implications.

Here a concept proposed by the Russian theoretician Mikhail Bakhtin is useful for studying the "privatizing" process through which *Jin Ping Mei* emerged as a crucial turning point in the development of the Chinese novel. In the essay "Forms of Time and Chronotope in the Novel," Bakhtin uses the concept of "chronotope" (time and space) to trace the development of the Western novel. He observes that changes in the prevailing chronotope succinctly reflect the development of this genre: from the road in the picaresque novel to the castle in the gothic novel to the parlor and salon in the nineteenth-century realistic novel, such as those by Balzac and Stendhal.[2] In the "privatizing" process in Ming fiction, we witness a similar pattern of change: from the court and battlefield in *Sanguo yanyi* to the road and battlefield motif in *Shuihu zhuan* and *Xiyou ji*, and, finally in *Jin Ping Mei*, to the bedroom and the garden, the second of which will become much more prominent in the eighteenth-century masterpiece *Honglou meng*.

2. Bakhtin, *The Dialogic Imagination*, pp. 245–47.

This change of chronotope succinctly reflects a subtle process of privatization—the focus of the novel shifts from the public to the private. In *Sanguo yanyi*, the court and battlefield are the main arenas in which the story of the novel unfolds. The private aspects of an individual character's life are relevant only insofar as they affect the outcome of public life (for example, how Lü Bu's infatuation with a woman or Liu Bei's marriage changes the balance of political power); in *Shuihu zhuan*, especially in the first seventy chapters, the main characters are often placed on the road, where the private and the public interact. However, the overriding concern is the fate of the collective cause of the uprising against the imperial government. In *Xiyou ji*, the pilgrims are constantly on the move and fighting the various evil forces trying to prevent them from reaching their destination. The novel's focus on the private life is never sustained long enough to achieve significance beyond the level of allegorical abstraction, albeit such abstraction can be compelling. In *Jin Ping Mei*, for the first time in a full-length novel, the domestic residence of an individual becomes the main arena for the action. Metaphorically as well as literally, "the battlefield" (which is a prominent motif in the other three novels) moves into the "bedroom." Stories of military encounters and of fighting by martial art specialists are replaced by those of the struggles among individuals for sexual and economic dominance. The fates of the characters in the novel are decided by what happens in the bedroom, just as those of the characters in the earlier novels are determined by what happens on battlefields, inside a tavern, or on the road. No Chinese novel before *Jin Ping Mei* exhibited such an obsession with the private lives of its characters. This novel, which is dominated by images of screens, shut gates, and closed blinds, is full of incidents of eavesdropping and peeping. Voyeurism, which depends on enclosed spaces, thus becomes one of the most important narrative features of *Jin Ping Mei*.

The urge to peep into others' private lives and to learn the details of their secret desires was a fact an increasing number of late Ming writers, specially fiction writers, were ready to face. Often the more private and more scandalous the details, the more appealing the novel was to its readers. Tu Long was convinced that it is a general rule that "people do not mention a word after hearing of virtuous deeds. However, they delight in endless gossip once they hear of something scandalous (淫縱破義之事)."[3] The writer Hu Yinglin

3. "Huoyu" (shang), 藿語(上), in Tu Long, *Hongbao ji*, 7.39b.

胡應麟 (1551–1602) once asked rhetorically: "Why are there so many fiction writers, and why has fiction become so popular?" Part of the answer, he concluded, was that "those well-respected gentlemen (*daya junzi* 大雅君子) like to read works of fiction, although they know in their heart that all of them are nonsense and morally questionable. During the day they condemn a fictional work that they later quote during the night. Obscene and scandalous works are especially appealing to them."[4] In typical tongue-in-cheek manner, the narrator in Li Yu's 李漁 (1611–80) famous erotic novel, *Rou putuan* 肉蒲團 (The carnal prayer mat), tries to justify the graphic pornography of the novel by claiming that no one, even the recipient of a free copy, reads moral tracts. In contrast, many, he asserts, are fascinated with stories about sex. In order to entice the reader to learn a moral lesson, he has to use those graphic details as "a date wrapped around an olive" (a sugarcoating for medicine).[5] Significantly enough, one character in the novel is a master thief who enjoys not only stealing things from other people but also peeping into their bedrooms. Taking pride in his skills as a thief/voyeur, he proclaims himself an "authority" on others' bedroom secrets.

Detailed stories of people coping with their private desires are a form of entertainment, and *xiaoshuo* was certainly the best medium for offering such entertainments in an age when mass media such as newspapers (not to mention radio and television) were nonexistent. Given Zhu Xi's famous observation that man's basic need for food is heavenly principle but that the wish to have good-tasting food is human desire (or selfish desire),[6] he would certainly have categorized the urge to enjoy fiction or other forms of entertainment as "human desire." Fiction was a commodity of leisure—one had to be able to afford both the expense and the leisure time in order to enjoy it. Many scholars have called attention to the intimate relationship between the rise of vernacular literature and the commercialization of the Ming economy and the rapid development of contemporary urban culture.[7]

4. Hu Yinglin, *Shaoshi shanfang bicong*, 13.5b–6a.

5. Li Yu, *Rou putuan*, p. 142. Elsewhere in one of his short stories, Li Yu, through the voice of the narrator, makes another equally humorous comment on the paradoxical transgressive nature of *xiaoshuo*: "Frivolous and lewd behavior must have something serious and proper about it if it is to be perpetuated" (see "Xiayi lou" 夏宜樓, in *Shi'er lou*, p. 75; and, "A Tower for the Summer Heat," in Hanan, trans., *A Tower for the Summer Heat*, pp. 5–6).

6. Zhu Xi, *Zhuzi yulei*, *juan* 13, p. 224.

7. See, e.g., Chen Dongyou, *Reyu de jiefang*. In his most recent book, *Reading Illustrated Fiction in Late Imperial China*, Robert E. Hegel has provided the best and most substantial study

Many *xiaoshuo* writers and commentators self-consciously advertised the entertainment value of fiction in promoting their "products": "Fiction is produced by private publishers to cater to the popular taste, and it is not the serious work of official history. Its main purpose is nothing more than to help people while away the time when they feel lonely during long nights or alleviate boredom and attain momentary emotional relief."[8] Some writers even tried to justify the entertainment value of literature by employing rhetoric similar to that which had been used by Zhu Xi to illustrate what he viewed as dangerous "human desire" (or selfish desire):

> I believe that if literature cannot provide its reader with enjoyment, then every piece of writing, except for the Six Confucian Classics, should be burned. The Six Confucian Classics are just like plants and crops, which can be cooked as food or used to produce clothes; literature is like exotic flowers and beautiful feathers, which can please one's senses as well as amuse one's mind. . . . One cannot live without food and clothes, but one's life would be rather miserable without the opportunity for enjoyment and pleasure. Therefore, neither of these two [literature and the classics] can be neglected.[9]

Moreover, Zhu Xi's very metaphor of "food" was used by another writer in a preface to an early Qing novel to defend *xiaoshuo*:

> The Four Books and Five Classics are like daily food without which people cannot survive, whereas fiction is like a special delicacy, which is indispensable if people want to treat themselves to something that tastes good. If one insists that people read only the Four Books and the Five Classics and not read fiction, this amounts to allowing people to have only basic food without the opportunity of enjoying delicious dishes.[10]

---

of the often-neglected physical features of traditional Chinese fiction and the important question of audience to date; see especially his discussions of the issue of "reading for pleasure," pp. 322–26, 335.

8. "*Xinke xubian Sanguozhi* yin" 新刻續編三國志引, in *Xinke xubian Sanguo zhi houzhuan* 新刻續編三國志後傳 (Wanli ed.), in Ding Xigen, *Zhongguo lidai xiaoshuo xuba ji*, p. 935.

9. "Zixu" 自序, in Zheng Yuanxun 鄭元勳 (1604–45), *Meiyouge wenyu*, 2b–3a.

10. Qiaoyun shanren, 樵雲山人 "*Feihua yanxiang* xu," 飛花艷想序, in Ding Xigen, *Zhongguo lidai xiaoshuo xuba ji*, p. 1275. Although Qiaoyun shanren was probably a writer of the early Qing, the sentiments expressed here are similar to those of the late Ming writer Zheng Yuanxun quoted above and could certainly have found support in fictional works produced during the late Ming.

Here both the desire to read fiction and to enjoy good-tasting food are justified as morally appropriate. It was precisely within this new and much expanded concept of "appropriate desire" that many late Ming writers tried to legitimate the production and consumption of fiction. The basic argument was that life was more than just survival. People had the right to material comforts and entertainment. And there is probably nothing more entertaining than reading about other people who desire what they are not supposed to desire.

Fiction or *xiaoshuo* is by definition a "transgressive" genre in that it often focuses on transgression in order to attract readers.[11] Fiction became transgressive in the eyes of conservatives precisely because of this, especially since, in Neo-Confucian moral theory, nothing more easily led to transgression than desire. Some fiction writers felt that in order to emphasize the entertainment value of their work they needed to exploit the transgressive nature of their topics by proclaiming that the focus on desire, with its tendency toward transgression, defined fiction as a new narrative genre. For example, the author of the late Ming collection of erotic stories *Huanxi yuanjia* 歡喜冤家 (Enemies in love) claimed that fiction writers should dwell on romantic love (*youxin yu fengyue zhi xiang* 游心於風月之鄉),[12] and the assertion of the publisher of the early Qing erotic fiction *Chundeng nao* 春燈鬧 (The celebration of the Lantern Festival) that since official history (*zhengshi* 正史) is concerned primarily with "righteousness" (*yi* 義), fiction should instead concentrate on *qing* suggests that fiction's value as an independent narrative genre lies precisely in its different focus.[13] Although not common, this is a bold and significant statement declaring that private *qing* and public morality are entirely different issues. Private desire is important enough to merit the

11. Keith McMahon (*Causality and Containment in Seventeenth-Century Chinese Fiction*, p. 1) characterizes *xiaoshuo* as concentrating on "exceptions to the norm" and the *xiaoshuo* writer as a "moralist" as well as "a trickster." He believes that "the argument is between the orthodox tradition and the unorthodox form of literature *xiaoshuo* has grown to be."

12. "Huanxi yuanjia xu" 歡喜冤家敘, *Huanxi yuanjia*, p. 77; also reprinted in Ding Xigen, *Zhongguo lidai xiaoshuo xuba ji*, p. 819.

13. See the Zizhou xuan zhuren's 紫宙軒主人 colophon on the title page of the Zizhou xuan edition of the novel *Chundeng nao*, p. 231. This early Qing novel was later reprinted by the publisher Xiaohua xuan 嘯花軒 with some minor changes (especially with regard to the ending) under the title *Dengyue yuan* 燈月緣; a facsimile edition of *Dengyue yuan* is available in the *Guben xiaoshuo jicheng*. For a brief discussion of its textual history, see *Chundeng nao*, p. 229; and Li Mengsheng, *Zhongguo jinhui xiaoshuo baihua*, pp. 275–79.

full attention of fiction, and fiction does not need to be justified in terms of moral appropriateness. By divorcing *xiaoshuo* from *yi*, he was almost proclaiming that *xiaoshuo* by generic definition is as naturally transgressive as desire tends to be. In a preface to Ding Yaokang's 丁耀亢 (1599–1669) *Xu Jin Ping Mei* 續金瓶梅 (A sequel to *Jin Ping Mei*), Xihu Diaosou 西湖釣叟 (The old fisherman of West Lake) argues that the "vulgar" discourse of *xiaoshuo* is able to compete with the classics and histories for an audience precisely because of its focus on *qing*.[14]

A frequent thematic concern of fictional works, many of them erotic, of this period is that disaster is bound to happen if one's desires, especially one's sexual desires, are not given adequate opportunities for gratification (emphasizing the transgressive potential of desire). In "The Case of the Dead Infant," a short story in Feng Menglong's collection *Jingshi tongyan* 警世通言 (Common words to warn the world), a widow commits suicide when her affair with a servant boy is about to be exposed. The narrator takes great pains to convince the reader that her fatal mistake lies in denying her own sexual needs by pursuing the empty reputation of a chaste widow and refusing to remarry.[15] There is a double message: because of its destructive potential, desire needs to be given an opportunity for adequate fulfillment, but it also has to be contained with great care. Of course, there are exceptions to this normative thinking on the transgressive nature of desire. Erotic novels such as *Langshi* 浪史 (A history of debauchery) celebrate sexual desire with little regard for contemporary social and ethical conventions. Its male protagonist, after involving himself in numerous relationships, both heterosexual and homosexual, finally achieves eternal bliss by becoming a reclusive immortal. The transgressions of the female characters in the early Qing novel *Dengcao heshang* 燈草和尚 (The candlewick monk), discussed in Chapter 5, are presented as excusable, if not completely justifiable, because a woman has the right to seek sexual fulfillment.

However, few works celebrate sexual desire with the verve of *Langshi*. The late Ming novel *Chipozi zhuan* 痴婆子傳 (Biography of a foolish woman), explored at length in Chapter 5, is ostensibly a woman's confession of her

14. "*Xu Jin Ping Mei ji xu*" 續金瓶梅集序, in Ding Xigen, *Zhonguo lidai xiaoshuo xuba ji*, p. 1118.

15. "Kuang taishou duan sihai'er" 況太守斷死孩兒, in Feng Menglong, *Jingshi tongyan*, p. 535; and "The Case of The Dead Infant," in Y. W. Ma and Joseph S. M. Lau, *Traditional Chinese Stories: Themes and Variations*, p. 123.

own sexual transgressions. However, she recounts her transgressions in such a way that the reader is compelled to wonder whether this is a show of repentance or a gesture of protest against an oppressive environment (a self-*vindication* camouflaged as a confession of transgressions). *Chipozi zhuan* is worth special notice because the main story is told by a first-person female narrator, a rarity in traditional Chinese fiction. This first-person narrative mode complicates an otherwise straightforward confession, and the focus on private desire foregrounds the issue of female sexuality.

Most works dealing with erotic desire, while seldom shying away from the alluring details, duly point out the dire consequences of being out of control (even the narrator of *Chipozi zhuan* pays lip service to this point). The transgressor has to be punished, and the transgressive potential of desire has to be contained. In fact, most works of erotic fiction follow a similar plot pattern: after a series of sexual escapades, the libertine protagonist repents and becomes a Taoist or a Buddhist monk. This is, for example the storyline of *Xiuta yeshi* 繡榻野史 (An unofficial history of the embroidered couch). Many such works appeal—briefly—to the concept of karmic retribution at the beginning or, more often, the end of a novel. At the end of *Rou putuan*, the male protagonist, after learning that his own wife has become a prostitute and slept with many men (presumably in retribution for his various adulterous affairs with married women), repents, castrates himself, and becomes a monk. However, the persuasiveness of the moral is seriously undermined by the apparent contradictions between the often perfunctory didactic ending and the lengthy, titillating, and graphic descriptions of sex that precede it.[16] There is an imbalance between transgression and punishment, with the narrative focus being on the former.

An easy explanation for the apparent inconsistency has been that the moralistic ending is only an excuse or a camouflage for the titillating accounts of erotic experiences—a "marketing" strategy commonly adopted by the writers and publishers of erotic fiction to fend off censorship. But this strategy was used so often by so many and sometimes in such a mechanical manner that someone—author, publisher, or censor—must have doubted its effectiveness as camouflage. Another possible explanation is that this was

16. Cf. Keith McMahon's (*Causality and Containment in Seventeenth-Century Chinese Fiction*, p. 67) observation on erotic fiction: "Even in a story which told of an aberration punished—very few did not—the final conformist and didactic stance would be lost on the already subversive and deleterious effects of the obscene portrayed."

simply a convention many erotic fiction writers slavishly followed even after it had lost its effectiveness as an apologetic gesture.

Some fiction writers and commentators offered a more subtle theory of apology: in order to drive home the message that excessive sex resulted in disaster, they had to describe excessive sex in graphic detail. The first to propose this theory was probably the author of the preface to the novel *Xiuta yeshi*: "I have tried to stop the spread of debauchery in this world but failed because so many people were already addicted. I have to make the best of the situation and try to reform them by [initially] following their inclination [and then teaching them a serious lesson]. I am sure people will have to change their ways."[17] This is reminiscent of Tu Long's remarks in the preface to his play *Tanhua ji* 曇花記 (The story of the night-blooming cereus):

> Since all the people in this world are crazy about singing and dancing [sensual pleasures], I [initially] have to go along with their desires [by describing such sensual pleasures]; then I deliver the important message that giving free vent to one's desire leads to tragedy; finally, I change to preaching the Taoist and Buddhist doctrines and the idea of karmic retribution. Consequently, people will reform themselves before they even become aware of it. . . . If you go along with their inclination, they will most probably do what you tell them to do.[18]

This is related to a slightly different argument couched in Buddhist terms that one has to experience "reality" (i.e., sex and attachment) in order to realize the empty nature of "reality" (*youse rukong* 由色入空).[19] In other words, to be effective, a didactic work about the dangers of excessive sex has to be erotic and graphic and detailed in its description of sex and is thus inherently paradoxical or self-contradictory.

17. Hanhan zi 憨憨子, "*Xiuta yeshi* xu" 繡榻野史序, in *Xiuta yeshi*, p. 95; also reprinted in Ding Xigen, *Zhongguo lidai xiaoshuo xuba ji*, pp. 1340–41.

18. "*Tanhua ji* xu" 曇花記序, in Cai Yi, *Zhongguo gudian xiqu xuba huibian*, p. 1212.

19. Of course, the most famous discourse on achieving enlightenment (the realization of the emptiness of reality) through the full experience of reality (*you se rukong*) can be found in the first chapter of the famous eighteenth-century novel *Honglou meng*; see *Honglou meng* 紅樓夢, p. 6. Wai-yee Li (*Enchantment and Disenchantment*, p. 177n32) suggests that this can be traced back to the cryptic passage on *se* and *kong* in the famous *Heart Sūtra*. The specific strategy of using desire to cure desire (*yiyu zhiyu* 以欲止欲) is explicitly proposed in the book of Buddhist doctrines *Zongjing lu* 宗鏡錄, which began to be circulated in printed edition during the early eleventh century; see *Taishō shinshū Daizōkyō*, vol. 48, *Zongjing lu*, *juan* 21, p. 529; see also Faure, *The Red Thread*.

Clearly these novels reflect the ambiguity felt by many late Ming literati about desire that I explore in Chapter 1. A writer of erotic fiction may have been sincere in preaching against excessive sex despite his delight in describing such sex. The best example of this is probably *Jin Ping Mei*. Its male protagonist, Ximen Qing, the reader is told, literally dies of overindulgence in sex (*tuoyang* 脫陽). Structurally, the novel devotes the first eighty chapters to Ximen Qing's zealous efforts to gratify his ever-expanding desire for sex, wealth, and power; the last twenty chapters depict the collapse of his household after his sudden death. The didactic message is obvious: the consequences of unrestrained desire are dire. Despite the novel's explicit didactic teleology, however, many readers come away with the impression that its author is indulging himself in lurid accounts of sexual escapades. Even the narrator, his frequent moral cautions to the contrary, enjoys describing the titillating details and is himself torn between the attractions of the sexual adventures being delineated and his simultaneous feelings of repulsion.[20] In a preface to the Wanli edition of *Jin Ping Mei cihua* 金瓶梅詞話, Xinxinzi 欣欣子, or the Master of Delights, observes: "As for those events that take place in the bedchamber, everyone feels attracted to them on the one hand and repulsed by them on the other."[21] This almost cliché-like remark, in light of the discussion in Chapter 1, may indeed capture the paradoxical nature of desire as it is represented in this novel. This is probably why many famous late Ming figures, such as the artist and critic Dong Qichang 董其昌 (1555–1636), insisted on having the novel burned while praising it profusely.[22] This may also explain why some modern students of the novel have proposed that Tu Long, with all his contradictory views on desire, is one of the most plausible candidates for its author (although one would like to see more hard evidence).

However, what is certain is that all these late Ming writers, including the author of *Jin Ping Mei*, shared in one way or another the complex and often

20. Cf. Patrick Hanan's ("Sources of the *Chin P'ing Mei*," p. 46) observation: "Use of such vocabularies implies anything but a detached attitude on the part of the author, and the attitude revealed in *Chin P'ing Mei* . . . is one of relish combined with an unmistakable note of jocularity as between author and reader."

21. *Jin Ping Mei cihua*, p. 6; and Roy, *Plum in the Golden Vase*, vol. 1, p. 4.

22. Yuan Zhongdao, *Youjue feilu* 遊居柿錄, *juan* 9, in idem, *Kexue zhai ji*, pp. 1315–16; also reprinted in Huang Lin, *"Jin Ping Mei" ziliao huibian*, p. 229. For more on Dong Qichang's views, see Chapter 6.

contradictory views of desire (contradictory, at least to us modern readers). To a certain degree, the appeal of *Jin Ping Mei* lies precisely in its unique ability to dramatize this ambivalence as well as the complexities of desire rather than in its ostensible attempts to provide the cautionary message against excess eagerly promised by its narrator. One might tentatively conclude that a better understanding of the ambivalence and contradictions of the late Ming concept of desire should help us find more convincing explanations for some of the perplexing phenomena of late Ming culture, such as the apparent "inconsistencies" of certain late Ming writers in trying to come to terms with desire. Fiction, understood as a didactic genre that paradoxically focuses on transgression with the double aim of entertaining and educating, was by nature a cultural phenomenon of ambivalence as well as self-contradiction. After all, for Neo-Confucians, the desire to be entertained by fiction was itself almost as dangerous as the uncontrollable craving for sex that such fiction cautioned the reader against, despite the author's claim that his only goal was to offer a cure for this very craving.

The enormous popularity of *Jin Ping Mei* and the controversies surrounding its often frank and detailed treatment of private desires seem to have added to the urgency of the question of how to achieve the proper balance between the focus on transgression and the emphasis on punishment, an issue to be further debated by many writers and readers following the appearance of *Jin Ping Mei*. It is probably accurate to say that any later fiction writer dealing with desire in a quotidian setting found it virtually impossible to ignore the issues raised by this sixteenth-century masterpiece. It set the standards against which later novels focusing on desire were judged. In fact, several seventeenth-century novels responded directly to what can be termed the "*Jin Ping Mei* problematik."

Ding Yaokang's *Xu Jin Ping Mei*, as its title explicitly advertises, is a sequel designed to address many issues its predecessor, according to this author, failed to address adequately; one of these is the "balance" between transgression and punishment. This same problem preoccupies the author of *Xingshi yinyuan zhuan* 醒世姻緣傳 (A marriage that awakens the world), which, I will argue in detail in Chapter 6, can be read as an elaborate rewriting of *Jin Ping Mei* in terms of a deliberate "structural reversal." Read in conjunction with *Xu Jin Ping Mei*, the latter work illustrates how the debate on the issue was reframed in this much more sophisticated *xiaoshuo*, in which the allegorical and the mimetic merge to present a graphic example of the deadly consequences of transgressive desire. An important issue raised in *Xingshi yinyuan zhuan* is the degree of personal responsibility for the consequences of one's desires. The author's insistence on deploying a *much more* carefully wrought moral structure of karmic retribution to frame the meanings of desire makes this novel an even more interesting comment on *Jin Ping Mei*, which, according to many, only halfheartedly flirts with the concept of retributive punishment.

So far I have explored the relationship between the novel and desire without taking into account the differing implications of *qing* and *yu* as conceived by late Ming writers and readers. As I discuss in Chapter 2, these two concepts, although overlapping in meaning, are sometimes contrasted, with *qing* referring to romantic sentiments and *yu* to physical desires. However, due to the ambiguities surrounding *qing* and its close association with *xing*, or inborn nature, which was considered morally perfect by Neo-Confucian thinkers, many preferred to use the term *qing* even though what they are trying to defend or promote was *yu* (physical desire). In the preface to the late Ming erotic novel *Langshi*, for example, we encounter a very different presentation of *qing*:

> In this world, for thousands of years, people simply could not read enough of those little books about what happens between a man and a woman in the inner chamber. Why? This is because of *qing*. The presence of *qing* brings about union, whereas its absence results in separation. This is why Confucius did not censor the love poems when editing *The Book of Poetry*, which has been able to serve the important functions of "stirring the mind," "contemplation," "expressing fellowship" and "showing resentment" (*xing guan qun yuan* 興觀群怨). The feelings of a loyal minister or a filial son may not necessarily be genuine *qing*, but in nine cases out of ten the love between a man and a woman cannot be false. A reading of the romance depicted in *Langshi* should transform a person without *qing* into someone with *qing*. *Qing* is first nurtured in the inner chamber; then it will expand and develop (*kuo er chongzhi* 擴而充之) in a person to enable him to become a loyal minister as well as a filial son.[23]

This preface, at least rhetorically, is reminiscent of Feng Menglong's much more famous preface to *Qingshi*, discussed in Chapter 2. Both authors emphasize that the most important *qing* is that between a man and a woman,

23. *Langshi*, p. 37. Here "expand and develop" (*kuo er chongzi*) was apparently employed by the author to remind the reader of Mencius' usage of this same phrase in his well-known remarks about the need to develop a person's innate goodness (or the so-called four sprouts *siduan* 四端); see Jiao Xun, *Mengzi zhengyi*, p. 140.

which is said to be the foundation on which other social relationships, such as those between a ruler and his ministers or between a father and a son, are based.[24] In other words, to be a loyal minister or a filial son, both authors insist, one has to become committed to *qing*, especially the kind of *qing* that exists between a man and a woman; both authors appeal to the authority of Confucian classics for rhetorical power.[25]

However, one crucial difference in *Langshi* is implicitly noted at the beginning of the preface: *qing* is defined as "what happens between a man and a

24. This rhetoric of advocating *qing* became so popular by the late Ming and early Qing that Wang Fuzhi found it necessary to clarify what he perceived to be the "confusion." Agreeing with the view that "love is not necessarily benevolence and that only the principle of love is benevolence" (愛未是仁, 愛之理方是理), he argued that "love (*ai* 愛) is feelings (*qing*), whereas principle (*li*) is nature (*xing*)" and pointed out: "Recently there has been a theory advocating that the fact that a person is capable of deep *qing* (鍾情正在我輩) should guarantee his becoming a filial son and a loyal minister. This sounds very persuasive but is extremely harmful to one's mind and body"; see "Gaozi shangpian" 告子上篇, *Du Sishu daquan* 讀四書大全, *juan* 10, in Wang Fuzhi, *Chuanshan quanshu*, vol. 6, pp. 1059–60; according to Wang Fuzhi, this was a result of confusing *qing* with *xing*. He believed that Mencius' so-called four sprouts (*siduan*), such as commiseration (*zeying* 惻隱), were *xing* rather than *qing* and that those who equated *qing* between man and woman with filiality and loyalty were simply trivializing benevolence (*ren* 仁) into sexual love (在兒女之情上言仁); "Gaozi xiapian" 告子下篇, *Du Sishu daquan*, *juan* 10, in Wang Fuzhi, *Chuanshan quanshu*, vol. 6, pp. 1065–66; see also his similar criticism of the practice of "changing [the meaning of] *xing* to accommodate *qing*" (遷性以就情); "Lun Jingnü" 論靜女, in "Beifeng," *Shi guangzhuan*, *juan* 1, in Wang Fuzhi, *Chuanshan quanshu*, vol. 3, p. 327.

25. The fact that both Feng Menglong's writings and the novel *Langshi* were closely associated with the cult of *qing* and *zhen* (the genuine) can be inferred from their shared use of the word *tongchi* 童痴 (childish foolishness). This harked back to Li Zhi's popular concept of *tongxin* (the childlike mind). One commentator on *Langshi* is named Tongchi, and Feng Menglong used the same word in the titles of his two collections of folk songs: *Tongchi yi'nong: gua zhi'er* 童痴一弄掛枝兒 and *Tongchi ernong: shan'ge* 童痴二弄山歌. If we accept Yuan-Hua Li Mowry's ("*Ch'ing-shih* And Feng Meng-lung," pp. 449–56) dating of *Qingshi* as completed between 1628 and 1632, then we have to seriously entertain the possibility that Feng had read *Langshi* and its preface (Youxuanzi 又玄子 was probably the author of both the novel and the preface) before he completed *Qingshi*. The theory that *Qingshi* was compiled before 1620 (see Wang Ling, *Qiren, qingzhong, qipin guan*, p. 128; and Li Mengsheng, *Zhongguo jinhui xiaoshuo baihua*, p. 92) would not completely exclude such a possibility. *Langshi* is mentioned in a preface (dated 1620) to the novel *Xutian zhai pidian Bei Song sansui Pingyao zhuan* 許天齋批點北宋三遂平妖傳, a work believed to have been rewritten by Feng Menglong based on the novel *Sansui Pingyao zhuan* 三遂平妖傳, which was attributed to Luo Guanzhong 羅貫中. For information on the textual history of *Langshi*, see "*Langshi* chuban shuoming" 浪史出版說明, in *Langshi*, pp. 15–19.

woman in the inner chamber," a difference that becomes abundantly clear when the novel proper begins to unfold. *Langshi* concentrates on the sexual adventures of the male protagonist—how he conquers various female beauties and finally becomes a Taoist immortal after achieving ultimate sexual gratification. As represented in this novel, *qing* refers to the pursuit of sexual gratification through promiscuity and has little to do with the values of *qingzhen* 情貞 (fidelity in love) that Feng Menglong advocated. In fact, Feng prided himself in *Qingshi* for being able to accomplish the task of "spreading *qing*" (*guang qing* 廣情) while not leading people down the path of lust (*daoyu* 導欲).[26] Feng's *qing* is conceived in opposition to *yu* (which to him means "excessive desire" or "lust" rather than "desire" per se).[27] But many of those interested only in lust or the "physical aspects" of desire also used the term *qing* because of its ambiguities as well as the bad reputation of the word *yu*. As a result, the distinction between what Feng Menglong called *guangqing* and *daoyu* became rather problematic.

The abuse and misuse of the term *qing* in works such as *Langshi* prompted many writers of the seventeenth century to attempt to restore the good name of *qing*. The late Ming fiction writer Zui Xihu xinyue zhuren 醉西湖心月主人 (The moon-heart master of the drunken West Lake) wrote two collections of homoerotic stories: *Bian er chai* supposedly focuses on exemplary *qing*; the other, entitled *Yixiang chunzhi* 宜香春質 (The pleasant fragrance of the spring), concentrates on transgressive or excessive *qing*. In the second collection, however, excessive desire is described as *dangqing* 蕩情 (dissipation or lecherous *qing*) or *boqing* 薄情 (lacking feelings or *qing*). In the latter case, a desire devoid of *qing* is presented as lust, although the author seldom celebrates *qing* as devoid of physical fulfillment. On the contrary, in the first collection, *Bian er chai* (to be discussed further in Chapter 7), physical desire is considered an integral part of a gratifying relationship of *qing*. Physical desire turns into lust only when it is deprived of the elements of *qing* or becomes *boqing*.

The seventeenth-century novel *Xixou bu* 西游補 (A supplement to *The Journey to the West*) attributed to Dong Yue 董說 (1620–86) is a detailed exploration of the psychology of *qing*. In this novel about the Monkey King's

26. "*Qingshi xu*," in Feng Menglong, *Qingshi*, in *Feng Menglong quanji*, vol. 37, 3b (p. 6).

27. Of course, Feng Menglong never tried to exclude "physical desire" from *qing*, as can be seen in many of his vernacular stories as well as in some of the stories in his *Qingshi*.

delusions, *qing* denotes all kinds of desire, physical as well as mental. Any attachment to worldly concerns is considered a form of *qing* as understood in the Buddhist sense of the word. What is particularly significant is the sequel's departure from its parent novel, the famous *Xiyou ji*. The Monkey King here becomes much more "human" in that he is now vulnerable to sexual temptation, something his predecessor in *Xiyou ji* is totally immune to. *Xiyou bu* offered perhaps the most profound Buddhist exploration of the ramifications of desire in a novelistic form up to that time.[28]

If, in *Bian er chai* and *Xiyou bu*, *qing* is not always presented in opposition to *yu*, this began to change dramatically with the appearance of a group of novels known as *caizi jiaren xiaoshuo*, or the scholar-beauty fiction, during the seventeenth century. Beginning from the early Qing, efforts to "rescue" *qing* took a more "Confucian" turn. The authors of the early Qing novels *Jin Yun Qiao zhuan*, *Dingqing ren* 定情人 (The worthy lovers), and *Haoqiu zhuan* 好逑傳 (The ideal mate), which I discuss in more detail in Chapter 8, took on the task of de-eroticizing *qing* by insisting on its asexual nature, even though the lovers in these stories marry each other at the end, as required by the generic conventions of the scholar-beauty fiction. What is emphasized in such works are the trials of the lovers and their triumphant ability to pass a series of tests in the most trying circumstances without compromising the moral integrity of their *qing*. The author often goes out of his way to desexualize *qing* by demonstrating how the lovers refuse to have a physical relationship until the most stringent Confucian moral codes have been observed. Here *qing* is often promoted as a Confucian virtue like faithfulness or chastity, and the emphasis is on spiritual affinity as exemplified in the idea of *zhiji* 知己 (soul mate).

A similar desexualization of *qing* can be found in another Qing novel, *Lin Lan Xiang* 林蘭香 (The three women named Lin, Lan, and Xiang), in which *qing* among several women (almost a sort of spiritual lesbianism) is contrasted with various examples of *yu* (especially "sexual lesbianism"),

28. There are many excellent studies in English on this novel; see, e.g., Hegel, *The Novel in Seventeenth-Century China*, pp. 141–66, Brandauer, *Tung Yüeh*; Hsia and Hsia, "New Perspectives on Two Ming Novels"; and Qiancheng Li, "Fictions of Enlightenment," pp. 166–93. I do not offer a discussion of this work in this study partly because of the many excellent studies already completed. Another important reason is that *Xiyou bu*, thanks to its fantastic nature, deals with the issue of desire largely in an allegorical manner, a continuation of the tradition of *Xiyou ji*; it thus lacks the kind of social or domestic ambiance we encounter in almost all the works to be explored in this study. It does not contribute *directly* to the "privatization" process I try to outline in this study.

which are condemned as "debauchery." Like *Bian er chai*, the concept of *qing* is further complicated in the novel's representation of homoerotic relationships. *Lin Lan Xiang* is apparently a work influenced by *Jin Ping Mei*, and it in turn anticipates in many ways the eighteenth-century *Honglou meng*. It has been considered by many to be part of a chain that links these two masterpieces.[29] *Lin Lan Xiang* is also a link in the sense that it marks a midpoint in the process of a changing focus in the fictional representation of desire from *yu* to *qing*, a point I explore in detail in the last four chapters of the study. Because *Bian er chai* and *Lin Lan Xiang* constantly appeal to the notion of *qing* in order to justify same-sex love, a close reading of these two works should enable us to appreciate better the impact of the promotion of *qing* on the mapping or remapping of gender boundaries in late imperial China. However, the attempts to redraw these boundaries are not as "radical" as they might first appear. In many works of fiction and drama, a same-sex relationship is defended as a deviation in form that vindicates the moral values of the norm (such as filiality or chastity in a heterosexual relationship). In the defenses of *qing*, this is familiar rhetoric (a man of *qing*, for example, is presented as more filial as well as more virtuous). In *Lin Lan Xiang* the spiritual lesbianism associated with *qing* is celebrated in part because, instead of challenging the patriarchal institution of polygamous marriage, it helps consolidate that institution. At the same time, sexual lesbianism, which is always associated with *yu*, is condemned, although the juxtaposition of the two in the novel is more complicated, as we shall see in Chapter 7. The familiar dichotomy between *qing* and *yu* is reformulated and thus attains new significance in the context of same-sex desire.

The dichotomy between *qing* and *yu* continues to be a major thematic concern in two long, eighteenth-century novels, *Guwangyan* 姑妄言 (Preposterous words) and *Yesou puyan* 野叟曝言 (The humble words of an old rustic). Both novels, especially *Guwangyan*, contain extended graphic and explicit descriptions of sex (something usually thought to be more typical of works produced during the late Ming and early Qing). In both novels, however, *qing* also occupies a prominent place and serves as a contrast to various forms of physical lust, or *yu*, and sexual excess is associated with evil forces in society. In *Guwangyan*, the evil officials, eunuchs, and bandits are invariably lecherous people who contribute directly to the downfall of the Ming,

29. Studies by others on this issue are cited in Chapter 7.

whereas the character Zhong Qing, an upright student and later a loyal official who is also a faithful lover, is represented as a man of exemplary *qing*. In *Yesou puyan*, the contrast between *qing* and *yu* is also carefully maintained in terms of good and evil in a fashion not unlike the theory of *zhengqing* and *bianqing* of the eighteenth-century dramatist Jiang Shiquan, briefly discussed in Chapter 2. Here, however, *qing* is often transformed along Neo-Confucian lines (*daoxuehua* 道學化), something already anticipated in many scholar-beauty novels such as *Haoqiu zhuan*. *Qing* is now redefined as the ultimate Confucian virtue, and plays a crucial role in the phenomenal public achievements of the male protagonist. One message of *Yesou puyan* is that a great Confucian does not have to be a puritan; he can, to borrow a term from the seventeenth-century writer Li Yu, be a "romantic Confucian" (*fengliu daoxue* 風流道學).[30]

However, by the mid-eighteenth century, expressions of *qing* had become so burdensome as well as so conventionalized that Wu Jingzi 吳敬梓 (1701–54), unlike the authors of *Guwangyan* and *Yesou puyan*, included them as targets of his satire in his famous *Rulin waishi*, a scathing critique of various contemporary literati mores. Chapter 30 of this novel presents a fascinating conversation between two literati characters, Du Shenqing and Ji Weixiao, which parodies some of the conventional motifs associated with the concept of *qing* as they had evolved in literature in late imperial China. This lengthy conversation merits a full quotation here. Congratulated by Ji Weixiao for marrying a concubine, Du Shenqing replies with a frown:

> "I am doing this simply to continue my family line, Sir. If not for the necessity of that, why should I take a concubine?"
>
> "A brilliant scholar and a beautiful girl (才子佳人)!" quoted Ji. "We should enjoy ourselves while we are still young. I can't understand why you have said this."
>
> "This shows you don't know me (*buzhi wo* 不知我) at all, Weixiao," said Du. "As our first emperor said: 'If not for the fact that I was born of a woman, I would kill all the women in the world!' Have you ever met a woman you could respect? I assure you, they affect me so painfully, I can smell a woman three rooms away!"...
>
> "Are you found of climbing mountains, or visiting rivers and lakes?" asked Ji.
>
> "My health is not up to it," replied Du. "I find these activities too strenuous."
>
> "Are you a music lover?"
>
> "I like to listen to music occasionally, but if I hear it too often it jars on my ears."
>
> A few more cups, and Du was a little tipsy.

30. See the concluding poem in the last scene of Li Yu's play *Shen luanjiao*, p. 528.

"Weixiao!" he said and heaved a long sigh. "Since ancient times no man has been able to see through the word *qing*."

"The *qing* between man and woman is certainly the greatest," replied Ji. "Yet you said just now you had no interest in women."

"And is *qing* confined to that between men and women? No, the *qing* of friends is more intense! Just look at the story of the Lord E and his embroidered coverlet. And in all history I consider Emperor Ai of the Han, who wanted to abdicate in favor of [his male lover] Dong Xian, shows the truest understanding of *qing*. Even Yao and Shun were no better than this, for all their polite deferring to others. But what a pity that no one understands this lofty *qing*!"

"True," rejoined Ji. "Have you never had a lover who truly understands you (*zhixin qingren* 知心情人)?"

"If I could live and die with such a man, I would not be grieving and pining away like this (*duochou shanbing* 多愁善病)! But I haven't been lucky enough to find a true friend (*zhiji* 知己), and this is why I so often give way to 'grieving under the moon and shedding tears in the wind (對月傷懷, 臨風洒淚)'!"

"You should look for this person among the actors."

"You really know nothing about this, Weixiao! To seek a true friend among actors is like looking for a female lover (*qingzhong* 情種) in the courtesans' quarter. Nothing could be more wrong! Such a relationship must be based on a spiritual affinity that transcends corporeality (相遇於心腹之間,相感於形骸之外). People involved in such a relationship must be the greatest men of all times!"

He struck his knee and sighed.

"But there's no such man in the world. No, Heaven has condemned me, Du Shenqing, for all my gallant spirit and grieving, to pine away alone." With this said, he began to shed tears.

"Why, this man is possessed!" thought Ji. "Let me play a trick on him."

"You mustn't say there is no such man in the world, Sir," he declared. "I know a young man who is neither an actor nor a scholar, but a Taoist priest. He is handsome and elegant, but not in any feminine way—he is a true masculine beauty. It always irritates me to hear people praise a handsome man by declaring he looks like a woman. How ridiculous! Anyone who likes feminine beauty can look at woman. But there is a masculine beauty too, which is seldom recognized."

"Only this remark of yours is worthy of being circled (*gaiquan* 該圈 [i.e., worth commending; examiners grading papers circled noteworthy phrases or sentences])!" cried Du, clapping the table. "But tell me more about this man."[31]

31. Wu Jingzi, *Rulin waishi huijiao huiping ben*, pp. 407–10; English trans. (modified) from Hsien-i Yang and Gladys Yang, *The Scholars*, pp. 326–28.

Among the familiar motifs of *qing* in literati literature being rehearsed here, a few of them are worth special notice: the narcissistic search for someone who can appreciate oneself, the self-pitying image of a pining-away woman, and the insistence on a relationship of spiritual affinity in terms of homosocialization (in the case of Du Shenqing, the insistence on a true friendship between two men).[32]

As discussed in Chapter 2, many disenfranchised literati tried to appropriate *qing* as a means of claiming, or maintaining their claim of, membership in the cultural elite. It may not be an exaggeration to suggest that the specific content of *qing* was largely invented as well as defined by many such literati writers. The degree to which a particular literary work can be judged to be a work of *qing* often correlates with the degree to which this work is "literatiized" (*wenrenhua* 文人化).[33] Anthony Yu, in discussing the early history of *qing*, has called attention to the intimate relationship between *zhi* 志 (another loaded term, often translated as "intention," "aspiration," or "ambition," depending on the context) and *qing* in early Chinese literature.[34] *Zhi* is

32. The term "homosocial" is borrowed from Eve Kosofsky Sedgwick (*Between Men*). She observes (pp. 1–2) that "'homosocial' is a word occasionally used in history and social sciences, where it describes social bonds between persons of the same sex; it is a neologism, obviously formed by analogy with 'homosexual' . . . and just as obviously meant to be distinguished from 'homosexual.' In fact, it is applied to such activities as 'male bonding,' which may, as in our society, be characterized by intense homophobia, fear and hatred of homosexuality. To draw the 'homosocial' back into the orbit of 'desire,' of the potentially erotic, then, is to hypothesize the potential unbrokenness of a continuum between homosocial and homosexual—a continuum whose visibility, for men, in our society, is radically disrupted."

33. For a discussion of the literati-zation of the Chinese novel, see my *Literati and Self-Re/Presentation*, pp. 15–26. Steven Roddy also focuses on the relationship between literati identity and several Qing novels in his more recent *Literati Identity and Its Fictional Representation in Late Imperial China*.

34. Anthony Yu, *Rereading the Stone*, pp. 83–86. Zhu Ziqing (*Shi yan zhi bian*, esp. pp. 34–42) argues that *zhi* originally referred to "public" aspirations, but writers in later ages (especially since the period of the Southern and Northern dynasties [420–589]) expanded the meaning of *zhi* to include private feelings so that they could appear to be following the tradition of *zhi* even though they were actually more concerned with the private *qing*. Citing Kong Yingda's 孔穎達 (574–648) gloss on a passage in *Zuozhuan*, which insists that *zhi* and *qing* are interchangeable (*Chunqiu Zuozhuan zhengyi* 春秋左傳正義, p. 406; reprinted in Ruan Yuan, *Shisan jing zhusu*, p. 2108), Guo Shaoyu ("Shilun *Wenxing tiaolong*," pp. 23–25) has argued the opposite—that *zhi* was originally a broad term not distinguishable from *qing* in terms of the concern with social reality. It formally began to be distinguished from *qing* only when Lu Ji put forward the theory of *shi yuan qing* (poetry follows one's *qing*). People of the

often associated with the idea of recognition—the recognition of someone with worthy *zhi* or political aspirations.[35] As we have seen, words such as *zhixin* or *zhiji* are important terms in the language in which Du Shenqing and his friend carry on their "pure talk" (*qingtan* 清談) on *qing* in *Rulin waishi*. "Recognition" becomes almost a defining quality of any relationship of *qing*, whether such relationship is sexual or not. In fact, it is precisely due to the importance attached to "recognition" that a heterosexual relationship can be, and often is, presented in terms of male-male friendship. The analogy is predicated on the *qing* of mutual recognition supposedly shared by these two types of relationships: the beauty of a woman is appreciated by her lover or husband just as a man's talent and worth are recognized by another man. This is captured in the saying "A man dies for one who appreciate his values [*zhiji zhe* 知己者], and a woman adorns herself for one who admires her [*yueji zhe* 悦己者]."[36] Both hinge on "recognition." Desexualizing the love between a man and a woman into a homosocial relationship of mutual appreciation is a common narrative strategy in scholar-beauty fiction, and the reverse strategy of using sexual love as a metaphor to describe a "political relationship" (say, between a powerful minister and a protégé) was a well-established convention in literati literature. Both, however, can be regarded as part of the repertoire of *qing*. This may account, presumably because of the compatibility between *qing* and *zhi*, for the common argument of many advocates of *qing* during the late Ming and early Qing that a faithful lover can be and has to be a loyal subject to his lord. Du Shenqing's professed distaste for women and his declared homoerotic yearning for a true male friend can also be read as one of his tactics to outdo his peers in presenting himself as a person of *qing*. The display of the intention to find a true friend among men, he hopes, will distinguish him from those suffering from the contamination of *yu* by making himself appear more spiritual. On the other

---

Southern Dynasties tended to interpret *qing* in the narrow sense of an attachment between man and woman. One thing that both Zhu and Guo, however, seem to agree on is the intimate relationship between these two important concepts. See also Steven Van Zoeren's discussions in *Poetry and Personality*, pp. 52–79. The bifurcation of *zhi* (understood as a broad concept) into *qing* and *zhi* (understood as a narrow concept) pointed out by Guo appears to have paralleled the process of gradual distinction between *qing* and *xing* in the early history of Chinese thought that I outline in Chapter 2.

35. For a discussion of the early tradition of "recognition," see Henry, "The Motif of Recognition in Early China."

36. "Cike liezhuan" 刺客列傳, in Sima Qian, *Shiji*, vol. 8, p. 2519.

hand, his self-image as a gentleman of *qing* needs a touch of the unconventional (viz., his professed misogyny and disinterest in the heterosexual), although his "vocabularies" of *qing* are hopelessly conventional.

The particular words Du Shenqing chooses to characterize himself, such as "grieving" and "pining away," are reminiscent of the familiar image of a lovesick woman pining away in her boudoir, an image prevalent in literary works—poems, plays, or fictional stories—that thematize *qing*. To desire is to be desired; a lovesick woman desperately searches for a worthy man to desire herself. The distinctions between desiring subject and desired object tend to collapse in the process of *qing*. The selfless search for a true friend for whom one is willing to give up one's life turns into a narcissistic gesture of self-aggrandizement. Selflessness and narcissism become indistinguishable in the act of *qing*. It is no accident that in *Rulin waishi* Du Shenqing is the character most anxious to show himself off as a man of great *qing*, since he is also the most narcissistic character in the novel. In one memorable scene, he chases his own shadow back and forth in the setting sun, a narcissistic gesture, a late Qing commentator reminds us, captured in the Chinese phrase "pitying one's own shadow and appreciating one's own romantic self" (顧影自憐風流獨賞).[37]

Although this study is concerned primarily with fiction, a brief digression to consider two famous works of drama, *Mudan ting* and *Taohua shan*, may be of interest here, since both are known for their focus on *qing*, and both are regarded as milestones in the history of literary representation of *qing* in late imperial China. Moreover, both, especially *Mudan ting*, exerted considerable influence on fiction. Tang Xianzu's *Mudan ting* has been celebrated as *the* drama of *qing* ever since it appeared during the late sixteenth century. It is the classic against which later narrative works of *qing* are often measured. The female protagonist Du Liniang (Bridal Du as she is known in English translation) has become the quintessential symbol of *qing*. She falls in love with a man in a dream and then dies of lovesickness, only to be revived later by the power of *qing* and (re)united with her lover. As suggested by the first name of her lover, Mengmei 夢梅 (literally, "dreaming of apricots"), the male protagonist is an "object of desire" *dreamed up* or invented by Du Liniang in order to "slake her thirst" (to fulfill her desire), which is in part caused by her reading the love poems (others' desires) in the *Shijing*. This is

37. Wu Jingzi, *Rulin waishi huiping huijiao ben*, 29.402.

underscored in the Chinese proverbs quoted in the lines sung by Liu Mengmei as he examines the self-portrait left by the now-deceased Du Liniang in Scene 26: "Just as I 'sketch a cake to appease my hunger' so she 'gazes at apricots to slake her thirst (*wangmei zike* 望梅止渴).'"[38] It is as if by looking at the portrait, he could somehow manage to appease his burning longing for the person portrayed. Furthermore, in that very portrait, the "sketched cake" Liu is using to appease his "hunger," Du Liniang portrayed herself as "gazing at the apricot tree in order to slake her thirst"—the lady in the portrait "invents" an apricot tree/lover in her dream to satisfy the desire stirred up in her by reading of others' desires. Consequently, someone's "self-representation" of her own attempts to "gaze at apricots to slake thirst" is being used by another as a representation of a cake (a "sketched cake") to "appease hunger." The desire of each lover is sustained by his or her own imagination, which is in turn based on the representation (imagination) of an "other." The desire of each is defined by the absence of its object; one is a figure accessible only in dreams, and the other is already dead and accessible only via a portrait. Representation becomes a form of desire precisely because of the absence of its object. Representation is necessitated by absence, much as the existence of desire is contingent on the absence of its object. Once the object becomes reachable and once fulfillment is achieved, desire no longer exists.[39]

Moreover, Du Liniang feels compelled to represent her own act of desiring once her desire is aroused through the reading of the representation of others' desires so that her imagined lover can continue to desire her even when she is not present. This highlights the subjective nature of *qing* or desire, which pre-exists its own object and which takes the absence of its object as a precondition for its own existence. Du Liniang first experiences desire in "representation" (reading and dreaming) and then invents an object to sustain that desire. If the dead Du Liniang is indeed resurrected by the magical

38. Tang Xianzu, *Mudan ting*, p. 156; English trans. from Birch, *The Peony Pavilion*, p. 145. As if to emphasize this symbolic meaning of the name of the male protagonist, Cyril Birch (*The Peony Pavilion*, pp. 42–43) translates the line sung by Du Liniang in scene 10 (曉來望梅關宿妝殘; *Mudan ting*, p. 53) as "Like one 'eyeing the apricot flower to slake her thirst' at dawn, cheeks blurred with last night's rouge, I gaze at Apricot Blossom Pass." The first part of the sentence is the translator's own interpretation of the possible significance of the "Apricot Blossom Pass."

39. Here we may recall the emphasis on "absence" and "representation" in many contemporary Western theories of desire as I briefly refer to in the "Introduction."

power of *qing*, then we may have to conclude that "desire" pre-exists not only its object but also its own subject in that not only is Liu Mengmei invented by her desire to be desired but so is Du Liniang herself, at least the Du Liniang that is resurrected.[40] Metaphorically, Du Liniang is (re)invented or resurrected by her own desire so that she can continue desiring after death.

There is an unmistakably narcissistic quality in *qing* as experienced by Du Liniang: *qing* is a self-generating process that feeds on itself—needing to sustain itself by constantly inventing and reinventing both the object and the subject. The dreamed-of (invented) Liu Mengmei is later reinvented as the "real" Liu Mengmei, and the dreaming Du Liniang is reinvented as Du Liniang the ghost and then reinvented again as the resurrected Du Liniang. This creational process of *qing* has puzzled many, starting with Du Liniang's father, who is not yet fully convinced at the end of the play that the Du Liniang he is seeing is not an impostor or a ghost. Ironically, he accepts the reinvented Du Liniang as "real" only after the emperor has examined her with a mirror, which is supposed to be able to tell a real human being from a ghost by showing whether she casts a shadow (a ghost is supposed to fear its own reflection in a mirror). As suggested by these images of mirror, reflection, and shadow, all of which have something to do with absence and the need to represent, *qing* is self-reflexive. To desire is also to be desired. There is probably no one better to serve as the symbol of *qing* than Du Liniang, who seems to be the very embodiment of self-love and self-pity:

> And yet, this bloom of springtime no eye has seen.
> What if my beauty should amaze the birds
> and out of shame for the comparison
> "cause fish to sink, wild geese to fall to earth,
> petals to close, the moon to hide her face"
> while all the flowers tremble? (scene 10, Tang Xianzu,
> *Mudan ting*, p. 58; Birch, *The Peony Pavilion*, p. 44)

Grieving and self-pitying (*shangxin zilian* 傷心自憐) are part of her very being (scene 12, *Mudan ting*, p. 67). Of course, images of self-pity and grieving are not uncommon in traditional poetry on *qing*, especially in works associ-

40. Wai-yee Li (*Enchantment and Disenchantment*, pp. 51–54) has an interesting discussion of the issue of "desire preexists and is in some ways independent of, the object of desire" and its relevance to *Mudan ting*, although I am not in complete agreement with her interpretation of the view of Ji Kang (ibid., p. 51).

ated with lovesick or abandoned women. What is significant is that now they are reframed in the new context of a long drama in which *qing* is celebrated as an all-defying force and in which desire is constitutive of the subject, which is the agency of that very desire.

Du Liniang's narcissism is best captured in her attempt to paint her self-portrait "lest the worst should suddenly befall me and no one then ever learn of the beauty of Bridal Du who came from far Sichuan" (Scene 14, Tang Xianzu, *Mudan ting*, p. 76; Birch, *The Peony Pavilion*, p. 67). The portrait is an attempt to "freeze" her own beauty in time so that she can continue to desire and be desired even after her death. And, moreover, her beauty must be "interpreted" or represented by herself. This is *her* rendering of her own self as reflected in the mirror. Her use of the mirror, however, here should call into question the authenticity of her self-representation. A "true" self-image is virtually impossible since the model reflected in the mirror is already a representation. Consequently, Du Liniang's self-portrait is at best a representation of another representation. Despite such doubts about the authenticity of self-representation, she will later ask Liu Mengmei to show the self-portrait to her father as proof that Liu is not an imposter but his real son-in-law, although her father is never fully convinced that his daughter has been resurrected, let alone married. It is crucial that the portrait be painted by Du herself because for Du, Liu, and probably many others, the portrait is truer than even her own real self (the audience, unlike Du's father in the play, is supposed to accept the resurrected Du Liniang as real). To be represented is to be truer partly because the representation can survive the real person being represented, just as Du Liniang's portrait survives herself. Here we may recall Du Shenqing in *Rulin waishi*, who expresses the wish to be considered one of the greatest men of all time by cultivating a spiritual affinity with a true *zhiji*. *Qing*-struck people are almost always obsessed with posterity. Du Liniang's self-portrait is only one of many tangible attempts at self-immortalization. In Du Liniang we can find many foreshadowings of Lin Daiyu, the narcissistic female protagonist of the eighteenth-century *Honglou meng*, and the ultimate symbol of melancholy *qing*.

If *Mudan ting* embodies full confidence in the supreme power of *qing*, then Kong Shangren's 孔尚任 (1648–1718) *Taohua shan*, written approximately one century later, questions that confidence by problematizing the autonomy of the world of *qing* in *Mudan ting*. *Taohua shan*'s female protagonist, the courtesan Li Xiangjun, is known for her singing talents, especially in the role of Du Liniang in *Mudan ting*. She aspires to be a worthy successor to Du Liniang as a heroine of great *qing*. Du Liniang was able to insist on inventing her own token of *qing* by painting a self-portrait for her lover, which is believed to be even more authentic than the subject it portrays because it is a *self*-portrait. The authenticity of the central symbol of *qing* in *Taohua shan*, the peach blossom fan, is in question the moment it is invented. When forced to marry a high official as a concubine, Li Xiangjun tries to commit suicide by knocking her head against the ground in order to remain faithful to her lover, Hou Fangyu. As a result, her blood accidentally stains the fan, which her lover has given her as a token of his love. Later the bloodstains on the fan are converted into "peach blossoms" by the painter Yang Wencong, a morally ambiguous character. The peach blossom fan is then sent to Hou as a reminder of Li Xiangjun's fidelity. The fan is eventually torn apart by the Taoist priest Chang because he believes that Hou Fangyu and Li Xiangjun, as subjects of the Ming monarch, should not indulge in personal *qing* when the nation has already been lost to the Manchus. Here the implications of *qing* become ironic: for the fan to become a symbol of her chaste love, Li has to rely on Yang, a person with no moral backbone. Self-representation in Li's case has become impossible—the peach blossoms have to be painted by someone else, even though her blood is used as "pigment."

The significance of the peach blossom fan becomes even more ironic when Li Xiangjun is granted another fan with peach blossoms painted on it by the totally incompetent Hongguang emperor precisely because she plays the role of Du Liniang so well! The Hongguang emperor's indulgence in theatrical performances of *qing* (including *Mudan ting*) and his total neglect of the well-being of the nation are symptomatic of the decadence of Ming culture, which was considered by many to be the ultimate cause for the fall of the dynasty. The Taoist priest's destruction of the peach blossom fan at the end of the play is the ultimate questioning of the authenticity of the kind of *qing* celebrated in *Mudan ting* at a time when the cultural sophistication of *qing* is seen as a curse that helped to bring down a nation. In other words, Du Liniang lost her authenticity as a model of *qing*, theatrical or real, when people lost their faith in the resurrecting power of *qing* and when the cause of resurrecting a fallen nation proved to be doomed. Here the realm of *qing* is no longer the autonomous world it appears to be in *Mudan ting*. *Qing* is now hopelessly entangled in the politics of betrayal (the wicked character Ruan Dacheng happens to be a master playwright of *qing*) and duplicity (the painter Yang Wencong, who has no moral stand); *qing* is now identified with narcissistic overindulgence in private desire and total obliviousness to the public crisis (the self-indulgent emperor and, to a lesser degree, the male protagonist Hou Fangyu). *Taohua shan* should prepare us for *Rulin waishi*'s parody of various clichés of *qing* and for the even more profound and subtler rethinking of *qing* in *Honglou meng* almost half a century later.

In fact, in *Rulin waishi*, Du Shenqing's dissatisfaction with the fad of finding a lover among courtesans was anticipated by *Taohua shan* many decades earlier, although ostensibly the play celebrates a courtesan's *qing* and her political loyalty.[41] Feng Menglong, who played a crucial role in the late Ming cult of *qing*, was fascinated with the story of the Song poet Liu Yong's romantic involvement with courtesans, a fascination not unrelated to his own affair with a courtesan. As some scholars have argued, the late Ming cult of *qing* was intimately related to the courtesan culture of that time. As a eulogy to late Ming culture, *Taohua shan*, which centers on the love between a courtesan and a talented scholar, is both a celebration and a profound critique of the culture of *qing* that flourished during that period.

The love between a talented scholar and a "chaste" courtesan is the main story of the mid-Qing novel *Guwangyan*. In that novel, the male protagonist, just as Hou Fangyu and Li Xiangjun are urged to do at the end of *Taohua shan*, becomes a hermit, renouncing the world of *qing* after the fall of the Ming monarchy. Although the exact dating of *Guwangyan* is difficult, the novel was probably written at about the same time as *Taohua shan* (around the turn of eighteenth century) or a bit later. Although, as an erotic novel, *Guwangyan* is quite different from the historical drama *Taohua shan*, the historical backdrop of both stories is the fall of the Ming, and in both works the concept of *qing* occupies an important place. At the end of both, the protagonists renounce the world of *qing* in order to demonstrate political loyalty to the fallen monarchy. However, if *qing* is often problematized as well as celebrated with unprecedented self-consciousness in *Taohua shan*, it remains largely unproblematic throughout *Guwangyan*, where it is conveniently con-

41. In Chapter 54 of *Rulin waishi*, a character named Ting Yanzhi 丁言志 (a pun on the famous poetic dictum *shiyan zhi* [poetry expresses intent]), who lacks the necessary cash, is being shown the door by a prostitute when he tries to persuade her to accept some of his poems. This is apparently another parodistic reference to the courtesan culture celebrated during the late Ming. For a discussion of this episode, see my "Stylization and Invention," pp. 105–6.

trasted with *yu* (understood as physical lust). This contrast is also conscientiously maintained in the novel *Yesou puyan*. Despite some moments of ambiguity, the polarizing pattern of *qing* versus *yu* is the main ethical structure within which various forms of desire are represented and valorized in both *Guwangyan* and *Yesou puyan*.

This contrast between *qing* and *yu* continues in *Honglou meng*, although the contrasting rationale itself is seriously questioned. The issue of *qing* versus *yu* is reformulated in *Honglou meng* in terms of "lust of intent" (*yiyin* 意淫) versus the "lust of the flesh" (*pifu lanyin* 皮膚濫淫) (we return to this issue in Chapter 10). The relationship between these two new concepts, however, is anything but unproblematic. Both Du Liniang and Jia Baoyu, the male protagonist of *Honglou meng*, can be considered characters of narcissistic *qing* (Baoyu's narcissism is much subtler). However, the author of *Mudan ting* does not seem to have felt any pressure to extract *qing* from *yu*. For Tang Xianzu, sexuality itself is not problematic. Many readers have been impressed by the rather explicit descriptions of the sexual union between Du Liniang and Liu Mengmei during their first encounter in Du's dream in scene 10. This sexual experience is repeated in scene 28, "Union in the Shades" ("Yougou" 幽媾). However, sexuality becomes a problem for Baoyu. The sexual initiation in both dream and real life early in the novel is the only sexual experience Baoyu has in the first eighty chapters. "Sexuality" becomes something Baoyu has to struggle to forget (or to suppress?) as he is growing up (although not in the last forty chapters, supposedly written by another author).[42] The supposed harmony between *qing* and *yu* in the sixteenth-century *Mudan ting* begins to disappear in the eighteenth-century *Honglou meng*. One central problem in the *Honglou meng* is how to redefine the relationship between *qing* and *yu*.

Many other issues raised in *Mudan ting* and *Taohua shan*, such as the narcissistic nature of *qing*, representation versus desire, and the illusionary nature of the autonomous world of *qing*, are further explored in *Honglou meng*, with great subtlety.[43] Given its complex textual history and the many revisions or rewritings of the novel, we might read *Honglou meng* almost as a meta-text that re-enacts within itself the subtle shifts in the representation

42. For a discussion of Baoyu's problematic sexuality, see Miller, "Children of the Dream," pp. 237–41.

43. For an interesting discussion of "representation and desire" in *Honglou meng*, see Anthony Yu, *Rereading the Stone*, pp. 203–9.

of desire in late imperial China—a gradual shift from a fascination with *yu* as manifested in works such as *Jin Ping Mei* to the kind of obsession with *qing* found in *Mudan ting, Taohua shan, Lin Lan Xiang,* and *Dingqing ren*. In this sense of a shifting process, *Honglou meng* can be regarded as a summation of all these works and as a profound novelistic rehearsal as well as rethinking of all the major motifs of *qing* throughout its history. This trajectory from *yu* to *qing* is also a history of desire becoming increasingly self-conscious of itself, as masterfully demonstrated in *Honglou meng*. Under the tremendous burden of conventions (when all expressions of *qing* have become so stylized, as satirized in *Rulin washi*), a new strategy of *qing* has to be proposed or invented—*qing* is now being redefined as a unique quality of being young in *Honglou meng*. The only hope one has for maintaining the authenticity of *qing* against the sheer burden of conventions and traditions is to seek to remain a child unbothered by sexual libido as well as by the burden of all the clichés of *qing*.

Some readers have tried to relate the novel's apparent obsession with *qing* to the influence of Li Zhi's famous theory of *tongxin* (the childlike mind).[44] If we consider *Honglou meng* a work that consciously addresses the issue of the legacy of the late Ming, then the idea of *tongxin* is shown to be only an aspiration that can never be realized, just as Baoyu has to admit that one day he has to outgrow his childhood and that he cannot forever pretend to be a child indulging in "lust of intent" in the company of his female cousins and his maids.[45] In a way, we can read the character of Baoyu almost as a personification of the burden of the claim of having a childlike mind—the predicament of someone who insists on being treated as a child by refusing to grow up. For Baoyu, the possibilities of *qing* are hopelessly predicated on his ability to (claim to) be a child, despite the inevitable maturing that ultimately diminishes his ability to make this claim.

In this study, the reading of specific works of fiction begins with Chapter 4 on *Jin Ping Mei* and ends with Chapter 10 on *Honglou meng*. Most of the works discussed in the study can be read, in one way or another, as responses to *Jin Ping Mei*, and the most remarkable response is unquestionably *Honglou meng*. Despite their obvious differences, both Ximen Qing and Jia

44. See Jing Wang, *The Story of Stone*, pp. 144–47.

45. Mizoguchi (*Zhongguo qian jindai sixiang*, pp. 195–202) has pointed out that the word *tongxin* was often used as a pejorative term in late Ming writings (meaning "childish" and "uncultivated"). This negative term was appropriated by Li Zhi to refer to what he had himself defined as the "childlike mind," or the uncorrupted mind of a man.

Baoyu are surrounded by women and bothered by their relationships with different women, a common novelistic situation of polygamous desire. Like Ximen Qing, Jia Baoyu also seems to be constantly troubled by a vague sense of discontent, often right after a moment of perfect gratification. Both have to constantly (re)invent the object of desire in order to sustain their desiring, although Baoyu's main problem is *qing* rather than *yu*. However, physical desire can by no means be relegated to the margins in *Honglou meng*. In Chapter 10 of this study, we shall see how successful the author of *Honglou meng* was in his attempt to differentiate his male protagonist from protagonists such as Ximen Qing. It is precisely in this effort to differentiate Baoyu that we are can discern a parallel to the evolution of desire in the Chinese novel during these two centuries. What is especially remarkable about *Honglou meng* is that this evolution is also fully re-enacted as the novel unfolds, or, as we the readers, in our reading, "reconstruct" the writing or rewriting (*chengshu guocheng* 成書過程) of this novel. Besides being a fascinating novel on the "desires," as they are experienced by its characters, *Honglou meng* also invites the reader to witness the interesting and yet seemingly never-ending process of *itself* trying to change from a novel dominated by *yu* (as suggested by one of its titles, *Fengyue baojian* 風月寶鑒 [A mirror for the romantic]) to a novel trying to propose a new concept of *qing*, a process that calls our attention to the complexities of the subtle relationship between these two important concepts of desire in Chinese cultural history.

CHAPTER FOUR
The Materiality of Desire and the Beyond in Jin Ping Mei

As mentioned in Chapter 3, *Jin Ping Mei* marks an important milestone in the history of the Chinese novel. It is probably the first Chinese novel to be written by a single author rather than being a product of a long process of textual evolution involving many hands. Of more significance, it is also the first full-length novel devoted to depicting the private lives of its major characters and their "private desires." It is a novel dominated by images of screens, windows, and bedroom curtains.

Jin Ping Mei's insistence on scrutinizing the private desires of the individual also captured the attention of its famous seventeenth-century commentator, Zhang Zhupo 張竹坡 (1670–98). Zhang drew attention to the important motif of *pozhan* 破綻 (cracks, rifts) in the novel:

> There are many episodes in the *Jin Ping Mei* in which the clandestine activities of some of the characters are disclosed to others [due to *pozhan*]. For example, Ximen Qing's sexual intercourse with Pan Jinlian during the funeral service for her husband is overheard by the monks outside the windows; Pan Jinlian's affair with Qingtung is discovered by Sun Xue'e, and the even more incriminating perfume sachet that Pan Jinlian has given him is also found on Qingtung's person; Pan Jinlian discovers Ximen Qing's secret assignations with Li Ping'er over the garden wall and stumbles upon Song Huilian's affair with Ximen Qing; Li Ping'er's remarks in the Feicuixuan

are overheard by Pan Jinlian, but her own antics in the grape arbor are witnessed by Tiegun.[1]

Although references to acts of eavesdropping and peeping are not uncommon in other works of fiction,[2] the frequency with which they are described or mentioned in *Jin Ping Mei* is indeed remarkable. Few private conversations or acts of intimacy go unwitnessed. Spying on others or overhearing them becomes almost a ritual in the novel.

Given the rapid urbanization that was taking place in the mid-Ming, it is tempting to speculate that the heightened consciousness of *si* 私 (the private, privacy) exhibited in *Jin Ping Mei* might be related to the dramatic increases in urban population density.[3] An enhanced sense of the need for personal privacy may have been related to the shrinking space within which people could shield themselves from the gaze of others and impingement by the public. In *Jin Ping Mei*, Ximen Qing's affair with Pan Jinlian soon becomes common knowledge among the neighbors, apparently because Pan's house is located on a crowded street. In Chapter 5, after murdering her husband, Wu the Elder, Pan Jinlian knocks on the wall of their bedroom to inform her next-door neighbor Dame Wang that the mission has been accomplished (5.51).[4] This certainly points to a relative lack of privacy even within their

1. "*Piping diyi qishu Jin Ping Mei* dufa" 批評第一奇書金瓶梅讀法, in *Zhang Zhupo piping "Jin Ping Mei,"* p. 27 (hereafter referred to as *Zhang Zhupo*); English trans. from David T. Roy, "How to Read the *Jin Ping Mei,*" in David Rolston, ed., *How to Read the Chinese Novel*, p. 207.

2. McMahon (*Causality and Containment*, pp. 35–36) has some interesting observations on various motifs of *pozhan* in many works of traditional Chinese fiction, although he does not specifically refer to this particular comment on *Jin Ping Mei* by Zhang Zhupo.

3. For the shortage of housing and the high housing costs in towns and cities during the Ming dynasty, see Han Dacheng, *Mingdai chengshi yanjiu*, p. 507. The issue of privacy, as far as I know, was rarely explicitly addressed in traditional China. A remark by Gong Zizhen 龔自珍 (1792–1841), although he lived two centuries after the novel was first printed, is of some interest here: "When wild cats copulate with each other, they never shun people, even during the day. This is because they have no sense of 'privacy' (*wusi* 無私). However, people must have the protection of boudoir and the shield of the curtains because they want to hide what they do in bed, and they won't do it if they are forced to feel embarrassed when exposed" ("Lunsi" 論私, in Gong Zizhen, *Quanji*, p. 92). For a discussion of the so-called sense of privacy in early Chinese thought, see Christina Whitman, "Privacy in Confucian and Taoist Thought." However, Whitman has failed to persuade me that the evidence she has marshaled from various early Chinese written sources is directly relevant to the issue of privacy.

4. Unless otherwise noted, all references to *Jin Ping Mei* are to *Jin Ping Mei cihua*, ed. Mei Jie. Chapter and page numbers are given in parentheses in the text.

residence. Wang Liu'er cannot keep her incestuous affair with her brother-in-law secret because her house is sandwiched between those of her neighbors on both sides. Someone even manages to see what is happening inside her bedroom from the top of the wall (33.361). No wonder Ximen Qing insists on her moving from her old house in Ox Hide Street to a new house in Lion Street as soon as he gets involved with her (39.433).

On the other hand, Ximen Qing is able to keep his affair with Li Ping'er a secret from the neighbors and consequently from Li's husband, Hua Zixu, largely thanks to the fact that they are next-door neighbors and that their gardens share a common wall: "As long as they did not go in and out the main gates, there would be no way for the neighbors in the vicinity to find out about their clandestine affair" (13.153; *Plum*, 13.267).[5] By climbing over the wall instead of entering her house from the street, he can make sure that no neighbor sees him visiting Li Ping'er (although, ironically, he is eventually caught by his own concubine Pan Jinlian on his side of the wall inside his own garden). Here the common wall, which is supposed to function as a boundary and a device of separation, is turned into a well-camouflaged "crack," or *pozhan*, through which Ximen Qing is able to carry on an illicit affair with his female neighbor without arousing the suspicions of their other neighbors. This unexpected function of a common wall also captured the attention of Zhang Zhupo, who, in his interlineal comments, kept careful track of the number of times "wall" (*qiang* 牆) occurs in that particular section of the novel.[6]

Defending one's privacy and protecting oneself from eavesdroppers and spies become major concerns for many characters in the novel:

> It so happens that well-to-do households are equipped with double windows, the outer layers of which are called shutters, and the inner layers, casements. When the woman sent her maidservants out of the room, she closed the two casements on the inside, so that even though the room was illuminated by lamps and candles, no one could see in from the outside. (13.134; *Plum*, 13.264)

5. David Roy's translation of the first twenty chapters of *Jin Ping Mei cihua*, *The Plum in the Golden Vase*, is referred to as *Plum*, and chapter and page numbers are cited in parentheses.

6. See the interlineal comments, *Zhang Zhupo*, pp. 205–9. Cf. McMahon's (*Causality and Containment*, pp. 26–27) general discussions of the "wall of self-containment" and the significance of the "crossing of boundaries" in traditional Chinese fiction.

Here the ability to protect one's privacy is dependent on one's financial resources. Only the well-to-do can afford this kind of double window. However, for a well-to-do household, which tends to have a large number of members, the main threat to privacy seems to stem from within the household itself.[7] Indeed, the protection offered by the double window soon proves to be totally inadequate, when Li Ping'er's maid Yingchun uses a hairpin to poke a hole in the window paper (13.135). Occasionally, being overheard turns out to be a blessing. Ximen Qing is quite touched when he happens to overhear Wu Yueniang's prayer to Buddha that demonstrates her genuine concern for him. This results in their unexpected reconciliation (21.219). More often, however, the results are fatal. There are many instances in the novel in which being spied on seals one's fate. The maid Qiujue reports Pan Jinlian's affair with Ximen Qing's son-in-law Chen Jingji to Wu Yueniang after she repeatedly eavesdrops on them (chap. 83). This leads to Wu Yueniang's decision to sell Pan Jinlian, a decision that will eventually lead to Pan's death at the hands of her murdered husband's brother Wu Song. Chen Jingji is killed by Zhang Sheng after he overhears Chen and Chunmei plotting to have him punished (chap. 99). Sometimes, the eavesdropper ends up paying with his or her own life. Ximen Qing's peeping at Lanshi, the wife of his new colleague, Mr. He (79.1039), proves to be fatal. He is so obsessed with the elusive Lanshi that he embarks on a deadly round of sexual escapades with several women in a short span of time, using these women to quench his unfulfilled desire for this unattainable woman. Ximen Qing finally collapses under Pan Jinlian (more about this later).

The fascination with acts of intrusion into others' privacy in *Jin Ping Mei* points to a heightened consciousness of such novels' obsession with the pri-

7. In his famous *Yuanshi shifan*, Yuan Cai 袁采 (*jinshi* 1163) made particular note of the importance of anticipating "eavesdropping" in a big family: "When living in a complex family, you should let the others know when you are coming or going by calling or by shuffling your sandals. Arriving silently is unacceptable because, should the others be discussing you, all concerned will be embarrassed and at a loss for what to do. . . . Do not assume that homes are secluded and vacant. If you are quick to find fault with others, you must always worry about whether they can hear you. There is a popular saying, 'The walls have ears.' It also said, 'By day speak not of men, by night speak not of ghosts.'" ("Tongju buke xiang jiyi" 同居不可相譏議, *Yuanshi shifan*, 1.16a–b; English trans. from Ebrey, *Family and Property in Sung China*, pp. 205–6). Obviously, by the time of the Song dynasty (960–1279), eavesdropping in large households had already became a problem serious enough for Yuan Cai to think it necessary to provide advice on this issue in his *jiaxun* (family instructions).

vate: *xiaoshuo* such as *Jin Ping Mei* make public the private experiences of an individual, a task that is inherently paradoxical: by focusing persistently and meticulously on the most intimate experiences of its characters (even their bedroom activities), the novel compels its reader to confront the full meaning of a private act; on the other hand, by making such an experience the object of representation to be shared by many "others" (the readers), the novel simultaneously undermines the private nature of these experiences.[8] Furthermore, reading a "morally compromising" *xiaoshuo*, unlike watching a play performed in public, is largely a secretive act and does in a way resemble eavesdropping and peeping through cracks or rifts.

The Chinese word *pozhan*, which can also mean "flaw" or "error" (99.1278), acquires new significance in reference to *Jin Ping Mei*; it not only refers to acts of voyeurism but also calls attention to the transgressive nature of both the act of voyeurism and what (such as an adulterous affair) is revealed by such an act. Never before in the history of the traditional Chinese novel was a work able to underscore so successfully the paradoxical nature of reading *xiaoshuo*: it is a private act that has deep "public" implications. Like any other voyeuristic act, reading *xiaoshuo* is always potentially "transgressive."

One way of appreciating the *Jin Ping Mei*'s focus on private desire is to study its relationship to *Shuihu zhuan*. *Jin Ping Mei* is developed from an episode in *Shuihu zhuan*, and a closer look at how the author of *Jin Ping Mei* appropriated and reworked this material illustrates the transition from *xiaoshuo* devoted to the public to those that concentrate on the private.[9] In *Shuihu zhuan* the story of Pan Jinlian's adulterous affair with Ximen Qing, the murdering of her husband, Wu the Elder, and Wu Song's subsequent revenge are only one of several incidents that force Wu Song to finally join the Liangshan rebels. This story is marginal in *Shuihu zhuan* and is significant only insofar as it explains Wu Song's decision. However, this single episode

8. Both Carlitz (*The Rhetoric of "Chin P'ing Mei"*) and Plaks (*Four Masterworks*, pp. 150–51) have emphasized the rhetorical importance of the figure of "voyeur" in the novel in terms of the involvement of the reader. Cf. Carlitz's (pp. 51–52) observation: "We watch these encounters through keyholes, we listen through walls. These other characters catch us in the act of watching Ximen Qing and his various partners, thus exposing our own frailties, demonstrating that the reader has as great a need for self-cultivation as do any of the characters in the novel."

9. For general discussions of the relationship between *Jin Ping Mei* and *Shuihu zhuan*, see Zhou Juntao, "*Jin Ping Mie* chaoyin *Shuihu zhuan* kaotan"; and Patrick Hanan, "Sources of the *Chin P'ing Mei*," pp. 25–32.

from *Shuihu zhuan,* with significant modifications, becomes a point of departure for another full-length novel, focusing on the private domain of Ximen Qing's large household. The author of *Jin Ping Mei* ingeniously postpones Wu Song's revenge for almost eighty chapters so that a series of lengthy stories can be told about the lives of these two adulterers as well as many others associated with them. Wu Song, the central character in the *Shuihu zhuan* episode, exits early in the novel only to reappear almost at the end of this novel to function as a sort of *deus ex machina,* whereas the two adulterers Ximen Qing and Pan Jinlian, both of whom are killed off by Wu Song in a story of only a few chapters in *Shuihu zhuan,* are now the protagonists of this one-hundred-chapter novel. In *Jin Ping Mei,* Wu Song's appearance is only significant in propelling the movement of the plot. As someone immune to the temptations of money and sex, Wu Song is by default exceptional, if not completely abnormal, in *Jin Ping Mei.* Unlike *Shuihu zhuan,* in which the sense of public justice and the values of the *haohan* 好漢 (manly heroes, with a strong sense of justice, who are usually unsusceptible to sex) are the narrative's central concerns, *Jin Ping Mei* presents a world in which almost everyone is consumed by desire: with few exceptions, the characters are preoccupied with money and sex. The author of *Jin Ping Mei* is deliberate in demonstrating how impossible it has become in his novelistic world for anyone to cling to a sense of justice, a far cry from *Shuihu zhuan.*[10]

One narrative strategy that underscores the impossibility of justice in *Jin Ping Mei* is to praise an official's sense of justice and then follow this with an undercutting acknowledgment that this official has to act against his own beliefs because of overwhelming pressures from his peers or superiors. For example, we are first told the prefect Chen Wenzhao is "an official of absolute integrity" (極是個清廉的官; 10.96). However, when his mentor Cai Jing and another high official intervene on Ximen Qing's behalf, he has to compromise his integrity by abandoning his attempt to redress the injustice done to Wu Song. The most he can do is to save Wu Song from the death penalty (10.98). In chapter 14, Ximen Qing bribes Cai Jing to interfere on behalf of Hua Zixu in a legal dispute. Cai pressures Prefect Yang Shi, another official of "absolute integrity," to render a judgment in Hua's favor

10. For a discussion of the *haohan* ideology in *Shuihu zhuan* and how it is replaced in the stories of Feng Menglong and Ling Mengchu, see McMahon, *Causality and Containment,* pp. 52–59.

(Cai can influence Yang because he was the examiner when Yang passed the *jinshi* exams). In chapter 92, Magistrate Huo is also said to be an official of honesty (*gengzhi* 鯁直; 92.1023), but we are soon told that he feels compelled to lessen Chen Jingji's punishment after receiving 100 taels of silver from him (92.1204–5).[11]

Read within the context of *Jin Ping Mei*, a passage incorporated from *Shuihu zhuan* about the hunters' response to Wu Song's killing of the tiger acquires new implications: "Strongman, are you a human or a god? You must have eaten the heart of an alligator, the liver of a leopard and the leg of a lion, or be made of gall! Otherwise, all by yourself, in the waning light, and without a weapon, how could you possibly have slain this man-eating tiger?" (1.6; *Plum*, 1.22). In the world of *Jin Ping Mei* heroic men (*haohan*) like Wu Song are indeed rare. *Shuhu zhuan*'s famous account of Wu Song's rebuff of Pan Jinlian's advances is now reframed in such a way in *Jin Ping Mei* that it compels the reader to view it as an isolated incident, because no other man in this novel is able to withstand such temptations. This new implication of the character of Wu Song did not escape the notice of Zhang Zhupo, who commented on Wu Song's resistance to Pan Jinlian's advances: "I did not expect to encounter a man like this in this novel" (不謂此書內有這樣一個男人).[12]

Indeed, there are only too few such *haohan* in *Jin Ping Mei*. As if to reinforce this impression, the author has several important characters from *Shuihu zhuan* appear in chapter 84. In that chapter Wu Yueniang is kidnapped by the bandits, and one of their leaders, Wang Ying (also known as the Dwarf Wang, who is one of the most lascivious rebels in *Shuhu zhuan*), tries to impose himself on her. Song Jiang tries to stop him and his reasoning is particularly interesting: "Brother, I understand you want to be a hero. However, you won't be able to become a *haohan* if you are addicted to something that will drain your marrow (犯了溜骨髓三個字)." He further argues that Wang will become a laughingstock among his fellow *haohan* if he imposes himself on this woman (84.1112). Coming almost at the end of the novel, this episode from *Shuihu zhuan*, just like Wu Song's story at the beginning, serves to remind the reader how distant the world of *Jin Ping Mei* is from that of *Shuihu*

11. The only exception is probably Zeng Xiaoxu, who handles the case of Miao Qing, but he is demoted and persecuted by Cai Jing (chaps. 48 and 49).

12. *Zhang Zhupo*, 2.46.

zhuan. All the manly qualities celebrated in *Shuihu zhuan* such as valor and celibacy are now no longer valid or even possible in *Jin Ping Mei*.

The Materiality of Desire

Rather than the ability to devise military tactics or to demonstrate martial skills on the battlefield (the public arena) of *Shuihu zhuan*, what counts in *Jin Ping Mei*, at least on surface, is one's skills in bed (the ultimate symbol of the private space) or in wheeling and dealing. It is Ximen Qing, with his knack for politics and business and his perceived sexual prowess, and not *haohan* like Wu Song, who triumphs (at least in the first two-thirds of the novel). *Jin Ping Mei* focuses squarely on the ramifications of private desires and how people are simultaneously driven and consumed by these desires. Never before in the history of the Chinese novel was desire as a phenomenon of the human psyche depicted with so much attention to its "materiality." What distinguishes *Jin Ping Mei* from its predecessors is its insistence on representing desire in the full context of its social and economic realities. Desire in *Jin Ping Mei* is so real and tangible that it can be measured and even quantified.[13] We are supposed to measure the enormity of Ximen Qing's desire by literally counting how many women he sleeps with (as the commentator Zhang Zhupo apparently did),[14] or how many taels of silver are involved in a transaction (business or otherwise), or even how many thrusts (*chou* 抽) he is capable of during sex. Some readers have even argued for a correlation between the number of taels of silver Ximen Qing spends in a transaction and the number of thrusts during the sexual encounter that immediately follows.[15]

The most impressive account of numbers in the novel is perhaps Ximen Qing's dying words to his son-in-law Chen Jingji. They read like a carefully kept ledger of business transactions:

> The silk shop is worth fifty thousand taels, but part of that belongs to our kinsman Qiao. Tell Fu to dispose of as much stock as is necessary, pay off our kinsman, then

13. This late Ming tendency toward quantification and calculation was probably related to the rapid development of a monetarized economy during that time. For a study of how some authors of practical handbooks for ethical behavior adopted an accounting method that enabled one to calculate the sum of one's moral deeds and moral merits or demerits to ensure a positive balance, see Brokaw, *Ledgers of Merit and Demerit*.

14. "Ximen Qing yinguo funü" 西門慶淫過婦女, "Zalu" 雜錄, in *Zhang Zhupo*, p. 5.

15. Satyendra, "Metaphors of the Body," p. 94.

close the shop. The thread shop of which Pan Si is in charge is worth six thousand five hundred taels, and the silk shop which Uncle Wu Er looks after, five thousand taels. Both these shops should be closed as soon as the stuff can be sold. If Li San gets the contract we have spoken about, it will be better not to go further in the matter. Ask Uncle Ying to get somebody else to take it up. Li San and Huang Si still owe me five hundred taels with interest amounting to another hundred and fifty. Ask them for payment. You and Clerk Fu can look after the household and the two shops that are here. The pawnshop is worth about twenty thousand taels and the medicine shop five thousand. Clerk Han and Lai Bao are still in Songjiang. When the river is free from ice, fetch them home again. They have about four thousand taels' worth of merchandise. Sell it and give the money to your mother. Liu, the Director of Studies, owes me three hundred taels. Hua owes me fifty. Xu Si, outside the city, owes me, including interest due, about three hundred and forty. We have all necessary documents, and you can ask them for payment at once.[16]

Even during his dying moments, Ximen Qing still has a clear sense of his financial holdings, although his death is caused by his serious miscalculation of the worth of his own sexual capital (see below).

The importance attached to quantities or numbers by the author of *Jin Ping Mei* can be seen from his great pains in altering numbers in some of the passages adopted from *Shuihu zhuan*. In chapter 23 of *Shuihu zhuan*, after killing the tiger single-handedly, Wu Song is rewarded with 1,000 strings of cash (*yiqian guan* 一千貫).[17] In chapter 1 of the *Cihua* 詞話 edition of *Jin*

16. Here I am following the Chongzhen 崇禎 edition (79.1153) where "pawnshop" 印子鋪 replaces the second reference to "silk shop" 緞子舖 in the Cihua edition (79.1059). The two mentions of the silk shop in Ximen Qing's remark in the Cihua edition do not make sense. The quoted English translation (with modifications) is from Egerton, trans., *The Golden Lotus*, vol. 4, pp. 97–98. In this study, all references to the Chongzhen edition are to *Xinke xiuxiang piping Jin Ping Mei*, ed. Qiyan et al. For general discussions of the textual history and the main extant editions of *Jin Ping Mei*, see Hanan, "The Text of the *Chin P'ing Mei*"; and Plaks, *Four Masterworks*, pp. 55–72.

17. See *Rongyutang ben Shuihu zhuan*, 23.324–25. It is impossible to determine which particular version of *Shuihu zhuan* the author of *Jin Ping Mei* was reading or had in mind when he was writing his own novel. However, it is certain that his *Shuihu zhuan* was a 100-chapter version (*baihuiben* 百回本) since the 120-chapter version came into circulation only after *Jin Ping Mei* was already completed. I will use the *Rongyutang* edition of *Shuihu zhuan* (dated 1610) because it is the most complete extant 100-chapter version. The 100-chapter *Tiandu waichen xu* 天都外臣序 printed edition, although dated several decades earlier, is incomplete, and furthermore, the extant copy was reprinted during the Qing period

Indira Satyendra ("Metaphors of Body," p. 93) notes this subtle change of number here in *Jin Ping Mei* to support her argument that the 30 taels of silver Wu Song receives as a reward

Ping Mei, however, the amount of the reward is changed to "thirty taels of silver." This subtle change seems to suggest that silver as a form of currency had become even more popular by the lifetime of the author of *Jin Ping Mei*.[18] Obviously, silver, as the most powerful symbol of wealth, occupies a much more important position in the lives of the people in *Jin Ping Mei*, and its author seldom failed to specify the amount of silver involved in any business deal or a case of bribery.[19] There are so many detailed accounts of transactions and deals that one critic accurately notes that "money is in the very fabric of the story" and the novel is "a mass of details about money and prices."[20]

Good at numbers, Ximen Qing is indeed a merchant with a knack for money. He is never stingy with his money nor is he nearsighted in business dealings. He seems to know exactly when and where he should spend his money to maximize the return on his investment. He never begrudges money when bribing officials or cultivating connections with powerful people. This is why he wins the goodwill of the imperial tutor Cai Jing and other high officials, who play such a pivotal role in his flourishing careers. Nor does he limit his dealings to officials in this world; he donates a large sum of money to a temple when he feels he needs religious blessings for his son or for himself. Ximen Qing is even generous with many of his poor friends. For example, he helps Chang Shijie with many taels of silver when Chang is under the threat of eviction because he cannot pay his rent (chapter 56). His friend's praise of his generosity provokes a surprisingly insightful observation from Ximen Qing: "That thing [money] likes action rather than staying quiet" (兀那東西是好動不喜靜的; 56.662). Ximen is apparently convinced that a wise man should know how to spend money in terms of

for killing the tiger is the same amount of money Mr. Zhang pays to purchase Pan Jinlian as a maid. However, although she does not cite a reference, she must have mistakenly observed that in *Shuihu zhuan* Wu Song's reward is 1000 taels of silver (instead of 1000 strings of cash as it is in all the editions of *Shuihu zhuan* that I have consulted) and thus fails to notice the significance of this change in currency. The large sum of 1000 taels of silver would not make sense in *Shuihu zhuan*.

18. In the Chongzhen edition of the novel (1.17–18), the number 30 taels is changed to "50 taels."

19. For studies of how silver became the main form of currency during the Ming dynasty and the monetarization of Ming economy, see von Glahn, *Fountain of Fortune*, esp. pp. 70–206; and Atwell, "Ming China and the Emerging World Economy."

20. Hanan, "A Landmark of the Chinese Novel," pp. 329–30.

good investment. In chapter 45, he agrees to make a loan to Li Zhi and Huang Si at a high rate of interest because otherwise the money would sit idle and bring in nothing (*xianzhe* 閒著; 45.505). Money will only reproduce more money or wealth will only multiply when it is in circulation or in the process of exchange (constant in action). Obviously, Ximen Qing's phenomenal and rapid successes in accumulating personal wealth have to be attributed to his intuitive knowledge of the active nature of money.

However, Ximen Qing seems to fail to realize the dangers inherent in the active nature of money or, for that matter, the active nature of his own desire. In traditional Chinese philosophical discourse (see Chapter 2), the phenomenon of desire, or *yu*, is largely defined by its active nature (*dong* 動). Desire is thought to be potentially dangerous precisely because of its tendency toward overreaction and violent movement. Ximen Qing's fatal mistake is his failure to comprehend the nature of *dong* and to heed the many warnings of the ancient sages. *Dong* can be an asset in the case of wealth because wealth can multiply only in circulation, but excessive movement may not be as good in the case of sexual desire. When desire (especially sexual desire) multiplies, it overwhelms a man since he has to overspend or overconsume his energy or wealth to gratify his multiplying desires. Consequently, an essential issue, the novel seems to suggest, is keeping a careful balance between production and consumption in this process of *dong* or circulation. Although Ximen is probably right in asserting that money likes action in the sense that money or financial capital can multiply and reproduce itself in the process of circulation and exchange, sexual capital may be an entirely different story. Ximen Qing's tragic end stems at least in part from his failure to comprehend the relationship between these two kinds of capital (*benqian* 本錢), the financial and the sexual. In fact, he is often confused about the two.

In Chinese *benqian* can refer to both financial capital (money and wealth) and sexual capital (sexual virility). Although it is fairly common for writers of erotic fiction to use the word *benqian* to directly refer to a man's sexual endowment,[21] the author of *Jin Ping Mei*, as far as I know, never resorts to such an explicit usage. However, a careful reader cannot fail to realize the frequent allusion to the close association between these two kinds of *benqian* or capital in this novel. In chapter 1 of the novel, after Mrs. Zhang discovers the affair between her husband and Pan Jinlian, Mr. Zhang concludes that he

21. See, e.g., chap. 6, Li Yu, *Rou putuan*, pp. 235, 237ff.

cannot keep Pan as a maid any longer. He decides to give her to Wu the Elder for free. Furthermore, "after Jinlian and Wu the Elder were married, Mr. Zhang made it a point to look after him. If he were short of capital [*benqian*] for his trade in steamed wheat cakes, he would slip him five taels of silver to make up the deficiency (與他做本錢). While Wu the Elder was out peddling his wares, Mr. Zhang would wait until there was no one about and then steal into their room for an assignation with Jinlian" (1.9; *Plum*, 1.27). The reader is later told that the sex-starved Pan Jinlian is frustrated because Wu the Elder is totally unattractive (suggesting that her new husband is probably not very good in bed). Here the reference to *benqian* or capital becomes interesting: Mr. Zhang gives "capital" to Wu the Elder to "make up" his "deficiency" as if to justify his sharing the latter's wife since the husband himself does not have adequate (sexual) capital. Mr. Zhang purposely chooses Wu the Elder as the recipient of Pan Jinlian precisely because of Wu's inadequate *benqian* (therefore, the need for and justification of his help in terms of supplying what Wu the Elder lacks—*benqian*).

In chapter 18, a man's lack of financial capital is once again associated with his inadequate sexual capital. After Li Ping'er marries the poor doctor Jiang Zushan, she gives her husband some money to open a herb shop. But Li soon begins to feel frustrated with her marriage because Jiang proves to be of little use in bed (his sexual capital is as inadequate as his financial capital). Later, after Li Ping'er marries Ximen Qing, he complains about her supplying Jiang with *benqian* to open a herb shop to compete with him (去拿本錢與他開鋪子; 19.202). Of course, Ximen Qing's point is that no matter how much (financial) capital she has supplied Jiang, she has to admit that Jiang, whom Ximen contemptuously calls "a dwarf cuckold" (矮王八; 19.202) in comparison to himself, remains far from adequate as far as sexual capital is concerned. Here, again, Jiang is said to be a dwarf, just like Wu the Elder, who also lacks *benqian* (both financially and sexually). Both Mr. Zhang and Ximen Qing seem to perceive, and to insist on, a close linkage between these two kinds of capital: a man without adequate financial capital must also be a man without sexual capital.

This perception of the close relationship between the two kinds of capital may explain Ximen Qing's fatal confusion of the two. His quick financial expansion and his seemingly impressive sexual successes blind him to a crucial fact: whereas money or financial capital can reproduce itself and multiply, his sexual energies cannot reproduce themselves quickly enough, even with the aid of aphrodisiac. The end result is that he is completely drained and exhausted thanks to his reckless overconsumption of his sexual capital, which can never keep up with his ever-expanding sexual appetites. The more active his sexual desire, the lower the capacity of his sexual energy (capital) to sustain such desire, as attested by the narrator's homily: "An individual's energy is limited, but the world's sexual lust is infinite" (一己精神有限, 天下色欲無窮; 78.1050)

The author of *Jin Ping Mei* meticulously explains why Ximen Qing becomes confused about these two forms of capital. At the beginning of the novel, Ximen is successful in acquiring both kinds of capital—the acquisition of Pan Jinlian as a concubine obviously has a lot to do with his ability to bribe officials and to pay busybodies such as Dame Wang (good use of his financial capital, so to speak), a fact receiving more emphasis in this novel than in *Shuihu zhuan* (in *Shuihu zhuan* Wu Song kills Ximen and Pan Jinlian before they can become husband and wife despite Ximen's attempts to bribe the officials; bribery does not always bring about results in that novel). This is certainly a case in which his financial capital (his many taels of silver) is properly invested, a success that must have led him to the false conclusion that his financial capital will automatically help to increase his sexual capital. There are other "facts" that boost Ximen Qing's self-confidence in this regard. In a reverse fashion, his attractive physical appearance and, perhaps more important, his perceived sexual prowess might also have helped him accumulate more wealth. His marriage with Meng Yulou brings considerable wealth into his household. The novel does not explain why Meng Yulou, after meeting Ximen Qing, becomes so determined to marry him despite the advice from a relative against such a marriage. It is interesting that when the matchmaker Auntie Xue first mentions Meng Yulou to Ximen Qing, her introduction begins with a lengthy and detailed account of her wealth but she brings up Meng's looks only later as if they are of less concern than her wealth (7.61–62). Obviously, what makes Meng Yulou so appealing to Ximen Qing is her wealth. But what attracts Meng Yulou to Ximen Qing? The reader may have to conclude that Ximen's impressive physique is a major factor in her final decision (the narrator never explicitly describes her impression of Ximen Qing).[22]

22. Of course, this is the case only in the Cihua edition (7.66). The editor of the Chongzhen edition must have felt that Ximen Qing's physical appearance should be a major

Whatever the reason behind Meng Yulou's decision, Ximen's physical appeal definitely plays a prominent role in his successful attempt to lure Li Ping'er, who will eventually bring him an even more impressive amount of wealth. In fact, the account of the adulterous affair between the two can be read as a detailed ledger of financial transactions—a minute record of the money and properties Li Ping'er sends bit by bit into Ximen Qing's household as they carry on their affair. The secret traffic over the wall is as much monetary as it is amorous: Ximen Qing enters Li's house by climbing over the wall via a ladder, and in turn trunks of money and other precious things are hoisted over the wall from Li's house. The reader is duly informed of the specific amounts of money and given an inventory of the valuable things transferred to Ximen Qing's house after each of his visits to Li Ping'er. The narrator is adamant in calling the reader's attention to the financial impact of their marriage on Ximen Qing's household:

> From the time that Ximen Qing brought Li Ping'er over his threshold, in the course of doing which he had picked up two or three dubious increments to his property, his affairs became more prosperous than ever. On his country estate outside the walls and in his residential compound:
>
> Everything was put on an entirely new footing,
> The rice and millet overflowed his granaries,
> His mules and horses became teeming herds,
> His slaves and servants were arrayed in ranks. (20.214; *Plum*, 20.420)

No wonder his servant Tai'an is convinced that Ximen Qing's show of grief over the death of Li Ping'er later in the novel is caused by the thought of how much money she has brought him rather than his distress over the loss of a beloved concubine (不是疼人,是疼錢; 64.779).

On the other hand, the narrator is unequivocal about Ximen Qing's appeal to Li Ping'er. After carrying on with Li Ping'er for some time, Ximen Qing suddenly stops seeing her because of his worries about becoming implicated in a political upheaval in the capital that involves the family of his in-laws. Confused and disappointed, Li Ping'er finds herself unable to wait and decides to marry Jiang Zhusan instead, who has helped her recuperate from an ailment. However, she soon begins to regret her choice of bedmate when she realizes that her new husband is incompetent in bed. After this

---

factor. That is why in that edition Meng Yulou is explicitly said to be attracted by Ximen Qing's handsome appearance (7.88), a fact not mentioned in the Cihua edition.

disappointing experience with her new husband, Li begins to miss Ximen Qing. To use her own words, Ximen is just like a wonderful medicine specially prescribed for her illness (醫奴的藥; 19.203). Furthermore, the sudden and mysterious transformation of Li from a shrew to a peaceful and sympathetic wife after she marries Ximen must be attributed at least in part to his sexual prowess and skills in bed (presumably because Ximen Qing, her new husband, is able to satisfy her sexually).

This "success story," however, is another—perhaps even more significant—case in which his sexual *benqian* (capital), Ximen Qing is led to believe, helps to generate financial capital for him. Successes as spectacular as this further convince Ximen Qing that these two kinds of capital are virtually interchangeable. His seemingly impressive successes in increasing his capital in both categories elevate his self-confidence to new heights, as reflected in his boasts to his wife Wu Yueniang:

> I've heard that the Buddha from the West wants to pave the ground of his residence with gold and that the guys in the ten palaces of the netherworld want paper money. Even if I rape Chang'e (常娥), or have an affair with the Weaving Lady, or abduct Xu Feiqiong (許飛瓊) and the daughter of the Queen Mother of the West, my prosperity should not be affected at all so long I spend some money for charity to accumulate merits. (57.576)[23]

Obviously Ximen Qing is convinced that so long as he has the money to make donations to Buddhist and Taoist temples and to bribe high officials, he can get away with anything, no matter how outrageous.

Here we may recall Ximen Qing's fatal encounter with the Indian monk in chapter 49. Ximen Qing is beginning to feel that his official career is on a promising track, especially after he has successfully spent a large sum of money to solidify his ties with two high officials, Censor Cai and Censor Song, by offering them lavish gifts and elaborate entertainments during their stay in the city. Apparently, in the mood for charity and spending money, he happily promises the abbot of the Temple of Everlasting Happiness

23. The belief that one's demerits can be canceled out by deeds of merit is directly or indirectly ridiculed in several fictional works of the seventeenth century, such as the 28th story in *Xingshi yan* 型世言 (Model stories for the world) and the ninth story, "A Daughter Is Transformed into a Son Through the Bodhisattva's Ingenuity," in Li Yu's *Wusheng xi* 無聲戲 (Silent operas); for an English translation of this story by Li Yu, see Hanan, ed., *Silent Operas*, 137–59.

(Yongfu si 永福寺) that he will donate money to the temple. This financial generosity results in an immediate reward. Ximen Qing meets an Indian monk whose strange appearance soon convinces Ximen Qing that the monk has some magic pills that can enhance sexual prowess. This, for Ximen Qing, is a case of his financial capital yielding profits in terms of sexual capital. Both the anonymous commentator on the Chongzhen edition and Zhang Zhupo noted the striking phallic imagery that dominates this particular section of the novel: not only is the monk said to personify a penis (his appearance is described with phrases such as "single-eyed dragon" 獨眼龍, "sunken-eye in leopard head" 豹頭凹眼, and "the color of a purple liver" 色若紫肝; 49.563),[24] but also the furniture and decorations in the hall of Ximen Qing's residence, presented from the perspective of this penis-like monk, remind the reader of the male sexual organ (the chairs are decorated with the carvings of the pattern of eel heads 泥鰍頭, that look like swelled veins 腫筋, and the pictures on the walls are mounted on purple rods with agate ends and silk binding 紫竹桿綾邊瑪瑙軸頭; 49.564). Even the food this penis-like monk is served by Ximen Qing resembles a male organ: in the soup are two meat balls with a garnished sausage between them. The reader is explicitly told that the soup is known as "One Dragon Playing with Two Pearls" 一龍戲二珠湯 (49.565).[25] It seems only appropriate that Ximen Qing should get his potency pills from a penis-like monk who eats penis-like food in a setting completely dominated by phallic images.

However, the true implications of these phallic images are not fully revealed till chapter 80, in the mock-serious elegy to the deceased Ximen Qing drafted by Licentiate Shui. Ximen is eulogized as a penis, or *diaoren* 鳥人, to use a double entendre by Zhang Zhupo (80.1299). In chapter 80, the phallic imagery reappears, after thirty chapters, only to remind the reader that Ximen Qing's death is a direct result of his own misuse of the potency pills

24. As early as in chap. 4, Ximen Qing's penis is compared to "a mad monk" (*fengseng* 風僧) in a verse (4.43).

25. See the comments in the Chongzhen edition: "Look at this monk. What does he remind you of?" and further on: "The appearance of the monk is actually not very different from that of a penis" (49.635). Zhang Zhupo comments on the phallic implications of Ximen Qing's furniture and decorations by referring to the phrase "one of those damned things" 一片鳥東西 from *Shuihu zhuan* (*Zhang Zhupo*, 49.728); in his interlineal comments on this section, he constantly asks the reader "What does this remind you of?" 像甚么 or uses the phrase "an exact duplicate" 很象 (49.728–29); cf. the relevant observations in Plaks, *Four Masterworks*, pp. 135f.

(Pan Jinlian also plays a role in this misuse, since she administers the pills to him in an attempt to arouse him when he is asleep and totally exhausted in chapter 79; of course, this in turn is reminiscent of the earlier incident in which Pan Jinlian murders her then-husband Wu Zhi with the poison provided by Ximen Qing). The very phrase used to describe the monk's penis-like appearance, "the color of a purple liver," in chapter 49 is used to describe the state of Ximen Qing's penis when he is about to collapse in his fatal sexual encounter with Pan Jinlian (79.1050). Ximen Qing's pill-driven penis literally costs him his life. In other words, Ximen Qing has overconsumed himself largely because of his misplaced faith in the potency pills given by the penis-like monk, who, the reader should remember, is fed penis-like food by Ximen Qing himself. The penis/monk symbolically devours penis. Deluded by a false sense of invincibility, partially created by the potency pills he received from the monk, Ximen Qing has grossly overestimated his own sexual capital, which has failed to grow in the same fashion as his financial capital.

Here the Temple of Everlasting Happiness takes on added significance. Besides being the place where Ximen Qing has his fatal encounter with the phallic Indian monk, the temple is also the setting where Ximen Qing entertains Censor Cai and other high officials and cements his connections with the powerful. Apparently pleased by his experience in the temple, Ximen Qing donates 500 taels of silver to its abbot as promised (chapter 57). So far the temple appears to have served as a witness to Ximen Qing's quick rise to wealth and power (financial as well as sexual). Its significance becomes more complicated, however, when we learn that Pan Jinlian, who plays a pivotal role in Ximen Qing's demise or self-destruction, is buried there after she is killed by Wu Song (88.1154). Pan Jinlian is probably no less self-destructive than Ximen Qing. The reader must be struck by her short memory and her blind willingness to marry Wu Song, while the latter has only revenge on his mind. More interestingly, Chen Jinji, the protagonist in the last twenty chapters of the novel as well as the successor of Ximen Qing in terms of their common sexual misadventures, is also buried in this temple (99.1283). Furthermore, the temple is also the place where Wu Yueniang (now a widow) meets Chunmei (now the wife of Commander Zhou). However, this time Ximen's formal wife and widow, Wu Yueniang, feels compelled to bow and show respect to Chunmei, her former maid but now the wife of a powerful person (chapter 89). This awkward encounter between

Wu Yueniang and Chunmei is a poignant reminder of the drastic decline of the Ximen household's fortunes, something Ximen Qing has feared would happen soon after his death. Having witnessed Ximen Qing's initial triumphs as well as quick demise, the Temple of Everlasting Happiness is far from being the place of everlasting happiness its name ironically suggests.

Here we may recall Zhang Zhupo's interesting interpretation of the significance of the temple in the novel:

> The Temple of Everlasting Happiness [Yongfu si] refers [homophonically] to what is pouring out from below one's abdomen (*yongyu fuxia* 湧於腹下). What can this thing be? One of the priests from this temple is called *huseng* 胡僧 [Indian monk] and the other Daojian 道堅 [hard thing]. The former refers to the appearance of that thing and the latter describes its supposed prowess. The Temple of Everlasting Happiness is indeed "the place where one is born as well as the place where one encounters death" (生我之門死我戶).[26] This is why all these people find their resting place here after they are dead. This is to underscore the consequences of lust and the reckless pursuit of profit.[27]

In Zhang Zhupo's reading, the temple is a phallic image as well as the ultimate symbol of the self-destruction of the phallic—the fatal attraction to *nüse* 女色. Of course, the conclusion of the novel provides the final twist to the symbolic meanings of the Temple of Everlasting Happiness. It is here that Wu Yuenian agrees to allow the monk Pujing to take her son Xiaoge as his disciple. She reluctantly consents only after receiving "divine" warnings in her dream and only after being convinced by the monk that Xiaoge is actually the reincarnation of her deceased husband, Ximen Qing. Now the temple becomes the place where Ximen Qing receives his ultimate retribution for his sins in the body of his son Xiaoge—the latter is supposed to seek redemption on behalf of the former.

Beyond the Materiality

Drunkenness, lust, avarice, and anger (*jiu, se, cai, qi* 酒色財氣) are the respective topics of the "Lyrics on the Four Vices" ("Sitan ci" 四貪詞) quoted just before the beginning of the story proper. Although the inclusion of

26. Here Zhang Zhupo is apparently referring to the warning about *nüse*, or fatal female attraction, at the beginning of chap. 1 in the Chongzhen edition (1.2).

27. "*Jin Ping Mei* yuyi shuo," *Zhang Zhupo*, 17.

warnings against indulging in these four vices was a conventional ploy in traditional fiction and drama,[28] *Jin Ping Mei* was certainly the first full-length novel to focus on the intricate relationships among these four vices as well as their dire consequences. As mentioned in Chapter 2, *Lunyu* implies that inappropriate or excessive *yu* is characterized as being *tan* 貪 (greedy). Lust, or *se*, and avarice, or *cai*, are unquestionably the main focus of the novel. Many characters are totally consumed by their desire for sex and money, and drinking, or *jiu*, is almost always part of the foreplay in an adulterous sexual encounter. However, the subtlest aspect of desire as it is experienced by many characters is probably *qi*. It is often *qi* that turns people like Ximen Qing into a monster for whom gratification (sexual or otherwise) is gauged in terms of the humiliation he can inflict on others and the triumph of taking possession of what does not belong to him.[29]

Qi is a loaded term with implications beyond those suggested by the English word "anger." Here it is worthwhile to have a close look at the lyric on *qi* in the novel:

Anger

Do not resort to violence or endeavor
    to show off your prowess;
By brandishing fists, rolling up sleeves,
    or displaying your spirit.
Once you let the flames of your temper
    escape your control;
You will subsequently stew with anxiety
    at the calamitous results.
Don't go overboard,
Avoid catastrophe;
Be advised, the best policy is to be
    tolerant in all things.
When it is appropriate to let things go,
    you should let them go;
When you can make allowances for people,
    you should make allowances. (*Plum*, p. 11)

28. See Roy, trans., *The Plum in the Golden Vase*, p. 463n1, for information on the possible author of these lyrics. The grouping together of these four vices as a concept can be traced at least to the Song dynasty.

29. See the commentator's interlineal comments on the relationship between *qi* and *cai*, or wealth, in the Chongzhen edition (1.2).

Compared with *jiu, se,* and *cai,* which are related more to the physical aspects of desire, the concept of *qi* points more to its psychological dimension. It has more to do with interpersonal relationships (thus it is more "societal") that involve competition; it suggests intolerance, pride, jealousy, and the need to feel superior to others. Often *qi* is the most dangerous element in *yu* precisely because it is a sort of "mental greed," which, unlike physical lusts, is not easy to define and consequently difficult to gratify. After Ximen Qing acquires Pan Jinlian and Meng Yulou as concubines, his *qi* seems to become especially strong; he becomes more self-confident as well as more arrogant. This is why he becomes so angry (bothered so much by his *qi*) when he learns of Li Ping'er's decision to marry Jiang Zhushan. "If you'd married anyone else, it wouldn't have bothered me. But that stunted little cuckold! What could he do for you? You brought him across your threshold and then supplied the capital [*benqian*] to set him up in business, opening a shop right under my nose, in order to take away my livelihood" (19.202; *Plum,* 19.398). What upsets Ximen is not so much Li Ping'er's favoring someone else but that man's being a particular kind of person—how could she feel attracted to a person as low as Jiang Zhushan after she has tasted his sexual prowess. Simply put, Ximen Qing feels insulted that Li Ping'er would choose a man with so little *benqian* (in terms of both sexual and financial capital) over him.

"Slut!" he demanded. "Come over here. Let me ask you. How do I stack up compared to that scoundrel, Dr. Jiang Zhushan?"

"How can he be compared to you?" the woman said.

> "You're the sky;
> He's shard of brick.
> You're higher than the Thirty-ninth Hell.

Quite aside from the fact that you are:

> Chivalrous by nature and open-handed with your wealth,
> Have a voice like plangent bronze and tinkling jade,
> Command a clear and articulate tongue,
> Dress in silk and wear brocades, and
> Are ever attended by three or five servants;

Thereby showing yourself to be:

> A Man above other men;

Even the delicacies that constitute your daily fare are such things as he would never see, were he to live for hundreds of years. How can he be compared to you? You're just the right medicine for me. Ever since I experienced love at your hands, by day and by night all I do is long for you."

This last statement had such an effect on Ximen Qing that:

> His delight knew no bounds. (19.203; *Plum*, 19.399; trans. modified)

Li Ping'er's flattering remarks, especially her praise of his impressive sexual *benqian*, finally make him feel vindicated, and his *qi* dissipates (怒氣消下些來了; 19.203).

Qi (understood here as the urge to dominate or to have absolute control over another person) is a useful concept in appreciating the true nature of Ximen's sexual relationships with many women. Often what he seeks from his numerous sexual partners in an adulterous relationship is not sexual pleasure per se but the feeling of power over and the sense of the total submission from these women. This need to feel dominant is best captured in the sadistic sexual scene in which he burns moxa on the wet nurse Ruyi's private parts:

> Soon the moxa was burnt to the part that began to touch her flesh. Knitting her brows and clinching her teeth, the woman was under tremendous pain. She moaned softly:
>
> "Please, Dearest Dad, please end this! I can't stand it any more!"
>
> Ximen Qing Yelled: "Zhang Si'er, you slut! Whose woman (*laopo* 老婆) are you?"
>
> "I am your woman," said the woman.
>
> "You should say that you are Xiong Wang's woman," Ximen Qing corrected her, "but today you belong to your dearest man."
>
> The woman answered: "This slut used to be Xiong Wang's woman, but today I belong to my dearest man."
>
> Ximen Qing asked again: "Am I good at fucking?"
>
> The woman answered: "You are indeed very good!" (78.1029)

Ximen Qing's correction of Ruyi is especially revealing. Trying to flatter Ximen Qing, Ruyi states that she is Ximen Qing's woman. But Ximen Qing wants her to acknowledge that she now belongs to him even though she is legally someone else's wife. Their affair becomes all the more "pleasurable" to him precisely because Ruyi is another man's wife. The fact that he can fornicate with the wife of another man whenever he likes has to be verbally confirmed by the very woman over whom he is exercising total dominance. This verbal confirmation enhances his sense of dominance. Furthermore, his dominance and his sexual partner's submission have to be not only *verbally* confirmed by the submissive other but also *visually* validated through his own eyes: during that sadistic sexual encounter, Ximen Qing moves the mirror stand near the bed so that he can observe himself in action (78.1029). He also derives special pleasure from a particular show of submission by Pan Jinlian and Ruyi: their willingness to drink his urine (72.903 and 75.955).

This may also explain why Ximen Qing seldom bothers with unmarried women, despite his enormous sexual appetite. He can only feel thrilled by taking another man's wife, taking what is understood to belong to others. Pan Jinlian's characterization of Ximen Qing's sexual greed is on the mark: "If you were allowed to get your wishes, you would like to sleep with every woman under heaven! (把天下的老婆都耍遍了)" (61.732). Note the word *laopo* here (which also appears in the conversation quoted above). It means both "wife" and "woman."

It is this sense of his absolute right to sleep with whatever woman he chooses that makes his greed so difficult to satisfy and, consequently, so dangerous, since he will never feel content with what he already has. Ximen Qing's final sexual escapade, which eventually leads to his death, is in large measure caused by this *qi* of his—the perpetual drive to get what seems beyond his reach or what should not be his. In this case, the ultimate symbol of forbidden fruit is Lanshi, the wife of his new colleague. Here the motif of peeping takes on added significance. One peeps at what one is not supposed to see. Peeping is motivated by the desire for the distant and the unreachable. However, it is the forbidden that is most attractive. If the ultimate desire is defined as the wish to acquire what one does not yet have—what is absent or what is beyond one's reach—then the act of peeping seems to capture this almost foredoomed nature of desire, whose existence is predicated on its being not fulfilled. A glimpse of the elusive Lanshi has stirred Ximen Qing's imagination/desire so much that he has to sleep with several women in succession in order to sustain the illusion that his wishes are indeed being fulfilled (that he is not just peeping but possessing what he is not supposed to see and have)—he insists on imagining that all these women are actually Lanshi, who has persistently eluded his reach. The more she eludes him, the more tempting she becomes and the more he lusts after her. The only way to alleviate his *qi* is to imagine all the other women over whom he can indeed have control to be the forever-beyond-reach Lanshi.

We should not underestimate the significance of Lanshi, who appears only briefly in the novel and remains a vague and even mysterious figure. However, it is precisely this vagueness and mysteriousness that point to the dangerous nature of Ximen Qing's *tanyu* 貪欲 (excessive desire or lust)—what Ximen Qing is doing is not pursuing any specific object of desire but attempting to perpetuate the act of desiring itself. Desire, the novel seems to suggest, really becomes dangerous when it turns itself into a kind of *qi* that insists on replicating itself. The ever-elusive figure of Lanshi in the novel can be read almost as an object invented by Ximen Qing's never-satisfied desire that has to constantly reinvent its object in order to ensure its own existence. This bespeaks the dangerous disparity between the infinite nature of desire and the always limited capacity to fulfil such desire, as attested by the homily in chapter 78. When Ximen Qing begins to ejaculate blood after a series of exhausting bouts of sex (most of which are a result of his unfulfilled desire for Lanshi), the narrator warns: "An individual's (*yiji* 一己) energy is limited, but the world's (*tianxia* 天下) sexual lust is infinite" (78.1050). Here *yiji* (an individual) and *tianxia* (the world) form a nice contrast that underscores the fatal disparity—how can an individual's energy be enough to fulfil a desire that seeks to possess everything in the world? We may also recall Pan Jinlian's apt remark that Ximen Qing wants to sleep with every woman/wife under heaven. The logical result of this disparity is violent and sudden death in which one's energy is literally drained by one's own ever-multiplying desire. In a sense, the murderous Pan Jinlian, whose sexual demands drive Ximen Qing to his death, is only a monster created by Ximen Qing's own desire (more on this in Chapter 5).

Chapter 57 represents a crucial stage in the development of Ximen Qing's desire. This chapter and chapter 56 are about the apogee of Ximen Qing's fortunes. He has never felt so self-confident and has never been so ready to be charitable or generous. He gives 12 taels of silver to save his sworn brother Chang Shijie from starving and promises him even more money to rent a new house (56.662). Then he donates 500 taels of silver to the Buddhist temple (57.675) and another 30 taels to defray the cost of printing copies of Buddhist sutras (57.679). Ximen Qing is in a charitable mood because, as he tells everyone, he is completely content with life (萬事已是足了; 57. 674). However, this is also a moment of new discontent. He chooses to reveal his malaise to his son, who is obviously too young to understand him: "Son, when you grow up, you should become a civil official. Don't follow your dad's example. Being a military officer, though a good job, would not bring you real respect" (57.672). Having got all he thought he wanted, Ximen Qing is feeling a bit bored. In order to sustain his desiring, he has to invent new targets to pursue. His earlier effort to acquire potency pills to enhance his sexual prowess is certainly part of this effort to win real respect, a manifestation of his *qi* (as expressed in the phrase *zhengqi* 爭氣).

Ximen Qing is bothered by *qi* up until the last moment of his life. He is particularly worried that his own wives and concubines might be taken by other men after he dies or, rather, that other men will do to him what he has always done to others all these years. He tells his wife Wu Yueniang: "After my death, if you give birth to a boy or a girl, please keep this family together with your sisters [Ximen's concubines] and don't split; otherwise this would become a laughingstock among people (惹人家笑話)" (79.1059). His posthumous reputation or his continuing desire for dominance even after death is apparently the overriding concern of the dying Ximen Qing. This reference to avoiding becoming a "laughingstock" is repeated by Ximen later (休要教人笑話; 79.1059). This is certainly a futile attempt, and he has ample reason to worry, as the last twenty chapters of the novel demonstrate—his concubines, almost all of whom he acquired through dubious means, are taken away one by one by other men (the exception is Pan Jinlian, who is killed by Wu Song in chapter 87 as the postponed judgment of revenge is finally executed). Ximen Qing indeed becomes a laughingstock and fails to win real respect, despite the dominance he achieved when alive. Paradoxically, it is his *qi*—his wanting real respect—that causes him to lose all respect.

One important achievement of *Jin Ping Mei* in its exploration of the ramifications of desire is its persistent focus on the deadly consequences that arise when desire tries to perpetuate itself by constantly reinventing its objects. Strictly speaking, there is no such thing as pure physical desire since *qi* is always part of desire, and *qi* is at least psychosomatic if not completely mental. *Jin Ping Mei* is able to demonstrate compellingly how desire is and, at the same time, is not about materiality (something that can be physically attained). People in the novel are constantly in pursuit of money and sex, and these things are "tangible." Most of them can even be quantified in terms of how many taels of silver a transaction involves or even how many thrusts one is capable of during sex. And yet, at the same time, numbers can never adequately measure the magnitude of the desires people like Ximen Qing experience. In the end, it is not Ximen Qing who is pursuing his desire, but desire that is pursuing him. Ximen Qing is literally consumed by his own desire. He is chased to his death by his own *qi*.

After the death of Ximen Qing, Chen Jingji begins to assume an increasingly important role in the last twenty chapters of the novel. Some critics consider him "an extension" of Ximen Qing. His sexual adventures or misadventures are "a recapitulation, at an accelerated pace, of the self-destructive excesses perpetrated by Ximen Qing in the body of the novel."[30] Chen Jingji does not, however, have Ximen Qing's ability to manage his financial capital and repeatedly falls victim to others' tricks. He is even less competent in managing his sexual capital compared with his formidable father-in-law. Instead of conquering many women, Chen Jingji literally survives at the mercy of the women whose favor he is trying to curry. He suffers dearly when one of these women happens to be less than responsive to his advances (such as Meng Yulou). He lacks Ximen Qing's self-assurance. Furthermore, he is often victimized by other men sexually, something inconceivable for Ximen Qing (Chen is repeatedly sodomized by other men, whereas Ximen Qing is the person who sodomizes others). If Chen Jingji is indeed a replica of the deceased Ximen Qing, then he must be an emasculated Ximen Qing who can no longer afford to have the kind of *qi* Ximen Qing had. In his homosexual relationships with other men, Chen is often reduced to the status of a woman and has to offer his body in exchange for favors from his sexual partners, just as Pan Jinlian, Wang Liu'er, and Song Huilian had to do with Ximen Qing.

Chen Jingji anticipates the weak and henpecked male protagonists of works such as the seventeenth-century *Xingshi yinyuan zhuan* (the focus of Chapter 6), in which men, partly because of their own uncontrollable desires, are completely dominated by women. In fact, this reversal of fortune between men and women starts in the last twenty chapters of *Jin Ping Mei*. Consequently, for the purposes of this study, Chen Jingji is more significant than Ximen Qing because he anticipates many similar characters in later novels. By the same token, the last one-fifth of the novel, although perhaps much less compelling than the first four-fifths for many readers, probably supplied later fiction writers with more reasons to write their own novel in order to provide a better ending for such cautionary tales about overconsumption and the lack of self-control, as we shall see in Chapter 6.

30. Plaks, *Four Masterworks*, p. 104.

CHAPTER FIVE
Women and Desire in Chipozi zhuan *and* Dengcao heshang

Since the appearance of *Jin Ping Mei*, the name Pan Jinlian has become almost synonymous with *yinfu* 淫婦 (lascivious woman). Pan Jinlian is not just a woman totally consumed by sexual desire. What makes her particularly *yin*, or lascivious, is that she is a woman of strong *qi*. Precisely because of her *qi*, she is one of the few women in *Jin Ping Mei* who is not ready to accept Ximen Qing's dominance. This controversial character is of the opinion that she is entitled to other men if Ximen Qing does not *give* her proper attention. In her own unique way, she is also trying to seek dominance—over Ximen Qing as well as over other women. As a woman constrained by her gender status, she has to be creative in her tactics and extremely manipulative. Her tactic is to allow Ximen Qing to have affairs with other women (such as Song Huilian, Li Ping'er, Wang Liu'er, and the wet nurse Ruyi) so that she can win concessions or favors from him on other issues. She then thinks of ways to take care of these women later if an opportunity presents itself. Indeed, she has a hand in the death of two of her rivals, Song Huilian and Li Ping'er. As a woman and as a concubine in a large polygamous household, she has to learn how to make the best of a bad situation: knowing that she cannot prevent Ximen Qing from having Li Ping'er, she concludes that the best she can do is to let him proceed while demanding a few favors in return:

"The first condition," the woman said, "is that you will have to give up frequenting the licensed quarter. The second condition is that you must do as I say. The third condition is that when you go over to sleep with her, when you come home, you must tell me all about it, without deceiving me by so much as a single word." (13.137; *Plum* 13.271)

The last condition is particularly interesting. If she cannot stop Ximen Qing, she wants at least to be informed of every detail of his affairs. Information, for Pan Jinlian, can mean power and control. After eavesdropping on Ximen Qing and Song Huilian during their rendezvous, Pan Jianlian purposely leaves a hairpin in the door latch to let them know that she has been spying on them and that everything they say or do is under her surveillance (23.247). This tactic works quite effectively. Song Huilian is intimidated enough to feel that she has to pay her respects to Pan Jinlian. Pan Jinlian enjoys a feeling of being in control in a polygamous situation in which she cannot directly control her husband's choice of sexual partners.

Her most effective tactic, however, is to have affairs of her own and get even with Ximen Qing. Chen Jingji, Ximen Qing's son-in-law, proves to be the perfect candidate, although ultimately she will pay with her life for this act of defiance (after the affair is exposed, she is sold by Wu Yueniang and thus becomes accessible to Wu Song, who eventually kills her to avenge the death of his elder brother by her hands at the beginning of the novel). Consequently, like Ximen Qing, Pan Jinlian's tragedy lies not so much in her desire for sex or even money as in her hunger for power and dominance. Of humble family background, Pan Jinlian feels especially powerless when forced to compete with Li Ping'er and Meng Yulou, who bring considerable wealth to Ximen Qing when they are married into the household. She is particularly resentful of Li Ping'er's ability to please every member of the household with gifts or money as well as the fact that Li has given birth to a son. Pan Jinlian's open attempt to challenge the authority of Wu Yueniang and to undermine her status in the family is also motivated by her *qi* or desire for power.

What makes Pan Jinlian such an evil character in the eyes of many traditional readers is not her indulgence in sexual desire per se but the fact that she is a woman who indulges her sexual desires. In other words, what is particularly disturbing about this character is her insistence on her own right to seek sexual fulfillment, although, compared with Ximen Qing, her sexual appetite is much more modest (Zhang Zhupo [*Zhang Zhupo*, 5–6] calculated that she had relations with five men compared with Ximen Qing's involvement with nineteen women and two men). Many consider her insatiable because, unlike Ximen Qing's other wives and concubines, most of whom accept the situation, Pan Jinlian is not content with what she is given by her promiscuous and polygamous husband. She never hesitates to take the initiative to compensate herself by cuckolding her current husband if he fails to interest or neglects her. Although sex is the reason she becomes a victim of Ximen Qing, it also becomes a weapon of revenge.

The attempt by the author of *Jin Ping Mei* to make Pan Jinlian's image as a *yinfu* more consistent can best be seen in the subtle changes he makes in her humble background when he incorporates materials from *Shuihu zhuan*. In *Shuihu zhuan*, a rich man gives Pan Jinlian to Wu the Elder to spite her for her refusal to succumb to his sexual advances when she is a maid in his household (chap. 24). Here Pan Jinlian is a woman with standards and unwilling to accept just any man for the sake of sex or money. However, in *Jin Ping Mei*, Pan Jinlian is the daughter of a poor tailor. She is first sold to the household of Imperial Commissioner Wang, where she is trained as a sing-song girl. Then she is resold into Mr. Zhang's household and later has an affair with Mr. Zhang. After his wife discovers the affair, Mr. Zhang arranges the marriage between Pan and Wu the Elder so that he can continue the affair with Pan. Shortly thereafter Mr. Zhang "came down with a venereal chill" and dies (apparently of sexual exhaustion).[1] Thus, even before the story proper begins, Pan Jinlian has already sent a man to his death, an event that foreshadows the other men who will suffer the same fate at her hands because of her insatiable, murderous sexual desire. She murders Wu the Elder because she wants to continue her affair with Ximen Qing, and later Ximen Qing meets his death as a direct result of her insistence on having sex with him when his sexual virility is drained. The image of Pan Jinlian drinking Ximen Qing's semen in that ghastly sexual encounter (79.1050) is reminiscent of the behavior of sexual vampires in many erotic novels.

The parallels in the manner in which Wu the Elder and Ximen Qing meet their death at Pan Jinlian's hands are hard to miss: both men die with Pan Jinlian sitting astride them and with her force-feeding Wu poison and

1. Many readers have noted that the representation of Pan Jinlian is more sympathetic earlier in the novel and that she becomes increasingly demonic as the plot progresses; cf. Plaks, *Four Masterworks*, pp. 140–41.

Ximen Qing the equally fatal potency pills.[2] Probably no other image testifies more eloquently to the fatal consequences of a woman's insatiable sexual desire than that of Pan Jinlian atop a sexually drained man. To reinforce Pan Jinlian's responsibility for Ximen Qing's death, the narrator goes out of his way to tell us that even after Ximen Qing has collapsed and is being treated by doctors, she insists on having sex with him the next night. Once again, she sits astride him, and her actions cause him to lose consciousness several times (79.1055).

Is Pan Jinlian a victimizer or a victim? The image of a woman atop a man can also be read as a defiant gesture: Pan Jinlian is refusing to succumb to Ximen Qing's sexual dominance. But Pan Jinlian is definitely a victim, too. In fact, in her relationship with Ximen Qing, she is more victim than victimizer, despite the fact that Ximen Qing dies *under* her. This becomes especially true if we read Pan Jinlian as serving the narrative function of hastening Ximen Qing's self-destruction. Hardly a sympathetic character, Pan Jinlian nevertheless makes *Jin Ping Mei* one of the earliest Chinese novels to raise the important issue of female sexual desire, an issue that would come to the forefront in many other novels during the late Ming and early Qing period.

When a Pan Jinlian Tells Her Own Story

The image of a woman shamelessly seeking fulfillment of her sexual desire can be traced to the mid-Ming *Ruyijun zhuan* 如意君傳 (The biography of Mr. Completely Satisfying), which many consider the first Chinese erotic fiction. As its title suggests, *Ruyijun zhuan* is a story about a woman searching for Mr. Right. The woman in question happens to be none other than Empress Wu Zetian 武則天 of the Tang dynasty (618–907), although this is a work of fiction rather than history. As the first full-fledged erotic novel, *Ruyijun zhuan* appears to have exerted a substantial influence on later works in this genre (including *Jin Ping Mei*), especially in terms of the vocabulary of explicit sexual description.

2. See the comments on this in the Chongzhen edition (79.1142): "How does this medicine [the potency pills] compare with the poison Wu the Elder has taken? Any differences between the way Wu the Elder takes his poison and the way Ximen Qing takes his potency pills?" 此藥較武大藥所差幾何?此吃法與武大吃法所差幾何? See also Zhang Zhupo's comments (79.1277).

Another novel that has a sexually insatiable woman as its protagonist is the sixteenth-century erotic novel *Chipozi zhuan* 痴婆子傳 (Biography of a foolish woman). Like *Ruyijun zhuan*, this is a short novel written in literary Chinese. What is remarkable about this novel, however, is that it is an erotic story told by a female first-person narrator, as if a Pan Jinlian had decided or, rather, been given an opportunity to tell her own story. A close reading of *Chipozi zhuan* together with *Ruyijun zhuan* will, I hope, throw some light on how the representation of female desire is complicated when the storyteller happens to be the *represented* woman herself. *Chipozi zhuan* adds several other dimensions to our reading of the figure of lascivious woman, or *yinfu*, that frequently appears in works of fiction during the late imperial period.

As with many works of traditional Chinese fiction, accurate dating of *Ruyijun zhuan* and *Chipozi zhuan* is virtually impossible. In *Dushu yide* 讀書一得 (Thoughts on reading), Huang Xun 黃訓 (1490–ca. 1540) wrote an essay entitled "Du *Ruyijun zhuan*" 讀如意君傳 (On reading the *Biography of Mr. Completely Satisfying*). This led some scholars to believe that the year *jiaxu* 甲戌, the date given in Huayangsanren's 華陽散人 preface, which is found in the earliest extant edition of the novel, must correspond to 1514 in the Western calendar. The fact that someone who died around 1540 had read this novel indicates that it must have been in circulation for some time before 1540, regardless of when that preface was attached.[3] As for *Chipozi*

3. See Sun Kaidi, *Zhongguo tongsu xiaoshuo shumu*, p. 177; and the entry on *Ruyijun zhuan* written by Liu Hui in Liu Shide et al., *Zhongguo gudai xiaoshuo baike quanshu*, pp. 422–23; see also Liu Hui's more detailed discussion in "*Ruyijun zhuan* de kanke niandai jiqi yu *Jin Ping Mei* zhi guanxi"; and Hanan, "The Erotic Novel," p. 26. Hanan (p. 2) and others have pointed out that as the first work in the tradition of the Chinese erotic novel, *Ruyijun zhuan* influenced many later works. Below I discuss in more detail this work's relationship to *Chipozi zhuan*. See also *Ruyijun zhuan* (*Siwuxie huibao* ed., 1995), pp. 15–20, for a brief account of this novel's textual history and the various extant editions.

The most thorough and detailed study of *Ruyijun zhuan* to date is Charles Stone's recently completed dissertation, "The *Ruyijun zhuan* and the Origins of the Chinese Erotic Novel." (It became available to me when the draft of this chapter was already completed. I thank Charles Stone for providing me with a copy.) Stone (pp. 322–71) suggests that Huang Xun might well be the author of this novel. In addition, he (pp. 415–21) believes that the preface attached to the extant edition of the novel was probably written by Wu Gongchen 吳拱宸 (ca. 1610–ca. 1662), who compiled and may have been the author of the collection of short stories titled *Yuanyang zhen* 鴛鴦針 (The mandarin duck needle), and that therefore the date of the preface should be 1634; see also his brief discussion of the dating and textual history of the novel

zhuan, judging from the fact that it is mentioned in other fictional works of the late Ming and early Qing period, we may determine, with considerable certainty, it was most likely written during the late Ming period. For example, *Chipozi zhuan* is mentioned in a preface to the novel *Dong Xi Jin yanyi* 東西晉演義 (The romance of the Eastern and Western Jin), which is dated 1612.[4] It must have been in circulation for some time prior to 1612. At the same time, internal evidence in *Chipozi zhuan* indicates that this work was completed after *Ruyijun zhuan*. We can therefore tentatively conclude that *Chipozi zhuan* is a work of the mid- or late sixteenth century, probably written around the same time as *Jin Ping Mei*.[5]

Chipozi zhuan is presented as the reminiscences of a good-looking, seventy-year-old woman, who, at the invitation of an acquaintance, tells the story of her life. When she (her first name, significantly, is E'nuo 阿娜, meaning "graceful")[6] was a teenager, she became acquainted the love songs in the *Shijing* (Book of poetry) and grew curious about what happened between man and woman. A female neighbor taught her all about sex. She tested her newly acquired knowledge by experimenting with her cousin Huimin. Several years later, she had an affair with a servant named Jun. At this point, she was married to Luan Keyong. Unable to stand the loneliness when her hus-

---

(pp. 433–35). Stone argues that *Ruyijun zhuan*, despite its sexually explicit nature, is a serious "allegorical" novel concerned with contemporary social and political realities.

4. See *Dong Xi Jin yanyi*, reprinted in the *Guben xiaoshuo jicheng* series (a reprint of the Dayetang edition 大業堂本), p. 2; this edition is thought to have been printed by the same publisher that published the edition recorded by Sun Kaidi in his *Zhongguo tongsu xiaoshuo shumu*, p. 45; Wuhu laoren 五湖老人 refers to *Chipozi zhuan* in his preface "*Zhongyi Shuihu quanzhuan* xu" attached to *Wenxing tang piping Shuihu zhuan* 文杏堂批評水滸傳, which was probably printed during the early seventeenth century; see Ding Xigen, *Zhongguo lidai xiaoshuo xuba ji*, p. 1469; and Ma Tiji, "*Shuihu*" *shulu*, p. 17. In Li Yü's *Rou putuan* (3.187), the male protagonist tries to give his bride a lesson in sex education by asking her to read *Chipozi zhuan*. Liu Tingji 劉廷璣 (b. 1653) also mentions the novel in his *Zaiyuan zazhi* 在園雜志, *juan* 2, reprinted in Huang Lin and Han Tongwen, *Zhongguo lidai xiaoshuo lunzhu xuan*, vol. 1, p. 383. All this indicates that by the early Qing *Chipozi zhuan* had achieved quite a reputation as an erotic novel.

5. Although the evidence of *Ruyijun zhuan*'s influence on *Jin Ping Mei* is abundant (see Hanan, "Sources of the *Chin P'ing Mei*," pp. 43–47; and Liu Hui, "*Ruyijun zhuan* de kanke niandai jiqi yu *Jin Ping Mei* zhi guanxi." pp. 57–59), we can find no trace of *Chipozi zhuan*'s influence on *Jin Ping Mei* or vice versa.

6. I believe that here 阿娜 is the same as 婀娜 and should be pronounced "e'nuo," literally meaning "graceful" or "beautiful"; see *Ciyuan*, p. 1774. The pronunciation "a'na" seems too modern for a Ming text.

band went to study elsewhere, she became involved with their servant Yinglang. However, she was forced to have sex with another servant, Datu, and with her husband's elder brother, Keshe, when she was caught having sex with Yinglang. She was also forced to sleep with her father-in-law when she happened to interrupt his affair with one of his other daughters-in-law, Shashi. During a visit to a Buddhist temple, she was forced to have sex with two monks at the machinations of Yinglang. When her husband's younger brother, Ketao, learned of the affair between her and his father, he blackmailed her into sleeping with him. She also had affairs with an actor and then with the husband of her sister. However, when she finally got involved with Gu Deyin, the tutor of her son, she became so attached to him, presumably because of his sexual capabilities, that she refused to have anything more to do with her previous paramours. This refusal made many of them bitter, and Huimin revealed her affair with the tutor to her husband. She was flogged and sent back to her mother's home. Ever since, she has been suffering shame and remorse and has stayed away from sex. She claims that she has remained celibate for almost thirty years.

This synopsis might give the impression that this is an erotic story about the adventures of a sexually insatiable woman, such as *Ruyijun zhuan*, which is about the notoriously amorous empress of the Tang dynasty and her quest for Mr. Right or, rather, "Mr. Right Size." Indeed, the resemblance between *Chipozi zhuan* and *Ruyijun zhuan* is substantial, and the indebtedness of the former to the latter is obvious. The intertextual reference to *Ruyijun zhuan* becomes quite explicit when the reader is told at the beginning of *Chipozi zhuan* that this seventy-year-old woman has gray hair and many missing teeth (*fabai chiluo* 髮白齒落; *Chipozi zhuan*, p. 107). In *Ruyijun zhuan*, Wu Zetian is said to still look very young, with fine hair and teeth (*chifa bushuai* 齒髮不衰), despite being at the advanced age of seventy when she acquires Mr. Right (*Ruyijun zhuan*, p. 46). The last name of the female narrator in *Chipozi zhuan* is Shangguan 上官, an apparent reference to Wu Zetian's notorious palace lady, Shangguan Wan'er 上官婉兒, who is known for her loose life-style and who also appears in *Ruyijun zhuan*.[7] Furthermore, Wu

7. All references to these two novels in this study are to the *Siwuxie huibao* editions (with page reference given in parentheses).These two cases of intertextual references have been pointed out by Hanan, "The Erotic Novel," p. 11; he (p. 5) also observes that the account of a woman's *pinwu* 牝屋 (uterus) in *Ruyijun zhuan* "appears in almost unaltered form" in *Chipozi zhuan*. See *Ruyijun zhuan*, p. 54; and *Chipozi zhuan*, p. 111.

Zetian and her affair with the future emperor Gaozong (Tang Gaozong 唐高宗) are specifically mentioned in *Chipozi zhuan* (*Chipozi zhuan*, p. 127). When the father-in-law tries to seduce Shashi, the wife of his eldest son, during her morning toilet, she playfully spits water onto his face. Then the father-in-law quotes the erotic lines that Wu Zetian speaks during her flirtation with Gaozong in *Ruyijun zhuan*: "Before enjoying the pleasures of wind and clouds behind the brocade bed curtain, / I have been already showered with the favor of rain and dew from the golden basin" (*Chipozi zhuan*, p. 127). The lines he quotes are spoken by Wu Zetian (then a palace lady of the emperor Taizong) in answer to a couplet recited by the future emperor Gaozong (at that time he is still the crown prince) when he spills water onto her face during their rendezvous (*Ruyijun zhuan*, p. 41). Strictly speaking, their affair is incestuous since Wu Zetian is the concubine of Taizong, Gaozong's father. This incestuous affair in *Ruyijun zhuan* parallels neatly the incestuous affair that is about to begin between the father-in-law and Shashi in *Chipozi zhuan*. What is more significant is that these two works also share some larger common features: both novels are explicit accounts of their female protagonists' sexual experiences and their quest for sexual gratification. Both women seem obsessed with the size of their sexual partners' penises. However, the differences between these two works serve as an interesting point of departure for this detailed discussion of *Chipozi zhuan*; this work consciously departs from *Ruyijun zhuan* and embarks on a different agenda that amounts almost to a parody of the earlier work.

Although the age of seventy figures significantly in both works, it has entirely different implications for the two female protagonists: E'nuo, at the age of seventy, has been a social outcast for thirty years due to her affair with her son's tutor, whereas Wu Zetian does not begin to enjoy ultimate sexual gratification until she reaches this age. One woman becomes socially excommunicated as soon as she gets hold of her Mr. Right; the other woman achieves satisfaction upon finding hers. Of course, the different fates of these two women are sealed by the obvious fact that one is an empress and the other is only an ordinary woman. Wu Zetian's success in finding sexual fulfillment is guaranteed by her imperial power. E'nuo's failure is a more realistic story of the fate of an insatiable woman in a patriarchal society—it tells what is more likely to happen to a woman who tries to find sexual fulfillment outside the limits imposed by the society. To a certain extent, *Chipozi zhuan* makes *Ruyijun zhuan* read like a fantasy of female sexual fulfillment (as suggested by the title—*Mr. Completely Satisfying*). If we regard the quests of both female protagonists as attempts to assert their own sexuality or, put more bluntly, to make their own decision as to whom they want to have sex with, Wu Zetian can have her way because she has all the political power of a male ruler, whereas E'nuo, in her more usual gender role as a woman, is forced to concede that the choice is not available to her and that female sexuality for her simply means submission to male sexual domination. Because of this important difference from *Ruyijun zhuan*, *Chipozi zhuan* as a fictional work focusing on the sexual experiences of an ordinary woman becomes all the more interesting.

In the novel, E'nuo has relationships with twelve men in addition to her husband (her list of partners is much longer than that of Pan Jinlian, although nowhere close to that of Ximen Qing). Since the main plot of the novel consists of a recital of her different affairs, the reader's impression of the high frequency of affairs (thus her promiscuity) is enhanced by the relatively short length of the novel. Among the twelve relationships, six are initiated by E'nuo, and the other six are forced upon her. The basic pattern is a self-initiated relationship followed by one or more forced relationships, some of which simply amount to rape. Sometimes a self-initiated relationship develops into a forced one. When E'nuo tries to choose a sexual partner, she often ends up being forced to have another, unwanted relationship. For example, Datu catches her having sex with Yinglang and blackmails her into having sex with him much against her will. What happens next is even more telling: before she can leave the scene, she is confronted by yet a third person, her brother-in-law Keshe.

"Why is Second Sister leaving in such a hurry?" my brother-in-law asked.

I felt so embarrassed that I didn't hold my pants tight; the pants fell down.

My brother-in-law smiled and said: "Second Sister must be having an affair with someone."

I didn't say a word, trying to leave.

But my brother-in-law grabbed my pants and said, "You should do me a favor. If you don't sleep with me, I will tell my brother what you've just done."

I said: "If you tell my husband, I will tell this to your wife."

My brother-in-law laughed and asked, "What have I done?"

I said, "You're trying to sleep with me."

"I haven't got you yet," my brother-in-law said, "You can say anything you want after I get you."

> . . . Yinglang's and Datu's semen was still there. My brother-in-law tried to wipe his hands and said, "Whose leftovers have got my hands dirty?"
>
> I said, "Don't soil my clothes."
>
> My brother-in-law said, "Your body is already soiled. Why worry about your pants?"
>
> Outraged and humiliated, I said, "Why are you so nasty when you try to sleep with me? This is not very kind." I pushed him onto the ground and tried to leave, not realizing that my brother-in-law was still holding the rope belt of my pants.
>
> He knelt down and begged me, "Please pardon my rude words."
>
> I refused. But my brother-in-law snapped the rope belt, pretending to be very angry, "Are you really refusing me?"
>
> "Yes." I said.
>
> My brother-in-law walked away with the rope belt in hand, saying: "With this evidence I'm going to tell everyone."
>
> I had to ask him to come back. (*Chipozi zhuan*, pp. 122–23)

The gender of an adulterous woman forces the protagonist/narrator to surrender herself repeatedly to men, including the servant and her brother-in-law. Since extramarital affairs on the part of a man were more or less accepted, her threat to her brother-in-law is simply brushed off as a joke, but the latter's threat of disclosure has to be taken seriously thanks to her lower gender status as a woman. Paradoxically, her attempts to control her own sexuality by choosing a sexual partner other than her husband become the reason she loses whatever limited control she found. It becomes all the more painful because she has to accept what she could otherwise have refused. Once she has an affair with a servant, her status as mistress of the household becomes meaningless: any servant can blackmail her because she is a woman and because a respectable woman is not supposed to have relationships with someone other than her husband (of course, the same rule does not apply to a master). Thus, she is treated according to her gender status as a "woman" rather than her social status as a "mistress." Here the normal social hierarchy is being rearranged within the context of gender inequality.

This is an interesting reversal of the situation in *Ruyijun zhuan*. Wu Zetian's enormous political power as an empress has in effect produced a new gender relationship in which the woman is the one who dominates and the man is the subordinate. Even when Wu Zetian insists that her relationship with her male "concubine" Xue Aocao 薛敖曹 be that between two lovers rather than that between a ruler and a subject, Xue always reminds her of the inviolable nature of the Confucian political hierarchy. Throughout *Ruyijun zhuan,* Xue Aocao insists on presenting himself as a loyal Confucian minister rather than as a lover, although what qualifies him as a minister is his penis rather than his Confucian learning, despite the fact he, we are specifically told, is a learned Confucian scholar. This becomes a constant source of anxiety and regret for Xue Aocao:

"There are normal channels for becoming an official. Now I will gain recognition from the empress merely because of my penis. What a shame! . . . A dutiful subject should attract his lord's attention by virtue of his talent. Now what kind of selection process is this [referring to his being summoned into the palace because of the unusual size of his penis]?" (*Ruyijun zhuan,* p. 50).

In fact, at one point, the empress reminds him that if he had become a minister by virtue of passing the examinations and his Confucian learning, there would have been no romance between them (*Ruyijun zhuan,* p. 64).

Xue Aocao has to resort to an unusual threat to achieve some degree of masculine control. In order to persuade Wu Zetian to restore her exiled son to the status of crown prince (a matter of great importance to the imperial succession in the eyes of many Confucian ministers), Xue Aocao threatens to castrate himself (*Ruyijun zhuan,* pp. 64–65).[8] His unusually large penis, before being graced by Wu Zetian's imperial favor, led to his being treated almost like a social outcast despite his talent and learning as a Confucian literatus. His penis made him a laughingstock, and no woman wanted to have sex with him or marry him, presumably because of the fear of being hurt during sexual intercourse. Paradoxically, once he begins to serve Wu Zetian,

8. In the sixth story in Li Yu's *Wusheng xi* (p. 122), "A Male Mencius' Mother Raises Her Son Properly by Moving House Three Times," the character Ruilang, in order to show his loyalty to his male lover, castrates himself (see Hanan, ed. and trans., *Silent Operas,* p. 120; see also Sophie Volpp's discussion of this story, "The Discourse on Male Marriage"). For a discussion of the relationship between castration and gender relationship in the late Ming and early Qing as evidenced in Pu Songling's 蒲松齡 (1640–1715) *Liaozhai zhiyi* 聊齋志異 (Strange stories from the Studio of Leisure), see Zeitlin, *Historian of the Strange,* pp. 98–106. Here one may be reminded of the famous historian Sima Qian's choice of the humiliating punishment of castration over death in order to complete his writing of *Siji.* Sima Qian turned being emasculated into an act of enhancing his Confucian manhood (he was willing to endure such punishment only for the purpose of fulfilling his important duties as a historian and as a filial son completing his father's work). For further discussion of the symbolic significance of Sima Qian's choice of castration over death, see my *Literati and Self-Re/Presentation,* p. 80.

castration or the threat of such action by Xue Aocao becomes an attempt to reassert his lost masculinity (to be valued as a man of Confucian ideals and learning rather than a sex object—an imperial "concubine"). That is to say, his giant penis, normally a powerful symbol of supreme masculinity, results in his emasculation and forces him to assume a submissive role usually played by a female (as Wu Zetian did when she was a palace lady).[9] In this situation of gender role reversal, castration becomes the only means for him to reclaim his lost masculinity.

In *Ruyijun zhuan* gender relationships always reproduce themselves politically. The presentation of a male as a favorite for a female ruler must have made the male author of *Ruyijun zhuan* feel uncomfortable enough that he went out of his way to underscore Xue Aocao's virtue as a political "subject" rather than his sexual appeal as an "object of desire," as we would expect in a typical account of a male ruler's relationship with a female favorite. In these accounts, the female is always represented as a cause of the ruler's deviation from his Confucian duties as an emperor. In *Ruyijun zhuan* this is reversed. Aocao's threat of self-castration should be read as a symbolic reminder of his own denied masculinity when he is relegated to playing the feminine gender role as a favorite of a ruler.[10]

Given the gender implications of the character of Xue Aocao, we might read *Chipozi zhuan* as a parody of *Ruyijun zhuan* that unmasks the male anxiety implied in the latter.[11] If pretending to castrate himself is paradoxically Xue Aocao's desperate gesture to reclaim his denied masculinity in *Ruyijun*

9. What is particularly interesting is that Wu Zetian used her own body when she was a palace lady to acquire political power, and this later enabled her to gain control over many male bodies once that political power was secured. However, this is a rare case of how the complicated mechanism of gender politics could work in favor of a woman in traditional China. In fact, Wu Zetian (*Ruyijun zhuan*, p. 55) is very aware of this reversal when she compares herself to the Duke Xian of Jin (Jin Xian'gong 晉獻公) during the Spring and Autumn period (770–476 B.C.), who alienated himself from his sons because of his infatuation with his concubine Liji 驪姬.

10. See also Charles Stone, "The *Ruyijun zhuan* and the Origins of the Chinese Erotic Novel," pp. 294–312, for a detailed discussion of Xue Aocao and the possible symbolic implications of his name (Stone believes that this character, who has no historical basis, was "invented" by the author).

11. Hanan ("The Erotic Novel," p. 8) considers Xue Aocao's relationship with Wu Zetian as described in *Ruyijun zhuan* a parody of the "whole stereotyped theme of the ruler's destruction at the hands of his favorite," although he does not elaborate on the implications of gender politics here.

zhuan, pretending to denounce her sexual transgressions by *telling* stories in her own words, by the same token, becomes E'nuo's attempt to reassert her deprived female sexuality. This leads us to an important feature of *Chipozi zhuan*—its unique narrative mode.

As an erotic novel focusing on female sexuality, what sets *Chipozi zhuan* apart from *Ruyijun zhuan* (and almost all other traditional Chinese novels) is its first-person narrative mode. The question that immediately comes to mind is whether we can trust the story told by such a narrator. One scholar, for example, has found the lack of "moral conscience" in this female narrator deeply troubling:

> The Foolish Woman's words cannot be taken at their face value. She consistently leaves out the moral implications of her actions. This is a story of promiscuity, adultery and incest, which omits the factor of conscience and glosses over the breakup of family and loss of husband and child. It is a tale told by a morally inadequate narrator, a Pan Jinlian who lacks only Pan Jinlian's lust for power.[12]

We may agree that we cannot take her words at their face value and that the remorse she expresses at the end of her story might not be that sincere. Yet *Chipozi zhuan*, as an "autobiography" of a fallen woman, is as much a confession of the sins of a female self as an indictment of the sins committed against that self by many male others. Indeed, it is this agenda of protest that complicates and qualifies the confessional nature of this female discourse and leaves us wondering whether the female narrator genuinely regrets her promiscuous past. The female narrator takes enormous pains to convince us that she is more sinned against than sinning.[13] For example, her incestuous relationship with her father-in-law (probably the most serious sin in the Confucian moral system, which valorizes family order) is the result of coercion by the latter:

> I cried out, "My father-in-law tries to rape me while my sister-in-law tries to stop me from escaping. You're acting like animals!"
>
> Shashi said, "Our father-in-law is our closest relative. Now if you serve him with your own body, this has to be considered an act of filiality."
>
> I laughed and said, "I've never heard that the opening which the son has entered can be entered by his father. If I become pregnant, how will people consider the baby—the son or the grandson of the family?"

12. Ibid., p. 11.
13. Patrick Hanan, "A Landmark of the Chinese Novel," p. 328.

My father-in-law smiled and said, "You two beautiful women are both my wives. Why bother talking about the dying mother-in-law or the dissolute son?" (*Chipozi zhuan*, p. 128)

It is her father-in-law and her sister-in-law who first commit the sin of violating the most sacred Confucian relationship, that between a father and a son.

Read from a slightly different perspective, this incident can tell us even more. In many traditional fictional works, a maid who accidentally interrupts her mistress's adultery is often forced to offer herself to her mistress's lover as a way of ensuring her silence (Chunmei, for example, does this at the request of Pan Jinlian when she interrupts Jinlian's dalliance with Chen Jingji in chapter 82 of *Jin Ping Mei*). Shashi's attempt to force the female narrator to join this incestuous affair appears to conform to this convention. However, when the reader recalls the earlier incident in which the narrator is forced to offer her body to another servant because he happens to catch her with another man, the possibility of a self-conscious parody becomes apparent. No matter what role our female narrator assumes, either a mistress caught by a servant or a daughter-in-law catching her father-in-law with another of his daughters-in-law, offering up her own body is the only way out for a woman.

The most poignant point in the story is perhaps how her husband learns of the narrator's affair with the tutor. What is extremely ironic is that until the very end of the story, the husband probably knows only of her affair with the tutor—he has no idea that his own father and brothers have also slept with his wife. What adds to the poignancy here is that her attempt to reject the promiscuous life-style becomes the cause of her undoing. If she had continued her affairs with all her paramours (presumably like her sister-in-law, Shashi), no one would have bothered to reveal the matter to her husband. In fact, it is her determination to assert control of her own sexuality—the right to choose and, more important, the right to refuse—that causes her to become a fallen woman in the eyes of the public. E'nuo's fall, according to many of her paramours, begins only when she decides to assert her right to be monogamous. The complicity among her male partners is most obvious when many of them condemn her for her exposed affair with the tutor. One of the most compelling scenes in her story is her father-in-law's straight-faced condemnation of her—"It is my second son's misfortune that his wife behaves so immorally" (*Chipozi zhuan*, pp. 142–43). Mimicking the rhetoric of the father, the commentator on the novel was quick to add that "it is the ancestors' misfortune that a father does not behave morally" (*Chipozi zhuan*, p. 143).

The impression that this story is an implicit indictment of a male-dominated society is strengthened by the possible symbolic implications of the names of E'nuo's husband and his two brothers. Her husband's name is Keyong 克慵. The character *yong* 慵 (laziness), which before the Han dynasty (206 B.C.–A.D. 220) was frequently written *yong* 庸,[14] also means "incompetence." The name of the elder brother, who blackmails E'nuo into sleeping with him, is Keshe 克奢. *She* 奢 is often associated with *yin* 淫, "excessive" and "debauched." The name of the younger brother, who also forces E'nuo to have sex with him, is Ketao 克饕. *Tao* 饕 means "greedy." The character *ke* 克, the common element in all three brothers' names, can mean "capable of." The names fit the three brothers perfectly. One is capable of being lazy and is probably incompetent (sexually inadequate?),[15] and the other two are either capable of acts of debauchery or being sexually greedy. Thus the reader is urged by the implied author (whether male or female) to conclude that the female narrator is a victim of her own husband's incompetence as well as of the greedy and excessive behavior of the two brothers-in-law.[16]

If the female narrator is successful in persuading her audience that she is a victim, the fact she is not punished more severely should be less troubling. The listener/reader is supposed to agree with this fallen woman that she is a victim of male domination rather than a transgressive and sexually insatiable woman. The basic rhetoric of this confession by a fallen woman is to compel the reader to condemn those who have condemned her (such as her father-in-law) and thus it undermines the validity of their condemnation.

Another of the narrator's subtle tactics for legitimating female sexuality is to associate female sexual desire with the *Book of Poetry*. Her curiosity about

14. *Ciyuan*, p. 625.

15. It is curious that, except for the first wedding night, her sexual experience with her husband is never mentioned in her story.

16. Of course, if we interpret the character *ke* according to one of its more common meanings, namely, "overcoming" or "prevailing against," as in the famous saying by Confucius: "To return to the observance of the rites through overcoming the self constitutes benevolence" (克己復禮爲仁; *Lunyu zhengyi*, ed. Liu Baonan, p.262; and Lau, *The Analects*, 12.1, p. 112), then the names of the three brothers yield similar ironic implications, emphasizing instead their utter failure to cultivate or control themselves.

sex is aroused in part by reading love poems in that anthology.[17] In fact, the reader is specifically told at the beginning of the novel that E'nuo is from a place that used to be a part of the ancient states of Zheng 鄭 and Wei 衛 during the Spring and Autumn period (770–476 B.C.; *Chipozi zhuan*, p. 107). Many of the love poems in the *Book of Poetry* were thought to have originated from that area. Furthermore, despite its explicitness, the female neighbor's lecture on sex is sometimes rather eloquent. At one point, she justifies sex in terms of procreation, a view not far from that of orthodox Confucian thinking on this matter (*Chipozi zhuan*, p. 110). The narrator's curiosity about sex and her later transgressions might be blamed in part on her parents, who do not even allow her to read those poems in the *Book of Poetry*; meanwhile her father has a sexual relationship with a servant (*waichong* 外寵; *Chipozi zhuan*, p. 118).

With this understanding of the implicit agenda of self-vindication on the part of the female narrator, we are now in a better position to appreciate the significance of the first-person female narrative voice. The sheer fact that she is able to survive to tell this story (she is not punished with death, nor has she committed suicide as all disgraced women were supposed to do after their affairs were exposed) has important implications.[18] Narration becomes the only means to reassert her sexuality, which the patriarchal environment has denied her, just like Xue Aocao, who has to resort to castration to re-

17. Of course, this was a well-established literary convention in traditional China. Almost all literary works that have something to do with sexual love seek legitimacy in the *Book of Poetry*. The sexuality of Du Liniang in *Mudan ting* is also awakened by reading the love poems from the *Book of Poetry*. Incidentally, in the ninth scene of this play, "Suyuan" 肅苑 (Sweeping the garden), the maid Chunxiang quotes Du Liniang as saying, "Even though the ospreys were shut in, they still had the freedom of the island: why should a human being be treated worse than a bird?" "Why should a human being be treated worse than a bird" is quoted verbatim from *Ruyijun zhuan* (p. 60; see Scene 9, Tang Xianzu, *Mudan ting*, p. 49; and Birch, *The Peony Pavilion*, p. 40). As Charles Stone ("The *Ruyijun zhuan* and the Origins of the Chinese Erotic Novel," p. 474) has pointed out, this figure of speech can be traced to the Confucian classic *Daxue*, in which Confucius is quoted as having made a similar observation on a line from one of the poems in the *Book of Poetry*. See Zhu Xi, *Sishu zhangju jizhu*, p. 5.

18. In the first story in Feng Menglong's *Yushi mingyan* 喻世明言 (Clear words to instruct the world), which is known for its relatively sympathetic treatment of an adulterous woman, the female protagonist at least has to make the gesture of trying to commit suicide; see Feng, *Yushi mingyan*, pp. 25–26; and "The Pearl Shirt Reencountered," in Y. W. Ma and Joseph S. M. Lau, *Traditional Chinese Stories*, p. 284. For the relationship between suicide and female chastity, see Chapter 8.

claim his denied masculinity in *Ruyijun zhuan*. Even the titles of these two novels parallel each other: both novels are *zhuan* (biographies or stories), one about an old woman's Mr. Right (*ruyijun*) and the other about a foolish old woman (*chipozi*). Wu Zetian, with the power of an empress, is able to achieve her ultimate sexual fulfillment by finding her *ruyijun* at the age of seventy; the female narrator in *Chipozi zhuan*, at the same age, has to cling to the opportunity of telling her own story about her "foolish past" to revalidate her sexuality. To a certain degree, telling, for this obsessed old woman, is much more than a passive act of merely talking about her past sexuality; for this woman (an old Wu Zetian without Wu Zetian's imperial power), talking about her own female sexuality is a sexualized act. It is almost her female sexuality itself.

This is all the more significant since few women in traditional China were granted a chance to tell their own stories, not to mention stories about their own sexuality. Patrick Hanan certainly touches on an important issue when he observes that *Chipozi zhuan* is "a tale by a morally inadequate narrator, a Pan Jinlian who lacks only Jinlian's lust for power." Would we still see Pan Jinlian as "a morally inadequate" woman if she, too, had had a chance to tell her own story? It is probably due to an acute awareness of the importance of "who is telling" that our seventy-year-old female narrator appears so eager to talk about her past, which is by no means glorious according to the moral standards of her male-dominated society. Before she begins her story, we are told that she never tires of talking about her past (喜談往事, 疊疊不倦; *Chipozi zhuan*, p. 107). Our narrator is so enthusiastic about her own past that her story lasts two days (she has to come back to continue her story the next day). When invited to tell her story, her answer is: "I would still tell you the story about my past even if you had not asked me":

> She was dressed in white and wore long sleeves; straightening her clothes and smiling, she leaned forward and began to talk in earnest: "Like the withering grass, I'm an old woman who does not have too many years to live. How could I allow my past romantic experiences to pass into oblivion?" (*Chipozi zhuan*, p. 107)

She ends her story with almost the same rhetoric: "Now I'm very old, and I don't mind being laughed at. This is why I've told you so much. Have you covered your ears all the time when I was talking?" (*Chipozi zhuan*, p. 144). Wu Zetian finally is able to achieve sexual fulfillment in her old age largely because of her political power; this female narrator is able to (re)assert her sexuality precisely because she does not have to worry about being silenced or about being condemned again.

She is granted a chance to tell her own story partly because she has led others to believe this is also an expression of her remorse. Another significant factor is the third-person male narrative framework that *contains* her narration in the novel. This male narrator's attitude toward E'nuo is surprisingly sympathetic. Despite his claim that E'nuo is a "foolish woman" and that her story is entertaining, his concluding remark calls the reader's attention to the fact that E'nuo is a victim:

> Shangguan had affairs with twelve men but was finally exposed only because of her involvement with Gu Deyin. All this is because she became "faithful" to one lover (*qingyou duzhong* 情有獨鍾). However, Keyong divorced his wife only knowing about her adultery with the tutor and nothing more. This is really something extraordinary! (*Chipozi zhuan*, p. 144)

The author of *Chipozi zhuan* is apparently following the convention of classical tales (such as Tang dynasty *chuanqi*) by presenting this novel as a biography (*zhuan* 傳).[19] By assuming the pose of a historian/storyteller and offering a concluding and authoritative comment on the meaning of this woman's words, the male narrator tries to alleviate the shocking effect of her autobiography. The male third-person narrator claims that by writing down this autobiographical story by a woman, he becomes the author of a "biography": "Because of her willingness to tell this story, we have something to laugh at. She must be a foolish woman. This is why I wrote this *Biography of a Foolish Woman*" (*Chipozi zhuan*, p. 144).[20] The transformation of a fallen woman's autobiography (*zizhuan* 自傳) into a male writer's biography (*zhuan* 傳) *of* a fallen woman may help to meet an important precondition for this ostensibly *oral* story's gaining access to the public: it gives rise to a secure sense of male control—the female voice is at least *contained* within a male discourse.

19. For a brief discussion of the narrative conventions of *chuanqi* of the Tang dynasty, see Shi Changyu, *Zhongguo xiaoshuo yuanliu lun*, pp. 173–82.

20. The word *chi* 痴 has implications other than "being foolish." It can also mean "obsession" or "infatuation." Thus by describing her as someone who is *chi*, the author may also try to call our attention to the fact that at the age of seventy, this woman is still obsessed with her past and with her own denied sexuality. This is another proof that she is by no means a woman who has totally renounced her past. For discussions of the significance of the phenomenon of *chi* in Ming-Qing China, see Zeitlin, *Historian of the Strange*, pp. 61–97; and Zhou Ruchang, *"Honglou meng" yu Zhonghua wenhua*, pp. 117–40.

It is partly due to a vague sense of male security created by this discursive containment that this subversive female voice is able to attain its textuality—becoming a printed text for circulation, a public event. Even before the foolish woman starts her tale, the third-person male narrator has promised her that he will seek to have her story published (*Chipozi zhuan*, p. 107), a promise that testifies to male access to and control of the public domain and therefore to the need for a woman's words to be embedded in a male discourse. The gender power structure has to be replicated in the novel's embedding narrative structure, despite, or precisely because of, the fact that what is embedded is meant to be a critique of this very power structure. Nonetheless, we should not underestimate the significance of the simple fact that a woman is finally given a voice, even though it is mediated through a male discourse.

It has been observed that the model for this embedding narrative structure may derive from *Ruyijun zhuan*, in which Wu Zetian recounts her past sexual experiences to Xue Aocao.[21] Besides the obvious fact that Wu Zetian's embedded narration is only a small part of the *Ruyijun zhuan* whereas *Chipozi zhuan* consists almost entirely of the embedded narration by a woman, another essential difference is that Wu Zetian's audience is limited to her lover and that her discourse is private, whereas E'nuo's discourse is potentially public (she tells this story to anyone who will listen, and the expectation is that it will become a published text), even though she does not have the political power of an empress to legitimize her voice. This is why *Chipozi zhuan* is even more scandalous. The act of a female talking publicly about her own promiscuity is perhaps more outrageous than the promiscuity itself.

The Vindication of Female Desire in *Dengcao heshang*

Chipozi zhuan is a unique erotic novel in which a woman is given the rare opportunity to (re)tell and (re)interpret her own sexual experiences, but there are several seventeenth-century erotic novels that relate a woman's sexual experience with varying degrees of sympathy in the more conventional third-person narrative mode. It was probably expected that erotic fiction would focus on sexual desire and its consequences. It was no coincidence that

21. Hanan, "The Erotic Novel," p. 11.

women characters became increasingly prominent as fiction began to focus on desire in the domestic realm, partly because the feminine was traditionally associated with the private and the domestic and partly because desire often finds its most compelling expressions in the domain of the private.[22] Erotic fiction as a transgressive genre seems occasionally to have offered more latitude for viewing deviations, especially those committed by women, with more tolerance. For example, in the late Ming erotic novel *Langshi* (A history of debauchery), after finding out that she has been tricked by her husband, Mei Suxian, into having sex with the servant Lu Shu, who is also her husband's male lover, Li Wenfei asks her husband why he has not blamed her for "failing to behave as a woman should behave." The husband offers a rather unexpected explanation: "Since you have allowed me to keep a concubine, why shouldn't I allow you to keep a male concubine (*xiao laogong* 小老公)?"[23] This rather "feminist" remark by a promiscuous husband is in-

22. We should, therefore, not be surprised by the fact that the first Chinese erotic novel, *Ruyi jun zhuan*, focuses on the sexual experience of a woman. For discussions of the increasing presence of women in Ming-Qing fiction, see McMahon, *Misers, Shrews, and Polygamists*, pp. 11–12, 99–125, 176–220; Yenna Wu, *The Chinese Virago*; and Epstein, "Beauty Is the Beast," esp. pp. 13–34. The increasing presence of women in these fictional works might, to an extent, be a result of the privatization process late Ming fiction (some of which began to focus on the domestic arena) was undergoing as an emerging narrative genre; see my "Dehistoricization and Intertextualization," pp. 57–58.

23. *Langshi*, 29.196. Of course, the male protagonist's offering of his own wife to his male lover in exchange for favors from the latter is a conventional plot in quite a few Ming-Qing erotic novels. Similar cases can be found in the late Ming erotic novel *Xiuta yeshi* and in some early Qing works such as *Chundeng nao* and *Taohua ying* 桃花影 (The shadows of the peach blossoms). However, Mei Suxian in *Langshi* was the first to make such a seemingly nonsexist claim about a woman's equal right to have more than one sexual partner. In *Chundeng nao*, in order to have sex with the male protagonist Zhen Chuyu 眞楚玉, Yao Zi'ang 姚子昂, who loves *nanfeng* 南風 (male homosexuality), has to allow Zhen Chuyu to sleep with his wife, Huiniang 蕙娘. Unlike Mei Suxian, however, Yao Zi'ang confesses that to gratify his own homosexual desires he has to violate his own belief that a man can marry many concubines but a woman cannot marry more than one husband (see *Chundeng nao*, 2.41). It is possible that *Xiuta yeshi* started this convention of exchanging sexual partners, if we accept the attribution of this work to Lü Tiancheng 呂天成 (1580–1618); *Langshi* was probably written sometime around 1620. For discussions of the textual histories and dating of these two works, see the editor's notes in *Xiuta yeshi*, pp. 15–23; and in *Langshi*, pp. 15–18.

A similar protest against the unfair convention that a woman is allowed to have sexual relations only with the man she marries whereas a man is entitled to many women is also voiced in the eleventh story in *Xihu erji* 西湖二集 (The stories of the West Lake, second collection) of the 1640s (11.201), and in the eleventh story in Ling Mengchu's 凌夢初 *Erke*

deed a surprise, a remark the equally promiscuous but much more chauvinistic Ximen Qing would never dream of making.

The first chapter of another late Ming novel, *Chanzhen houshi* 禪眞後史 (Later tales of the True Way), contains a lengthy and graphic account of how a widow suffers tremendous physical "torture" when her long-repressed sexual desire is reawakened by witnessing a pair of moths mating (probably a motif from *Ruyijun zhuan*). She then tries to seduce her children's tutor but is rejected. She then attempts to cope with her aroused sexual urges:

> She stood with her hands hugging a black lacquer pillar, her feet crossed below; and up and down she slid, without stopping, a hundred and more times, until all at once she felt a wave of pleasure. Her whole body became numb, as if buckets of water had been poured from her breast all the way down to her womb. She twisted a while until there was a loud rupture and an object fell out of her womb. Then she felt her limbs become paralyzed.[24]

Many years later before she dies, she vehemently advises her daughters-in-law against widowhood based on her own personal experiences, which seem to have convinced her that a widow's sexual desire is simply too strong to suppress.[25] All these can be considered rare "feminist" moments in these otherwise quite conventional erotic novels, which as a whole do not follow a coherent agenda of re-examining the implications of female sexuality.

A more interesting work that focuses on a woman's right to seek sexual fulfillment is the early Qing erotic fiction *Dengcao heshang* 燈草和尚 (The candlewick monk).[26] Although a bit crude in terms of plot and character development, the novel contains many rather innovative and sometimes even ingenious moments. In this short novel, the candlewick monk (so named be-

---

Pai'an jingqi, p. 225. Many stories in *Huanxi yuanjia* also exhibit very tolerant attitudes toward adulterous women. *See* McMahon, *Misers, Shrews, and Polygamists*, pp. 51–52 and 69–72, for discussions of this issue in some fictional works of that period.

24. *Chanzhen houshi*, 1.70. English translation from McMahon, *Causality and Containment*, p. 120; see also his discussion of the representation of female desire, pp. 119–23.

25. *Chanzhen houshi*, 14.172–74. A similar message can be found at the beginning of the 35th story in Feng Menglong's *Jingshi tongyan* 警世通言 (Common words to warn the world), pp. 523–24; and "The Case of the Dead Infant," in Y. W. Ma and Joseph S. M. Lau, *Traditional Chinese Stories*, p. 123.

26. Most scholars agree with Sun Kaidi (*Zhongguo tongsu xiaoshuo shumu*, p. 181) that *Dengcao heshang* is an early Qing work. For information on this work's textual history, see "*Dengcao heshang* chuban shuoming" 燈草和尚出版說明, in *Dengcao heshang*, pp. 15–18.

cause he can appear from and disappear into a burning candle at will), has the magical ability to transform himself into different heights or sizes (sometimes only three inches and sometimes eight feet tall) and creates chaos in the family of Magistrate Yang by seducing many of its female members. All this is indirectly triggered by the fact that Madame Wang (Magistrate Yang's wife) is sexually frustrated because of her husband's neglect and sexual incompetence. One day, an old female magician is invited to entertain the family. Her magic enables a three-inch tall monk to jump out of the burning candle. The monk suddenly climbs onto Madame Wang and begins to caress her. The candlewick monk proves to be superb in bed in part thanks to his ability to shrink or enlarge at will. His sexual prowess soon proves to be a source of happiness for several women in the family, Madame Wang, her daughter Changgu, and the maid Nuanyu. Later Magistrate Yang is literally frightened to death by a display of magic by the candlewick monk. Madame Wang eventually marries a certain Mr. Zhou, who used to be a Taoist priest and who, ironically, becomes sexually involved with Madame Wang during the funeral of her deceased husband. They live happily ever after.

What is shocking is the revelation at the end of the story: the candlewick monk tells Madame Wang that he came to wreak havoc only because Magistrate Yang had once sentenced an official's wife and her servant to a public flogging for having an adulterous affair. This sentence, which was extremely lenient by the standards of the time, is, however, deemed too harsh by Heaven (*shangtian* 上天). Deeply upset, Heaven sends down the candlewick monk to punish Magistrate Yang: his own wife is to have affairs with other men without being punished at all. In other words, Magistrate Yang's punishment for showing so little sympathy to an adulterous woman takes the form of being cuckolded. And his adulterous wife is even rewarded for her sins, whereas the magistrate eventually pays with his own life. It is indeed very rare, even in an erotic novel, that an adulterous woman is allowed to go unpunished for her sexual transgressions against her own husband, let alone being rewarded. Of course, the fact that one of her lovers is an emissary from Heaven should make her transgressions more excusable.

The novel's ultimate message seems to be that when a man cannot fulfill his duties as a husband by giving his wife proper sexual satisfaction, his wife's recourse to affairs with another man should be judged with sympathy and understanding. In the novel, one of the female spirits sent to seduce

Magistrate Yang voices the most daring declaration of a woman's right to seek sexual fulfillment outside marriage: "Although we four sisters are married, our husbands cannot control us. The world is the same for everyone. Who among our women does not want to have affairs with a few men (*tou jige nanzihan* 偷幾個男子漢)?" (1.91–92). The four female spirits sent to punish Magistrate Yang by sexually draining him (because he has tried to kill the candlewick monk) are named after the four seasons—Sister Spring, Sister Summer, Sister Autumn, and Sister Winter—names that underscore the naturalness of female sexuality as an inviolable force of nature.

Dengcao heshang is apparently indebted to the Song dynasty *huaben* 話本 story "Denghua popo" 燈花婆婆 (Auntie Candleflame), which is, in turn, based on the story "Liu Jizhong" 劉積中 in the collection of literary anecdotes and tales *Youyang zazu* 酉陽雜俎 by Duan Chengshi 段成式 (ca. 803–63). "Denghua popo" relates that an old woman three feet tall jumps out of a burning candle, wreaks havoc in an official family, and is finally subdued with the help of the Boddhisavtta.[27] In the novel, the three-feet-tall candlewick woman becomes an old female magician, who conjures up a three-inch-tall monk, who can change the size of his body and the size of his penis at will. Because the monk can shrink and enlarge himself, he can not only have sex with a woman as a full-size man but also enter a woman as if his entire body, when three inches tall, were a male organ. At this size, it is less likely that others will discover what he is doing with their wives and daughters. Like the penis-like monk in chapter 49 of *Jin Ping Mei*, the candlewick monk illustrates the resemblance often assumed in traditional erotic discourse between the male sexual organ and a bearded monk with a shaved head.[28]

This ingenious image of a ductile monk (or penis) can almost be read as an embodiment of willful desiring by a sexually frustrated woman such as Madame Wang. This sexually gratifying "monk" can conveniently be concealed when shrunk (in the novel, this technique is called *suoyang fa* 縮陽法

27. Duan's story can also be found in *Taiping guangji*, *juan* 363, pp. 2888–89; The original Song *huaben* story is lost, but it is incorporated by Feng Menglong into the beginning of his novel *Pingyao zhuan* 平妖傳, 1.1–2. Based on information in the prefaces to certain Ming editions of *Shuihu zhuan* and on clues from other sources, some scholars believe the story "Denghua popo" might have been part of the introduction in some early versions of *Shuihu zhuan* but was deleted in later versions of the novel; see He Xin, *"Shuihu" yanjiu*, pp. 115–21.

28. In the eighteenth-century erotic novel *Guwangyan* (SH ed., 2.274), discussed at length in Chapter 9, a man's sexual organ is referred to as a "little monk" (*xiao heshang* 小和尚).

or "the magic of penis shrinking"; 1.45),[29] and yet he can also become a full-sized man if kissing and hugging are desired in addition to sexual intercourse (as wished by Madame Wang; 2.54). This reading is supported by another interesting episode in the novel—the four female spirits have the magical ability to spit out (*tu* 吐) handsome men so that they can copulate with them; in turn these men can produce beautiful women by the same method. These spirits can have sex with whomever they want whenever they want thanks to this unique magical power of being able to create their own sexual partners with their mouths.[30] With this magic, one's sexual desire can fully and conveniently be satisfied.

On the other hand, the fact that this candlewick monk is a god or spirit (*yaoguai* 妖怪) should make a mortal woman such as Madame Wang appear rather innocent in an adulterous situation, since she is a pawn in Heaven's plot. There is reason to believe that the author of *Dengcao heshang*, who is unusually sympathetic to women's need for sexual fulfillment, must have been inspired by various legends and stories associated with the cult of God Wutong 五通神, which was extremely popular during the Ming-Qing period.[31] This god was believed to be unpredictable and easily upset. He either brings wealth to people or ruins their lives. One of the nasty things he enjoys doing is debauching women.[32] In fact, *biji* 筆記 (random notes) and other

29. Later in the story (3.57), the Magistrate Yang tells his wife of a certain monk who masquerades as a nun to defile many women using this method of *suoyang*. In chapter 18 of *Guwangyan*, a man is said to use this method to defile many women by cross-dressing himself as a nun.

30. Here the novel is obviously influenced by the story "Yangxian shusheng" 陽羨書生, in Wu Jun's 吳鈞 (469–520) *Xu Qixie ji* 續齊諧記, which is about a scholar who can perform the magic of spitting things or even human beings out of his mouth (he also sleeps with the woman he spits out; that woman spits out another man, who will in turn spit out yet another woman to flirt with). The story is also known as "E'long shusheng" 鵝籠書生, since the scholar initially asks to be caged together with a goose despite his full-size body as a man. It has been collected in many anthologies of *xiaoshuo* since the Southern dynasties; see *Taiping guangji*, *juan* 284, pp. 2266–67. In fact, this story is specifically mentioned in *Dengcao heshang* (5.95), when, after witnessing Sister Summer expectorate human beings, Magistrate Yang exclaims, "Oh, yes! I remember the story of "E'long shusheng."

31. For studies of the cult of this god and attempts to suppress this cult in late imperial China, see von Glahn, "The Enchantment of Wealth"; and Cedzich, "The Cult of the Wu-t'ung/Wu-hsien in History and Fiction."

32. Von Glahn, "The Enchantment of Wealth," pp. 682–87.

anecdotal writings of the period contain stories of women who tried to cover up their affairs by claiming that they had been seduced by gods.[33] In *Dengcao heshang*, long before the candlewick monk's arrival, Madame Wang had an affair with one of her servants. Thus, even the excuse of being seduced by a god does not work in her case. When the candlewick monk stops seeing Madame Wang after her husband's death, Madame Wang, during a trip to a temple, casually consents to sleep with two monks. As a result, the candlewick monk tells her that she will no longer be allowed to practice Buddhism (不便修行) because she and the two monks have defiled the sacred place of Buddhism (污了佛他; 12.191). However, the candlewick monk reveals that she will be blessed with a new marriage and a good son and will live to the age of seventy (12.193). Given all the transgressions Madame Wang has committed, the punishment of not being able to practice Buddhism sounds almost absurd. Few traditional novels are as adamant as *Dengcao heshang* in trying to vindicate a woman's right to sexual fulfillment.

Dengcao heshang and especially *Chipozi zhuan*, by virtue of their focus on female sexual experiences from a woman's perspective, seem to have been an important step toward establishing what has been called the "feminine authority" in fictional narrative.[34] In these two novels, the female protagonists are presented not as "objects of desire" but as "desiring subjects." This is also true of *Ruyijun zhuan*, although Wu Zetian's status as a desiring subject is sustained, to a large extent, by her imperial power, which, ironically, according to the orthodox view, she usurped. In *Chipozi zhuan*, E'nuo is not only a desiring subject but, what is more significant, also a speaking subject, who had the discursive power to define and interpret her own subjectivity. Despite the fact that we do not have enough information to determine the

33. "Huang Zhen" 黃震, in *Zhinang bu* 智囊補, *juan* 7, in Feng Menglong, *Quanji*, vol. 35, pp. 469–70.

34. "Feminine authority" is a term used by Nancy Armstrong in "Postface: Chinese Women in a Comparative Perspective," p. 402. However, in earlier work, she uses the term "female authority" (*Desire and Domestic Fiction*, p. 30): "Although concerned mainly with the vicissitudes of courtship and marriage, and fictional courtship and marriage at that, fiction that represented gender from this gendered viewpoint exerted a form of political authority." See also ibid., pp. 28–58.

gender of its author,[35] *Chipozi zhuan* should probably be considered one of the first fictional narratives in China that promoted "feminine authority."[36]

An unexpected but logical result of the obsession with the intimate details of desire in many works of erotic fiction is a new awareness of issues associated with women's sexuality and their undeniable subjectivity as women. Even if we accept the premise that erotic fiction was largely written by and for men, its transgressive generic nature, intentionally or not, gave rise to a new consciousness of the gendered ramifications of desire—among them, the suppressed subjectivity of women (women's capacity as desiring subjects). In this implicit gendered consciousness lie the possibilities of a serious challenge to the otherwise dominant patriarchal ideology, which, ironically, may have been the main force behind the rise of erotic fiction in late imperial China. In the next chapter, we will examine how such challenges produced deep anxieties in certain men and, consequently, horror stories about shrews.

35. "Feminine authority," as defined by Nancy Armstrong, is not necessarily dependent on "female authorship."

36. The study of the history of female authorship of fiction has been exasperated by the lack of data and the time-honored convention of anonymous authorship of fiction. Ellen Widmer ("Ming Loyalism and the Women's Voice in Fiction After *Honglou meng*," p. 368) speculates that the late Ming, early Qing female writer Wang Duanshu 王端淑 (1621–ca. 1706) might have written a novel or *tanci* (poetic narrative). So far the earliest documented evidence that a woman wrote a novel during late eighteenth century can be found in Mei Shujun's 梅樹君 (1770–1844) collected writings. Mei wrote a postscript for a sequel to *Honglou meng* titled *Honglou juemeng* 紅樓覺夢 authored by a certain Madame Tiefeng (鐵峰夫人). The postscript contains some information on this female novelist. However, the work itself is no longer extant; see Zhao Jianzhong, "*Honglou meng*" *xushu yanjiu*, pp. 31–36. The earliest known work of fiction by a female author still extant is probably the famous Qing poet Gu Taiqing's 顧太清 (1799–1876) *Honglou meng ying* 紅樓夢影, which was published posthumously in 1877; see Widmer, "Ming Loyalism," pp. 393–96; and Zhao Botao, "*Honglou meng ying* de zuozhe ji qita."

CHAPTER SIX
Desire and Karmic Retribution in Xingshi yinyuan zhuan

The Problem of *Jin Ping Mei*

The earliest extant reader response to *Jin Ping Mei* is probably Yuan Hongdao's letter, dated 1596, to Dong Qichang:

> A month ago, Shikui 石簣 [Tao Wangling 陶望齡] came to visit me, and we spent five days in delightful talk. After that, we set off by boat to tour the Five Lakes and to see the outstandingly beautiful places among the Seventy-two Peaks. When we had completed the tour, we returned to my studio in the official residence. Our discussion ranged over every conceivable topic, both trivial and important. My illness had receded a little because of his visit, and my regret was that you were not there with us. Where did you get the *Jin Ping Mei* from? I glanced at it from time to time, while lying in my bed, and find it well written (*manzhi yunxia* 滿紙雲霞) and far superior to Mei Cheng's *Qifa* 七發 [Seven stimuli]. Where is the latter part? Please let me know where I can return it to you, once it has been copied, and exchange it for the other part.[1]

Reading *Jin Ping Mei* had obviously made Yuan Hongdao feel less ill, and this was probably the immediate reason he compared the novel to Mei

1. "Yu Dong Sibai" 與董思白, in Yuan Hongdao, *Ji*, *juan* 6, p. 289; Huang Lin, *"Jin Ping Mei" ziliao huibian*, p. 227; English trans. based on Hanan, "The Text of the *Chin P'ing Mei*," pp. 39–40.

Cheng's 枚乘 (d. 141 B.C.) *Qifa*, a famous *fu* 賦 (rhapsody) in which a long talk by a guest cures an ailing prince of the state of Chu.[2] However, Yuan's comparison might be more significant than his casual reference to feeling better after reading the novel suggests. It bespeaks the ambivalence of many of Yuan's contemporaries toward the novel despite their enthusiastic advocacy of vernacular literature. In *Qifa*, the guest who comes to inquire about the health of the prince diagnoses his illness as a result of overindulgence and suggests that the best cure is to listen to "essential and marvelous doctrines" (*yaoyan miaodao* 要言妙道). He then proceeds to describe for the prince a series of enticements or stimuli, such as beautiful music, delicious food, and an exciting chariot ride. The proposed stimuli fail to arouse the prince's interest except for the seventh and last one, a promise to introduce him to the words of the sages. Upon hearing this, the prince is miraculously cured. For many readers, *Qifa* presents a typical dilemma faced by literature of "persuasion" (*shui* 說), especially those works that rely on the method of "criticism by indirection" (*feng* 諷). In order to be effective, persuasion has to be couched in a language that sustains the interest of the person one is trying to persuade, and in *Qifa*, most of the guest's long speech on various sensual pleasures is supposed to serve this purpose. The desire to instruct the prince in the need to stop indulging himself and to reform conflicts, however, with the necessity to entertain him by talking, at least initially, about the pleasures of further indulgences. Critics of later ages were rather ambivalent about *Qifa*'s impact on later *fu* writers; in trying to emulate Mei Cheng's model, many writers failed to achieve the proper balance between instruction and entertainment and focused on the entertaining rhetoric at the expense of the didactic agenda.[3] Yuan Hongdao may have sensed the similarities between *Qifa* and *Jin Ping Mei* in terms of their common strategy of using the enticing rhetoric of indulgence to persuade readers to stop indulging themselves. Thanks to its generic nature as a full-length novel, *Jin Ping Mei*

2. See *Qifa*, in *Quan Shanggu Sandai QinHan Sanguo Liuchao wen*, vol. 1, pp. 448–49; for a discussion of Mei Cheng's *Qifa*, see Knechtges, *The Han Rhapsody*, pp. 30–34.

3. See, e.g., the view expressed by Zhi Yu 摯虞 (d. 311) in his "Wenzhang liubie zhilun" 文章流別志論, in Xu Zhixiao, *Lidai fulun jiyao*, pp. 11–12; and also in *Quan Shanggu Sandai QinHan Sanguo Liuchao wen*, vol. 4, pp. 802 (where the title of the essay is given as "Wenzhang liubie lun," p. 801); for a discussion of Yang Xiong's anxiety about and dissatisfaction with *fu*, the kind of writing he himself had once so enthusiastically practiced, see Knechtges, *The Han Rhapsody*, esp. pp. 89–108.

had more space to focus on debauchery (*yinyu* 淫欲), and despite its author's declared purpose of warning people about the dangers of such activities, readers' reactions to the erotic nature of many passages in the novel were intense and often ambivalent. Some found Yuan Hongdao's praise of *Jin Ping Mei* simply excessive.[4] Dong Qichang, for example, though fascinated, had serious qualms. As attested in Yuan Zhongdao's diary, Dong Qichang insisted that *Jin Ping Mei* should certainly be burned (*juedang fenzhi* 決當焚之), although he did not hesitate to praise it as an excellent (*jijia* 極佳) novel.[5]

This conflicting image of *Jin Ping Mei*—an excellent novel that should be burned—would become a perennial problem for many fiction writers and readers of later ages. The commentators and authors of the prefaces to different editions of *Jin Ping Mei* expended considerable energy in justifying its author's decision to present debauchery in graphic and explicit detail. This task was seen as especially urgent as well as necessary since the author of *Jin Ping Mei* never explicitly explained or defended in the novel or elsewhere his inclusion of explicitly erotic passages, a "mistake" many later writers of erotic fiction have tried to avoid committing. Both Niangong 廿公 (Twentieth Master) in a colophon and Dongwu nongzhuke 東吳弄珠客 (Pearl Juggler of Eastern Wu) in a preface to the novel took on themselves the task of defending the author. Dongwu nongzhuke's rationale in his defense is especially interesting:

> I have remarked that "he who reads the *Jin Ping Mei* and responds with a feeling of compassion is a Bodhisattva; he who responds with a feeling of apprehension is a superior man; he who responds with a feeling of enjoyment is a petty person; and he who responds with a feeling of emulation is no better than a beast." (p. 4; *Plum*, p. 6)

Here the responsibility is being shifted from the author to the reader. The reader must read this supposedly cautionary work properly in order to derive its intended message.

This insistence on the reader's role is echoed in Zhang Zhupo's short essay "On the First Book of Genius Not Being a Debauched Book" ("*Diyi caizi*

4. Li Rihua 李日華 (*jinshi* 1592) argued that Yuan's excessive praise of the novel was due to his obsession with the bizarre and strange (好奇之過); see idem, *Weishuixuan riji* 味水軒日記, *juan* 7, p. 496; and Huang Lin, "*Jin Ping Mei*" *ziliao huibian*, pp. 229–30.

5. Yuan Zhongdao, *Youjue feilu*, *juan* 9, in idem, *Kexue zhai ji*, pp. 1315–16; and Huang Lin, "*Jin Ping Mei*" *ziliao huibian*, p. 229.

shu fei yinshu lun" 第一才子書非淫書論) in his commentary-edition of the novel: "Those who see the debauched are themselves debauched" (淫者自見其爲淫耳; *Zhang Zhupo*, p. 20).[6] In "How to Read the *First Book of Genius, Jin Ping Mei, with Commentary*" ("*Piping diyi qishu Jin Ping Mei* dufa" 批評第一奇書金瓶梅讀法), Zhang elaborated on this point:

> Those who read it and find it enjoyable are a source of anxiety to the *Jin Ping Mei*; anxiety lest they not know why it should be enjoyed and only enjoy it for its licentiousness. Where this is the case, the *Jin Ping Mei* may do the reader an injury (則金瓶梅誤人矣). But, in fact, it is not the *Jin Ping Mei* that injures him, but he who injures himself (人自誤之耳). . . . People who are not good readers are careless and superficial. If you give them the Classics and histories to read, they will not be able get all the way through them. By contrast, they may enjoy reading the *Jin Ping Mei* but will dislike the second half (*xiaban* 下半) of the book. In such a case, the *Jin Ping Mei* may be thought to do the reader an injury. (*Zhang Zhupo*, pp. 45–46)[7]

According to Zhang, it is the reader's own responsibility to "gain enlightenment in the sagely learning" (悟聖賢學問) by reading this story of the "debauched world" (淫欲世界; pre-chapter commentary, *Zhang Zhupo*, 25.376).

The problem is that most readers, according to commentators, are not up to the task and are interested only in the first half of the novel in which Ximen Qing enjoys one success after another. They ignore the second half and especially the last fifth of the novel in which Ximen Qing's household undergoes a drastic decline after his sudden and violent death in chapter 79. The writer Liu Tingji 劉廷璣 (b. 1653) expressed a similar concern:

> When it comes to depicting the quotidian world of daily life (*renqin shiwu* 人情世務), there is no better novel than *Jin Ping Mei*. It is indeed a marvelous work. In order to stop debauchery, one has to describe debauchery, and in order to lead people from delusion to enlightenment, one has to induce them into delusion first (欲要止淫, 以淫說法; 欲要破迷, 引迷入悟). . . . Those who want to read *Jin Ping Mei* have to take into serious consideration (*tiren* 體認) the remark made in the preface: "He who reads the *Jin Ping Mei* and responds with a feeling of compassion is a Bodhisattva, and he who responds with a feeling of emulation is no better than a

6. For a discussion of Zhang Zhupo's reading strategy, see my "Author(ity) and Reader in Traditional Chinese *Xiaoshuo* Commentary," esp. pp. 56–57.

7. English trans. from Roy, "How to Read the *Jin Ping Mei*," in Rolston, ed., *How to Read the Chinese Novel*, p. 237.

beast." The problem is that nowadays most readers only want to read the first 79 chapters and are unwilling to read the last 21 chapters. Are they not beasts?[8]

Since "readers cannot control themselves" (*duzhe meizhi liudang* 讀者每至流蕩) despite authors' noble intentions of providing implicit cautionary messages (*zuozhe benyu quancheng* 作者本寓勸懲) and since "incapable readers" (*bushan dushu zhe* 不善讀書者) far outnumber "capable readers" (*shan dushu zhe* 善讀書者), Liu proposed that all erotic novels should be banned for the sake of public morality.[9]

What has made the defense of the *Jin Ping Mei* even more difficult is the impression of many readers that the author is inconsistent in denouncing the activities of some characters in the novel. To these readers, the author/narrator apparently enjoys describing some of the obscene scenes in the novel. This is perhaps why even today, approximately four centuries after the appearance of *Jin Ping Mei*, almost every critic who admires this novel still feels compelled to defend its author's obsession with graphic sexual scenes by trying to connect them more effectively with his explicit didactic messages and to establish a morally consistent stance in the novel.

Jin Ping Mei is much more than an erotic novel, however. It contains too many other dimensions to fall comfortably within the generic boundaries of erotic fiction. This multidimensionality may well complicate its exploration of the issue of desire. The novel is a mass of details in which sex is closely intertwined with other forms of desire, such as those for money and power. The explicit message about overindulgence is unmistakable, and yet the graphic depiction of indulgence is not always convincingly cautionary. Sometimes, the author/narrator himself seems bedazzled by the details he is throwing at the reader. He becomes a victim of his own success.

Although the author of *Jin Ping Mei* "redeems" himself "ethically" with the last twenty chapters in which all the major evil characters receive retributive punishment, many later erotic novels, though adopting this retributive formula, appear even less persuasive as well as less sincere in their didactic efforts. To an extent, this retributive formula becomes a generic marker for most works of erotic fiction. Most such works follow a plot pattern in which the libertine protagonist, after a series of sexual escapades, repents and be-

8. Liu Tingji, *Zaiyuan zazhi* 在園雜誌, *juan* 3, reprinted in Huang Lin, "*Jin Ping Mei*" *ziliao huibian*, p. 253.

9. Ibid., p. 254.

comes a Taoist or Buddhist monk, for example, the late Ming erotic novel *Xiuta yeshi*.

Of course, not every author of an erotic novel felt the need to appear didactic. The protagonists of the late Ming *Langshi* and the early Qing *Dengcao heshang*, discussed in Chapter 5, go unpunished after their sexual escapades. However, such works are in the minority. Most fiction writers bowed to pressures to appear didactic, and some even seem to be sincere, despite their failure to be consistent. It is probably no exaggeration to say that since the appearance of *Jin Ping Mei*, every writer of fiction focusing on the quotidian world and especially on the issue of desire has had to come to grips with the problem of how far to go in being graphic and explicit in describing passions and desires. *Jin Ping Mei* was a work no future writer of fiction could ignore.

The contemporary response to *Jin Ping Mei* was so immediate and overwhelming that the writer Shen Defu 沈德符 (1578–1642) reported that the author of *Jin Ping Mei* wrote a sequel titled *Yu Jiao Li* 玉嬌李. According to Shen, in this sequel, the author describes in detail how Ximen Qing and the others suffer further punishments in their next lives.[10] Although this sequel is no longer extant, we can infer from Shen's brief description that it was intended to answer readers' complaints about a perceived lack of moral justice in *Jin Ping Mei* (Ximen Qing and others get off too easily) and the author felt pressured to change this perception of the novel's moral teleology.

This was also the goal of another writer, Ding Yaokang, who wrote a novel entitled *Xu Jin Ping Mei* 續金瓶梅 (A sequel to *Jin Ping Mei*), which, unlike *Yu Jiao Li*, does survive. Ding claimed that one reason he wrote the sequel was that the author of *Jin Ping Mei* had devoted too much of his attention to *se* 色 (sensual experiences). In contrast, he had decided to emphasize *kong* 空 (emptiness).[11] According to Ding, the excessive focus on sensual experiences in *Jin Ping Mei* has led to the unintended result that many readers are riveted on the first half of the novel and ignore the second half (*hou banjie* 後半截) on retribution, despite repeated explicit messages (*gong'an shenming* 公案甚明) from the author.[12] Ding Yaokang, therefore, felt that he should concentrate in detail on the further punishments the evil characters receive. This does not mean that Ding Yaokang refrained from explicit

10. See Shen Defu, *Wanli yehuo bian*, *juan* 25, p. 652; in Huang Lin, "*Jin Ping Mei*" *ziliao huibian*, p. 230.

11. Ding Yaokang, *Xu Jin Ping Mei*, 43.412.

12. Ibid., 31.285.

descriptions of the passions or that he did not touch on *se*. However, he did show more restraint and always apologized for being explicit:

Now I want to talk about what will happen to these two characters [Pan Jinlian and Pang Chunmei] in their next lives and their ups and downs. If I don't spice the story up a little bit (*zhuangdian de huoxian* 妝點的活現), people won't read it. If I spice it up too much, people will become too aroused (*dongqi huolai* 動起火來), and then I would be accused of continuing the spread of debauchery (*daoyu xuanyin* 道欲宣淫) in the manner of the author of *Jin Ping Mei* rather than illuminating the dharma by describing worldly experiences (*jieshi shuofa* 借世說法). I could only write some hot passages and then follow them with some cold ones, to titillate the reader so that he could discern in my writings the ultimate unpredictability of the workings of the universe.[13]

Ding Yaokang is, however, often distracted from his self-imposed task of detailing the further punishment of the *Jin Ping Mei* characters by his more urgent concern with the fall of the Northern Song dynasty, his own allegorical effort to come to terms with the fall of the Ming dynasty he himself personally experienced. Critics such as Katherine Carlitz and Andrew Plaks have argued in their interpretations of *Jin Ping Mei* that there is a subtle analogy between the moral corruption of Ximen Qing's household and the political chaos of the nation that is so masterfully suggested in the novel, a link between the household and the nation originally outlined in the Confucian classic *Daxue* (Great learning).[14] This concern is of even more importance in Ding Yaokang's sequel, and he was quite explicit about this point:

To caution the lecherous men and women of the world, the author of *Jin Ping Mei* confines his story to what happens within the boudoir. How could he also include the gentry and officials in his story? The moral state of the society and behavior of the virtuous women and righteous men are closely related to the appropriate appointment of upright officials and the proper disciplines imposed by the government. . . . One has to trace the problem to its ultimate origins so that the reader will understand that both the national disaster and the wide spread of moral decay stemmed from the moral lapses on the part of the scholars-bureaucrats (*shidafu* 士大夫). . . . A good reader of *Jin Ping Mei* should realize that the nation is bound to fall and personal morality is bound to go from bad to worse if all scholars-

13. Ibid., 31.285–86.
14. Carlitz, *The Rhetoric of "Jin Ping Mei,"* pp. 28–44; and Plaks, *Four Masterworks*, pp. 159–67.

bureaucrats emulate Ximen Qing and all women emulate Pan Jinlian, Li Ping'er, and Pang Chunmei.[15]

Unfortunately, the author of *Xu Jin Ping Mei* never managed to integrate the two main storylines (the punishment of characters from *Jin Ping Mei* and the fall of the nation) into a coherent and smooth narrative. Despite, or because of, the novel's explicit argument for the existence of a morally determined universe, the rigid workings of karma delineated in the novel and the author's impatience with the development of the stories of various individual characters result in many characters appearing to be puppets caught in a giant machine of retributive justice. *Xu Jin Ping Mei* never achieves the depth and novelistic successes of its "parent" novel, especially in terms of exploring the ramifications of individual desire.

Xingshi yinyuan zhuan as a Response to *Jin Ping Mei*

For a work that comes close to *Jin Ping Mei* in terms of dealing with individual desire, we have to turn to another seventeenth-century novel, *Xingshi yinyuan zhuan* 醒世姻緣傳 (A marriage that awakens the world; hereafter *Xingshi*). As in *Xu Jin Ping Mei*, the concept of karmic retribution plays a prominent role in *Xingshi*. This, together with some other factors, has led some scholars to believe that both novels were authored by Ding Yaokang.[16] The evidence for this attribution is less than fully convincing, however. In

15. Ding Yaokang, *Xu Jin Ping Mei*, 34.314.

16. Relying mainly on certain similarities between *Xu Jing Ping Mei* and *Xingshi*, Zhang Qingji ("*Xingshi yinyuan zhuan*" *xinkao*) proposes that Ding Yaokang was the author. While refuting Zhang's theory, more recently Xu Fuling ("*Xingshi yinyuan zhuan*" *zuozhe he yuyan kaolun*, pp. 1–132) has suggested that Jia Fuxi 賈凫西 (1589–1675) was the author of *Xingshi*. However, neither offers conclusive evidence to support their respective attribution. In general, the dating and authorship of *Xingshi* are still unresolved issues among scholars. Hu Shi, in his pioneering study "*Xingshi yinyuan* kaozheng," was the first to try to prove that Pu Songling was the author. For discussions in English, see Yenna Wu, "Marriage Destinies to Awaken the World," chap. 1; and Andrew Plaks, "After the Fall," pp. 554–56. Based on the available data, I tend to accept the theory that *Xingshi yinyuan zhuan* was most probably completed before 1661. Huanbi zhuren's 環碧主人 preface (*bianyu* 弁語) is dated *xinchou* 辛丑, which could be 1601, 1661, or 1721. But evidence for 1661 seems to be the strongest. See Zhang Qingji, "*Xingshi yinyuan zhuan*" *xinkao*, pp. 204–16; and Xu Fuling, "*Xingshi yinyuan zhuan*" *zuozhe he yuyan kaolun*, pp. 21–31. For arguments for a late Ming date for the novel (also accepted by Xu Fuling), see Cao Daiwei, "*Xingshi yinyuan* de banben yuanliu he chengshu niandai"; and Hu Wanchuan, "Guanyu *Xingshi yinyuan zhuan* de chengshu niandai."

comparison to *Xu Jin Ping Mei*, the presence of *Jin Ping Mei* in *Xingshi* is less conspicuous (although still quite significant). Unlike *Xu Jin Ping Mei*, which was written as a sequel to *Jin Ping Mei*, *Xingshi* does not explicitly claim such a relationship to the famous sixteenth-century classic. I will argue, however, that *Xingshi* owes much more to *Jin Ping Mei* than has so far been recognized by students of the Chinese novel. A close examination of how *Xingshi* can be read as a response to *Jin Ping Mei* should help us better appreciate the different ways in which the issue of desire is framed and explored in this important seventeenth-century novel.

Xingshi, which, like *Jin Ping Mei*, contains 100 chapters, can be generally divided into two parts: chapters 1–22 and 23–100. The first part concerns Chao Yuan and his various misdeeds, such as his murder of a fox-spirit, mistreatment of his wife, adultery, and unfiliality. Chao Yuan is killed in chapter 19, but the second part about the family into which he is reborn does not start till chapter 23. The second part relates how, as a result of karmic retribution, Chao Yuan, in this reincarnation known by the name of Di Xichen, is being tortured by two women, his wife Sujie and his concubine Jijie, who are, respectively, the reincarnations of the fox-spirit killed by Chao and Chao's abused wife, Jishi.[17] Throughout the second part of the novel, the narrator constantly reminds the reader that Di Xichen's seemingly inexplicable sufferings at the hands of his wife and concubine are payment for the sins committed by Di's previous incarnation, Chao Yuan. The much longer second part compels the reader to witness the full effect of the ruthless operation of moral retribution. And the message is obvious: one is punished for one's sins, if not in this life, then in the next.

What is particularly significant about the structure of *Xingshi* in light of its relationship to *Jin Ping Mei* is that organizationally it is almost an exact reversal: the *Jin Ping Mei* devotes eighty chapters to indulgence and twenty chapters to retribution; roughly a fifth of *Xingshi* is given over to describing indulgence, and the remaining four-fifths deal with retribution. In *Jin Ping Mei*, Ximen Qing's punishment in the form of the drastic decline of his household does not formally begin until chapter 80 (by which time Ximen has already died of sexual exhaustion). In fact, one major complaint of ethically minded traditional readers has been that the author of *Jin Ping Mei* de-

17. Of course, the first part could also be considered a lengthy prologue to the second part, the main story of the novel.

voted too little space to describing how Ximen Qing and others pay for their sins. This brevity, some readers believed, contributed to many impressionable readers concentrating on the first eighty chapters and ignoring the last twenty. A related complaint is that Ximen Qing gets off too easily by being allowed to die before all begins to unravel.[18] As noted above, Ding Yaokang's *Xu Jing Ping Mei* can be read at least in part as a response to such complaints. However, *Xingshi* is a much subtler as well as a more elaborate response and is unburdened by the usual obligations of a formal sequel.

To put it more precisely, *Xingshi* is deliberately structured as a *response* to *Jin Ping Mei* to address the issue of retributive justice. Chao Yuan is killed in chapter 19 of *Xingshi* (81 chapters before the end of the novel), a death that parallels in a reversed manner that of Ximen Qing in chapter 79 of *Jin Ping Mei* (21 chapters before the conclusion of that novel). Whereas Ximen Qing dies of sexual exhaustion after a series of sexual escapades, Chao Yuan is killed by a man whose wife he is having an affair with; it is as if Ximen Qing's servant Laiwang were now able to avenge himself for being made a cuckold by his master in *Jin Ping Mei*. For the author of *Xingshi*, however, death at the hands of someone whom one has cuckolded is obviously not enough. As Di Xichen, Chao Yuan is to suffer far more from those he has abused. *Xingshi*'s emphasis is unmistakably on retribution and punishment, an emphasis many traditional readers found lacking in *Jin Ping Mei*. Furthermore, compared with *Jin Ping Mei*, *Xingshi* also shows much more restraint in describing sexual scenes, further testimony of its author's views on the thorny question of the proper narrative balance between sins and their consequences.

The fact that *Jin Ping Mei* was very much on the mind of the author of *Xingshi* is confirmed by other textual evidence within the novel.[19] In chapter 3 of *Xingshi*, Chao Yuan's concubine Xiaozhen'ge quotes "Pan Jinlian": "Just as Ximen Qing's Pan Jinlian said, a three-legged toad is hard to find, but you

18. "Reading *Jin Ping Mei*, I initially found it quite contemptible, but later I realized that its author had a good sense of moral justice when I found out that all the evil characters have died unnatural deaths with Wu Yueniang being the only character blessed with a good end. But Xiemeng Qing should be executed in public instead of being allowed to die of illness" (Xue Gang 薛岡 [ca. 1561–1642], *Tianjia tang biyu* 天爵堂筆余, *juan* 2, reprinted in Huang Lin, "*Jin Ping Mei*" *ziliao huibian*, p. 235).

19. For a brief discussion of the relationship between *Xingshi* and *Jin Ping Mei*, see Xu Shuofang, "Lun *Xingshi yinyuan zhuan* jiqi he *Jin Ping Mei* de guanxi," in idem, *Xiaoshuo kaoxin bian*, pp. 202–4.

can have as many thousands of two-legged cunts as you want" (3.40).[20] Here Xiaozhen'ge is arguing that Chao Yuan should not succumb to pressures from his primary wife, Jishi (there are too many available women out there for Chao Yuan to care about Jishi). In *Jin Ping Mei* this remark is made not by Pan Jinlian but by Commander Zhou's butler Zhou Zhong, who is furious when Dame Wang refuses to lower her asking price for Pan Jinlian.[21] Xiaozhen'ge's penchant for quoting Pan Jinlian certainly links these two *yinfu* (lecherous women) (like Pan Jinlian, Xiaozhen'ge also has an affair with a servant), although her misattribution may have deeper ironic implications. Not only does she have a bad memory, but she is also a bad reader who fails to see that what happened to Pan Jinlian after she is sold to Wu Song has implications for the consequences of her own behavior. Furthermore, reflecting the character of the person who misquotes, Xiaozhen'ge's version is more vulgar than that of Zhou Zhong in *Jin Ping Mei*.[22]

In chapter 66 of *Xingshi*, Di Xichen's classmate Zhang Maoshi is able to free himself from Sujie only after his wife, Zhijie, pulls downs his pants to embarrass her into releasing him, and it is his naked body that saves him from further blows from Sujie. This tactic was obviously inspired by a similar act by Chen Jingji in *Jin Ping Mei*: in chapter 86, Chen Jingji escapes by exposing himself when he is surrounded and being beaten by Sun Xue'e and other maids at the order of Wu Yueniang. Even the manner in which the two men's naked bodies are described is somewhat similar (cf. the Chongzhen edition, 86.1230).[23] But whereas Chen Jingji is being punished for a serious misdeed—his incestuous affair with his "mother-in-law" Pan

20. Unless otherwise noted, all references to *Xingshi* are to *Xingshi yinyuan zhuan* published by Shanghai guji. I choose this edition because it is not only a carefully collated modern typeset edition that is widely available but also conveniently annotated. A major complaint is that some "sexually explicit" words or phrases are expurgated from this edition. I will refer to other editions whenever the expurgated materials are significant to my discussion.

21. The Chongzhen edition, 87.1242; the wording here is the same as that in the *Cihua* editions (87.1142). Since the edition of *Jin Ping Mei* available to the author of *Xingshi* was most likely the Chongzhen edition, I cite this edition in my discussion of the relationship between this novel and *Jin Ping Mei*.

22. Of course, another possibility we have to entertain is that the author was recalling this passage from memory and did not doublecheck it.

23. For passages censored from the modern typeset edition, see the Tongde tang 同德堂 edition entitled *Chongding Xingshi yinyuan zhuan* reprinted in the *Guben xiaoshuo jicheng* series, 66.9a (p. 1799).

Jinlian—Sujie beats Zhang Maoshi simply because he made the arrangements for a party at which Di Xichen was entertained by a singsong girl. The beating of Chen Jingji is, at least in appearance, intended to vindicate the late Ximen Qing. In contrast, the beating of Zhang illustrates a husband's loss of his "legitimate" right to be entertained by a singsong girl. This subtle difference illustrates how inferior the man's position has become in *Xingshi*.

In *Jin Ping Mei*, Ximen Qing is able to further his official career and become a local power broker because he maintains, with the help of money and gifts, a good relationship with powerful people in the capital. Chao Yuan's father secures a lucrative appointment because he is able to bribe the powerful eunuch Wang Zhen with the help of two actors. The detailed description of the two actors' mission to the capital in chapter 5 of *Xingshi* is reminiscent of similar stories in chapters 19 and 55 of *Jin Ping Mei*.

Chao Yuan's primary wife, Jishi, commits suicide by hanging herself when she can no longer stand the abuse meted out by her husband and his actress-concubine Xiaozhen'ge. Jishi's family then sues Chao Yuan and Xiaozhen'ge. Ximen dajie (Ximen Qing's daughter) hangs herself as a result of Chen Jingji's physical and verbal abuse following his marriage to the prostitute Feng Jinbao. Wu Yueniang then sues Chen for driving Ximen dajie to death (chapter 92).

Another less explicit but probably more significant reference to *Jin Ping Mei* can be found in the couplet/title of chapter 79, "Xichen finds his land of bliss in a wrong place / Jijie wreaks havoc under the grape arbor" (希陳誤認武陵源, 寄姐大鬧葡萄架). This reference to a grape arbor calls to mind the notorious scene in chapter 27 of *Jin Ping Mei*, which is titled "Li Ping'er shares an intimate conversation in the Kingfisher Pavilion / Pan Jinlian goes on a drunken rampage in the grape arbor" (李瓶兒私語翡翠軒, 潘金蓮醉鬧葡萄架). To punish Pan Jinlian for her jealousy toward Li Ping'er, Ximen Qing accidentally almost kills Pan by sexually tormenting her in the grape arbor in their family garden. This chapter contains one of the most graphic sexual scenes in *Jin Ping Mei*.[24] Incidentally, in Ding Yaokang's *Xu*

24. In "Puns and Puzzles in the *Chin P'ing Mei*," Katherine Carlitz offers a detailed reading of this chapter. She argues (esp. p. 237) that the sexual game in which Ximen Qing shoots plums into Pan Jinlian's vagina is a key to understanding the title of the novel—*Jin Ping Mei* or *The Plum in the Golden Vase*. Xu Shuofang ("*Jin Ping Mei xifang lunwen ji* qianyan" 金瓶梅西方論文集前言, reprinted in idem, *Xiaoshuo kaoxin bian*, p. 300), however, finds this argu-

Jing Ping Mei, the second line of the couplet/title of chapter 44, "Jingui becomes possessed in the Grape Arbor" (金桂姐鬼魅葡萄架) also refers to the grape arbor scene in *Jin Ping Mei*. In that chapter, Jingui, Pan Jinlian's reincarnation, repeatedly dreams of her rendezvous with her lover under a grape arbor and becomes physically drained. This soon renders her unable to function sexually, and she become a "stone woman" (*shinü* 石女). Elsewhere in *Xu Jin Ping Mei*, the author/narrator denounces readers who are interested only in the sexually graphic scenes in *Jin Ping Mei* such as that under the Grape Arbor (那金瓶梅前集說的那潘金蓮和春梅葡萄架風流淫樂一段光景,看書的到如今津津有味).[25] Obviously, by the time of *Xu Jin Ping Mei*, thanks to the popularity of *Jin Ping Mei*, for many people the term "grape arbor" had become almost synonymous with "sexual escapade."[26]

What is particularly intriguing about this reference to the grape arbor in the title of chapter 79 of *Xingshi* is that the text of the chapter does not mention a grape arbor at all. This conspicuous "mistitling" is, I believe, deliberate and compels the reader of *Xingshi* to *recall* the significance of *Jin Ping Mei* in order to make sense of the chapter title and its relationship to the chapter's content.[27] Not only is a grape arbor not mentioned, but there is also no sexual escapade in this chapter. Instead, we are told how Di Xichen is tricked by his shrewish concubine Jijie into mistaking her for the maid Xiaozhenzhu (Little Pearl) and is consequently caught trying to flirt with a maid. He subsequently receives a thorough beating from Jijie. The only similarity between Jijie in this chapter and Pan Jinlian in chapter 27 of *Jin Ping Mei* is the jealousy both feel as a result of their husband's interest in another woman. But it is the differences between the two chapters about a jealous concubine get-

---

ment unpersuasive because, he contends, people use the English word "plum" to translate the Chinese words *li* 李 and *mei* 梅 (which is actually a kind of apricot), and that in the novel Ximen Qing is shooting *li* and not *mei*.

25. Ding Yaokang, *Xu Jin Ping Mei*, 31.285.

26. The motif of a grape arbor also appears in the eighteenth-century novel *Yesou puyan* for a different reason; see the discussion of this novel in Chapter 9.

27. Cf. Keith McMahon, *Misers, Shrews, and Polygamists*, pp. 74–75: "Although there is no actual 'grape arbor' in the scene in *Xingshi yinyuan zhuan*, the words appear in the title, thus making Jijie's abuse of her husband's penis into a type of intertextual revenge across a century or so of narrative history." As McMahon (p. 75) points out, in chapter 58 of *Xingshi* the grape arbor (see p. 832) is the setting for Di Xichen and Xiang Tongxu's discussions of wife-fearing husbands and where Xiang is later attacked by Sujie (58.839).

ting upset with her promiscuous husband that will help us see the larger parodistic intention on the part of the author of *Xingshi*. The grape arbor in *Jin Ping Mei* is the setting in which Ximen Qing as a tyrannical husband exercises his dominance (both sexual and political) over his rebellious concubine Pan Jinlian, forcing her to renounce her jealousy, at least on the surface and temporarily. The situation in *Xingshi* is completely reversed: although Di Xichen can be as promiscuous as Ximen Qing, he is completely dominated by his shrewish wife and concubine. Curiously enough, the title of chapter 27 of *Jin Ping Mei* is also misleading, since the focus of the chapter is Ximen Qing's abuse of Pan Jinlian's genitals rather than her drunken rampage in the grape arbor (醉鬧葡萄架), as the title seems to suggest. In other words, it is Ximen Qing who has a rampage (*nao*) rather than Pan Jinlian. This is again reversed in chapter 79 of *Xingshi*. It is now Jijie who abuses Di Xichen's genitals by marking his penis so that she can check whether he is faithful to her.[28] It is the concubine who is now exercising control and asserting her dominance. The grape arbor in *Jin Ping Mei* is appropriated in the title of chapter 79 of *Xingshi* to underscore this complete reversal of fortune on the part of a husband. The absence of a grape arbor in the text of that chapter merely brings home the reality that, for Di Xichen, the land of bliss (Wuling yuan 武陵源) is available only to tough men like Ximen Qing. Di Xichen can never aspire to the status of his predecessor Ximen Qing as a man and as a husband. This leads us to a more significant issue—the issue of "male degeneration."

The male protagonists in many novels focusing on sexual relations between man and women written after the appearance of *Jin Ping Mei*, especially in works in which the direct influence of *Jin Ping Mei* is discernable, bear witness to a gradual but distinct trend of "male degeneration." As I observe at the end of Chapter 4, the male degeneration is already visible in the

28. The passage in which Jijie leaves marks on Di Xichen's penis is expurgated from the modern typeset edition published by Shanghai guji; see *Chongding Xingshi yinyuan zhuan*, 79.11b (p. 2164); see also McMahon, *Misers, Shrews, and Polygamists*, p. 75. In fact, the device of a shrewish wife leaving marks on her husband's penis in order to prevent him from being unfaithful can be traced to the late Ming novel *Cu hulu* 醋葫蘆 (The vinegar gourd). In chapter 4 of that novel, Tushi has a seal specially made to stamp her husband's penis so that she can check him everyday. The description is more elaborate and almost hilarious. This tactic will be adopted by another wife in the early eighteenth-century novel *Guwangyan* (3.455), a work to be discussed in Chapter 9.

image of Chen Jingji, the male protagonist in the last twenty chapters of *Jin Ping Mei*. The process seems to have accelerated after *Jin Ping Mei*.

In the late Ming erotic novel *Xiuta yeshi*, the male protagonist's *hao* 號 (sobriquet) is Dongmen sheng 東門生 (presumably because he was born in the area of Yangzhou known as the East Gate; 1.103), which may be a parodistic reference to Ximen Qing's surname, "West Gate." Throughout the novel, the male protagonist is addressed as Dongmen sheng, and his formal name, Tao Tongxin, is seldom mentioned. Dongmen sheng's wife is addressed as Jinshi 金氏, Madame Jin, probably a reflection on Pan Jinlian's given name, Jinlian. However, in his relationship with his wife, Dongmen sheng, unlike Ximen Qing, is obviously in an inferior position. Ximen Qing prides himself on his sexual prowess, which is supposed to have played a crucial role in his triumphant conquering of women such as Li Ping'er, but Dongmen sheng is sexually inadequate, a result of his dissolute youth. In fact, until he is able to improve his sexual stamina with a drug, he is an object of ridicule, even from his own maid (1.131).[29] Of course, Ximen Qing also uses a drug to enhance his already impressive prowess. Thanks to his sexual inadequacy, Dongmen sheng is reduced to playing the role of a voyeur when he arranges for his own wife, Jinshi, to sleep with his male lover and friend Dali, something Ximen Qing would never even dream of doing.[30] In *Rou putuan*, the male protagonist Weiyang sheng is also ridiculed because his *benqian*, or penis, is considered too small.

Much less explicit in its treatment of sex, *Xingshi* is concerned with male degeneration more in terms of general competence rather than sexual stamina per se. At the beginning of the novel, the narrator tells us that Chao Yuan is henpecked. He begins to feel confident enough to ignore his primary wife, Jishi, only after his family suddenly becomes wealthy and powerful when his father, by sheer good luck, is appointed the magistrate of an important county. Unlike Ximen Qing, Chao Yuan has no sense of money and business. The things he purchases are either completely useless or worthless. For example, he is conned into buying the "Heart Sutra" cat when the seller convinces him that the cat can pronounce the name of the Bodhisattva (chap. 6) when tickled. Whereas Ximen Qing's wealth is largely the

29. Incidentally, an Indian monk also supplies a drug in *Xiuta yeshi* (*huseng gongbao* 胡僧貢寶), 1.115.

30. For a discussion of possible references to *Jin Ping Mei* in *Xiuta yeshi*, see Hanan, "The Erotic Novel," pp. 9–10.

result of his own efforts, Chao Yuan is capable only of squandering the fortune made by his father, a point the novel emphasizes repeatedly. Ximen Qing never encounters a problem in gaining access to the wife of any of his servants. When Song Huilian's husband, Laiwang, complains and make threats after he finds out what is going on between his wife and his master, he is quickly framed by Ximen Qing and later sentenced to deportation by the local magistrate. Ximen Qing's resourcefulness in dealing with this affair are in sharp contrast to the incompetence of Chao Yuan, who pays with his own life when Xiaoya'er beheads Chao upon finding out that Chao has been sleeping with his wife, despite the fact Xiaoya'er is a poor leatherworker and a tenant of one of the houses on Chao's farm.

After Chao Yuan is reborn as Di Xichen in the second part of *Xingshi*, the contrastive parallels with Ximen Qing continue. In chapter 11 of *Jin Ping Mei*, Ximen Qing receives quite a fanfare for deflowering (*shulong* 梳籠) the prostitute Li Guijie.[31] However, in chapter 37 of *Xingshi*, the situation is just reversed: the sixteen-year-old Di Xichen is instead "deflowered" by the prostitute Sun Lanji, who asks Di not to forget that it was at her hands that he lost his virginity: "Don't forget me. It's me who has deflowered (*shulong* 梳籠) you" (37.549), as if he were a virgin just initiated into prostitution by her!

Instead of beating his wives as Ximen Qing often does, Di Xichen is the object of physical abuse by his wife Sujie and concubine Jijie, despite the fact that as a man he is supposed to be physically stronger. His beatings are much more constant and much more severe than those Ximen Qing inflicts on his women. The narrator takes great pains to depict in graphic detail how this poor man is physically abused and tortured by his wives.

To assert his dominance over "his" women, Ximen Qing takes great delight in abusing their private parts (such as burning moxa on Pan Jinlian, Lady Lin, and Wang Liu'er). Again this is reversed in *Xingshi*. In a show of complete submission, Di Xichen, as mentioned above, has to consent to letting his concubine mark his penis. It is now the woman's turn to assert her possessiveness of her spouse by marking his genitals.

In reading *Xingshi* with *Jin Ping Mei* in mind, we are almost tempted to think that Sujie and Jijie are exacting revenge on behalf of the women abused by Ximen Qing and other men in *Jin Ping Mei*, as if *Xingshi* were designed to

31. The word *shulong* appears in the title of chapter 11 as well as in the text of this chapter in *Jin Ping Mei* (Chongzhen ed., 11.137).

show what would happen if Pan Jinlian and others like her were able to turn the tables. *Xingshi* seems to present the most nightmarish scenario that could happen to a man in a supposedly male-dominated society when that man fails to perform his duties as a man properly. Despite its deep anxiety over female dominance, however, *Xingshi* is not a work of true misogyny. In fact, it demonstrates how men are ultimately responsible for their own miserable sufferings and how so-called shrewish women sometimes serve as the vehicle of punishment for incompetent and self-indulgent men.

The Karmic Framework of *Xingshi*

Any attempt to interpret *Xingshi* has to come to grips with its persistent emphasis on karmic retribution. An important part of *Xingshi*'s complicated response to *Jin Ping Mei* is its greater thoroughness in carrying out retributive justice by showing the workings of karma in great detail. Many key incidents in the novel are presented in such a way that they appear to be readable only as retributive karma in action, and the reader is periodically reminded of this point not only routinely in the opening verses of many chapters but also, more deliberately, at various points in the unfolding of a specific plot segment. For example, the reader is repeatedly told that Sujie's virulent hatred of Di Xichen is revenge for his previous incarnation's murder of her previous incarnation. Sujie often complains that for some inexplicable reason the mere sight of Di Xichen drives her crazy:

> This is something I myself can't figure out. In fact, my parents-in-law are not difficult at all, and they love me a lot. Even my husband never dares to do anything to displease me; in spite of the abuse on my part, he never complains. I understand perfectly well that I should be dutiful to my parents-in-law and be respectful to my husband. But the moment I see my husband, I lose control of myself, as if there is a deep enmity between him and me, and as if I cannot coexist with him for a single moment. . . . Now that my husband is not here, I seem to understand everything and really regret what I've done and would swear that I will reform myself. But as soon as I see him, everything is changed. I suppose this must be due to a deep hatred toward him incurred in my previous life. I can't control myself because I am possessed by ghosts and spirits. (59.850)[32]

32. For similar statements, see 44.651 and 45.661.

The night before her marriage, Sujie dreams that a ghost gives her an evil heart to replace her old heart. She is specifically informed in the dream that since she is marrying Di, she no longer needs her original heart, which is probably a kind one (44.646). Thus, Sujie's inexplicable cruelty toward her husband can be explained by the fact that Sujie is the karmic avenger of her previous incarnation, the fox-spirit.

Chao Yuan/Di Xichen, the fox-spirit/Sujie, and Jishi/Jijie are not the only examples of karmic reward and punishment in the novel. Significant portions of the much longer second part of the novel are devoted to Chao Yuan's family, especially his mother, Madame Chao. This saintly woman is rewarded for her many good deeds (her son Chao Liang is a reward for her kindness toward an actor, who, out of deep gratitude, ends his own existence in "this life" in order to be reborn as her son).The narrative focus of the second part constantly shifts between the two main storylines of Chao Yuan's relatives and friends after his death and Di Xichen and his household. Sometimes the focus shifts at a particular poignant point to draw the reader's attention to the ironic contrast between the two opposite aspects of retribution (punishment and reward). If the story of Madame Chao illustrates "immediate retribution in this life" (*xianshi bao* 現世報), then the story of Chao Yuan's punishment in his reincarnation as Di Xichen is a more eloquent example of "retribution postponed to next life" (*zhuanshi bao* 轉世報). Furthermore, there are numerous anecdotes about many other characters, such as Chao Wuyan 晁無宴 (probably a pun on *wuyan* 無厭 "insatiable") or Chao Sicai 晁思才 (*sicai* 思財, "greedy about money"), who receive their immediate retribution in their present life. To an extent, some readers' impression of the episodic nature of the novel arises in part from its tendency to complement the two main stories about Di Xichen and Madame Chao with the stories of minor characters that are designed to demonstrate different facets of the workings of retribution.

The novel's enthusiastic embrace of the concept of karmic retribution, however, also exposes some problematic aspects of this idea of moral justice. An immediate problem is that the seemingly endless cycle of rebirth and retribution tends, sometimes paradoxically, to lessen the individual's moral responsibility. For example, Sujie, as a reincarnation of the fox-spirit, is an avenging spirit. Therefore, one cannot judge any of her wickednesses (her cruelty toward Di Xichen, her unfiliality in driving her own parents and parents-in-law to death) as manifestations of her own moral makeup. Her actions are beyond her own control; a higher force is dictating her actions. Sujie "is only taking revenge according to the order from Heaven, and her actions are by no means personal," as Di Xichen is told in a dream at the end of the novel (100.1429). This "amoral" nature of Sujie undercuts much of the novel's moral indignation at its many "evil" characters. In this karmic process, a particular evil always assumes the retributive function of punishing another evildoer and consequently the process negates any legitimate moral basis for judging such action. Sujie is "evil" only because her evil is intended as a punishment of Chao Yuan; Chao Yuan could make similar claims of "innocence."

Furthermore, the logic of karmic retribution offers some people an excuse for being evil: people grant themselves the privilege of committing evil in the name of being instruments of karmic punishment. Here "retribution" becomes something to be manipulated as an excuse for furthering one's personal interests at the expense of others. For example, Chao Sicai claims that the reduction of Chao Wuyan's family fortune to nothing and his new widow's immediate betrayal after his death are retribution for the sins Chao Wuyan committed while alive (57. 878). There is a certain measure of truth in Chao Sicai's statement because Chao Wuyan indeed committed many misdeeds, including the illegal appropriation of Chao Jinren's property. His remarks provoke from Madame Chao an exclamation of admiration for the "mighty power of immediate retribution" (*xianbao*; 57.878). However, one reason for Chao Sicai's emphasis on retribution is to justify his taking Cao Wuyan's orphan to be his slave (presumably as a further punishment for Chao Wuyan). Cao Sicai appeals to the idea of retribution to sanctify his own scheme of enslaving Cao Wuyan's son in the name of predestined retribution. By the same token, monks play on the common people's fear of *diyu* 地獄 (hell) to extort money from them (69. 990–91).

The author of *Xingshi* was apparently conscious of the dilemma inherent in overemphasizing the rigid workings of karmic retribution. A few characters are allowed to assume a more active role in changing this retributive process. To explain why Ma Zhonggui, the son of Ma Congwu, is spared from death while both of his parents are killed for their sins, the narrator observes:

Judging from their sins, Ma Congwu and his wife should not have had a son. Then how can the son be allowed to have a proper family? Although there is a saying that one has to suffer the retributive consequences of one's parents and grandparents,

Heaven will figure out another plan for that person if he cultivates himself and establishes his own destiny (*xiushen liming* 修身立命). If one has to suffer for what one's father or grandfather has done, regardless of one's own merits and demerits, and if the retribution continues to punish the son or grandson, then karmic retribution is really unfair. (27.402)

On a few occasions in the novel, characters complain about possible prejudices in karmic retribution. After the death of Xichen's mother, Sujie again makes a public spectacle of herself by physically abusing Xichen. In front of the grave of his wife, Di Binliang (Di Xichen's father) bursts into a tearful complaint and openly questions why Heaven has punished him so severely even though his ancestors, his wife, and he himself have committed no sins whatsoever (73.1044). Indeed, the novel offers no explanation why Di Xichen's parents have to suffer so much, even though their son's suffering is always justified as a result of karmic retribution for the sins committed by his previous incarnation. All this gives rise to an impression that the workings of retribution may not be always impartial. A bigger problem in this regard is that the novel's central story—the muddleheaded but harmless Di Xichen is made to suffer endless cruelties at the hands of Sujie and Jijie—is not always morally persuasive, although the reader is constantly reminded that his ordeal is due to the sins of his previous reincarnation. This is largely because Di Xichen is presented as a character who has his own moral makeup as well as his own will, someone morally independent from his previous incarnation, Chao Yuan. Paradoxically, the more successful the author is in presenting Xichen as a fully rounded character in the second part of the novel, the less convincing the retributive scheme becomes. A scrupulous insistence on karmic retribution may turn an individual character into a helpless pawn in the game of punishment and reward and thus seriously undercut the didactic persuasiveness of the novel.

Probably to compensate for this lack of persuasiveness, the narrator occasionally tries to underscore the role played by environment in the shaping of a person's moral character. In chapter 1, the narrator emphasizes the importance of education and the parents' duty to shape the moral character of their children. For example, the narrator blames Chao Yuan's parents for doting on him and the bad company he keeps for pushing him toward evil (this fact should problematize the saint-like image of his mother, Madame Chao, which the author is at pains to construct in the novel, in the sense that she is also partly responsible for her son's failings). Given the significance of the concept of *xi* 習 (practice and habit) in the intellectual discourses on human nature in the late Ming and early Qing,[33] we should not be surprised to find that this word is frequently used in *Xingshi* to refer to the importance of education and environment in phrases such as *xijiu xingcheng* 習久性成 (what is long practiced becomes part of one's nature or character; 1.2). Another such usage can be found in *xiran chengfeng, guanxing chengxing* 習染成風, 慣行成性 (what is often practiced becomes a popular habit while what becomes a habit is part of one's nature; 26.378). In describing Di Xichen's first sexual adventure (or misadventure; see above), the narrator emphasizes that the age of fifteen and sixteen is a critical stage in a person's life when he or she can be led to become either a good person or a bad person (40.587). One of the three happy things mentioned by Mencius (quoted in the *yinqi* 引起, or "Introduction," to the novel) is to be able to educate a talented youngster. Indeed, the narrator repeatedly calls attention to education and the proper way to raise a child. An important implication of this emphasis on the influence of the environment and education is that there are many factors that can shape a person's moral character.

The Allegory of Lust

Another factor that further undermines the explanatory power of karmic retribution is the novel's persistent attention to the issue of excessive desire and its moral consequences. Underneath the novel's mimetic surface, in addition to the more explicit fable of a meticulous process of retribution, is a carefully wrought, though more implicit, allegory about self-cultivation (*xiushen* 修身 is the word used by the narrator) and self-control. Many modern readers of *Xingshi* have been bothered by the persistent link between Chao Yuan's killing of the fox-spirit in the first part of the novel and the retributive consequences Di Xichen has to suffer in the second. First of all, there is little malice involved in the killing (it happens during a hunt), and Chao Yuan's act is in no way proportionate to Di Xichen's sufferings. Second, the

33. The *locus classicus* for this is found in Confucius' *Lunyu*: "Men are close to one another by nature. They diverge as a result of repeated practice" (Liu Baonan, ed. *Lunyu zhenyi*, p. 367; Lau, *The Analects*, 17.2, p. 143). Plaks ("After the Fall," p. 579) also briefly mentions this point. The shift in focus from discussions of human nature (*xing* 性) to emphases on the role of practice and environment (*xi* 習) that emerged in the philosophical discourse of the late Ming and early Qing is relevant here. However, a detailed discussion of this topic has to await another occasion.

fox-spirit is by no means an innocent victim. To the contrary, it has long been entertaining a scheme to entrap Chao Yuan:

> This fox-spirit had an evil heart and had long fancied Chao Dashe [Chao Yuan].... Seeing that Chao Dashe was a womanizer and that he was hunting games with prostitutes, ignoring all the rules of propriety between men and women, the fox-spirit thought to herself that this was the best opportunity to seduce him. The fox-spirit immediately transformed herself into a beautiful young girl of twenty. (1.12)

This "beauty" immediately bewitches Chao Yuan and arouses him. The hunting dogs and falcons, however, see through the deceptive human appearance of the fox-spirit and begin to chase her. In a panic, the fox-spirit betrays her true form. She runs to Chao Yuan for protection. Seeing her true form, Chao Yuan kills her instead. This act of killing, we are told, sets in motion the karmic cycle that constitutes the main plot of the novel. What may puzzle the reader is that Chao Yuan's act does not seem to deserve the punishment it receives in the second part of the novel (even if killing is a sin in Buddhist belief) partly because the fox-spirit does have evil intentions. Chao Yuan's killing is to a certain degree justifiable.

This becomes less puzzling, however, if we read the later sufferings of Di Xichen not so much as a direct result of this act of killing but as a warning about the dangers of a lust for *se* 色, or sex (both Chao Yuan and Di Xichen suffer from this fatal attraction). The detailed and often graphic account of Di's sufferings is compelling in the symbolic sense that they arise from his lack of self-control rather than being a case of karmic retribution. In fact, the fox-spirit's desire to seduce Chao Yuan is triggered by his loose behavior (such as hunting animals with a prostitute). After the hunt, Chao Yuan dreams that his grandfather blames him for entertaining the evil thought (*xiexin* 邪心) of having an affair with the fox-spirit when he first catches sight of her in the form of a pretty woman: "The fox-spirit came to me and told me in detail the reason why you killed her. She said that if you had not had that evil thought (*dong le xiexin* 動了邪心) and had felt attracted to her, she would have kept her distance" (3.32). Thus the fox-spirit bothers Chao Yuan only because of his own lust. Within this context, the fox-spirit can be read allegorically as a symbol of Chao Yuan's (as well as Di's) sexual desire, which needs to be restrained. In other words, the fox-spirit is a reflection of Chao Yuan's own lust. In a well-established literary convention, a fox-spirit was often associated with a fatal sexual attraction that leads a man to commit social transgressions. In this convention, a charming but dangerous temptress is always called a *huli jing* 狐狸精 (fox-spirit).[34] Read in this light, the fact that Chao Yuan kills the fox-spirit only when she is deprived of her deceiving appearance can be interpreted as a symbolic reference to his lack of self-awareness—he does not foresee the ultimate consequences of losing control over his own desire.

Soon after the hunt, both Chao Yuan and his concubine Xiaozhen'ge are tormented by illness and nightmares. The opening verse of chapter 11 is explicit in suggesting that ghosts and spirits in a nightmare or hallucination are often the workings of a mind tormented by guilt: "The ghost is one's own mind" (鬼是自家心; 11.155). Later, after Chao Yuan's first wife commits suicide, Chao Yuan and Xiaozhen'ge are again bothered by illness and haunted by ghosts, and the narrator breaks in to remind the reader once more that all the ghosts and spirits Chao Yuan sees are hallucinations caused by his own sense of guilt, or *guixin* 鬼心 (17.245).[35] Chao Yuan and Xiaozhen'ge are being punished for their own excessive lust (Xiaozhen'ge is certainly one of the most lustful women in the novel). Significantly, the reader is told twice that Chao Yuan's wife, Jishi, who will later be reborn as

34. For example, probably because of this very common association between female sexual temptation and the fox-spirit, the narrator feels a special need to explain that even though Chao Yuan's wife, Jishi, had been a fox-spirit in her previous incarnation, in her present life, she is not particularly skilled at seducing a man (8.117). In her Ph.D. dissertation "Beauty Is the Beast: The Dual Face of Woman in Four Ch'ing Novels," Maram Epstein (pp. 94–95) also makes the point that the fox-spirit and Sujie are "a projection of Xichen's desire" (p. 90); see also her discussions of the tension between what she calls desire and reason in the novel (pp. 89–108). Epstein's arguments seem to be shared by Keith McMahon (*Misers, Shrews, and Polygamists*, pp. 73–74), who observes that "in the causal scheme of the book, she [Sujie] is only reacting to wrongs suffered in a previous life at the hands of a man. In metaphysical terms, cause and effect are respectively characterized as male and female, so that husbands and fathers are the prime moral movers, and the woman is the expression or concrete manifestation of the man." For a discussion of the image of the fox in traditional tales of the supernatural, see Fatima Wu, "Foxes in Chinese Supernatural Tales," pp. 121–54.

35. The words in the couplet/title of this chapter also point to this fact (*xinxu jian'gui* 心虛見鬼). This is reminiscent of *Xiyou ji*, in which the spirits and demons are often meant to be understood as embodiments of the lack of self-cultivation on the part of the pilgrims. See Plaks, *Four Masterworks*, pp. 244f, 258; note especially a commentator's observation quoted by Plaks (p. 270), "The Demons are none other than the individual self." In fact, Sujie in the novel (86.1222) is literally compared to the Baigu jing 白骨精 (Demon of White Skeleton) or Baigu furen 白骨夫人 (Lady White Skeleton), as she is called in *Xiyou ji*. This demon is famous for her scheme to seduce Pigsy by appearing as a beautiful young woman in that novel.

Jijie and who will torture Chao Yuan in his next life, is also the reincarnation of a fox-spirit.[36] Thus, allegorically, what is tormenting Chao Yuan is his own "fox-spirit"—his uncontrollable lustful mind. Of course, the ultimate cause of Chao Yuan's death at the hands of Xiaoya'er is precisely his inability to keep this lust in check.

In the second part of the novel, Sujie and Jijie can also be understood as having the same symbolic implications in their allegorical relationship with Di Xichen. Like his previous incarnation, Di Xichen suffers from a lecherous mind, although he is even more incompetent and more cowardly. Numerous incidents suggest that not all his ordeals can be explained as the fulfillment of retribution and that many of them are self-inflicted. Di Xichen, though much less wicked than Chao Yuan, is a womanizer, too. His seduction and initiation into sex by the prostitute Sun Lanji when he is sixteen paints a picture of a susceptible young man who henceforth will repeatedly fall victim to women because of his own uncontrollable lusts. Di Xichen is so infatuated with this prostitute that he refuses to leave the provincial capital, where his new love lives, even after the examinations are over and he no longer has any excuse to stay there. Later, Di Xichen agrees to return to his hometown only when he is led to believe that there are also singing girls there. Thus, like Chao Yuan, Di Xichen is always involved with prostitutes, and for this he will suffer tremendous physical as well as psychological abuse from his wife and later from his concubine. On another occasion, he "overspends" himself almost to death when several sexually starved nuns prey on him for several days (64.922).

A reader might wonder why, since his wife is so abusive, he doesn't leave or divorce her. Part of the answer can be found in a confession he makes. Beaten up by Sujie and at the end of his wits, Xichen seeks help from a fortuneteller. He is told that he is destined to suffer in marriage, and the only way that he can be saved is divorce and life as a bachelor. Di Xichen is reluctant. He finally makes the sad confession: "Several times I couldn't stand her torture any more, and I almost decided to divorce her. But she is so pretty, and she can be quite tender to me when we are on good terms. Only she changes quickly. That is why I don't have the heart to di-

36. Madame Chao dreams that Jishi is a fox-spirit in her previous incarnation. She is able to be reborn as another female, Jijie, instead of a fox due to the merits she accumulates by reciting Buddhist sutras (30.446). Earlier, the narrator specifically mentions this fact (8.117).

vorce her" (61.878).[37] A certain bewitching power in Sujie makes him reluctant to leave her.

Allegorically, Di Xichen is suffering from his own "fox-spirit"; he is being punished for his lust, of which Sujie is a reincarnation as well as a symbol. On many occasions the immediate cause of the physical abuse he suffers at the hands of Sujie is his involvement with another woman (often a prostitute). Sujie once beats him severely because she happens to come across the gifts Sun Lanji has given to him (chap. 52). Sun, significantly enough, resembles Sujie, his abusive wife, in appearance (a fortunetelling nun predicts that Di Xichen will marry a girl who resembles Sun Lanji; 40.589). Symbolically, the fox-spirit punishes Xichen for being attracted to "herself"; in other words, Xichen is being punished by, as well as for, his own sexual lust. On another occasion, Di Xichen is invited to a party at which a prostitute is entertaining. He enjoys the presence of this attractive singing girl so much that he forgets he cannot stay in such a place because he will pay dearly when his jealous wife finds out about this. But he cannot help himself, because "whenever he sees a pretty woman, he acts as if he were a leech seeing blood" (66.941). Ironically, he has to cut himself on the arm in order to escape the grasp of his friend to run back to Sujie when he is told that she has found out what he is doing, and it is the sight of the blood on his clothes that saves him a sound beating. Later in the novel he is physically punished by Jijie after she finds him flirting with the maid Xiaozhenzhu, who, significantly, is the reincarnation of Xiaozhen'ge, a singing girl whom Chao Yuan married as a concubine.

A more subtle explanation as to why Di Xichen suffers almost willingly at the hands of Sujie and Jijie is his lack of will to control his own sexual desire. This vulnerability shared by both Di Xichen and Chao Yuan is further emphasized by the fact that the prostitute Sun Lanji, Di Xichen's first seductress, is also the reincarnation of Xiaobanjiu, the prostitute with whom

37. Later in the novel, after Sujie tries to kill him, Xichen decides to investigate the possibility of a divorce. But he is stopped by his always-resourceful adviser Zhou, who argues that Xichen cannot divorce her largely because this is a marriage made in Heaven; he has to repay the debt of revenge and hatred he accumulated in his previous life by suffering at the hands of his wife. If he divorced her, he would then have to continue to pay the debt in his next life (98.194–98). This is an apparent reference to the logic of the karmic retribution the novel seems to advocate. However, this can be read in another way; namely, Di Xichen's sufferings will not end till he rids himself of the "fox-spirit" symbolized by Sujie.

Chao Yuan is briefly involved when Xiaozhen'ge is in jail (40.587–88). Di Xichen is largely responsible for his own sufferings.

Di Xichen suffers because he cannot control his "fox-spirit." This is probably why many readers of the novel often feel that Di Xichen's sufferings are self-willed and even somewhat masochistic:

Finding Sujie showing a bit of tenderness, Di Xichen feels as elated as An Lushan 安祿山, when the latter was allowed to take a bath in the palace of Yang Guifei 楊貴妃. He utters no words of protest, not even a sign of disappointment. What explanation could one offer except to say this must be due to the disaster seeded in one's previous life? Xue Rubian thought to himself, "It's really a shame that a man can have so little self-respect; he is like a dead dog that can't be forced onto a wall [someone totally hopeless]. That's why his wife can humiliate and torture him to such a degree!" (63.909)

Elsewhere, Xichen is said to be so mischievous that he will not behave without a beating and that he soon forgets the taste of a beating and gets out of control if he has not been beaten for a while (95.1359). Therefore, allegorically, Di Xichen inflicts physical suffering on himself (punishment by the reincarnation of the fox-spirit, a symbol of *se* or sexual lust) for his own weak moral character, just as his previous incarnation, Chao Yuan, has to bear the ultimate consequence for his own (sexual) transgressions.[38]

This fatal vulnerability to sexual temptation is shared by many other male characters in the novel, and several of them die of overindulgence in sex. Wang Weilu, the hooligan-like old licentiate (*xiucai* 秀才), ruins his own health, we are told, soon after marrying the sixteen-year-old daughter of Wei Cai (chap. 39). Likewise, Chao Wuyan dies of sexual overindulgence after he marries a young widow, Guoshi (chap. 53). What makes this ironic is his confession before dying:

Although we are just married, the attachment between us is even deeper than that between those who have been married for several decades. This disease of mine is the result of my loving you too much. . . . Although I'm not rich, there should be enough to support you and your son if you could remain faithful to me . . . and do not marry again after my death." (53.765)

38. For discussions of the parallels between Chao Yuan and Di Xichen, see Yenna Wu, "Repetition in *Xingshi yinyuan zhuan*," p. 62; and Zhu Yanqing, "*Xingshi yinyuan zhuan* yanjiu," pp. 128–30.

We learn later that his widow decamps with all his money as soon as he dies. The fifty-year-old Zhou Longgao also dies not long after remarrying the young and lustful Sister Cheng 程大姐 (chap. 72); the two monks in the Xianyan Temple die of sexual exhaustion (chap. 93). The point all these deaths seem to emphasize is the importance of controlling one's desires and the consequences of the lack of such control, something very close to what the fox-spirit symbolizes at the beginning of the novel. What makes this message about the importance of self-control even more interesting is that Sujie, the vehicle of karmic retribution, sometimes forgets her function as an avenging angel and becomes sexually vulnerable, too: "Intoxicated by the smell of the wine, Sujie's desire was aroused. Even though she knew that Di Xichen was her foe in her previous life, she could no longer contain herself and had to make use of him to satisfy her present need" (61.881). Of course, Sujie's sexual arousal should not come as a surprise, considering her symbolic associations with the fox-spirit in the novel.

Indeed, there are many moments in the novel when the behavior of a character has to be explained according to something other than the laws of karma. Besides the bondage of retribution, what prevents the otherwise horrendous marriage between Di Xichen and Sujie from breaking apart is *se*, or sexual desire. Allegorically, the fox-spirit is the symbol not only of sexual lust but also of the dangers associated with such lust. This partly explains the curious fact that many of the important and lustful women in the lives of Chao Yuan and Di Xichen are associated with fox-spirits in one way or another. They are either reincarnations of fox-spirits or resemble someone who was a fox-spirit in a former incarnation.

The emphasis on environment (as discussed above) and the novel's implicit allegory on the significance of self-control and self-cultivation are, at least on the surface, contradictory to the novel's explicit message about karmic retribution. If everyone is a reincarnation of a previous being and has to carry the full load of the moral consequences of the actions of his or her previous incarnation and if everything is predetermined by what has taken place in a previous life, there is little room for the environment to exert an influence and for the individual to exercise initiative. Although moral justice seems to be maintained during the cycle of rebirth and reincarnation (one's sins, which cannot be redeemed in this life, are redeemed in the next), there is little moral justice in terms of the life of a specific individual, who can exist only in the form of one incarnation at a time. Within a single life-span, one's fate is pretty much predetermined by the action of one's previous incarnation, and "practice" or "environment" and one's individual will are largely irrelevant in this perpetual cycle of rebirth and retribution. An important problem in reading this complex seventeenth-century work is how to reconcile all the seemingly conflicting signals it sends out to its readers. But they may not have seemed so contradictory to the author or his contemporaries. Or, this may never have been a problem for the author in the sense that it is now to us as modern readers.[39] Before addressing this complicated aspect of the novel, however, we need to examine closely the clues provided by the novel itself regarding the possible reasons for its apparent embrace of the theory of karmic retribution despite its many other concerns that contradict this theory.

The Unraveling of the Confucian Order

Xingshi is full of social transgressions, evils, and moral corruption; everyone is consumed by lust. Besides many specific and detailed cases, the author presents the moral degeneration of the society in general. The most impressive story of moral decline is probably that of Mingshui 明水 village. The author first paints a picture of a village utopia during the early Ming, when almost no trace of evil can be found (chaps. 23 and 24).[40] Then all of a sudden, almost inexplicably,[41] rapid moral degeneration sets in (chaps. 26 and 27). Only one person or two out of a hundred are good, and eight or nine out of ten are evil (28.414). The immorality of Mingshui village becomes so overwhelming that the Jade Emperor unleashes a devastating flood to punish the corrupt people. It is in the middle of the account of this rapid moral regres-

39. Cf. Robert Hegel's (*The Novel in Seventeenth-Century China*, p. 138) comment on Yuan Yuling's 袁于令 (1592–1674) novel *Suishi yiwen* 隋史遺文 (The forgotten tales of the Sui dynasty): "This blend of attitudes that appear mutually contradictory to modern readers was not necessarily so to Yüan Yü-ling; he attributes the responsibility for human action to both Heaven and man on different occasions."

40. Many passages in the novel express nostalgia for the early Ming (see, e.g., 24.354 and 27.390). Such nostalgia for the good old days of the early Ming is typical of many other narrative works produced during the late Ming (when the Ming monarchy was collapsing) and the early Qing (when the Ming just became a "fallen dynasty"); see Hanan, "The Fiction of Moral Duty," p. 190.

41. The narrator briefly refers to the theory of dynastic cycles as a possible explanation for this sudden change (24.363).

sion that the reader is introduced to Di Xichen and Sujie (the respective reincarnations of Chao Yuan and the fox-spirit in the first part of the novel) and their families. In other words, the protagonists of the second part of the novel are introduced within the context of the unraveling of the long-existing moral order; the result is an even stronger sense of moral chaos.[42] According to the novelist, the "abnormal" phenomena of shrewish wives and henpecked husbands, which are among the most important thematic concerns of the novel,[43] are only symptoms of a more profound social malaise or moral disorder; in the words of Judge Wu in the novel, it is a world of *yangxiao yinzhang* 陽消陰長 (the *yang* element wanes, and the *yin* element waxes): "In a world where *yang* is dominated by *yin*, where men of virtue are in fear of men of mean character and where people are in fear of ghosts, how can a husband not be afraid of his wife?" (91.1304). This is a moral universe turned upside down, a world in which the Confucian social and patriarchal gender hierarchies are completely disrupted.

In this chaotic world, the traditional moral teachings of the Confucian classics are increasingly irrelevant. An important and common tactic in this novel for exploring the implications of the irrelevance of a disintegrating moral tradition is to associate people of compromised moral character with *related* teachings in the Confucian classics; this gives rise to many comic scenes that testify to a rapid moral degeneration. Here, the satire is often double-edged—both the cogency of the moral teachings of the Confucian classics and the moral fiber of the people who quote them are thrown into doubt.

When Chao Yuan informs his father-in-law that he is going to divorce his wife, Jishi, he appeals to the authority of the Confucian classics by reciting a passage that he thinks is found in the *Daxue*: "Don't look unless it is in accordance with the rites; don't listen unless it is in accordance with the rites; don't walk unless it is in accordance with the rites; don't speak what is

42. The graphic descriptions of moral corruption that permeate the novel often make the story of the good old days of Mingshui 明水 village appear too remote to be believable; the author seems to reinforce this impression by comparing it to the neverneverland of the Peach Blossom Spring (23.241). This isolated story is inserted partly to underscore the absence of such a world and the poignancy of a remote memory.

43. For studies of the figures of shrewish wives and henpecked husbands in traditional Chinese fiction, see Yenna Wu, "The Inversion of Marital Hierarchy"; idem, *The Chinese Virago*; and McMahon, *Misers, Shrews, and Polygamists.*

against propriety." The passage is actually from the *Analects*, and, due to poor schooling, Chao Yuan not only misattributes but misquotes by altering the wording of the original by changing the word *wu* 勿 to *bu* 不 and *dong* 動 to *zou* 走 (8.119).[44] Furthermore, Chao Yuan is in fact doing just the opposite of what is encouraged in this passage—he is divorcing his wife based on the slanders of his concubine (certainly an act against propriety). Chao Yuan's claim that, although Xiaozhen'ge was a singing girl, once she married him as a concubine she became a respectable wife adds to the satirical effect because this is anything but "decent." The phrase Chao Yuan uses—*rumen weizheng* 入門為正 (8.119)—is perhaps a double-entendre; it can be read to mean either that "once married to him, she became a woman of decency" or "once married, to him she became the formal wife" (replacing Jishi as the first wife). A prostitute's replacing his original wife as the de facto formal wife (*zheng* 正), as Chao Yuan proposes, is obviously a clear violation of the Confucian sense of propriety.

Like Chao Yuan, Di Xichen is also a poor student who often misquotes the Confucian classics:

> Di Xichen thought to himself, "Although parents and brothers are considered one's Heavenly endowed kin (*tianqin* 天親), there are many private things which a man can't tell them but which he can tell his wife. . . . Doesn't this mean that husband and wife are the closest to each other? . . . I vaguely remember a passage from the *Analects* that reads: 'I should do my best in tilling the fields and discharge the duties of a son, and if my parents do not love me, what is that to me?' It seems that all this is predetermined by Heaven." (61.873–74)

The quotation is from the *Mencius* rather than the *Analects*,[45] and the original gives priority to one's duties to one's parents. Di Xichen believes that he has found canonical authority for his view that one's relationship to one's spouse is more important than that to one's parents, a view apparently at odds with the message in the classic but a view shared by the author himself, as we will discuss below. This misquotation indicates first that Di Xichen does not understand the *Mencius* and second that the view espoused in the classic merits

44. The original passage from *Lunyu* reads: "Do not look unless it is in accordance with the rites; do not listen unless it is in accordance with the rites; do not speak unless it is in accordance with the rites; do not move unless it is in accordance with the rites" (see Liu Baonan, *Lunyu zhengyi*, p. 262; and Lau, *The Analects*, 12.1, p. 112).

45. See Jiao Xun, *Mengzi zhengyi*, p. 360; Lau, *Mencius*, 5A.1, p. 138.

qualification, as the narrator tries to do throughout the novel with his persistent emphasis on the importance of the conjugal relationship. The irony lies in the fact that the passages quoted from the classics often preach something very different from what the people in the novel are actually doing, and that their relevance can only be understood from a perspective of derision.

The examination topics (which are usually selected from the Confucian classics) given to students also provide the narrator with opportunities to address the issue of the irrelevancy of Confucian teachings to the daily moral practices of ordinary individuals and to satirize the moral makeup of a particular character. During the *tongsheng* 童生 examinations, Di Xichen's essay topic is a passage from the *Mencius*: "Together they reviled their husband and wept in the courtyard. The husband, unaware of all this, came swaggering in show off his to his womenfolk" (37.543).[46] The husband of this story always comes home drunk and well fed; he brags to his wives that he has been in the company of many important and rich people. However, the wives later find out that their husband feeds himself by begging food from those visiting the graves of their relatives. The husband in this passage displays the incompetence and vanity that Di Xichen will come to symbolize later. The incompetence of men and the dominance of women are important themes in the novel.[47]

Later, during the examinations for the *xiucai* 秀才 degree, Xichen is given an essay topic from the *Analects* as his topic for the examination on the *Sishu* (Four books): "I [Confucius] never dreamt the joys of music could reach such heights" (38.557).[48] The narrator comments that Di Xichen is overjoyed because this happens to be the topic on which he has prepared an essay in advance; for him the joy is as great as if he had just seen Sun Lanji, the prostitute he is currently romancing. By virtue of this subtle reference to the classic, Xichen's infatuation with a prostitute and his joy over being able to guess the right examination topic (a questionable way of preparing for the examinations) are ironically compared to the Master's ecstasy over hearing the ritual music of antiquity. To reinforce the ironic effect of this juxtaposition of the sage with our anti-hero, the author arranges that Di Xichen's *Jing*

46. Jiao Xun, *Mengzi zhengyi*, p. 358; Lau, *Mencius*, 4B.33, p. 137.

47. In fact, the narrator refers to this story from the *Mencius* in the "Yinqi" (Introduction; pp. 3–4) when he tries to argue that a wife plays an important role in the moral well-being of a husband.

48. Liu Baonan, *Lunyu zhengyi*, p. 141; Lau, *The Analects*, 7.14, p. 87).

經 (classic) essay topic is a line from a song in the *Shijing*: "The loved one is just in the middle of the water" ("Jianjia" 蒹葭 from the "Qinfeng" 秦風 section). This song was usually interpreted as a love song or as a political allegory blaming the King of Qin for not following the rituals of the Zhou dynasty.[49] Of course, this line fits Xichen's situation almost perfectly, though not without irony. Throughout the examinations, Xichen's mind has seldom been on his essays, which are supposed to test his understanding of the moral teachings of the sages, and, despite his Confucian education, this sixteen-year-old boy's young heart is already the captive of a prostitute. Thus the mention of this classical song refers both to Di Xichen's romantic adventures and to his questionable moral character. Earlier, Di Xichen, after much effort by his new teacher, has finally learned to compose a proper opening sentence for an examination essay (*poti* 破題) according to a topic based on quotations from the Confucian classics (an important part of writing *bagu* 八股, or eight-legged essays). When he is given as a topic a passage from the *Analects*: "The Master went to see Nanzi. Zilu was displeased,"[50] Di Xichen works out the following opening sentence to illustrate the meaning of this topic: "The sage admires a beautiful girl, and the wise man is able to caution against sexual temptation" (37.540). Here, again, the reference to Di Xichen's romance with the prostitute and his own vulnerability to sexual temptation are subtly suggested. He is once more juxtaposed with the sage. The Confucian classics are given a new relevance in an extremely ironic manner. All these examples seem to demonstrate that Confucian teachings have to be understood from a new perspective because they are either irrelevant or require updating.[51]

In the "Yinqi" (Introduction) to the novel, the narrator openly questions the Confucian classics when he argues that one further kind of bliss—that of husband and wife—should be added to the three kinds of bliss listed by

49. For interpretations by the traditional commentators, see Hao Zhida et al., eds., *Guofeng shizhi zuanjie*, pp. 473–79.

50. Liu Baonan, *Lunyu zhengyi*, p. 131; Lau, *The Analects*, 6.28, p. 85. This is a very controversial passage. Some commentators believe that Confucius met Nanzi, a woman of lewd character, under special circumstances and that he was misunderstood by Zilu; see Liu Baonan, *Lunyu zhengyi*, pp. 131–32.

51. Of course, not all essay topics presented in the novel are meant to satirize the character who is writing an examination essay; for example, the case of Chao Liang's 晁梁 essay topics is at least ambivalent (46.669).

Mencius.[52] Obviously, the narrator feels that Mencius failed to pay enough attention to what he considers an important aspect of human society—the conjugal relationship. In fact the entire novel seems designed to make this point, a point Di Xichen comes to realize only after some extremely painful experiences. This has reminded people of the radical view expressed by the iconoclastic, late Ming thinker Li Zhi that the relationship between husband and wife should be considered more important than that between father and son, an implicit challenge to the rigid hierarchical structure suggested in the orthodox Confucian idea of *san'gang* 三綱 (the three bonds).[53] Related to this questioning attitude toward the Confucian tradition is the scant respect shown in the novel to the two Neo-Confucian giants, Cheng Yi 程頤 (1033–1107) and Cheng Hao 程顥 (1032–85):

> If she finds the wife in the family is an upright person, the nun assumes a very sincere appearance as if she was wearing the face of the two Neo-Confucian Masters Cheng Yi and Cheng Hao, always rattling on such pedantic and tiring topics as "being sincere" and "righting the mind" and "the Way of the king." (8.117)

Even Confucius himself is openly ridiculed in the novel. When discoursing on the practical need to feed oneself before one can talk about studying, the narrator specifically mentions Confucius:

> Sages have always advised students to be content with being poor while enjoying the Way (*anpin ledao* 安貧樂道). . . . But the sage who said this, I would say, must have led a comfortable life himself so that he could afford to feel content with being poor and still enjoyed the Way. . . . When Confucius was in the country of Chen, he and his people were without food for several days, and many of them became sick. . . . Although Confucius forced himself to insist: "It comes as no surprise to the gentleman to find himself in extreme straits. The small man finding himself in extreme straits would throw over all restraint."[54] I think this was surely not a fun time, but someone of later age made this even more straightforward in his remark that "learning is more important than making a living (*zhisheng* 治生)." (33.478)

This direct satire of the sages (especially Confucius himself) is by no means frequent in literary works from late imperial China.[55] The author is

52. See Jiao Xun, *Mengzi zhengyi*, pp. 533–34; and Lau, *Mencius*, 7A.20, p. 185.

53. See "Fufu lun" 夫婦論 (On husband and wife), in Li Zhi, *Fenshu*, *Xufenshu*, pp. 90–91.

54. Liu Baonan, *Lunyu zhengyi*, p. 331; Lau, The *Analects*, 15.2, p. 132.

55. The sayings of the sages are parodied in Li Yu's fictional works, such as *Rou Putuan*; however, Li Yu's narrators seldom show serious moral indignation.

openly questioning the relevance of the Confucian classics to daily life. Significantly, this ridicule of sages' quixotic insistence on *anpin ledao* is followed by a lengthy account of many *xiucai* 秀才 degree holders who have to go hungry because their classical learning does not earn them enough to feed themselves and their families (probably an accurate reflection of the situation in the author's own time). Traditional Confucian learning and wisdom are often the target of satire and ridicule.

Some critics have deplored the fact that after chapter 20 the author of *Xingshi* begins to lose sight of "the microcosm-macrocosm analogy" and fails to pull together such an "analogy as *Ch'in Ping Mei* does in its powerful conclusion."[56] Given the utter disappointment with Confucianism as an effective ideology manifested in the novel, we have to entertain the possibility that the author might also have lost confidence in the explanatory power of the "microcosm-macrocosm analogy" envisioned in *Daxue*. Skepticism about the perceived "natural" link between the self-cultivation of an individual and the well-being of the nation can also be found in some of the leading thinkers of the seventeenth century, such as Wang Fuzhi, Li Gong 李塨 (1659–1733), and Tang Zhen 唐甄 (1630–1704).[57] This in turn should explain, at least in part, why the notion of karmic retribution became so appealing to the author of *Xingshi*.

The Search for Theodic Accountability

All this and the numerous stories of moral corruption and degeneration in the novel give strong testimony to the author's profound anxiety about a world without a moral authority to follow. This anxiety, which arises from a loss of faith in the effectiveness and relevance of the moral doctrines in the Confucian classics, may partly account for the novelist's eagerness to embrace the Buddhist concept of karmic retribution as a means of containing the "moral chaos" created by people's uncontrollable desires. If people cannot be taught to be virtuous, a belief quite contrary to the Mencian conviction of human perfectibility and the convictions of orthodox Neo-Confucians, perhaps they can at least be scared into good behavior by the

56. Plaks, "After the Fall," p. 574.

57. Mizoguchi (*Zhongguo qian jindai sixiang*, p. 291) has some very interesting observations on this issue.

gruesome consequences of moral misconduct as demonstrated in this novel's meticulous scheme of karmic retribution. The void created by the unraveling of the Confucian moral order desperately needs to be filled, and one solution suggested by the novel is the Buddhist doctrine of karmic retribution, which, by the seventeenth century, had become an integral part of popular moral culture. In a world that is dominated by evil, that has no human justice, and where people will not behave (i.e., Confucian teachings have become irrelevant), the concept of karmic retribution provides a psychologically much-needed faith: justice will eventually prevail, if not in this life, then in the next life. A person who has apparently committed no wrongdoing but is nevertheless suffering hardship or misfortune must have done something evil in a previous life. In fact, the theory of karmic retribution, when domesticated in China, became a theory about the postponement of justice.[58]

One of the rationalizing strategies of this doctrine is to explain the apparent absence of justice in reality in terms of its eventual arrival in a future life. To put it simply, it is a tactic of deferral. The moral consequences of a person's action can be understood fully only in his or her next life, and what is happening to that person now can be explained by what he or she has done in a previous life, as suggested in the following saying from a Buddhist sutra quoted in a story from the *Erke Pai an jingqi* 二刻拍案驚奇 (Slapping the table in amazement, second collection): "To know the cause rooted in the previous life, one has to look at what is happening in this life; to know what is going to happen in the next life, one has to look at what is happening in this life."[59] The judgment of the moral consequences of one's action always has to be deferred to another life.

In the last chapter of *Xingshi*, when the monk Hu Wuyi reveals to Chao Liang that the reason Di Xichen has been suffering all these hardships is because in his previous incarnation Chao Yuan committed many sins, Chao Liang wonders why Chao Yuan did not receive an even severer punishment, such as being reborn as an animal rather than as a man. Hu Wuyi explains that Chao Yuan was originally a virtuous woman prior to being reborn as a man. Thus, his retribution is accurate as well as fair. Here again the

58. For discussions of the Indian influence on the Chinese concept of retribution, see Liu Daochao, *Zhongguo shan'e baoying xisu*, pp. 81–91; and Yün-hua Jan, "The Chinese Understanding and Assimilation of Karma Doctrine."

59. Story no. 24 in Ling Mengchu, *Erke Pai'an jingqi*, p. 481.

present is explained in terms of the past or even a very distant past (three reincarnations ago, or *sanshi qian* 三世前; 100.1425). The present is rationalized *away* by being dissolved into (the cause in) the past and (the effect in) the future. This kind of present-dissolving rationale must have a tremendous appeal to someone who cannot account for the dominance of evil in the present. Appealing to the concept of karmic retribution can be considered mainly an attempt at theodicy:

> The most complete formal solution to the problem of theodicy is the special achievement of the Indian doctrine of *karma*, the so-called belief in the transmigration of souls. The world is viewed as a completely connected and self-contained cosmos of ethical retribution. Guilt and merit within this world are unfailingly compensated by fate in the successive lives of the soul. . . . What may appear from the viewpoint of a theory of compensation as unjust suffering in the terrestrial life of a person should be regarded as atonement for sin in a previous existence.[60]

This observation of Max Weber may be better understood in comparison with a remark made by a character in one of the stories in the *Yuewei caotang biji* 閱微草堂筆記 (Random jottings from the Cottage of Close Readings) by the eighteenth-century scholar and writer Ji Yun 紀昀 (1724–1805):

> Confucianism is like daily food: go without it for one day, and one feels hungry; go without it for several days, and one would die of starvation. Buddhism and Taoism, like medicine, can have a crucial role in saving one's life and in making one sad or happy. They are more effective than Confucianism in terms of being able to account for apparent injustice and relieving one's frustrations; especially, for those who are unenlightened, the theory of retribution is more impressive than the Confucian teachings in terms of being able to scare them into good behavior.[61]

Despite the expedient tone here, the concept of karmic retribution is regarded mainly as a means to maintain moral order, something also suggested in Weber's remark (although the latter tends to be more "metaphysical"). In a word, this is a solution to the problem of theodicy, a problem of special urgency in seventeenth-century China, which was experiencing tremendous social turmoil.[62]

60. Weber, *Sociology of Religion*, p. 145.

61. "Luanyang xiaoxia lu" 灤陽消夏錄, *juan* 4, in Ji Yun, *Yuewei caotang biji*, p. 93. For a discussion in English of this work in terms of the late eighteenth-century literati's attitudes toward the supernatural, see Leo Tak-hung Chan, "Narrative as Argument."

62. For a more detailed discussion of the possible reasons behind the surge of interest in

This leads us to an otherwise curious passage in the novel. In a description of the prelapsarian Mingshui village, the narrator says that the old ethical order that kept people morally upright for so long is pre-Buddhist:

> This was a time of vitality and simplicity when almost everyone was virtuous because those who morally didn't fit all died early in their lives. All the year around, families big or small only knew that paying homage to the ancestors meant filiality, and never knew about praying to the Buddha or being vegetarians or burning incense to call upon the Buddha. (23.340)

In this passage, the narrator goes out of his way to remind us that all this happened before the coming of the Buddhist concept of karma. Here we may better appreciate the author's choice of the pen name Xizhousheng 西周生. In the novel, the good moral order of Mingshui village is carefully compared to that of the Western Zhou (Xi Zhou) dynasty, the moral golden age cherished in the Confucian tradition (26.378). The narrator here is obviously being nostalgic for an age when people were still unaware of the Buddhist concept of karmic retribution (or, more bluntly, when there was as yet no need to use such a concept to scare people into desirable behavior as suggested by Ji Yun). This seems to contradict the novel's apparent championing of the universality of karmic retribution. However, it may not have appeared contradictory to the author since he uses karmic retribution only as an expedient to make sense of a world in which the traditional Confucian ideologies seem to be increasingly irrelevant and as a moral deterrent to scare people into virtuous behavior.

Interpreted from the perspective of expediency and the psychological need for moral "intelligibility," the novel's emphasis on karma can be understood as the author's desperate attempt to find a workable substitute for a rapidly unraveling moral order. For this novelist, who appears to have been pessimistic about the moral status of his fellow beings, *Xingshi*'s retributive structure is absolutely necessary in the sense that it provides a stabilizing moral vantage point from which he can confront all the horrendous cases of moral corruption exposed and condemned in the novel. The novel somehow needs to impose a moral pattern on the various social phenomena that seem to defy the application of the usual standards (such as those derived from

---

the concept of karmic retribution exhibited in many fictional works of seventeenth-century China and its possible relationship to the chaotic and violent dynastic transition, see my "Karmic Retribution and the Didactic Dilemma in the *Xingshi yinyuan zhuan*," pp. 398–404.

conventional Confucian wisdom). In this sense, karmic retribution is indeed the best solution possible when other ideologies fail to explain the dominance of evil.

Furthermore, the framework of karmic retribution provides the novel with a much-needed license to devote so much space to graphic accounts of social transgressions or evils without incurring the kind of criticism *Jin Ping Mei* received. These evils now can be understood as the result of divine wrath or as a punishing vehicle of karmic retribution (such as the case of Sujie's sadomasochism).

To a certain extent, the novel's proclaimed belief in karmic retribution is more than an act of expediency. Structurally, the novel needs to impose a moral coherence on the "chaotic stories" that threaten to disrupt its narrative flow and structural teleology. The reader is often bothered by the novel's constant digressions and the elaborate "prologues" at the beginning of many chapters.[63] There is an interesting tension between the neatness the novel's framework of karmic retribution seems to promise and its episodic narrative (the novel is full of digressions, independent short stories about seemingly unrelated incidents or persons). On the other hand, the narrator's frequent impatient intrusions into the narrative to remind the reader of the workings of karmic retribution also create a distance between the narrator and his characters, a distance that allows the narrator to maintain authority in navigating through the ethically chaotic world of the novel by offering appropriate interpretation and passing moral judgments. The narrator's knowledge of the operations of karmic retribution, which the characters in the novel are apparently denied, seems to elevate him onto a much higher moral plateau, from which he (almost like a god) can look down at sentient beings, exposing, laughing at, and satirizing their human follies. Paradoxically, the novel's elaborate allegory of human lust and its dire consequences, which appears to undermine the notion of karmic retribution, also depends on this very notion for its rhetorical power. As demonstrated above, the intricate allegorical relationships among Chao Yuan, Di Xichen, Sujie, Jijie, and others are, to a

63. For some typical examples, see chaps. 34, 36, 62, and 90. These lengthy prologues often remind the reader of the *ruhua* 入話 device favored by writers of vernacular stories such as Feng Menglong and Lin Mengchu; for a discussion of the use of prologue by these writers, see Hanan, *The Chinese Vernacular Story*, pp. 127–28, 149–50. Indeed, without the teleological containment provided by the novel's framework of karmic retribution, a large portion of *Xingshi* would read like a collection of many short stories of different lengths.

large degree, based on as well as enhanced by the karmic connections between these characters (for example, the fact that both Chao Yuan and Di Xichen suffer from an uncontrollable sexual lust is much easier to understand allegorically since the latter is the reincarnation of the former). Thus, the karmic framework and the allegory of lust are not necessarily always contradictory; sometimes they are complementary. For the sake of moral coherence, desire, which has proved to be difficult to control with Confucian teachings, has to be contained even if it means appealing to a not so perfect Buddhist theory of karmic retribution.

Because the basic structure and main narrative content of *Xingshi* are deeply shaped by an unprecedented concern with the effectiveness of karmic retribution and because the narrator relies on this concept for his narrative authority as well as strategies, we should not dismiss it merely as a deplorable folk superstition or the author's reluctant bow to the narrative conventions of traditional vernacular fiction. He is apparently making a conscientious effort to employ such conventions to his own advantage. Alternatively, to treat karmic retribution in the novel only as an aesthetic or formal function devoid of any serious ideological implications is equally questionable, because, as the preceding discussions have sought to demonstrate, it is an integral part of the novel's moral structure, no matter how problematic and ambiguous it may often appear.[64] More subtly, the concept of karmic retribution is important in the paradoxical sense that the novel alludes to the impossibility of explaining every human phenomenon according to this concept despite (or because of) its very "neatness," but, at the same time, it also successfully compels the reader to face the possible moral and social consequences if such a theodic concept of retributive justice were not available.

64. Cf. Plaks's observation ("After the Fall," p. 577) that "the entire framework of karmic retribution may be reduced to essentially a structural function, one of aesthetic rather than doctrinal significance." This view seems to be shared by Eve Alison Nyren, who observes that "the karmic framework appears to be used merely as a structural convenience" ("Translator's Note," *The Bonds of Matrimony*, p. ix).

CHAPTER SEVEN
Qing and Homoerotic Desire in Bian er chai *and* Lin Lan Xiang

In the fictional works examined above, desire is usually represented in general terms, with little conscious or deliberate effort to distinguish *qing* from *yu* (understood in the narrower sense of physical desire), although various phenomena of *yu* were explored. Of course, this does not mean that the word *qing* does not appear or that romantic sentiments are never mentioned. However, the character *qing* is more often employed to refer to sexual attraction, as in *qingse* 情色, without evoking its common associations with romantic sentiment. For fiction that conscientiously explores the romantic aspects of *qing*, we have to turn to other works, especially those produced in the seventeenth and eighteenth centuries, which exhibit a distinct shift from a fascination with *yu* to an intense interest in *qing*.

In the late Ming collection of homoerotic stories *Bian er chai* 弁而釵 (Hairpins beneath the cap), the concept of *qing* is the central rationale for defending and celebrating male homosexual love, as reflected in the titles of the four stories in the collection: "Qingzhen ji" 情貞紀 (A story of chaste love), "Qingxia ji" 情俠紀 (A story of chivalric love), "Qinglie ji" 情烈紀 (A story of sacrificing love), and "Qingqi ji" 情奇紀 (A story of extraordinary love).[1] The author's tactic of categorizing *qing* may have been influenced by

1. It is generally agreed among scholars that the two collections of homoerotic stories *Bian er chai* and *Yichun xiangzhi* 宜春香質 (Fragrance of the pleasant spring) were authored by the

Feng Menglong's famous *Qingshi*, in which all the stories are classified into different categories to illustrate what Feng perceived to be the different aspects of *qing*.

At the very beginning of the first story, "A Story of Chaste Love," the narrator declares that his protagonists bring honor and glory to male homosexuality (大爲南風增色) because the two lovers first fall in love with each other for the sake of *qing* and then pursue their love to the end in order to seek complete fulfillment of this *qing* (始以情合,終以情全).[2] A central message of these four stories is that it is the deep *qing* of the male protagonists that makes them become what they are.

In "A Story of Chaste Love," *qing* is celebrated as having the power to "transcend" gender boundaries: after consummating their relationship, Zhao Wangsun sighs that he, as a man, is willing to offer his body as a woman would only because he has been moved by his lover's deep love (*chiqing* 痴情). His lover Feng Xiang offers this paean to *qing*:

---

same writer, The Moon-Heart Master of the Drunken West Lake (Zui Xihu xinyue zhuren 醉西湖心月主人), and were first published during the Chongzhen reign period (1628–44). For information on the author and the extant editions of these two works, see the "Qianyan" 前言 (forewords) written by Xiao Xiangkai 蕭相愷 for *Bian er chai* and *Yichun xiangzhi* in Mingdai xiaoshuo jikan, series no. 2, 2: 575–76, and 759–61; "*Bian er chai* chuban shuoming" 弁而釵出版說明 in *Bian er chai*, Siwuxie huibao series, pp. 17–20; and "*Yichun xiangzhi* chuban shuoming" 宜春香質出版說明 in *Yichun xiangzhi*, Siwuxie huibao series, pp. 17–20. See also Wu Cuncun, "*Bian er chai yu Yichun xiangzhi* de niandai kaozheng." The Mingdai xiaoshuo jikan versions of these two works, according to editor Xiao Xiangkai, were based on the edition printed by the publisher Bigeng shanfang 筆耕山房 and were most probably printed during the early Qing. Extant copies of this edition are held in the Tenri Library in Japan and in the Beijing Municipal Library. The Siwuxie huibao version of *Bian er chai* is based on another early Qing edition published by Bigeng shanfang, an extant copy of which is held in the Palace Museum Library in Taipei. In discussing these two works, I refer to the Mingdai xiaoshuo jikan versions, mainly because these collated versions, compared with those in the Siwuxie huibao series, seem to have fewer missing characters or words. However, all extant copies of the Bigeng shanfan printed edition appear to have suffered different degrees of obliteration, probably due to damaged printing blocks (apparently first produced during the Chongzhen reign period) that were reused for printing during the early Qing. However, the Siwuxie huibao version of *Bian er chai* contains some interlineal comments, which do not appear in the Mingdai xiaoshuo jikan editions.

2. *Bian er chai*, in Mingdai xiaoshuo jikan, 1.797. Further references to *Bian er chai* are given in parentheses.

The place where *qing* is most concentrated is precisely among people like ourselves (情之所鍾,正在我輩). What we've done today is wrong if judged by the standard of *li* [reason/principle]; however, if judged by the logic of *qing*, it is possible for a man to become a woman or for a woman to become a man, or for the living to die or for the dead to come back to life. Those who are bound by the distinctions between man and woman or life and death have not lived their *qing* to the fullest. As I've said before, the sea may dry up, and rocks may erode. Only *qing*, however, will never perish since it is not bound by the logic of *li*. (1.818)

As pointed out by Keith McMahon, this inspired speech is reminiscent of Tang Xianzu's famous manifesto on *qing* in his preface to *Mudan ting*.[3] What is significant here, however, is that the transcendent power Tang Xianzu attributed to *qing* is cited for the sake of redefining conventional gender boundaries. The dichotomy between *qing* and *li* envisioned by Tang is underscored here to legitimize homosexual love. This logic of *qing* is pushed even further in the opening poem of chapter (*hui*) 1 of "A Story of Sacrificing Love":

From *qing* both life and death originate,	生死繇來只一情
Both life and death are worthy of glory if *qing* is genuine.	情眞生死總堪旌
Qing becomes endearing only when it is understood through death,	以死論情情始切
Death becomes a chaste act only when it is for the sake of *qing*.	將情償死死方貞
The void of death only could *qing* fill,	死中欠缺情能補
In death union remains when *qing* is persistent.	情內乖張死可盟
If *qing* is untrue, the body does not die,	情不眞兮身不死
Since ancient time no person of deep *qing* is afraid of death. (1.875)	鍾情自古不偷生

3. McMahon, *Causality and Containment*, pp. 74–75. For a more detailed discussion of *Bian er chaizhai*, see Vitiello, "Exemplary Sodomites," pp. 83–132. In Chapter 2, I mention Feng Menglong's insistence that achievement in *qing* should be considered a fourth in addition to the traditional three kinds of cultural immortality (*san buxiu* 三不朽; namely, achievements in moral self-cultivation, public service, and writing or *lide*, *ligong*, and *liyan* 立德，立功，立言). Feng was in fact referring to homosexual *qing* when he made this "bold" statement. See Feng Menglong, "Qingxian qu xu," *Taixia xinzou*, in idem, *Quanji*, vol. 15, 1.18b–20a (pp. 40–42); and Xu Shuofang, "Feng Menglong nianpu," pp. 427–28.

The omnipresence and transcendence of *qing* are underscored by the repeated use of the word, which appears in every line of this brief poem. In the story that follows, Wen Yun, a female impersonator/actor, tries to reciprocate Yun Han's love by sacrificing his own life in order to vindicate his chastity; he then returns to life as a female ghost and sells himself/herself to an official as a concubine to raise funds to enable his lover to take the examinations. As this brief summary of the story suggests, sacrificing one's life for one's lover and then returning to life as a ghost to continue that sacrifice after death are carefully demonstrated to be made possible by the all-defying power of *qing* (here the author appeals to the death-transcending power of *qing* in *Mudan ding* for the sake of homosexual love). "A Story of Extraordinary Love" has a similar plot: Li Youxian, to repay Kuang Shi for rescuing him from the humiliating and painful life of a male prostitute, first masquerades as a woman to live with his lover as a concubine and then risks his own life to raise Kuang's son after Kuang is wrongly imprisoned. Later, the son, after becoming an adult and achieving top honors in the examinations, reunites with his parents and takes revenge on their persecutor.

Despite this emphasis on *qing* as reciprocal appreciation and as loyalty or chastity, the physical aspects of homosexual love are not ignored in *Bian er chai*; love is ultimately fulfilled and consummated in physical union.[4] In "A Story of Chaste Love," the narrator describes Feng Xiang's physical attraction (*yu*) to Zhao Wangsun in explicit terms, such as "he is quite aroused" (*shenshi dong huo* 甚是動火; 3.808), "his burning desire is blazing" (*yuhuo zhengshi* 慾火正熾; 3.813), or "his face above is glowing with burning desire, while his penis below is as hard as iron" (臉上慾火直噴, 腰間孽根鐵硬; 3.812). To emphasize the inseparability of *qing* and *yu*, the narrator sometimes uses the words *qinggen* 情根 (literally, the root of *qing*) to refer to a lover's penis ("A Story of Sacrificing Love," 2.889) and *qingku* 情窟 (literally, the "cavern of *qing*") to refer to his partner's anus (ibid., 2.889; see also "A Story of Chivalric Love," 3.855).

Throughout these four homoerotic stories, the body is represented as an important site where *qing* subverts and, at the same time, duplicates or even reinforces in the context of a homosexual relationship the conventional gen-

4. Cf. McMahon's (*Causality and Containment*, p. 75) observation: "Another facet of his [the author's] theme is to show that emotional fulfillment in *qing* cannot be complete without its sensual complement."

der hierarchy between a "man" and a "woman" typical of a patriarchal and polygamous society. As pointed out before, Feng Xiang argues in justification of homosexual love that *qing* makes the usual gender distinctions between a man and a woman irrelevant; paradoxically, however, in *Bian er chai* homosexuality is defended by showing homosexual lovers outdoing their heterosexual counterparts in vindicating patriarchal gender values. These lovers, despite or because of their homosexuality, can be and indeed are more chaste and more filial than "straight people." With the possible exception of "A Story of Chivalric Love," the lover who takes the passive role is expected to behave as an "honorable" woman should behave in a heterosexual relationship. The ultimate act of *qing*—the commitment of love on the part of such a lover—is the offering of his body to his partner. In "A Story of Chaste Love," Zhao Wangsun confesses to the sick Feng Xiang that he has decided to stay in order to nurse him back to health: "Since I have already promised to offer you my body (*yeyi shen xu xiong* 業已身許兄), I should certainly stay to take care of you" (3.816). It is Feng Xiang's expectation that Zhao will definitely offer his body if he is truly moved by *qing* (*yinqing juanshen* 因情捐身; 3.816).

In "The Story of Sacrificing Love," in order to show his gratitude to Yun Han for saving him from harassment and persecution by a local bully, Wen Yun deliberately dresses as a woman to seduce Yun Han and offers him his body as the ultimate gift, because he is convinced that the only valuable thing he has to give his benefactor as a token of gratitude is his own body (我將何以爲謝, 只此一身, 庶幾可報萬一; 2.888). In a poem, Wen Yun characterizes the yielding of his body to his lover as "sacrificing his body for the sake of thanking his soul mate" (*sheshen chou zhiji* 捨身酬知己; 2.890). Later he pledges that he will die rather than allow another man to take advantage of his body and thus dishonor his soul mate (我當以死報兄, 斷不辱身以爲知己丑; 3.895). Assuming the role of a woman, the passive lover is supposed to protect his chastity once he has given his body to his lover; that lover is supposed to play the "active" role (i.e., the gender role of a man).

In "A Story of Extraordinary Love," Li Youxian, to raise money to pay his imprisoned father's fine for the loss to bandits of government food supplies under his supervision, decides to sell himself for 100 taels of silver. However, he is worried that, as a man, his body is not worth that much (兒系男身, 安能值得百金; 1.920), a view confirmed by many in the story.

However, impressed by his feminine appearance, a brothel owner decides to pay this amount. Without realizing it, Li Youxian sells himself into a male brothel (*nanyuan* 南院), in which the male prostitutes dress in women's clothing and address one another as "sister." Thus, the cash value of the body of a socially inferior and poor man is determined by how feminine that male body appears to be, because only a woman's body can become a commodity with a commercial value. Furthermore, after falling in love with another man, Li behaves like an exemplary concubine and risks his own life to raise the son of his lover/husband Kuang Shi by the latter's formal wife.[5] To be an exemplary concubine, his body has to be feminized, too. He washes his feet in a special liquid so that they shrink enough to appear to be a pair of bound feet (3.943). He even signs a letter to Kuang as "your male concubine" (*nanqie* 男妾; 4.955).[6]

In "A Story of Chivalrous Love," which, unlike the other three stories, does not duplicate the patriarchal gender hierarchy,[7] the masculine Zhang Ji, who is a military strategist and a martial art specialist (thus someone who possesses both superb military and civil skills, or *wenwu shuangquan* 文武雙全), is drugged by Zhong Tu'nan. While he is in a deep sleep, Zhong sodomizes him. In sleep, Zhang gradually begins to enjoy the experience so much that he is no longer sure whether his body is that of a man or that of a woman (幾不知此身是男是女也; 3.856). Although Zhang is always the receiving party in this homosexual affair, the narrator, surprisingly, seldom

5. A lover who assumes the passive role in a homosexual relationship and tries to repay his lover's favor by insisting on becoming an exemplary woman or concubine is a common theme in homoerotic stories of that period. See, e.g., Li Yu's story "A Male Mencius's Mother Raises Her Son Properly By Moving House Three Times," in *Wusheng xi*, pp. 107–31; English translation in Hanan, trans. and ed., *Silent Operas*, pp. 97–134. In that story, in order to make sure that he become a perfect woman, not only ethically but also physically, Ruilang, the passive lover, not only has his feet bound but also has himself castrated. For a discussion in English of this story, see Volpp, "The Discourse on Male Marriage." Li Yu's story is unique in the sense that the homosexual relationship there takes the form of marriage, unlike most stories on male homosexual love (including those in *Bian er chai*) where the relationship is often provisional, as has been pointed out by McMahon (*Causality and Containment*, p. 78).

6. A woman in traditional China was supposed to use the word *qie*, which also meant "concubine," to refer to herself (it was almost a feminine reflexive first-person pronoun).

7. Another story on male homosexual love that does not explicitly duplicate the patriarchic gender hierarchy typical of heterosexual relationships of that time is the last story in Xi Langxian's 席浪仙 *Shi diantou* 石點頭 "Pan Wenzi Finds Male Love in a Grave of Mandarin Ducks" (see *Shi diantou deng sanzhong*, pp. 304–23).

emphasizes his feminine qualities. Moreover, "body" becomes a notion to play with in Zhong's verbal attempt to appease Zhang's anger when the latter realizes what has transpired:

> Now that I have fulfilled my wishes, you can just behead me so that two glorious things can be achieved: future generations will remember that a Scholar Zhong was willing to give up his life/body (*sangshen* 喪身) for the sake of *qing*, while a Scholar Zhang killed his wicked friend because that friend took advantage of his body [literally, "made him lose his body" or *shishen* 失身]. Both of us will be immortalized in people's memory. (3.856)

Although the loss of body in the literal sense is loss of life, or *sangshen*, in the case of Scholar Zhong's willingness to die, the loss of body (*shishen*) in the metaphorical sense, as in the case of Zhang's being sodomized by another man, has to be understood as assuming the gender of a "woman" whose body is being penetrated by a man. "Body" is capable of quite different gender implications in relation to the different partners in a homosexual relationship: the body that penetrates is male; the body that is penetrated is female. Zhang is so moved by this eloquent expression of *qing* on Zhong's part that he quickly forgives him and is now willing to accept the role of a concubine or a woman (*ganwei qiefu* 甘爲妾婦) in their homosexual relationship, even though he has just married two beautiful girls, a polygamous marriage that fully testifies to his gender status as a man.

But no matter how deep the love or *qing*, there is always a sense of profound shame when a man is reduced to a woman and asked to offer his body in a homosexual relationship. This sense of shame is apparent in Zhao Wangsun's confession to his lover Feng Xiang:

> "I lost/offered my body (*shishen* 失身) to you because I was so moved by your love (*chiqing* 痴情). However, I can never wash clean my shame even if I jumped into a river or a lake. As a man, I have been studying hard, trying to establish myself in the world. Now I am willing to act like a woman (甘爲婦人女子之事). What a shame!" (3.818)

It is this expression of shame by Zhao that provokes Feng Xiang's eloquent speech on *qing* and its gender-defying power quoted above. Paradoxically, for a passive partner such as Zhao Wangsun, the more humiliated he feels about offering his body, the greater his sacrifice to *qing* appears to himself as well as to others. In other words, the degree of *qing* symbolized by an act of sacrificing one's body is in direct proportion to the humiliation that sacrificial act is perceived to visit on the person who performs the act. Zhao loves Feng so much that he is willing to suffer the humiliation of being a woman. Consequently, within the context of male homosexuality, a gesture of *qing* is much more expressive precisely because it can affirm the patriarchal gender hierarchy typical of a heterosexual relationship. A passive partner is able to demonstrate his devotion or *qing* to his lover by giving up his rights as a man and becoming a woman, a sacrifice unavailable to a "real" woman in a heterosexual relationship since she is *already* in the inferior position. She cannot claim that she has made a sacrifice by lowering herself further since as a "real" woman she is already in the cellar of the gender hierarchy.

One important aspect of *qing* in *Bian er chai,* therefore, is the heroic act of sacrifice performed to prove the purity of the body by a passive lover in the interest of his partner. A story often begins with the active lover making a sacrifice for the passive lover, a sacrifice that later leads to much more substantial sacrifices by the passive lover. It is these sacrifices that are the main focus of the narrative. The passive lover either offers his body for the sole enjoyment of the active lover or destroys his body to avoid its being contaminated by others. Here the logic of *qing* sees any violation of chastity as seriously compromising the sanctity of the ritual of offering one's body. Both acts (sacrificing and destroying the same body) are meant to be viewed as powerful tokens of the passive partner's deep gratitude or reciprocal *qing.* This gratitude, however, can acquire its expression only after being inscribed on the body of the passive lover (as we shall see in Chapter 8, a woman often has to make a similar statement with her body in a heterosexual relationship). For a passive lover or a passive partner, the body is almost the only effective medium through which he can articulate his *qing.*

If the Moon-Heart Master's *Bian er chai* is meant to be a collection of exemplary stories of the perfect union between *qing* and *yu* in a homosexual relationship, then his other collection of stories, *Yixiang chunzhi* 宜香春質 (Fragrance of the pleasant spring), was obviously written to demonstrate the dangers of excessive *yu* or lust in a homosexual relationship. The four stories in this collection are entitled "Fengji" 風集 (The wind), "Huaji" 花集 (The flowers), "Xueji" 雪集 (The snow), and "Yueji" 月集 (The moon). The four words "wind," "flower," "snow," and "moon," when read together as *fenghua xueyue,* usually refer to overindulgence in sexual romance. At the beginning of the first story, the narrator launches into a long harangue on *qing* and the need to avoid excess:

A sage forgets his *qing*; the lowest beings are not even capable of having *qing*. But the place where *qing* is most concentrated is precisely among people like ourselves. If people like ourselves do not have *qing*, there will be no *qing* in the world. Our having *qing* means we are capable of becoming good; not having *qing* means that we are capable of becoming bad. Dissipation (*dangqing* 蕩情) is capable of becoming good or bad. If this world is without *qing*, I want *qing* to be there. If this world is overindulging in *qing*, then I will worry about dissipation. If *qing* develops into dissipation, it will harm the world. Dissipation originates from *qing*, but it can harm *qing*.[8]

All the stories in this collection are designed to serve as warnings about the consequences of excess. In his "self-comments" (*ziping* 自評) at the end of the first chapter of the last story, the author calls attention to the futility of trying to escape from *qing*: "Those affected souls proclaim themselves to be high above *qing* and beyond *qing*'s control, not knowing that they are already trapped in *qing*."[9] He seems to suggest that the only feasible approach is to confront *qing* and that one can achieve enlightenment only after experiencing intense *qing*. This is demonstrated in the last story, which relates how its protagonist became a Taoist immortal after undergoing various trials of *qing* in a long and tortuous dream.[10]

If *qing* is a powerful concept appropriated to bring honor to male homosexuality, as the narrator proclaims at the beginning of the first story in *Bian er chai*, this same concept again plays a crucial role in defining as well as complicating gender relationships in the Qing novel *Lin Lan Xiang* 林蘭香 (The three women named Lin, Lan, and Xiang). Although not as nearly explicit as male homosexuality in *Bian er chai* and *Yichun xiangzhi*, woman-to-

8. *Yichun xiangzhi*, Mingdai xiaoshuo jikan, 1.611. For another discussion of *Yichun xiangzhi*, see Vitiello, "Exemplary Sodomites," pp. 133–80.

9. *Yichun xiangzhi*, 1.726. This "self-comment" seems to be somewhat contradicted by the comment at the end of this chapter by Bubu shanren 不不山人, which is much more positive about *qing*: "I used to regret that there was not a manual of *qing* (*qingpu* 情譜). People of *qing* in this world have models to follow (*fanyi* 販依) now that the Moon-Heart Master has revealed the true nature of *qing*. This is really marvelous!" (1.725). At the end of chapter 3 of "A Story of Chivalric Love" in *Bian er chai*, the author's "self-comment" is also contradicted by Hehe daoren's 呵呵道人 comment (3.857). This complicates Wu Cuncun's argument that the comments attributed to these two were actually written by the author himself; see her "*Bian er chai yu Yichun xiangzhi de niandai kaozheng*," p. 67.

10. For a discussion of this story, see Vitiello, "Exemplary Sodomites," pp. 163–80; and idem, "The Fantastic Journey of an Ugly Boy."

woman or lesbian relationships are an important issue in the novel's exploration of the ramifications of *qing* and *yu*.[11]

As a novel that focuses on *qing* and the image of women in a large family, *Lin Lan Xiang* is considered by some to have anticipated in many ways the eighteenth-century masterpiece *Honglou meng*. Some scholars have specifically argued that *Lin Lan Xiang* is an important historical link between *Jin Ping Mei* and *Honglou meng*.[12] Although the influence of *Jin Ping Mei* on *Lin Lan Xiang* is rather obvious, the latter's relationship with *Honglou meng* is complicated by its dating. The dating of *Lin Lan Xiang* is a serious problem not only because we know little about its author, Suiyuan xiashi 隨緣下士 (by no means an uncommon case in dealing with traditional fiction), but also because the earliest extant edition of this novel dates to 1838. Consequently, the novel is variously held to have been written during the late Ming, the early Qing, or as late as the Jiaqing 嘉慶 (1796–1820) or Daoguang 道光 (1821–50) reign periods of the Qing.[13] Based on the limited data available, I tend to accept the theory that *Lin Lan Xiang* was written during the early Qing. In the only relatively substantial discussion of the dating of this novel known to me, Chen Hong provides some persuasive clues suggesting that the novel probably was written during this period, although most of his evidence is circumstantial.[14]

11. "Lesbian" and "lesbianism" are loaded terms that defy easy definition. I use these terms in a rather broad sense that includes what have generally been understood as "romantic friendships," which can be homoerotic, though not necessarily homosexual, as understood and explored in Adrienne Rich, "Compulsory Heterosexuality and Lesbian Existence"; and in Lillian Faderman, *Surpassing the Love of Men*. Of relevance to my discussion here is also Cosslett, *Woman to Woman*. Aware of the possible risks involved in applying such a hotly contested and deeply politicized term from the West to a little-studied but very complex cultural and social phenomenon in late imperial China, I wish there was a better alternative. The understanding of what constitutes "a lesbian identity" is an especially thorny issue in dealing with the "history" of lesbianism before this century. For general discussions, see Vicinus, "Introduction": and idem, "'They Wonder to Which Sex I Belong.'"

12. See, e.g., Yu Zhiyuan, "*Lin Lan Xiang* lun" (a slightly different version of this same article was published as an appendix, or "Fulu" 附錄, in *Lin Lan Xiang*, published by Chunfeng wenyi chubanshe, pp. 498–516); Zhang Jun, "Lun *Lin Lan Xiang* yu *Honglou meng*"; Rolston, "*Lin Lan Xiang* yu *Jin Ping Mei*"; and idem, "A Missing Link Between the *Jin Ping Mei* and the *Honglou meng*?" I am grateful to David Rolston for providing me with the copies of these two essays.

13. See Cao Yibing's preface to *Lin Lan Xiang* (facsimile reprint of the 1838 ed.), p. 1.

14. Chen Hong, "*Lin Lan Xiang* chuangzuo niandai xiaokao." Chen bases his arguments mainly on the descriptions of the city of Beijing in the novel and on their relationships to the

As many have pointed out, the three characters in the title *Lin Lan Xiang* derive from the names of the three central female characters: *lin* refers to Lin Yunping, the first wife of Geng Lang, the male protagonist; *xiang* refers to Ren Xiang'er, the fourth wife; and *lan* refers to Yan Mengqing, the second wife. Obviously, the character *lan* does not appear in Yan Mengqing's name; rather, it alludes to *Zuozhuan* 左傳 (The Zuo commentary): Duke Wen of Zheng's favorite consort, Yanji, dreamed (*meng*) of *lan*, or orchid (Yanji *menglan* 燕姞夢蘭).[15] The practice of entitling a work of fiction by combining elements from the names of female characters became quite common after *Jin Ping Mei*. The resemblances do not end there, however. The commentator Jilü sanren 寄旅散人 repeatedly draw parallels to *Jin Ping Mei* in his comments on *Lin Lan Xiang*.[16] Like *Jin Ping Mei*, *Lin Lan Xiang* is about a polygamous family composed of six wives and a husband, and the male protagonist Geng Lang shares Ximen Qing's credulity and susceptibility to his

---

historical changes the city underwent. He concludes that the novel was most probably written during the Kangxi 康熙 reign period (1662–1722). Chen's conclusions have been accepted by many other Chinese scholars; see Qi Yukun et al., eds., *Zhongguo gudai xiaoshuo yanbian shi*, p. 377; and Zhang Jun, *Qingdai xiaoshuo shi*, p. 146.

15. *Lin Lan Xiang* (Chunfeng wenyi), 1.1. See "Xuangong sannian" 宣公三年, in Yang Bojun, *Chunqiu Zuozhuan zhu*, pp. 673–74. Further references to the novel, unless otherwise noted, are to this edition, which is, as far as I know, the only modern typeset edition. One problem with this edition is that all the interlineal comments in the 1838 edition are printed at the end of each chapter in the form of "endnotes," which, to say the least, are inconvenient to the reader and force the reader to re-create the immediate context of the comments.

16. Chapter-end comments, 58.451 and 62.480; comment no. 46 (63.490; from this point on, interlineal comments are cited with three numbers: chapter number followed by page number and then by comment number). Jilü sanren's comments are quite substantial and often very illuminating, and I refer to them frequently below. Some scholars believe that the commentator and the author might be the same person (see, e.g., McMahon, *Shrews, Misers, and Polygamists*, p. 207). However, the nature of some of the comments is such that, without newly unearthed independent evidence outside the text of the novel, we may have to conclude that the commentator was someone other than the author himself. For instance, consider the comment at the end of chapter 54: "Throughout *Lin Lan Xiang* there are many unnecessary descriptions (*zhuibi* 贅筆) like this. However, I was not able to have them expunged" (54.420). The commentator seems to be suggesting either that the author did not follow his advice (if he knew the author personally) or that he was unable to do a thorough editing/rewriting when the novel was being published or republished (in traditional China an editor/commentator always took such liberties with a fictional work when publishing or republishing it). For a discussion of the complicated relationship between "commentator" and "author," see my "Author(ity) and Reader in Traditional Chinese *Xiaoshuo* Commentary."

concubines' slanders of one another.[17] However, what is more interesting for my purposes here is how *Lin Lan Xiang* consciously or unconsciously departs from *Jin Ping Mei*.

Unlike *Jin Ping Mei*, in which physical desire, or *yu*, is the dominant factor, *Lin Lan Xiang* focuses on the ramifications of *qing*. Furthermore, what is carefully explored in this novel is not only the role played by *qing* in a heterosexual context (say, that between Geng Lang and his wives) but also, perhaps even more significantly, that played by *qing* among women, especially among several of Geng's wives. In *Jin Ping Mei*, the relationships among women are often characterized by rivalry and animosity. Almost every woman is vying for the attention and favor of Ximen Qing, the man of the household. In *Lin Lan Xiang*, although competing with other wives is still an important issue for certain women, such as Ren Xiang'er, who resembles Pan Jinlian in many ways, a new element emerges in the relationship of the three wives Lin Yunping, Yan Mengqin, and Xuan Ainiang—their mutual attachment. Xuan Ainiang consents to marry Geng Lang, whom Lin Yunping and Xuan Ainiang have already married, not because she feels attracted to him but because this is the only way she can fulfill her wish to live with the two women she loves. In other words, what brings them together is their *qing* for one another as *women* rather than their common feelings for the same man.

The stories of how the three women become so attached to one another before they marry Geng Lang are the focus of the early part of the novel. First, we are told that Lin Yunping and Xuan Ainiang are relatives. They grow up together and become deeply attached. They wish they could stay together forever (自幼相親, 本期長久; 11.84). The second line of the couplet/title of chapter 4 is "The Two Girls Have a Love Talk in a Secret Room" (二小姐密室談情). In this chapter the two girls engage in a sort of "pure conversation" (*qingtan* 清談) while drinking tea and appreciating the snow-covered garden. Viewing the snow-covered trees and hills, they compare each other to *yushan* 玉山 (jade mountain) and *yushu* 玉樹 (jade tree). In traditional literature, both terms were often used to describe someone's beauty, especially that of a talented young man.[18] Xuan Ainiang, feeling the

17. For a more detailed discussion of the relationship between *Jin Ping Mei* and this novel, see Rolston, "*Lin Lan Xiang* yu *Jin Ping Mei*."

18. For an example of this usage, see the biography of Pei Kai 裴楷 attached to the biography of Pei Xiu 裴秀 in *Jinshu*, *juan* 35, p. 1048. On the same page, Pei Kai is also referred to

inadequacy of the gender bias of the linguistic convention, asks Lin Yunping why these two terms are not used to describe women too. Lin Yunping then asks: "How about my comparing you to 'jade tree' and 'jade mountain'?" However, the power of convention can nevertheless be felt in Xuan Ainiang's answer: "If you compare me to jade tree and jade mountain, you must be my jade person (*yuren* 玉人)!" (4.27). Here Xuan Ainiang builds on Lin Yunping's comparison of herself (Xuan Ainiang) to jade tree and jade mountain by saying that she, as a "man," must have a jade person, or a female lover, to match. "Jade person" is a euphemism for lover (either male or female). For example, in the famous romantic Tang tale *Yingying zhuan* 鶯鶯傳 (The story of Yingying), one line from the poem by the female protagonist Yingying reads: "When the flower shadow on the wall moves, / I thought it was my jade man coming" (拂墻花影動, 疑是玉人來).[19] At the same time, however, Xuan Ainiang is herself reaffirming the gender bias of the linguistic convention that she initially tried to challenge when she assumes the voice of a "man." This reaffirmation is shared by Lin Yunping when she retorts: "If I become a man, you must address me as 'jade tree' and 'jade mountain,'" an acknowledgment that both terms, which may seem rather phallic to a modern reader, should only be used to describe men.

In other contexts, *yushan* can also refer to one's body, as in the famous erotic scene "Xunmeng" 尋夢 in *Mudan ting*: "As he laid down my body (*yushan*), 'smoke issued from jade in warm of sun'" (待把俺玉山推倒, 便日暖玉生煙).[20] This particular usage of *yushan* as referring to "body" is confirmed in *Lin Lan Xiang* by Lin Yunping's maid Zhi'er, when she quotes a line from Li Bai's 李白 (701–62) poem "Xiangyang ge" 襄陽歌: "The jade mountain collapses by itself without being pushed down by others" (玉山自倒非人推) (4.27).[21] Li Bai, in his poem, is talking about being drunk, a typical privilege enjoyed by a man. But Zhu'er quotes this line to describe the two women's *qing*, or admiration, for each other. Underscoring the sapphic nature of their conversation, Xuan Ainiang's maid Xi'er jokingly re-

---

as *yuren*. This indicates that sometimes both *yushan* and *yuren* can be used to describe a handsome or beautiful person. For *yushu*, see "Yanyu" 言語 in Liu Yiqing, *Shishuo xinyu jiaojian*, p. 82.

19. "Yingying zhuan," in Wang Bijiang, *Tangren xiaoshuo*, p. 136.

20. Tang Xianzu, *Mudan ting*, p. 66; see also Birch, *The Peony Pavilion*, p. 59. Birch translates *yushan* as "jade limbs" instead of "body."

21. Li Bai, *Quanji*, *juan* 7, p. 371.

marks that she wishes one of the two mistresses and one of their maids could become men so that they could all marry each other as husbands and wives (4.28). Later, Madame Hua, Lin Yunping's aunt, reiterates this wish by observing that the two girls are so close that they look like an inseparable young couple. "If one of them were a man, the parents could have saved themselves the trouble of having to look for two sons-in-law" (4.29). The commentator Jilü sanren labels what has just happened between the two women an important "pledge of love," or *dingqing* 定情 (4.31.32); and later in chapter 13 the narrator uses this same word *dingqing* to describe what transpires between Yan Mengqing and Xuan Ainiang (13.98). This interesting exchange between the two female lovers, or *qingren*, captures the ambiguous nature of "lesbian" discourse in the novel as a whole: in trying to challenge the norms (in this case, the heterosexual norms), it often ends up duplicating and even reaffirming the values of the norms (more about this later). On the one hand, the female protagonists try to challenge the gender bias associated with words such as "jade tree" or "jade mountain," and, yet, on the other hand, they cannot help relying on such biased linguistic convention to communicate their *qing*.

After Lin Yunping marries Geng Lang, Xuan Ainiang misses her so much that one day she inscribes a poem on a wall when she and her family are on an outing to sweep the ancestors' graves. This poem is seen by Yan Mengqing, who is able to guess from the four-line riddle attached to the poem that its author is probably a woman. She begins to ponder:

> This woman must be full of *qing* (*duoqing* 多情). Having grown up in the boudoir, I haven't met in person anyone who can be my soul mate (*zhiji*), and even now I can only read a poem by such a woman. . . . Following her rhyme, I must compose a matching poem to be inscribed beside hers on the wall. If by any chance she comes here again, we will be able to empathize with each other and become a pair of soul mates without even seeing each other (不見面的知己). (7.51)

After finishing the poem, Yan Mengqing forgets to pick up a gold hairpin she removed a moment earlier. The poems by Xuan Ainiang and Yan Mengqing center on the theme of separation and loneliness. Later, Xuan Ainiang, after reading Yan Mengqing's matching poem on the wall, which reveals that its author is suffering from the same frustrations as she is (*tongbian xianlian* 同病相憐), is able to identify the author as Yan Mengqing, who is a well-known figure because of her filial act of offering herself to receive her father's punishment for his alleged wrongdoings. This experience makes Xuan Ainiang wonder whether finding a soul mate is really as difficult as others have suggested (7.52). Meanwhile, Yan Mengqing has become anxious because she is not sure about the gender identity of the writer of the poem. It would be scandalous, she feels, if she has inadvertently matched a poem written by a man. For Yan Mengqing, whom the commentator repeatedly dubbed a "puritan" (*daoxue* 道學),[22] an exchange of poems of this nature between two women is acceptable only as long as no man is involved.[23]

A few years later, in chapter 11, much to the delight of the two women, they discover that they are neighbors when a chunk of the wall between the gardens of their households collapses after a heavy rainfall. After they confirm the authorship of the poems, Yan Mengqing sighs: "We didn't find out that we have been soul mates (*zhiji*) for three years until today. We would not have even known this if we hadn't met each other by coincidence today!" (11.84). Then Xuan Ainiang complains that she lost Lin Yunping when Lin married Geng Lang and now she is going to lose Yan Mengqing because Yan is about to marry the same man. "Now you are going to desert me and marry Mr. Geng in order to be with Sister Lin for ever" (11.84). This provokes a long, inspired speech on *qing* from the "passionate" puritan Yan Mengqing:

This is the fate for many people of *qing*. If one's *qing* can find a perfect match in another (*qing de xiangqi* 情得相契), then even death becomes as good as being alive; if

22. Consider the interlineal comment (7.55.29): "Mengqing is a puritan (*daoxue ren* 道學人), but she is capable of writing love poems (*yanqing zhizuo* 言情之作). Even people such as Guangping [Shu Lin 舒璘, 1136–99] of the Song dynasty could produce 'Rhapsody on Plum Blossoms' ('Meihua fu' 梅花賦), which expresses the feelings of happiness, anger, sadness, and delight." Elsewhere (7.55.34) the commentator again blames Yan Mengqing's regret over writing the matching poem on "the bad habit shared by all the 'puritans'" (*daoxue tongbing* 道學通病).

23. Cf. Dorothy Ko's discussions of the friendship among Ming-Qing women poets in *Teachers of the Inner Chamber*, pp. 262–74. She notes (pp. 270, 272) that "although explicit references to another woman's bewitching waist or swaying steps [in a woman's poems] may have been considered in bad taste, attraction between women itself was acceptable in the gender system of seventeenth-century China" and that "erotic feelings" for another woman were expressed in poems by women poets. Ko, however, does not use the term "lesbianism" to describe such female friendships; see also ibid., p. 344*n*49. R. H. van Gulik (*Sexual Life in Ancient China*, p. 163) observes that female homosexuality was "quite common" and "viewed with tolerance" in traditional China. Except for a brief reference to Li Yu's play *Lianxiang ban*, van Gulik does not elaborate or provide further "evidence." See also Hinsch, *Passions of the Cut Sleeve*, pp. 173–78, for a brief discussion of "lesbianism" in traditional China.

one's *qing* cannot find an outlet (*qing bude shen* 情不得伸), then being alive is no better than death. My heart has been as dead as ashes since my late father was charged by the court with wrongdoing. However, my *qing* was stirred when I read your poem. This *qing* of mine found its first chance of an outlet in today's meeting with you. I am not sure if I will live or die for the sake of *qing*. From now on could we often exchange *qing* with each other? (11.85)

Yan Mengqing and Xuan Ainiang agree that the best way to sustain the *qing* among the three of them (including Lin Yunping) is for Xuan Ainiang to marry Geng Lang too (*tongshi* 同事; 11.85). The reality of the situation forces them into this: "A man can find his soul mates (*zhiji*) everywhere in the world. But for a woman, the chance is almost once in a thousand years (千秋難遇)" (11.85). The commentator is quick to point out that "Ainiang consents to this marriage because she wants to be with her soul mates rather than because she feels attracted to the handsome young man Geng Lang" (愛娘之嫁,爲知己而然,非私耿朗美少年也; 11.87.40). The commentator uses the derogatory word *si* 私 to characterize Xuan Ainiang's possible heterosexual feelings toward a man and to contrast them with the more admirable attachment of *qing* between her and another woman (more about *si* below).

Later Yan Mengqing gives Xuan Ainiang another of her gold hairpins as a token of her pledge of *qing* (the other gold hairpin, which she left on the wall, was picked up by Geng Lang): if in future she does not follow through on her pledge of *qing*, she will suffer the fate of a short marriage (伉儷不得長久), just like the separation her pair of gold hairpins have suffered (11.85). Here she is rather ambiguous as to whether the word *kangli* 伉儷 (a married couple) refers to her marriage with Geng Lang or is a metaphor for her relationship with her women friends/lovers. However, other images in the chapter such as repeated references to a pair of flying dragonflies (11.83–84) and the words the women use (such as "men and women in love" or *youqing nannü* 有情男女; 11.85) seem to give this exchange of *qing* between them an implicit significance that is at least potentially lesbian.

Much later in the novel, Yan Mengqing paints Xuan Ainiang's portrait. Xuan Ainiang has a suggestion: "Since we are so attached to each other (*tongxin* 同心), why don't you also paint yourself into [my] portrait so that we can be companions to each other in the picture (何不將自己也畫上作個伴侶)?" Yan Mengqing does so in order that their mutual love will be preserved even after her death (34.265). Significantly, the author uses the word *qingren* or "lover" in the second line of the couplet/title of chapter 34: "Paint a Portrait of the Dead in Advance to Keep a Lover Companion" (寫遺肖情人作伴). Commenting on Xuan Ainiang's initial request that Yan Mengqing paint her portrait—"Sister, please don't begrudge the time spent in painting a portrait of me because I cannot see my own appearance" (34.265), the commentator specifically quotes a poetic couplet from the legendary female talent Xiaoqing 小青: "The slender figure reflected in the spring water, / you should pity me while I pity you" (瘦影自臨春水照, 卿須憐我我憐卿) to emphasize Xuan Ainiang's narcissism (34.267.25),[24] an important aspect of *qing* also celebrated in the "Self-portrait" scene in *Mudan ting,* in which Du Liniang, before dying, paints a self-portrait for her dream-lover (see Chapter 3). Of course, Du's lover is a man. Xiaoqing was the most celebrated female reader of *Mudan ting,* and she is said to have died from reading the play. Obviously, the commentator expected readers to get the implicit intertextual reference to *Mudan ting.* However, what makes the reference more interesting is the possible lesbian implications suggested in the novel. The commentator further points out:

> The only thing under Heaven that cannot be falsified is *qing.* Whether it is love between a man and a woman that will last one hundred years or a man with another man or a woman with another woman, so long as they love each other wholeheartedly (*qingtou yihe* 情投意合), they will make a pledge of eternal union. This is why Mengqing and Ainiang are painted together. Now they can be considered a loving couple in this world (*shijian qinglü* 世間情侶). (34.267.27)

Nor are the novel's appropriations limited to *Mudan ting.* Motifs common in scholar-beauty romances of heterosexual love, such as a chance encounter through a hole in the garden wall, an exchange of poems, and the accidental leaving and picking up of ornaments like hairpins are used in this novel to describe the flowering of a lesbian relationship.

Love between two women who eventually marry the same man is also the theme of the play *Lianxiang ban* 憐香伴 (The fragrant companion) by Li Yu; Du Liniang is also the model of *qing* emulated by one of the female lovers, Miss Cao Yuhua, in that play.[25] *Lixiang Ban* was written around 1651,

24. For discussions of the legends surrounding the figure of Xiaoqing and her role in the female reception of *Mudan ting,* see Widmer, "Xiaoqing's Literary Legacy"; and Ko, *Teachers of the Inner Chambers,* pp. 91–112.

25. Li Yu, *Lianxiang ban,* vol. 4, pp. 69–70.

and the author of *Lin Lan Xiang* may have read it, if we accept the theory that *Lin Lan Xiang* is a work of the Kangxi period. There are some similarities between this play and the novel in terms of the relationships between women who eventually marry the same man and the vocabulary used to describe such a relationship. Like the relationship between Yan Mengqing and Xuan Ainiang, the love of Cui Jianyun and Cao Yuhua in *Lianxiang ban* is initiated by an exchange of poems when they meet by chance in a temple. To ensure that they can live together in the future, Cui Jianyun proposes that Cao Yuhua marry Cui's husband. Their *qing* is also described in the traditional vocabularies of *zhiji* and the mutual appreciation of talent and beauty.[26] Like the joking conversation between Lin Yunping and Xuan Ainiang on becoming husband and wife in *Lin Lan Xiang*, Cui Jianyun and Miss Cao also discuss the question who will be the "husband" and who the "wife." And their maids, like those in *Lin Lan Xiang*, also debate this same question. Later, when Cui Jianyun and Miss Cao perform the wedding ritual (*baitang* 拜堂), Cui dresses in men's clothing (something that does not happen in *Lin Lan Xiang*). And the word *kangli* 伉儷 (married couple) is used to describe their union: in Scene 5, the Buddha expresses his determination that these two women form a couple (*jiecheng kangli* 結成伉儷; p. 17).

Sometimes, the *qing* between the two comes very close to the erotic, and they are not shy about expressing their attraction. Admiring Miss Cao's beauty, Cui Jianyun sighs: "Look at the way she appears without any effort of makeup. Pure natural charm! She is really a rare beauty. Not to mention a man, even I, a woman, am aroused by her" (動起好色的心來; p. 20). In Scene 10, after the "wedding" ceremony, Cui Jianyun again is very explicit: "Looking at your pretty face, I can't help becoming wild (不覺輕狂起來). . . . As I become wild, your 'spring heart' should also be stirred" (p. 33). In their relationship, since Cui Jianyun is the "husband," she often views things from a male perspective and takes the aggressive, active role; Miss Cao, as the "wife," always takes the passive role a woman is expected to assume. She pledges that since a chaste woman does not marry twice (烈婦不更二夫), she is determined to live with Cui Jianyun forever by marrying Cui's husband (p. 33). Of course, in such a relationship, marrying a man, which is a precondition for their union, does not compromise their chastity. Conse-

26. Scenes 5, 6 and 10, in Li Yu, *Lianxiang ban*, pp. 17, 21–22, 34. Hereafter page references are given in parentheses in the text.

quently, as in the male homosexual relationships described in *Bian er chai*, the patriarchal gender hierarchy of heterosexuality has to be reaffirmed here in this lesbian relationship.[27]

Moreover, the author is careful to assure us that nothing "real" happens between these two women. Cao Yuhua's maid tells us in scene 13 that "although the husband-wife relationship is not real, [her mistress's] lovesickness is real" (p. 42). Later in scene 21, through the voice of Miss Cao, the author reassures the audience about the platonic nature of their love: "Stupid maid, you only know the cause of lovesickness, but you don't know how to distinguish between *qing* and *yu*. What arises from one's heart is *qing*, whereas what happens in the bedroom is *yu*. If one gets lovesick because of bedroom desire (*siqing* 私情), even if one dies of lovesickness, one will become nothing more than a ghost of lust (*yugui* 欲鬼) and can never be considered a real lover (*qingchi* 情痴). Du Liniang is the only person of *qing* throughout all of history" (pp. 69–70). Then she continues to compare her situation to that of Du Liniang and insists that she and Cui Jianyun will die for love of each other. Despite the homoerotic innuendoes, the emphasis in *Lianxiang ban* is on *qing*, in this case a sort of "spiritual lesbianism," as a solution to the problem of jealousy among the wives in a polygamous marriage,[28]

27. Cf. Hanan's (*The Invention of Li Yu*, p. 162) observation: "Throughout, Miss Cui's thoughts have been erotic and practical, Miss Cao's passionate and idealistic, expressed in moral terms. The two maids, in their farcical imitation of their mistresses' wedding, are coarse and ribald, supplying the explicit physical reference that is lacking even in Miss Cui's speech and song."

28. Here we may recall a "lesbian" incident in chapter 58 of *Honglou meng*. The actress Ouguan, who usually plays the male *xiaosheng* 小生 roles, falls in love with her fellow actress Diguan, who usually plays female *xiaodan* 小旦 roles. After Diguan dies, Ouguan falls in love with another actress, Ruiguan, who replaces Diguan in playing the *xiaodan*. Ouguan, however, continues to commemorate her former lover, even though she is now in love with another actress. Her rationale is that it is permissible for her to behave this way because a man may remarry as long he does not forget his deceased wife. This is certainly a grand gesture of genuine *qing*. No wonder Baoyu is so moved by this story (*Honglou meng*, 58.827). What is interesting, however, is that in this lesbian relationship, Ouguan obviously views herself as the active partner and thus entitled to enjoying the privileges of a man. For instance, it would not be right for Ruiguan to fall in love with another actress even if Ouguan somehow dies, since she is the passive partner in this relationship and therefore she should behave as a "woman" should in a heterosexual relationship. For a woman to remarry is not an honorable thing to do, just as Miss Cao claims in her pledge of her love to Cui. From this example in *Honglou meng*, we can see how the gender values of patriarchal gender hierarchy are reaffirmed in an even more subtle manner in this otherwise very loving lesbian relationship.

a message to be repeated in *Lin Lan Xiang*, although with some serious complications.

One thing that distinguishes *Lin Lan Xiang* from *Lianxiang ban* is that in the novel, although nothing sexually explicit ever transpires among the three wives, sexual acts that are explicitly lesbian are indeed depicted. This substantially complicates the implications of lesbianism in the novel. Widow Li is disappointed when a blind male fortuneteller fails to show up and resorts to a sexual tool called *jiao xiansheng* 角先生 (dildo) for self-satisfaction. Later she begins to share this secret pleasure with Hongyu, the maid of Ren Xiang'er. The two become a loving couple (*moni* 莫逆) with one playing the role of a male and the other the role of a female (*huxiang cixiong* 互相雌雄). When their affair is exposed, both are expelled from the household. However, the commentator has a very interesting view of this scandal: "There are many sexually deprived or starved women and girls such as Widow Li and Hongyu. The *jiao xiansheng* would render a great service if its use can prevent adulteries (*chanxue yuqiang* 鑽穴逾墻)" (28.222.49).[29] Ironically, "adulterous acts" such as *chanxue yuqiang* (sneaking through an opening or climbing over the wall) are exactly what Yan Mengqing and Xuan Ainiang do when they meet each other for the first time in the garden. Obviously, for the commentator, only heterosexual affairs are scandalous, because lesbian affairs (even those involving explicit sexual activities) are something a woman resorts to in order to compensate for the unavailability of man. The novel *Xu Jin Ping Mei* contains more graphic as well as much more detailed descrip-

---

See the reference to the issue of "jealousy" in scene 12 of *Lianxiang ban*, pp. 40–41. Scholars have speculated that *Lianxiang ban* might have something to do with Li Yu's own polygamous marriage situation. See the preface to the play written by the author's friend Yu Wei 虞巍 (p. 3) and the discussions in Sun Kaidi, "Li Liweng yu *Shi'er lou*," in idem, *Cangzhou houji*, p. 177; and Hanan, *The Invention of Li Yu*, pp. 15–16. The kind of lesbian love among wives married to a same man celebrated in *Lianxiang ban* became so famous that in the eighteenth-century author Shen Fu's 沈復 (b. 1763) autobiography *Fusheng liuji* 浮生六記 (Six records of a floating life), the play is explicitly mentioned when the wife tries to arrange for one of her good friends, a prostitute, to marry her husband as a concubine. For a discussion of *Fusheng liuji*, see Ropp, "Between Two Worlds" (for the issue of implicit lesbianism in this work, see ibid., pp. 114–18).

29. This comment on lesbian sexuality, although surprisingly tolerant, is nevertheless very sexist. However, elsewhere, the commentator does express his displeasure with man's obsession with women's "bound feet" (10.80.59). If we accept the dating of *Lin Lan Xiang* as a work of the Kangxi period and see the commentator as a contemporary of the author, then this anticipated Li Ruchen's similar view in his novel *Jinghua yuan* of more than a century later.

tions of lesbian sexual acts between Guijie (Pan Jinlian's reincarnation) and Meiyu (Chunmei's reincarnation) in chapters 32 and 41. Once again, their homosexual activities are presented more as their attempt to compensate for the unavailability of the "real thing." Moreover, in *Xu Jin Ping Mei*, the very need to seek compensation is meant to illustrate the karmic retribution these two "lecherous" women receive for their sins in *Jin Ping Mei*.

Lesbian sexuality as a substitute for heterosexual sex is presented as qualitatively different from the "spiritual" love of Lin, Yan, and Xuan; their relationship is nonsexual and thus defendable as an expression of pure *qing* instead of the physical *yu* that characterizes sexual lesbianism. Whereas lesbian *qing* is celebrated, lesbian *yu* is categorically denounced (as condemned by Miss Cao in scene 21 of *Lianxiang ban*). In fact, in *Lin Lan Xiang*, sexual lesbianism is deliberately contrasted with spiritual or nonsexual lesbianism, which, significantly, is emphasized as posing no threat to the absolute male dominance of a polygamous household. On the contrary, the novel seems to suggest, as does Li Yu's *Lianxiang ban*, that a husband should find nonsexual love among his wives and concubines desirable since such lesbian *qing* will help minimize jealousy and rivalry among them, a rare "blessing" for a polygamous man (as demonstrated in the cases of Ximen Qing in *Jin Ping Mei* or Chao Yuan and his reincarnation Di Xichen in *Xingshi*). In a way, this may even be read as a solution to the problem raised in *Jin Ping Mei* of the deadly disputes and competition among jealous wives and concubines in a polygamous marriage. Of course, not every wife or concubine in *Lin Lan Xiang* subscribes to "female attachment": Ren Xiang'er insists on playing the role of Pan Jinlian and wreaking havoc in this polygamous household. However, once lesbian love develops beyond the "spiritual" and becomes an explicitly sexual relationship, it is to be viewed with disapproval and not tolerated. Therefore, women who engage in physical affairs with each other, such as Widow Li and Hongyu, have to be punished accordingly.

What is so intriguing about the representation of lesbianism in *Lin Lan Xiang* is that sometimes the distinctions between the sexual and the nonsexual become problematic and difficult to maintain. These two kinds of lesbian relationships are not as different as they may first appear to be. The potentially homoerotic nature of many poems and the various suggestive remarks exchanged among them notwithstanding, Yan Mengqing and her female friends or, more precisely, *qingren* or lovers, as they are sometimes called in the novel, are quite conscious of the potential danger of failing to differentiate themselves from those "sexual lesbians." After the affair between Widow Li and the maid Hongyu is exposed, Yan Mengqing remarks jokingly that she would not mind sharing a bed with Xuan Ainiang, as long as Xuan does not bring along the gadget (*wujian* 物件) that Widow Li used to trick the maid (30.235). Such self-consciousness belies an uneasiness on the part of Yan Mengqing that their *qing* may give rise to the appearance of impropriety.

Whereas the condemned lesbian sexuality is presented as arising from an attempt to compensate for the absence or unavailability of men, the nonsexual or spiritual lesbian love seems to be caused by a disappointment with men or at least a "deficiency" in men, despite the three women's efforts to keep their love an "innocent" female friendship. It is nevertheless compensatory in the sense that women such as Yan Mengqing, when frustrated in a heterosexual marriage, need to find, within the restrictive confines of the inner chambers in a polygamous environment, a "domestic community" to turn to for emotional consolation if not sensual diversion. For a virtuous woman such as Yan Mengqing, a relationship with her fellow wives is a means of coming to terms with what would otherwise be a painful polygamous marriage by making the best of a bad situation and celebrating the opportunities for female comradery and emotional fulfillment among the wives and concubines (something a monogamous marriage paradoxically may not be able to offer), although such relationships are not supposed to be sexual. This is quite different from the situation in *Lianxiang ban*, in which the husband is a perfect *caizi*, or a handsome and talented young man. In *Lin Lan Xiang*, Geng Lang fails to be impartial in his relationships with his wives (somewhat like Ximen Qing in *Jin Ping Mei*).

What further problematizes the explicit condemnation of lesbian sexuality is the novel's rather curious conclusion, in which the expelled sexual lesbians Widow Li and Hongyu reappear. No longer a widow, Li is addressed as "Grannie Li" and is now married to a teacher who trains actors, a profession known as a hotbed for homosexual relationships. The narrator informs the reader that since all the people associated with the Geng family have passed away, no one mentions it any more. Fortunately, many years ago, Grannie Li, who witnessed the family's ups and downs, wrote a play based on them. The play, however, is not staged until several years after the death of Grannie Li. When it is, it becomes very popular. Then after the play loses its popularity, Hongyu, who was a brothel madam for many years and is now a blind *tanci* 彈詞 (poetic narrative) writer and singer, composes a script based on the stories of the Geng family and begins to perform it. This, too, becomes very popular until she decides to take religious vows (*chujia* 出家). The novel ends with the following passage in which the author/narrator directly addresses the reader: "To record all the events that have happened during this one hundred years, I wrote this marvelous tale (*she yi qitan* 設一奇談) for the descendants of these lovers. Should the author of this marvelous story consider himself someone outside the dream world of theater and *tanci* 彈詞? Someone might say yes. But I don't think so" (64.495). Obviously, by comparing this story to *tanci* and drama, the author/narrator is identifying himself/herself with the two lesbian characters, Widow Li and Hongyu, and suggesting to the reader that the novel is probably told from the perspective of these two women, who used to be lesbian lovers.[30] This suggestion becomes all the more significant because *tanci* was a popular narrative genre closely associated with women; by Qing times, most *tanci* were written by and for women.[31] It is tempting to speculate that the author of *Lin Lan Xiang* might have been a woman, although there is no hard evidence either for or against such speculation.

Appropriated in *Bian er chai* and *Lin Lan Xiang* to defend same-sex love, the ambiguous concept of *qing* almost always serves a paradoxical double function. On the one hand, the appeal to *qing* creates a space within which certain deviations from the norm, such as homosexuality, can be tolerated or even celebrated; on the other hand, this tolerance or celebration is based on the argument that this seemingly deviant behavior, when motivated by

30. Cf. McMahon's observation (*Misers, Shrews, and Polygamists*, p. 210): "What appears to be an actual case of lesbianism thus becomes a means of compassionate survival for these two women and a vehicle of eulogy for other women destroyed by their involvement with men." Of course, strictly speaking, Widow Li is also involved with men after her lesbian affair with Hongyu is exposed since she later marries the teacher.

31. For studies of *tanci* in English, see Sung, *The Narrative Art of Tsai-sheng-yüan*; and Siao-chen Hu, "Literary *tanci*." Of course, there are precedents in works of fiction and drama; often a *tanci* singer is said to retell the plot of a particular fiction or drama in this popular form to create a special "distance." For example, in chapter 12 of *Xiyou bu* Tripitaka and the Small King of the Moon are said to be listening to three blind women singing a *tanci* story titled *The Story of the Journey to the West* (*Xiyou tan* 西游談), and in Hong Sheng's (1645–1704) *Changsheng dian* 長生殿 (The palace of eternal youth), scene 38 is entitled "Tanci," and in that scene the musician Li Guinian tries to sing the story of the tragedy of Yang Guifei. What is significant in *Lin Lan Xiang* is that the female *tanci* singer is a lesbian and that her *tanci* story is at least in part a lesbian story.

genuine *qing*, vindicates the norms, such as chastity, filiality, and even polygamy, better than supposedly "normal" behavior can.[32] Here a same-sex relationship is defended by using the same strategy often employed to defend *qing*. Just like *qing*, which is said to enable people to become not only faithful lovers but also upright officials or chaste wives, same-sex love, although deviant according to many, is capable of being more normative than the norms if it is motivated by proper *qing*.

Of course, in *Lin Lan Xiang* the significance of *qing* is by no means confined to the representation of lesbianism. As pointed out above, lesbian desire is closely related to other forms of desire in the novel, and there is a constant and conscientious effort to distinguish *qing* from *yu* by desexualizing the former. The deliberate contrasting of spiritual lesbianism with sexual lesbianism is only one of many such discriminating tactics. In terms of heterosexual relationships as they operate in Geng Lang's polygamous household, the three wives who form a sort of alliance of lesbian *qing*, Lin Yunping, Yan Mengqing, and Xuan Ainiang, are contrasted to the other two, much-sexualized wives, Ren Xiang'er and Ping Caiyun. Just as they have managed to maintain their chastity in their spiritual lesbianism, the three women tend to resist, to varying degrees, the attempts by Geng Lang to sexualize or eroticize their conjugal relationships.

This tendency appears to be particularly strong in Yan Mengqing. This may account in part for the strained relationship between her and Geng Lang. Geng Lang's inclination to insist on eroticizing his relationship with Yan Mengqing becomes clear when they first meet each other after their engagement is canceled due to Yan's decision to offer herself to be punished in place of her father: in Geng Lang's eyes, Yan Mengqing's waist appears to be more slender than that of Bai Juyi's famous singsong girl Xiaoman (欺小蠻之楊柳),[33] and her bound feet are more delicate than those of the royal Consort Pan of the King of the Southern Qi monarchy (勝潘女之金蓮; 2.13).[34] Both of these historical figures are known for being sexy; one was a

32. This tactic is also employed by the narrator in Li Yu's story "A Male Mencius' Mother Raises Her Son Properly by Moving House Three Times." Ruilang, the gay lover, who assumes the passive role, turns out to be a "woman" more chaste than other "real women" and a better "mother" than all other "real" mothers.

33. "Shigan" 事感, in Meng Qi, *Benshi shi*, 13b–14a.

34. See the biographies of Feidi Donghun hou 廢帝東昏侯 and Wang Mao 王茂, in *Nanshi*, *juan* 5, p. 154, and *juan* 55, p. 1352, respectively.

sensuous singing girl, the other a seductive royal consort who turns the head of a king. The unusual reference to Consort Pan (Panfei 潘妃) as Pannü (潘女) should also alert the reader to the possible association with the notorious *yinfu* or woman of debauchery, Pan Jinlian, in *Jin Ping Mei*, since this six-character sentence, coincidentally or not, contains the full name of Pan Jinlian (潘金蓮), and it can also be read as "[her bound feet are] are more delicate than those of the woman whose last name is Pan."[35] Pan Jinlian, as her name suggests, is known for her delicate bound feet. The commentator tries to call the reader's attention to the author's possible motive for this description of Geng Lang's response to Yan Mengqing:

> The author does not mention how Yan Mengqing responds to Linzhao (Geng Lang) for fear of degrading (*tangtu* 唐突) Yan Mengqing. Only Linzhao's response is described so that the reader can see how infatuated he has become (*qingsi teshen* 情私特甚). I assume that the maid Chunwan is bound to tell her mistress later during the night that his eyes had been glued on her, apparently with no good intention (大不畜好意也). (2.15.77)

Here again the commentator uses the pejorative word *si* to describe Geng Lang's sexualized *qing*. Such *yu* or sexualized *qing* (*siqing* 私情) is precisely what, as a virtuous wife, Yan Mengqing later will try to shun in their relationship, as testified to by her comment to Geng Lang in his dream: "I do not want to burden you with passion (*er'nü siqing* 兒女私情) day and night" (37.286). This is one of the reasons Yan Mengqing has alienated Geng Lang, and the "sexy" Ren Xiang'er is able to secure his love for herself. The narrator again appeals to the concept of *siqing* to explain the reasons for Geng Lang's outpouring of sorrow after Ren Xiang'er's death: "Usually, in a sexual relationship, *qing* is more important than *li* [principle]. *Li* is the principle of a married couple, whereas *qing* is the sexual attraction between a man and a woman (*ernü siqing*). Since Geng Lang had been most intimate (*sixia* 私狎) with Xiang'er, their *qing* was therefore the deepest" (51.392).

In discussions of the implications of *qing* in the novel, several scholars have argued that the author is prioritizing *qing* over *li* by referring to the first sentence in the passage quoted above.[36] However, the entire remark presents a much more ambivalent view of *qing* (at least as *qing* is defined in the specific

35. I do not think this is a misprint. "Pannü" also appears in the 1838 edition of *Lin Lan Xiang*, 2.9a (p. 37).

36. See, e.g., Zhang Jun, "Lun *Lin Lan Xiang* yu *Honglou meng*," p. 71.

context here). This distaste for physical intimacy or "sexualized" *qing* is obviously shared by the commentator, who observes in his chapter-end comment on chapter 28, one of the two chapters with explicit descriptions of sex associated with lecherous characters in the novel:

> Throughout the entire novel, only chapter 10 and this chapter contain explicit scenes of fantasizing sex, and yet none of these is actually materialized [the commentator does not consider lesbian sex as "real" sex]. This is because it becomes boring as soon as people have actually done it (蓋成事實便索然矣). Imagine how tender a couple's feelings are (*heyang qingzhi* 何樣情致) before sexual intercourse and how they feel after sexual intercourse. This is something very obvious. (28.221)[37]

For Yan Mengqing, her main duty as a wife is to offer sound advice to her husband (or to remonstrate with him when necessary) and to help him manage the household, just as a royal minister is supposed to help his lord. She sees the relationship in terms of duty rather than passion. She should win respect and perhaps even *qing* from her husband because of her intelligence and virtue rather than because of the allure of her sexualized body. This reluctance to be sexualized may account for the humiliation Yan Mengqing feels when she is forced to allow Geng Lang to be intimate with her as part of her attempt to reconcile with him after her remonstration has alienated him. But he again turns away from her when he is accidentally reminded of her remonstration by his drink-soiled clothes. When Xuan Ainiang tries to arrange for the two to spend the night together to mend their damaged relationship, it must be the deeply felt humiliation that causes Yan Mengqing to burst out:

> No! This will never do. My meeting with him during the day was already an effort to use my body to win favor (*yise meiren* 以色媚人). Now my trying to please him again during the night is simply a case of surrendering my own self by appealing to [his] lust (*yiyin zixian* 以淫自獻). One cannot use sex and lust to force another to accommodate oneself. What would you do with me if he does not accommodate me? (32.248)

However, right after this outburst, Yan Mengqing is given a rare chance to offer her body to Geng Lang, this time in a manner completely devoid of

37. This view of purified *qing* finds more extreme as well as more elaborate expressions in the eighteenth-century novel *Yesou puyan*; see the discussion in Chapter 9.

sexual implications. Geng Lang gets sick, we are told, presumably because of his dissolute life-style (too much drinking and sex, precisely the activities Yan Mengqing has desperately tried to dissuade her husband from doing not only through her verbal remonstrations but also through her reluctance to allow her own body to be sexualized). Persuaded that one's flesh can help cure another's illness, she determines that this time her body be put to good use for her husband. She cuts off a finger to make a medicinal broth for him. Her desexualized body, literally as well as metaphorically, is good for her husband's health, which was ruined precisely because of his involvement with sexualized bodies (i.e., his overindulgence with his sexy concubines Ren Xiang'er and Ping Caiyun [*jiuse guodu* 酒色過度; 32.248]).[38] Of course, this is not the first time Yan Mengqing has sacrificed her body. Earlier in the novel, in order to save her father from punishment, she offers to become a palace lady, although she is able to maintain her chastity thanks to the help of a eunuch. Here we may recall Li Youxian in *Bian er chai*, who sells himself into a male brothel in order to pay his father's fine. His filial good intentions can be fulfilled in large part because he is able to attract a buyer with his feminine looks. Only a woman's body or the body of a feminine man can make possible such an expression of filiality.

Besides spiritual lesbianism, Yan Mengqing, a reader in a post-Freudian age is tempted to suspect, might be trying to find in such heroic acts of filiality or chastity a sublimated outlet for her long-repressed desires, which may be sexual or not. Conscientious denial of her own sexuality, like her repeated sacrifices first for her father and then for her husband, becomes the only effective way of vindicating her worth as a talented and virtuous woman, who is, however, never appreciated by the supposedly most important person in her life—her husband. This is probably why her friendship with Lin Yunping and Xuan Ainiang has become so important to her. Her life, after her marriage, can even be read as a persistent but frustrated effort to seek the recognition denied her by her husband. The commentator in his chapter-end comment on chapter 34 deplores that Yan Mengqing's marriage with her husband is in large measure ruined by her pursuit of empty fame (*xuming zhiwu* 虛名之誤; 34.266). Of course, as noted in Chapter 3, seeking

38. One section of McMahon's discussion of the novel (*Misers, Shrews, and Polygamists*, pp. 213–17) is entitled "The Polygamist's Sexy Concubines."

recognition of one's value and recognizing the worth of others are essential components of *qing* as defined in literati culture.

In contrast to the story of Yan Mengqing, passages dealing with Geng Lang's concubines, Ren Xiang'er and Ping Caiyun, are often dominated by sexual images, although the author of *Lin Lan Xiang* was much more restrained in this regard than the authors of *Jin Ping Mei* and *Bian er chai*. Chapter 10 is probably the most sexually explicit chapter in the novel. Mao Dagang 茅大剛, the most lecherous male character in the novel, meets his death as a result of overindulgence in sex (apparently he is intended to be read as another Ximen Qing). Although the name Mao Dagang has obvious phallic implications, the commentator (10.71.45) calls attention to his rather ironic *zi* 字 (courtesy name) Sirou 思柔 (thinking about the soft). When Mao Dagang begins to use potency pills to enhance his sexual prowess (10.75), alerting the reader to the intended parallel with Ximen Qing, the narrator repeats the cliché that one's desire is infinite but one's energy is limited, which the narrator of *Jin Ping Mei* cites when Ximen Qing collapses from sexual exhaustion. It is also in this "sexiest" chapter that Ping Caiyun meets a handsome young man riding a horse and shooting arrows. The descriptions of this young man—"he is in full control of his speed and rides back and forth in perfect rhythm" (控縱合宜來回有度), "catching the butterflies on the flower petal" (捕花蛺蝶), and "the dragonflies dipping over the water" (點水蜻蜓)—suggest that Ping Caiyun is probably hallucinating that she is having sexual intercourse with the man (10.73–74).[39] Later in this chapter, we learn that the woman with whom Mao Dagang had sex with the help of the black magic of a Taoist priest in the previous chapter is the sexually starved Ping Caiyun. Later Ping Caiyun is kidnapped by a villain and then saved by a knight-errant, who puts her in a box placed on Geng Lang's property. She is discovered by Geng and becomes his fifth wife. As the commentator points out in his chapter-end comment on chapter 28, chapters 10 and 28 are the two most explicit chapters in the novel as far as "debauchery" (*yindang* 淫蕩) is concerned (28.221). Whereas chapter 10 is a story of heterosexuality, chapter 28 contains scenes of lesbian sexuality; both

39. Butterflies and dragonflies are conventional metaphorical references to sexual acts. See, e.g., the verse near the end of chap. 6 of *Jin Ping Mei* (6.58); Roy, trans., *Plum in the Golden Vase*, 1: 491n26.

are cases of *yu* that are contrasted with the *qing* represented by the three wives, Lin, Yan, and Xuan.

The other sexy concubine, Ren Xiang'er, is married to Geng Lang after her father decides to give her to Geng as a token of gratitude for helping win his release from jail. The two maids who serve Ren Xiang'er are named Lüyun 綠雲 and Hongyu 紅雨; the final characters in their names, when combined, become *yunyu* 雲雨, a common Chinese euphemism for sexual intercourse. Hongyu later will be expelled from the household because of her lesbian affair with Widow Li. However, the maid who replaces her is given the same name Hongyu. These names are apparently designed to enhance the sexualized image of Ren Xiang'er.

Although indulgence in physical desire, or *siqing*, is explicitly condemned in the novel, the kind of puritanical (*daoxue*-like) *qing* represented by Yan Mengqing is also implicitly questioned. The author tries to present a better alternative in the person of Tian Chunwan, who is Yan Mengqing's personal maid and will eventually be promoted to be the sixth wife of Geng Lang after the death of her mistress. Tian Chunwan is a woman of *yi* 義 (righteousness), but her tactics in dealing with Geng Lang are much more effective than those of her mistress.[40] Making a virtue out of her humble origins as a maid, she is able to make Geng Lang feel much more comfortable, whereas Yan Mengqing, because of her reputation as a filial and chaste woman and her education, always makes him feel insecure. Moreover, Tian Chunwan manages to attract her husband by oscillating between "loving" and "cold" (似有情又似無情; 43.331). Her explanation of this ambivalence to Geng Lang itself epitomizes *youqing* and *wuqing*:

> Although I am asked by the Madame to serve you day and night, I have to observe the principles of the distinctions between servants and masters as well as those between men and women. I serve you wholeheartedly. This is why I may have appeared to be *youqing*. But I have to avoid the slightest appearance of improprieties. That is why I may have appeared to be *wuqing*. (43.331)

When asked by Geng Lang why she did not respond to his earlier flirtations, she explains:

> Not being plants or rocks, who among us people could claim to have no feelings at all? But I must not do harm to the morality of the family or violate the codes of

40. See McMahon's discussion in *Misers, Shrews, and Polygamists*, pp. 217–19.

proper behavior. Besides, a mistress would look down upon a maid, once the maid has a secret affair (*yousuo si* 有所私) [with the master]. Otherwise, how could I have hoped to enjoy the situation [I do] today? (43.331)

The dilemma, as the narrator observes, is: "When a talented young man's *qing* becomes excessive, it inevitably harms *yi*, whereas if a beautiful girl insists on *yi*, she will appear as if she were oblivious to *qing*" (正是才子情深, 過情則未免傷義; 佳人重義, 守義則恰似忘情; 51.395). Tian Chunwan's *yi* has tamed Geng Lang's *qing*: "I cannot allow a pretty girl who insists on being righteous (*shouyi jiaren* 守義佳人) to laugh at a talented young man deep in love (*duoqing caizi* 多情才子) such as myself" (51.396). However, Tian Chunwan as a character who is supposed to achieve the proper balance between *yi* (sometimes interchangeable with the concept of *li*) and *qing* is not always that convincing. The task of finding the perfect balance between *yi* and *qing* will continue to obsess many fiction writers of the seventeenth- and eighteenth-centuries, as we shall see in Chapters 8 and 9.

CHAPTER EIGHT
Qing and the Virtuous Body in Three Scholar-Beauty Romances

The seemingly sudden appearance of scholar-beauty fiction during the seventeenth century had not been adequately explained until fairly recently when scholars began to pay serious attention to a group of long-neglected fictional texts dating from the late thirteenth to the sixteenth century.[1] Students of traditional Chinese fiction have usually traced the origins of scholar-beauty fiction to stories of the love affair between Sima Xiangru 司馬相如 (179–117 B.C.) and Zhuo Wenjun 卓文君 (fl. 150–115 B.C.) of the Han dynasty and the famous Tang tale "Yingying zhuan." This left a gap of several centuries, however.[2] Some have also attempted to trace seventeenth-

1. The most comprehensive study of Yuan and Ming literary romances to date is Chen Yiyuan's *Yuan Ming zhongpian chuanqi xiaoshuo yanjiu*; see esp. chap. 1, "Xulun" (pp. 1–18), for a "generic" description of these texts. This study also provides detailed discussions of the textual evolution of many of these tales.

2. Chen Dakang (*Zhongguo tongsu xiaoshuo de lishi guiji*, pp. 33–66) deplores what he terms "a stagnant period of two hundred years" (approximately from the late fourteenth century to the mid-sixteenth century) in the history of Chinese fiction. This is exactly the period when the literary romance was popular. However, to judge from his recent article "Lun Yuan Ming zhongpian chuanqi xiaoshuo," which is one of the most substantial discussions of the relationship between the Ming literary romance and seventeenth-century scholar-beauty fiction that I have so far read, Chen has apparently revised his view of the "stagnant period."

century scholar-beauty fiction to dramatic works such as the *Xixiang ji* produced during this gap.[3]

An examination of long-neglected literary romances from the Yuan and Ming periods should convince us that they were the immediate predecessors of the scholar-beauty fiction of the seventeenth century.[4] Ye Dejun has estimated that approximately forty or more such literary romances were produced during the Ming.[5] About half of them are extant, largely because they were collected in a genre that became very popular during the Ming—the "anthologies of popular writings" (*tongsu leishu* 通俗類書), such as *Guose tianxiang* 國色天香 (The beautiful and the fragrant), which was compiled in 1587.[6]

These romances share several characteristics. They are written in literary Chinese. They usually deal with romantic love between a handsome and talented young man and an equally talented and beautiful young woman. The exchange of poems is almost always an important ingredient in the tale. Often there are extensive intertextual borrowings among these texts despite the fact they may have been produced a century or more apart. They are usually 20,000–30,000 characters long. The longest work, *Liu sheng milian ji* 劉生覓蓮記 (The story of Scholar Liu acquiring the lotuses), is close to 40,000 characters. This is fairly long compared with most literary tales from the Tang and Song periods, but much shorter than most novels. Some scholars have referred to them as "the romance-novella of the Yuan and Ming periods" (*Yuan Ming zhongpian chuanqi xiaoshuo* 元明中篇傳奇小說); others

3. See, e.g., Hessney, "Beautiful, Talented, and Brave," pp. 38–115. For a study of the scholar-beauty theme in Ming-Qing drama, see Yao, "*Cai-zi jia-ren*: Love Drama During the Yuan, Ming, and Qing Periods."

4. Wang Zhongmin was probably one of the first scholars to point out that these Ming literary romances were the immediate predecessors of the scholar-beauty fiction of the seventeenth century; see the entry on *Xiugu chunrong* in his *Zhongguo shanben shu tiyao*, p. 399. Although Wang's book was published in 1983, eight years after his death in 1975, Wang finished the book manuscript between 1939 and 1949. For another discussion of the possible influence of the literary romances of the early Ming on the development of scholar-beauty fiction, see Lin Chen, *Mingmo Qingchu xiaoshuo xulu*, p. 63. However, Lin considers *Jiaohong zhuan* 嬌紅傳 (also known as *Jiaohong ji* 嬌紅記) to be an early Ming work, a view shared by quite a few scholars, such as Hou Zhongyi and Liu Shilin (*Zhongguo wenyan xiaoshuo shigao*, 2: 110).

5. Ye Dejun, "Du Mingdai chuanqi wen qizhong," p. 535.

6. Sun Kaidi (*Riben Dongjing suojian xiaoshuo shumu*, p. 127) was probably the first to use the term *tongsu leishu* to refer to the kind of anthologies of miscellaneous writings (ranging from letters and jokes to fiction), which became extremely popular during the Ming.

use the term "romance novels" (*changpian chuangqi xiaoshuo* 長篇傳奇小說).[7] *Jiao Hong ji* 嬌紅記 (The story of the two women Jiao and Hong), attributed to Song Meidong 宋梅洞 (fl. late thirteenth century), which is usually considered the first such romance, inspired many other literary romances during the Ming. Obviously indebted to "Yingying zhuan," *Jiao Hong ji* is a much more elaborate romantic story (close to 20,000 characters long). Unlike the male protagonist in "Yingying zhuan," who deserts his lover (Yingying), Shen Chun is a young man deeply in love with Wang Jiaoniang. The lovers here are much more resolute and determined in pursuit of their happiness, although both eventually die for love. Together with *Xixiang ji*, *Jiao Hong ji* became one of the most celebrated love stories during the Ming.[8]

The appearance of *Zhongqing liji* 鍾情麗集 (A beautiful book on deep passions), attributed to Qiu Jun 邱濬 (ca. 1421–95), marked an important milestone in the development of the Ming literary romance. In this novella, *qing* is given unprecedented emphasis. Probably for the first time in a story of this kind, love triumphs, and the tale has a happy ending (a happy ending is one of the important generic markers of the scholar-beauty fiction of the seventeenth century). Despite the work's emphasis on *qing* and faithfulness in love, the topic of sex is not shunned. Compared with the love scenes in *Jiao Hong ji*, the descriptions in *Zhongqing liji* are significantly more detailed as well as more explicit, although they are still couched in euphemisms.[9] In *Jiao Hong ji* and *Zhongqing liji* the relationship between *qing* and *yu* is unproblematic in that the two are not presented as mutually exclusive. The bifurcation of desire into *qing* and *yu*, however, came to characterize later works.

In works such as *Tianyuan qiyu* 天緣奇遇 (The heavenly destiny and marvelous encounter), *Xunfang yaji* 尋芳雅集 (A refined book on seeking fragrant flowers), and *Li sheng liuyi tianyuan* 李生六一天緣 (The heavenly destiny of Scholar Li), *yu*, or physical desire, is the focus of the narrative, and

7. Both Chen Yiyuan (*Yuan Ming zhongpian chuanqi xiaoshuo yanjiu*) and Chen Dakang ("Lun Yuan Ming zhongpian chuanqi xiaoshuo") have used the term *zhongpian chuanqi*. He Changjiang ("Lun Yuan Ming changpian chuanqi xiaoshuo de fanzhan licheng") uses the term *changpian chuanqi*.

8. The attribution of *Jiao Hong ji* to Song Meidong is still controversial. For discussions of the textual history of *Jiao Hongji* and its influence, see Chen Yiyuan, *Yuan Ming zhongpian chuanqi xiaoshuo yanjiu*, pp. 19–46; and idem, "Ming Qing xiaoshuo li de *Jiao Hong ji*." See also Wang Gang, "The Cult of *Qing*"; and Cheng Yizhong, *Song Yuan xiaoshuo yanjiu*, pp. 198–210.

9. For a discussion of *Zhongqing liji*, see Wang Gang, *Langman qinggan yu zongjiao jingshen*, pp. 114–35.

promiscuous sex is described in fairly graphic detail, although the descriptions never reach the level of explicitness encountered in erotic fiction during this period, such as *Ruyijun zhuan* or the later *Chipozi zhuan*.[10] Literary romances such as *Tianyuan qiyu* would exert great influence on erotic romances written in vernacular Chinese such as the late Ming *Langshi* and the early Qing *Chundeng nao*, *Taohua ying* 桃花影 (The shadows of the peach blossoms), and *Xiuping yuan* 繡屏緣 (The embroidered screen), which are often about the promiscuous adventures (*yanyu* 艷遇) of a handsome young man and his polygamous bliss.[11]

On the other hand, the emphasis of literary romances such as *Shuang Qing biji* 雙卿筆記 (Random notes about the two sisters) and *Liu sheng milian ji* is on chaste *qing*, especially chastity on the part of the female protagonists.[12] Interestingly, in *Liu sheng milian ji*, *Tianyuan qiyu*, which is known for its promiscuous male protagonist, is singled out for criticism.[13] Obviously, the

10. Erotic fiction written in literary Chinese produced during the same period does not share some of the most important features common to these literary romances, such as the number of poems and the focus on the love between handsome and talented young men and women. On the other hand, erotic fiction features much more explicit and detailed descriptions of sex.

11. For discussions of these literary romances and their possible influence on later works, see Chen Yiyuan, *Yuan Ming zhongpian chuanqi xiaoshuo yanjiu*, pp. 212–15, 244–45. Wang Gang has a detailed discussion of *Tianyuan qiyu* in his *Langman qinggan yu zongjiao jingsheng*, pp. 135–82. Li Mengsheng (*Zhongguo jinhui xiaoshuo baihua*, p. 59) also argues that *Tianyuan qiyu* may have influenced the erotic fiction of later periods. For discussions of some of these early *Qing* vernacular erotic romances, such as *Taohua ying* and *Xiuping yuan*, see McMahon, *Misers, Shrews, and Polygamists*, pp. 126–49. For an examination of how the concept of *qing* is hijacked in *Xiuping yuan* to defend the male protagonist's promiscuous sexual adventures, see my "Sentiments of Desire," pp. 179–83.

12. For a discussion of the textual history of *Liu sheng milian ji* and its possible influence on later works, see Chen Yiyuan, *Yuan Ming zhongpian chuanqi xiaoshuo yanjiu*, pp. 219–38. He Changjiang ("Lun Yuan Ming changpian chuanqi xiaoshuo de fazhan licheng") has argued that there were two stages in the development of the Ming literary romance: the first being that of the "roaring passions" (*qingbo benyong* 情波奔涌) and the second, the "return to ritual" (*huigui lizhi* 回歸禮制). Although one might quibble with his particular "chronological ordering," He's characterization of the two increasingly distinct trends in the Ming literary romance are, in my view, accurate.

13. "Liu Xihuan milianji" 劉熙寰覓蓮記, in *Xiugu chunrong*, p. 97. The texts of the same literary romance in different anthologies, such as *Guose tianxiang* and *Xiugu chunrong*, vary considerably. For example, the title "Liu sheng milian ji" is changed to "Liu Xihuan milian ji" in *Xiugu chunrong*. For a discussion of the different versions of this work, see Chen Yiyuan, *Yuan Ming zhongpian chuanqi xiaoshuo yanjiu*, pp. 222–23.

author of *Liu sheng milian ji* tried to distinguish his work from works such as *Tianyuan qiyu*. Much more attention is paid in these tales to the need to keep *qing* within the boundaries of *li* (ritual).[14] The preservation of premarital virginity becomes an important aspect of *qing*.[15] At the end of this story, during the wedding night, the two female protagonists proudly proclaimed that they are still virgins.[16] Works such as *Liu sheng milian ji* in which the female protagonists try hard to shun premarital sex are not in the majority as far as Ming literary romances are concerned. However, they anticipated the trend in the seventeenth-century scholar-beauty fiction in which premarital abstinence became the norm.[17] It is probably accurate to say that literary romances such as *Liu sheng milian ji* played a significant role in shaping the tradition of chaste *qing* in seventeenth-century scholar-beauty fiction. Consequently, during the late Ming and especially the early Qing, there were two fairly distinct kinds of vernacular romances: the "chaste romance" (also known as scholar-beauty fiction) and the "erotic romance." The chaste romance was the much more dominant form during the early Qing, and chaste romances significantly outnumbered erotic romances.[18]

The three chaste romances *Jin Yun Qiao zhuan* 金雲翹傳 (The story of one gentleman and two sisters), *Dingqing ren* 定情人 (The worthy lovers), and *Haoqiu zhuan* 好逑傳 (The ideal mate) can be read as representative of a more conscious effort during the early Qing to harmonize *yi* (righteousness) and *qing* by purifying the latter. These works can even be viewed as a possible reaction against the tendency to promote the cause of desire by ignoring

14. See, e.g., "Liu Xihuan milian ji," in *Xiugu chunrong*, pp. 114, 118.

15. Ibid., pp. 125, 129.

16. Ibid., p. 132.

17. Cf. the charts of the common features of the Yuan and Ming literary romances and of the works of scholar-beauty fiction in Chen Dakang, "Lun Yuan Ming zhongpian chuanqi xiaoshuo," pp. 55, 62.

18. The terms "chaste romance" and "erotic romance" are borrowed from McMahon, *Misers, Shrews, and Polygamists*, pp. 103–7. Commenting on the differences between Ming erotic fiction and early Qing erotic romances, McMahon (ibid., p. 147) observes: "In late Ming erotic fiction, lovers also met without a go-between or parents' permission but could not marry and thus redeem their illicit involvement; they mostly encountered disastrous endings. In the [erotic] Qing romance, sex is domesticated by being brought into the sphere of marriage. The enjoyment of sex no longer subverts social order but instead belongs to that order." An examination of such Ming literary romances as *Tianyuan qiyu* or *Li sheng liuyi tianyuan* reveals that many of the features McMahon attributes to Qing erotic romances were anticipated in these Ming literary romances.

the assumed distinctions between *qing* and *yu* as exemplified in works such as the late Ming erotic novel *Langshi* and the apparent emphasis on *yu* at the expense of *qing* in works such as *Jin Ping Mei*. *Qing* is almost always oversexualized in *Langshi* (physical desires are emphasized as the main aspect of *qing*). A counter-trend in many of these early Qing chaste romances (traces of which we have already encountered in *Lin Lan Xiang*) is an effort to desexualize *qing*.[19]

One thing shared by the three early Qing novels examined in this chapter is the enormous pains their authors took to demonstrate that sex is irrelevant and often even detrimental to the *qing* celebrated in their works. In these three novels, all the protagonists not only successfully refuse to stoop to premarital sex, but even sometimes avoid conjugal sex for the sake of completely vindicating chastity. In *Haoqiu zhuan* and *Dingqing ren*, *qing* finally triumphs precisely because the lovers abstain from physical relations until they have fulfilled the most stringent Confucian prescriptions for the proprieties, despite overwhelming circumstances. *Jin Yun Qiao zhuan* significantly expands the concept of chastity and presents sex as unnecessary or "improper" even in marriage. In an effort to reclaim the purity of *qing*, these early Qing fiction writers try to reinvent the content of *qing* by redefining "chastity." A careful examination of this endeavor is crucial to an understanding of the ramifications of *qing* in the fictional discourse of this period and its possible influence on later works.

Qing and the Sufferings of a Chaste Body in *Jin Yun Qiao zhuan*

The novel *Jin Yun Qiao zhuan* is apparently based on the "life" of Wang Cuiqiao, a woman who lived around the mid-sixteenth century. Little was actually known about her, and several literati writers supplied details about her, probably based on rumor or their own imagination. Her life attracted the interest of writers largely for her supposed involvement with the notorious pirate leader Xu Hai 徐海 (d. 1556) and her possible role in the dramatic downfall of this formidable brigand. She was believed to have persuaded Xu to surrender to the Ming government, which eventually executed him. So

19. See also McMahon's (*Misers, Shrews and Polygamists*, pp. 148–49) discussion of "desexualization" in those scholar-beauty novels or chaste romances.

many literati writers have written on her that it would be no exaggeration to call the tales associated with this woman a "Wang Cuiqiao story complex." The first relatively detailed record of Wang Cuiqiao was a short biography written by Xiehu laoren 謝湖老人 (The old man of Lake Xie), which is still available today because it happened to be printed as an appendix to the famous writer Mao Kun's 茅坤 (1512–1601) account of the Ming government's campaign against Xu Hai, titled "Ji jiao Xu Hai benmo" 紀剿徐海本末 (A chronological account of the campaign against Xu Hai).[20] The story of Wang Cuiqiao continued to attract literati writers' attention. Wang Shizhen 王世貞 (1526–90) included a biography of her in the "Jinü" 妓女 (Courtesan) section of his *Yanyi bian* 艷異編 (Collected stories of the romantic and the strange).[21] Interestingly enough, in Huang Zongxi's *Ming wenhai* 明文海 (The sea of prose essays from the Ming dynasty), the biography of Wang Cuiqiao is anthologized in the "Lie'nü" 烈女 (Chaste women) section, possibly a reflection of Wang's elevation in the minds of many literati who had just experienced the traumatic dynastic transition.[22] Wang Cuiqiao is now mainly remembered and even celebrated as a "chaste courtesan," who sacrificed her life for the cause of the nation. The same sentiments are also echoed in Xu Huai's 徐懷 (1616–93) biography of Wang Cuiqiao.[23]

The story of Wang Cuiqiao began to be adopted into works of vernacular fiction during the last few decades of the Ming dynasty. In Zhou Qingyuan's 周清源 (fl. 1619–54) *Xihu erji* 西湖二集 (Stories from West Lake, second collection), the thirty-fourth story focuses on the suppression of the pirates by governmental forces led by Hu Zongxian 胡宗憲 (d. 1565). However, in this story Wang Cuiqiao is a marginal figure. In another seventeenth-

20. I have been unable to locate Xiehu laoren's biography of Wang Cuiqiao in the recently published, modern typeset edition of Mao Kun's *Ji*, although it includes "Ji jiao Xu Hai benmo" (pp. 817–24). Mao Kun's piece is also reprinted in the *Baibu congshu jicheng* series, but, again, Xiehu laoren's biography is not appended to it. This biography (about 500 characters), however, is quoted in its entirety by Dong Wencheng in his study of the evolution of the story of Wang Cuiqiao, "*Jin Yun Qiao zhuan* de gushi yanhua," p. 30. Also note Mao Kun's poem on Wang Cuiqiao, in Mao Kun, *Ji*, *juan* 1, p. 8. Dong's article is the most detailed study to date of the evolution of the story of Wang Cuiqiao.

21. Wang Shizhen, *Xu Yanyi bian* 續艷異編, *juan* 6, in idem, *Yanyi bian*, pp. 1583–87.

22. Huang Zongxi, *Ming wenhai*, 414.17–20 (vol. 5, pp. 758–59). The biography, however, is titled "Li Cuiqiao zhuan."

23. Zhang Chao, *Yuchu xinzhi* 虞初新志, 8.4–6 (pp. 255–56). A biography of Wang Cuiqiao can also be found in Feng Menglong's *Zhi'nang bu*, *juan* 26, *Quanji*, vol. 36, pp. 1594–97.

century collection of vernacular short stories, *Xingshi yan* 型世言 (Model stories for the world), attributed to Lu Renlong 陸人龍, the younger brother of the more famous publisher and writer Lu Yunlong 陸雲龍 (ca. 1586–1644), the seventh story concerns Wang Cuiqiao's role in the downfall of Xu Hai. The image of Wang Cuiqiao in this story is much closer to that of the female protagonist of *Jin Yun Qiao zhuan* than those in other versions in this story complex. In *Xingshi yan*, Wang Cuiqiao is presented for the first time as an exemplary filial daughter, who sells herself in order to save her father, a petty official, when he is jailed because a granary under his supervision burned down. Compared with previous stories of Wang Cuiqiao, the *Xingshi yan* version contains more details of how she is first sold as a concubine and then later resold as a prostitute. The presentation of Wang Cuiqiao in *Xingshi yan* may have influenced the writing of *Jin Yun Qiao zhuan*.[24]

A quick comparison of *Jin Yun Qiao zhuan* with other versions of the Wang Cuiqiao story will clarify what is significantly new about this novel and its rather different novelistic agenda. Although the earlier image of Wang Cuiqiao as a courageous woman with a strong sense of justice (*yixia nüzi* 義俠女子), as emphasized in the story in *Xingshi yan*[25] and elsewhere, is still present in *Jin Yun Qiao zhuan*, it devotes much more effort to underscoring a new image: a chaste *cainü* 才女 (woman of talent) of great *qing*. What is probably most significant to this examination of the implications of *qing* in the novel is its author's painstaking and somewhat uneasy attempt to contain Wang's story within the framework of the scholar-beauty romance. This tension between the image of a *xiayi nüzi* and that of a chaste *cainü* provides clues to the novel's new agenda for *qing*. In *Jin Yun Qiao zhuan* we are told in detail that before selling herself to gather funds to save her father, Wang Cuiqiao has been seeing a handsome young scholar (*caizi*), Jin Zhong, and the two have secretly pledged their love. The story of Wang Cuiqiao's

24. Most scholars date *Jin Yun Qiao zhuan* to the early Qing; see, e.g., Lin Chen, *Mingmo Qingchu xiaoshu shulu*, p. 257; and Li Zhizhong, "Jiaohou ji" 校後記, in *Jin Yun Qiao zhuan* (Chunfeng wenyi chubanshe, ed.), pp. 216–24. Li speculates that the novelist might be Xu Huai, the famed author of *Banqiao zaji* 板橋雜記. Some scholars believe that *Jin Yun Qiao zhuan* is a late Ming work; see, e.g., Dong Wencheng, "*Jin Yun Qiao zhuan* banben kao"; idem, "*Jin Yun Qiao zhuan* banben kao buzheng"; and Ouyang Jian, "*Jin Yun Qiao zhuan* de kanben yu chaoben." I find the evidence supporting an early Qing date more persuasive.

25. See *Xingshi yan*, 7.151.

involvement with the pirate leader Xu Hai and her supposed key role in his suppression by the Ming government is relegated to the periphery, taking up only three chapters in this twenty-chapter novel, significantly less space than that devoted to the "scholar-beauty" beginning, which takes up almost six chapters. All previous versions in the Wang Cuiqiao story complex focus on her role in the eventual demise of the pirate leader Xu Hai, and her life is significant only to the degree that she helps end his rebellion. This changes dramatically with the appearance of *Jin Yun Qiao zhuan*. Now the private life of Wang Cuiqiao rather than her public role in quelling the formidable pirate force becomes the narrative focus.

Wang Cuiqiao's love-at-first-sight meeting with Jin Zhong obviously fits the scholar-beauty formula. Following a meeting with the Wang sisters, Jin Zhong happens to pick up a hairpin Wang Cuiqiao dropped. Jin returns the hairpin and uses the opportunity to express his feelings to Wang Cuiqiao. Their love develops rapidly with the exchange of poems and other love tokens, although she twice rebuffs his sexual advances. However, before their love can progress further, Jin Zhong, like the male protagonist in many scholar-beauty novels, has to take his leave and travels to a distant place to transport the body of a dead uncle back to their hometown. Almost at the same time, Wang Cuiqiao's father is wrongly implicated in a case of robbery. It seems that the only way to gather the necessary sum of money to save her father is for Wang Cuiqiao to offer herself for sale (by now a familiar trope). Before leaving, Wang Cuiqiao is able to secure a promise from her family that they will marry her younger sister Yunqiao to Jin Zhong in her place to fulfill her pledge to him. From this point on, the plot begins to deviate from the storyline of a typical scholar-beauty novel. Without realizing it, Wang Cuiqiao has sold herself into a brothel. Then she is secretly married to a young rich man, Shu Shou, as a concubine. However, his wife discovers this and devises an elaborate scheme to have Wang Cuiqiao kidnapped and then makes Wang her personal maid. Too afraid to admit the truth to his wife that Wang Cuiqiao is his concubine, Shu Shou cannot prevent his wife from torturing Wang. Later Wang manages to escape, only to be sold to another brothel. Xu Hai, the formidable pirate leader, falls in love with her and takes her as his wife. With the help of Xu Hai, Wang Cuiqiao is able to take revenge on those who harmed her, including the pimp, the madams of the two brothels, and Shu Shou's wife.

Having repeatedly failed to contain the forces of Xu Hai, the general commander of the Ming governmental forces, Hu Zongxian, sends a messenger to attempt to persuade Xu Hai to surrender. Although failing to accomplish his mission, the messenger does find out that Wang Cuiqiao might favor surrender. Hu Zongxian sends two women to serve as her maids. These two women encourage Wang to talk Xu Hai into surrendering. Pretending to accept Xu Hai's surrender, Hu Zongxian's troops instead ambush him and his group and are finally able to defeat them. Xu Hai is killed in the fighting, and Wang Cuiqiao is captured. During the victory celebration, Hu Zongxian gets quite drunk and attempts to take advantage of Wang Cuiqiao. The next morning, however, Hu regrets his action and gives Wang to one of his generals as a concubine. Feeling responsible for the demise of Xu Hai, Wang Cuiqiao tries to commit suicide by jumping into a river. Miraculously, Wang is rescued by a nun she used to know and is able to reunite with Jin Zhong, who is now married to her sister, Cuiyun. At the insistence of Jin Zhong, her sister, and her parents, Wang Cuiqiao reluctantly agrees to marry her former lover, although she refuses to consummate the marriage on the grounds that her body is no longer clean. The novel concludes with two sisters married to the same man; hence the title *Jin Yun Qiao zhuan* or, more literally, *The Story of [One Gentleman] Jin and [Two Sisters] Qiao and Yun*. Like a typical scholar-beauty fiction, the novel has a happy ending, despite the heroine's reluctance to participate in it.

As this synopsis suggests, the main part of the novel (approximately chapters 7–19), which consists of accounts of Wang Cuiqiao's bitter experiences as a prostitute and as a concubine and her dramatic fate as the wife of a pirate leader, is anything but typical of a scholar-beauty novel. There is a tension between the *caizi jiaren* (scholar-beauty) *framing* chapters of the novel and the *framed* story of the female protagonist's (mis)adventures. The tension is generated in large part by the conflict between Wang Cuiqiao's image as chaste beauty or *jiaren* (like almost every female protagonist in a typical scholar-beauty fiction) and her experiences as a promiscuous *wanren qi* 萬人妻 (a woman who has slept with ten thousand men; 1.3).[26]

In the framing scholar-beauty chapters of the novel (the first six chapters and the final chapter), the focus is Wang Cuiqiao's persistent defense of her

26. All references to the novel, unless otherwise noted, are to *Jin Yun Qiao zhuan* published by Chunfeng wenyi chubanshe; chapter and page numbers are given in parentheses in the text.

chastity and, at the end, her attempt to redeem her chastity by redefining "genuine" chastity. In the first six chapters of the novel, the Chinese character *shen* 身, or "body," appears frequently (besides numerous appearances in the text proper, it also appears in the titles of chapters 4, 6, and 7). As in *Bian er chai*, the body is represented in *Jin Yun Qiao zhuan* as a crucial symbolic site where the meanings of chaste *qing* are contested, renegotiated, and inscribed. Wang Cuiqiao's *qing* and her chastity (the two are almost interchangeable in the novel) are literally inscribed on her body—whether she yields her body to a man, and, when she eventually does, why she yields, and the abuse her body is subjected to once it is yielded.

Wang Cuiqiao's virginity is initially presented as an emblem of her chaste *qing*. Although she quickly accepts Jin Zhong's love, she twice refuses to yield her body to him because premarital sex as exemplified in "Yingying zhuan" is incompatible with the chaste *qing* she is pursuing:

> If a girl yields to her lover because of deep *qing*, she will not be a virgin on the wedding night. . . . A girl will regret it greatly if she does not cherish herself, because this will lead to contempt on the part of a man. . . . If Yingniang had refused Scholar Zhang's request, she would not have suffered the fate of being deserted by him later. . . . Unfortunately, Yingniang casually yielded her body (*qingshen* 輕身) to please Zhang. Although Zhang took her body (*shen sui nizhi* 身雖暱之), he actually despised her in his mind. I hope your plan for us envisions a long life together. I must behave according to what is right. We can play music and write poems to express our "scholar-beauty" sentiment (才子佳人情致) and avoid degenerating into fornicators. . . . We should set ourselves up as a model of "Confucian romance" (*mingjiao fengliu* 名教風流) (3.19)

Later Wang Cuiqiao launches another lecture when Jin Zhong again fails to control himself:

> A woman should protect her body like a fragile vase (*shoushen ru shouping* 守身如守瓶). Once a vase is broken, it can never be repaired. Once a woman's body is stained, how could it regain its chastity? Then what kind of body could I present to you on our wedding night? . . . Taking this into consideration, you should kill me with a knife if I were to have this kind of idea and thus avoid debauchery as soon as [the thought of] it arises. (3.25)

As Chen Yiyuan points out, Wang Cuiqiao's remarks were probably inspired by the similar remarks of Jiaofeng when she refuses to yield herself to

Scholar Wu in the Ming literary romance *Xunfang yaji*.[27] Interestingly enough, *Xunfang yaji* is notorious for its graphic descriptions of premarital sex. By virtue of this intertexual reference to *Xunfang yaji*, the author of *Jin Yun Qiao zhuan* seems to have deliberately underscored the differences between Wang Cuiqiao and Jiaofeng, who does eventually yield her body to Scholar Wu. Wang Cuiqiao can be read as a carefully constructed image deliberately designed to repudiate a tradition in which the female protagonist of a scholar-beauty romance succumbs to the temptations of premarital sex. In fact, chapter 3 is devoted to relating how Wang Cuiqiao spends a whole night with Jin Zhong and yet is able to keep her body intact, as emphasized in the second line of the chapter's couplet/title "After a Whole Night of Pleasure, the White Jade Still Remains Stainless" (通宵樂白璧無暇). In chapter 1, Wang Cuiqiao tells her sister that a woman's ultimate reputation depends on whether she cherishes her own body (女人之身, 重之則太山, 輕之則鴻毛; 1.7). Her painstaking insistence on being different from previous *jiaren* models, such as the famous Yingying (or Yingniang as she is called in the novel; Wang Cuiqiao also discusses the female protagonist of *Jiao Hong ji*, 3.21), in terms of her avoidance of premarital sex becomes even more significant, although not without irony, when she decides, for the sake of her father, to sacrifice the very body (the word *sheshen* 捨身 repeatedly appears in chapter titles and the text proper of the novel) she has tried so hard to protect. Her argument for this drastic change of attitude is eloquent:

> You [Yunqiao] should become a "conscientious minister" (*liangchen* 良臣) and take good care of our parents, while I will be a "loyal minister" (*zhongchen* 忠臣) who sacrifices her body to fulfill an act of virtue (*shashen chengren* 殺身成仁). . . . I have decided to give up my body (*sheshen*) for the sake of our family. This act of suffering should also be an act of happiness. Indifferent to what god will do, I have seen through this body of mine (看破此身).[28] (4.30)

Wang Cuiqiao further rationalizes: "Previously I preserved the chastity of my body (*shoushen*) for the sake of Jin Zhong. This is in accordance with the

27. "Wu sheng xunfang yaji" 吳生尋芳雅集, in *Xiugu chunrong*, p. 20. For other "borrowings" from *Xunfang yaji* in *Jin Yun Qiao zhuan*, see Chen Yiyuan, *Yuan Ming zhongpian chuanqi xiaoshuo yanjiu*, p. 195.

28. Here the character *shen* may be understood as *sheng* 生 (life), as is further demonstrated in the discussion below. Thus, "I have seen through this body of mine" can also mean "I have seen through this life." There is a tendency in the novel to replace the character *sheng* with *shen*, probably due to the need to underscore the symbolic significance of body.

norms (*daoqi chang* 道其常). Now because of this disastrous event, I won't be able to dictate my fate any more since a woman's life/body (*nüzi yishen* 女子一身) is ultimately controlled by others" (4.31). Here a woman's life is referred to as her *shen* (literally, "body"). Wang Cuiqiao's "life" or the story of her life, as the novel demonstrates, is indeed a history of her body: how its chastity is initially maintained, then lost, and finally revindicated.

Obviously, Wang Cuiqiao is convinced that her duty to her father is more important than her love for Jin Zhong, as argued by the anonymous commentator (孝重于情, 情爲孝奪).[29] That is to say, a father's claim to his daughter's *shen* (body/life) could be even more legitimate than that of the daughter's husband, because, according to this view, the *shen* (body/life) of a daughter is first of all a gift from her father, as eloquently proclaimed by Tianhuazang zhuren in his preface to the novel:

> The reason that she refuses to view the defilement of her own body (*rushen* 辱身) as a defilement is due to her utter filiality; the reason that she can accept such suffering as no suffering at all is due to her absolute willingness. How is this so? This is because her body is a gift from her father. Now she gives up that body for the sake of her father. If this body is already given up, it will turn into soil, wood, and be dead. It is sheer luck that she should have a second chance of life. How could she again aspire to the dream of a virgin girl (*zuo guige xiang* 作閨閣想). (p. 1)

On the other hand, Wang Cuiqiao never fails to point out to others that what she is selling is her "physical body" (*roushen* 肉身; 4.34); the implication is that her "true" body or chastity can never be for sale.

Once she has decided to sell herself, Wang Cuiqiao, however, begins to rethink the significance of her previous refusal to allow Jin Zhong to claim her body:

> Previously I did not comply with the request of Jin Zhong, because I wanted to keep the integrity of my body (*quan cishen* 全此身) and because I was afraid that I would have nothing to present during our wedding night. My refusal was all for the sake of my lover. If I had anticipated today's event, there would have been no need to protect my body from him. (4.32)

29. *Jin Yun Qiao zhuan*, Asakusa ed., 4.19a (p. 35). Since none of the modern typeset editions of the novel that I have consulted reprints the commentator's pre-chapter comments, I refer to the facsimile reprint of a copy of the Kangxi edition collected in the Asakusa Bunko 淺草文庫 in Japan, when quoting the commentator.

Of course, precisely because the chastity of Wang Cuiqiao's body has been so scrupulously maintained up to the point, her sacrifice becomes all the more laudable and virtuous. At the same time, Wang Cuiqiao feels that she has to ask her sister to marry Jin Zhong so that her lover will eventually have her "body," albeit in the form of a symbolic substitute. To fulfill her duty as a future wife to Jin Zhong, she has to have a body that is chaste enough to be presentable as that of a virgin bride. Consequently, as a woman, she has to be ready to give up her body for her husband as well as her father. After all, the body, the novel seems to suggest, does matter.

By the time the reader finishes the last page of the novel, he or she is compelled to feel that in fact all that matters in the novel is "body." *Qing* or, for that matter, female virtue ultimately depends on the body for signification. In the concluding chapter, when Wang Cuiqiao is finally reunited with Jin Zhong, she reluctantly consents to marry him. On their wedding night, however, Wang Cuiqiao reprises her act as a chaste girl from the beginning of the novel—she refuses to yield her body to Jin, this time seemingly for an entirely different reason. The reader is urged to see the parallel between her previous action when, as a virgin, she protected her chastity from Jin Zhong during their courtship and her action as a defiled woman at the end of the novel. In both cases, she refuses him not once but twice. Previously, she refused him to protect her body's chastity. Now she refuses because her body is no longer chaste, although Jin Zhong's request is sanctioned by the institution of a formal marriage, a sanction whose absence she has previously used to justify her refusal to yield her body. She is convinced that, after having been the "wife" of so many men, she is no longer worthy of Jin Zhong. In other words, she refuses because her contaminated body would compromise the "chastity" of Jin Zhong, although as a man he is entitled to have more than one wife. A man's bodily "chastity" is presented here as a woman's responsibility. A defiled female body will defile a man's body. And yet she agrees to be his wife, as if by marrying him without offering her body, Wang Cuiqiao is able to vindicate her chastity with her very defiled body. Of course, Wang Cuiqiao now has additional justification, since Jin Zhong is married to her younger sister, Yunqiao: thus he is by no means deprived of his right to conjugal bliss, and, more important, his family line will be continued.

During their wedding night, Jin Zhong and Wang Cuiqiao enjoy all the nuptial pleasures except for sex. The narrator claims that they have become a married couple and yet are able to avoid polluting their *qing* with sex. This is exactly the kind of romance (*fengliu*) that is worth being transmitted in the form of a novel (20.213). The significance of this *fengliu* story lies precisely in the absolute absence of a physical relationship between its male and female protagonists throughout the entire novel. Body is most relevant to *qing* (at least in the case of a chaste woman such as Wang Cuiqiao) only when it is excluded from a relationship, although to show her total devotion and to fulfill her responsibility as a dutiful wife and as a heroine of *qing*, Wang Cuiqiao has to supply another "body" in the form of her younger sister to Jin Zhong to compensate him for the unavailability of her own body. Although body is most relevant to a woman's *qing* when it is absent, for a man's *qing*, body has to be present, since a man's *qing* needs to be authenticated by the physical act of procreation, the most important Confucian duty for a man. Consequently, *qing* transcends body and yet, at the same time, paradoxically, it relies on body for its signification. In the case of a chaste woman, the physical dimension of *qing* becomes meaningful only when body is deliberately excluded.

Besides the complex implications of the female body in the novelist's attempt to illuminate what is genuine *qing* for a chaste woman, another important quality that defines *qing* in the novel is suffering—the experience of a beautiful and chaste female body being defiled or symbolically destroyed (*suishen* 碎身; 5.39). In his pre-chapter remarks to chapter 1, the anonymous commentator argues that the two most important concepts in the novel are *qing* and *ku* 苦 (suffering); he even proposes a new concept of *qingku* 情苦 (suffering for the sake of *qing*) to characterize Wang Cuiqiao's experiences.[30]

The central part of the novel shows, sometimes in graphic detail, how a beautiful *cainü* (talented woman) is reduced to a "wife of ten thousand men." Wang Cuiqiao is forced to lose her "body," or virginity (*shishen* 失身), when she is deflowered by an utterly worthless pimp, Ma Kui, who has paid 450 taels of silver to purchase her. Immediately after this *shattering* experience, with the ruthless pimp sound asleep, Wang Cuiqiao picks up a writing brush and composes a poem to express her sorrow, as if to show how her poetic talent, just like her chaste body, is being wasted. Later she is tricked into eloping with a young man, Chuqing; actually he has been sent by the brothel madam as part of a plan to punish and tame her. After being caught,

30. Ibid., 1.1a (p. 1).

Wang Cuiqiao is stripped to her waist (*chishen luti* 赤身露體; 9.80), and her foot-bindings are removed. Her naked body is whipped repeatedly. Wang Cuiqiao feels that her body is being violated again. The exposure of her body to public view and the whipping of that same body are meant to be further assaults on her chastity. Later when she is kidnapped by the agents of Huanshi, the wife of her then-husband, Shu Shou, Wang Cuiqiao is again physically tortured, and her body once more becomes the target of physical assault. Paralleling the obsession with the chaste body in the framing "scholar-beauty" chapters of the novel is an intense interest in the body in these chapters. Here, the focus is on the defiling and abusing of this chaste body. In chapter 18, Wang Cuiqiao, now the wife of the pirate leader, in turns tortures and mutilates the bodies of all those who previously tortured her. Given the immense interest in the female body expressed in the novel, the physical nature of her revenge should come as no surprise.

The defilement of Wang Cuiqiao's chaste body gains added significance when the reader realizes that she has almost sought out an opportunity to be defiled. Well before Wang Cuiqiao is forced to sell herself for the sake of her father, she fully anticipates that a woman is born to suffer. She is known for her musical talents, and the music she composes is entitled "On Ill-fate" ("Boming yuan" 薄命怨). It often moves people to tears, although nothing tragic has happened in her life up to that point in the novel. When she passes the grave of the courtesan Liu Danxian, she feels such an affinity with the dead woman that she deplores Liu's tragic fate, as if she is anticipating that she herself will soon suffer the same fate. When her sister and brother express surprise that Cuiqiao should be so saddened by a dead courtesan, whom she hardly knows, she offers a philosophical though rather far-fetched explanation:

> That beautiful women cannot dictate their own fate has been a fact throughout history. Liu Danxian was not born a prostitute. . . . How do you know that our fate will not be a repetition of hers? Besides, one cannot avoid being sick and eventually dying of old age. It is often these beautiful women that have won the most sympathy from people. Look at those women in the past, such as Xishi and the Imperial Consort Yang—who among them has had a good ending? (1.4)

Later she dreams that the Goddess of Sorrows (Duanchang jiaozhu 斷腸教主) asks her to compose poems on ten topics, all on the theme "an ill-fated beautiful woman" (*hongyan boming* 紅顏薄命); nothing is said to indicate what in her past or present life could explain such deep pessimism on her part. Early in the novel, Wang Cuiqiao is so insistent that she is an ill-fated woman that the reader begins to suspect that she delights in viewing herself as a victim, although she is not masochistic in the sense that she likes to inflict physical pain on herself. However, she certainly likes to inflict psychological pain on herself. Her decision to sell her body, a body she has taken so many pains to protect from her lover Jin Zhong, is almost a long-awaited event, as if all her efforts to preserve its chastity were designed to enhance the tragic effect of her sacrifice. To a degree, the destruction of this body is self-willed by its owner, Wang Cuiqiao, a self-fulfilling prophecy of her self-image of a suffering beauty.

If Wang Cuiqiao's insistence on chastity in the framing chapters of the novel is sincere, then the destruction of that chastity in the main part of the story is meant to vindicate her virtue as a woman as well as a daughter. In the last chapter of the novel, when she refuses to defile Jin Zhong's chastity with her own already defiled body, her chastity is resurrected as well as reconfirmed. Or, to quote the commentator, allowing her chaste body to be defiled is another way for her to assert her chastity (*rushen zhi wei jieshen* 辱身之爲潔身).[31] Here we may recall some of the "business tricks" the brothel madam teaches Wang Cuiqiao to attract patrons. One such method is the *kurou ji* 苦肉計 (inflicting harm on one's own body to show one's devotion; 10.89). To keep a customer, a prostitute burns moxa on her body, and the burn scars are often considered tokens of devotion. Another trick is called *xianshen shuofa* 獻身說法 (to make a statement by offering one's own body; 11.92).[32] A prostitute is supposed to "demonstrate" every part of her body to attract a customer. Understood in the context of Wang Cuiqiao's virtuous act of self-sacrifice, the two tricks have rather ironic implications: Wang Cuiqiao's willingness to allow her body to be defiled to save her father (so that she will be remembered as a filial daughter) is certainly a case of *kurou ji*, or "inflicting harm on one's own body in order to show devotion" as well as a case of *xianshen shuofa* or "making a statement by offering one's own body." For this act, she will be immortalized (*mingchuan buxiu* 名傳不朽), as Wang Cuiqiao herself openly acknowledges (5.39). After all, like the profes-

31. Pre-chapter comment to chap. 8 in ibid., 8.8b (p. 84).

32. This phrase is a pun on the proverbial expression *xianshen shuofa* 現身說法 (using one's own experience as proof to argue a point).

sion of prostitution, the enterprise of chastity is a body business. One exchanges the body for money; the other exchanges the body for fame. In the novel, thirteen years after selling her body, she reclaims it as an emblem of her chastity. In other words, just as her defilement has to be written on her body, her chastity has to be inscribed on it in order to be seen as a physical emblem of her female virtue. On the other hand, the overwhelming sense of sadness that such a beautiful and chaste body has been defiled is precisely one of the most important qualities of *qing*, or *qingku*, as it is being defined in the novel.

In fact, this insistence on pathos as an essential quality of *qing* is the first point the narrator makes at the beginning of the novel, when he refers to the legendary *cainü* Xiaoqing. If, he asserts, Xiaoqing had not suffered so greatly, she would not achieved her present immortality. He decides to tell the story of Wang Cuiqiao because she is comparable to Xiaoqing in terms of her miserable fate. Her sufferings impose on him the duty of immortalizing her. For male literati writers and readers, nothing was more moving than witnessing a beautiful and talented woman suffering and languishing.[33] In defending Wang Cuiqiao's failure to commit suicide after being sold to the pimp, the commentator argues that suicide would have been the easy way out. An early death would have deprived her of the opportunity to demonstrate her great chastity (*dajie* 大節) by experiencing suffering, and people would not have remembered her so much.[34] There is a lot of male anxiety invested in this novelistic image of a suffering beautiful *cainü*. Wang Cuiqiao is said to have compared herself to the ultimate male literati figure of suffering, Qu Yuan 屈原 (fl. fourth century B.C.) (4.31). Of course, in many literati writings, Xiaoqing was also closely associated with Qu Yuan, the exemplary tragic figure.[35] Interpreted within this context, the pseudonym of the author of *Jin Yun Qiao zhuan*, Qingxin cairen 青心才人, yields some interesting meanings: first, it obviously refers to the concept of *qing* since the character *qing* 情 is composed of the *xin* 心 radical and the *qing* 青 phonetic. Moreover, *qingxin* is also a homophone of *qingxin* 傾心, "admiration." Consequently, this pseudonym can also mean "an admirer of talented beauty."

33. Cf. my *Literati and Self-Re/Presentation*, p. 84.

34. *Jin Yun Qiao zhuan*, Asakusa ed., 8.8b (p. 84).

35. See the story of Xiaoqing in the early Qing collection of literary tales *Nücaizi shu* (A book of female talents), p. 1.

Throughout the novel, an important aspect of Wang Cuiqiao's *qing* is her ability to claim such *qingxin*, or admiration, by virtue of her tremendous sufferings.

Stabilized *Qing* in *Dingqing ren*

Compared with *Jin Yun Qiao zhuan*, *Dingqing ren* is a much more typical example of scholar-beauty fiction. Determined to find a worthy and talented beauty, the male protagonist, Shuang Xing, embarks on a search disguised as a study tour. He falls in love with Jiang Ruizhu, the daughter of a good friend of his father's. Just as they are about to marry, his mother orders him to leave to take the examinations. During his absence, Hao Yan, the son of a high official, hears of Jiang Ruizhu's fame as a talented beauty and tries to force her to marry him. Rejected and upset, Hao Yan convinces Eunuch Yao to select her as a palace lady for the crown prince. To save her parents from persecution, Jiang Ruizhu pretends to be willing to travel with Eunuch Yao to the capital, but she is actually determined to commit suicide to demonstrate her faithfulness to Shuang Xing. Before her departure, she arranges for her parents to adopt her maid Caiyun and leaves a letter for Shuang Xing asking him to marry Caiyun as her substitute so that her parents can enjoy the benefits of having a daughter and a son-in-law to look after them in the future. Returning after winning the top honors in the examinations, Shuang Xing reluctantly agrees to marry Caiyun to fulfill the wishes of Miss Jiang but, thanks to his determination to remain faithful to Miss Jiang, insists on abstaining from any physical intimacy with Caiyun, despite pressures from his parents-in-law. In the end everything turns out to be perfect: Miss Jiang is able to reunite with them after being rescued from the river as soon as she tries to drown herself. The novel concludes with both Miss Jiang Ruizhu and her maid Caiyun married to Shuang Xing in a happy polygamous marriage.

The plot of *Dingqing ren* shares some important similarities with that of the scholar-beauty framing chapters in *Jin Yun Qiao zhuan*. Each pair of lovers exchanges poems. Both male protagonists have to leave suddenly before they can marry their respective lovers. Something disastrous happens, and the female protagonists end up belonging to someone else. Before being sent away, however, they arrange for a substitute bride for their lover. Both female protagonists are miraculously rescued after they try to commit suicide by drowning. Both male protagonists have to go through a marriage that remains unconsummated. And both novels eventually conclude with a happy polygamous marriage, although the reader is supposed to understand that the nominal marriage between the male and female protagonists in *Jin Yun Qiao zhuan* is not a temporary arrangement as it is in *Dingqing ren*—Wang Cuiqiao's defiled body will always keep her from consummating her marriage with Jin Zhong. However, it is the differences between these two novels that are even more important.

As the title suggests, the concept of *qing* occupies a more conspicuous position in *Dingqing ren*. In his preface to the novel, Suzheng tang zhuren 素政堂主人 (The master of the Hall of Plain Governing) argues that *qing* is difficult to stabilize because although it appears to be very similar to heart/mind (*xin*), it is not mind itself, and even though it is very similar to nature (*xing*), it is too active to be nature. Then he lists historical figures who could not stabilize their *qing* by remaining constant in their love, because, he contends, they did not find lovers with qualities good enough to enable them to stabilize their *qing*. The message is that it is not as difficult to stabilize one's *qing* as it is to find someone worthy of such a commitment of stabilized *qing* (情不難于定,而難于得定情之人).[36]

As Shuang Xing complains, none of the girls others have introduced to him is worthy of his committed *qing* (不足定人之情; 1.4). However, whether a girl can be considered one's *dingqing ren*, or worthy lover, depends on a judgment based on his subjective *qing* (憑吾情以爲衡量; 1.5): "If my *qing* is not moved by her, then she is not the one worthy of my committed love" (吾情既不爲其所動,則其人必非吾定情之人) (1.6).[37] By the time this novella was written, that one must marry someone one can love wholeheartedly had become a cliché of long standing. However, the author reformulates this idea in terms of his concept of *dingqing* and emphasizes its subjective nature. What is important is finding the person worthy of the pledge of eternal love. Shuang Xing argues that "the proper relations between ruler and subject and between father and son are based on nature [*xing*], and therefore one's nature can fully manifest itself in acts of loyalty and filiality. However, a harmonious relationship between husband and wife depends on not only [the couple's] *xing* but also [their] *qing*" (1.6; cf. the nar-

36. "*Dingqing ren* xu" 定情人序, in *Dingqing ren*, p. 154. Future references to this novel are given in parentheses in the text, citing chapter and page numbers.

37. See also *Dingqing ren*, 5.42, 11.101.

rator's view of the relationship between *li* and *qing* in *Lin Lan Xiang*, discussed in Chapter 7). The reader is told at the beginning of the novel that a man's desire for a pretty woman is a result of both *xing* and *qing* (好色原兼性和情). Because of *qing*, however, "human desire becomes more dangerous and difficult to control" (故令人慾險難平; 1.1). This leads to the important question of how to maintain the purity of *qing* by keeping it in line with *xing*.

Thus far the novel's title *dingqing ren* has been understood as referring to "the person worthy of eternal love." In fact, the novel's main focus is on the question of how to fulfill this pledge of eternal love once it is made. Here *dingqing ren* should be understood as referring to "the person who follows through on the pledge of love." In other words, a worthy lover is someone who is able to be faithful and constant in love. Miss Jiang, when asked by her maid why she is hesitant about committing herself to Shuang Xing, explains: "Although he is handsome and talented, I know little about his personality (*xingqing* 性情). If his nature is not stabilized (*xing buding* 性不定), he will change his mind quickly. If he is not deep in *qing*, then I cannot entrust him with the rest of my life" (4.31). Here Jiang Ruizhu is trying to legitimize her view of *qing* by associating the concept of *dingqing* with the Neo-Confucian concept of *dingxing* 定性 as elaborated in the Song thinker Cheng Hao's theories.[38] Later, Miss Jiang is able to secure evidence of her lover's "stabilized *xing*" when he falls seriously ill after a maid misquotes her mistress as saying that he would commit incest by marrying her mistress since he has already become the adoptive son of her father, an incident that may have inspired the author of *Honglou meng*. In chapter 57 of that novel, Jia Baoyu gets sick after Zhijuan lies to him and tells him that Lin Daiyu is already engaged to someone else (many of the small details in these two works are similar).[39]

What is particularly interesting about *Dingqing ren* is how the "test of chastity" is focused on its male protagonist. Later in the story, presumably because of his devotion to Miss Jiang, Shuang Xing declines a marriage pro-

38. For a study of Cheng Hao's *Dingxing shu* 定性書 (On stabilizing nature), see Zhang Yongjun, *Er Cheng xue guanjian*, pp. 1–36.

39. For a discussion of the possible influence of *Dingqing ren* on *Honglou meng*, see Li Zhenyu, "Yibu dui *Honglou meng* chansheng guo yingxiang de xiaoshuo." More recently, in the article "*Jin Yun Qiao zhuan* dui *Honglou meng* yishu chuangxin de duochong yingxiang," Dong Wencheng discusses the possible influence of *Jin Yun Qiao* on *Honglou meng*, although some of the evidence presented is less than fully persuasive.

posal made by the influential official Tu Lao 屠勞 (a pun on *tulao* 徒勞, or futility) on behalf of the latter's daughter after he gains the top honors in the civil-service examinations, as heroes of scholar-beauty fiction are supposed to do. But he does more. He even tries to commit suicide by smashing his head against a pillar after learning of the supposed death of Miss Jiang, an act of chastity normally expected of a woman. (Miss Jiang, as the novel's female protagonist, has already proved her chastity by trying to drown herself in a river.) This is a gesture *Jin Yun Qiao zhuan*'s male protagonist Jin Zhong fails to make. What is even more remarkable is Shuang Xing's refusal to consummate his marriage with Caiyun, although they live together as a couple in every other way, an arrangement reminiscent of that between Wang Cuiqiao and Jin Zhong in *Jin Yun Qiao zhuan* (however, in that novel it is the female protagonist who refuses to consummate the marriage). Shuang Xing consents to a nominal marriage only after reading the will left by his fiancée. The difference is, of course, that the marriage between Shang Xing and Caiyun is consummated once Miss Jiang is reunited with Shang Xing and once the all-important hierarchy of first and second wives is properly determined. No reader of *Jin Yun Qiao zhuan*, however, expects the marriage between Jin Zhong and Wang Cuiqiao to be consummated. What is particularly significant about *Dingqing ren* is that it is the male protagonist who is insistent on his chastity. During their wedding night, Shuang Xing appeals to Caiyun not to force him to bring dishonor to *mingjiao* (the teachings of the sages), as if his pledge of love to Miss Jiang is somehow related to the strict behavioral codes of Confucianism (in fact, sleeping with one's wife would violate no Confucian teachings whatsoever), just as Miss Jiang herself earlier insisted on the causal relationship between "stabilized *qing*" and "stabilized *xing*." After Caiyun assures him that she will never press him, he thanks her for allowing him to maintain his "reputation of chastity" (*mingjie* 名節), a term usually applied to a woman (for example, it is used of Wang Cuiqiao in *Jin Yun Qiao zhuan* [20.209]; this term is also used to describe a male subject's loyalty to his lord).

Shuang Xing's femininity is a fact emphasized in the novel: his feminine appearance (女兒一般標致; 2.17), his susceptibility, the way in which he attempts his suicide—smashing his head against the pillar of the house (*zhuangzhu* 撞柱; 14.127)—and finally the way he perceives his commitment to Jiang Ruizhu as a demonstration of his chastity or *jie*. It seems that this novel's emphasis on *dingqing* has led to a new gender fluidity in fiction, a tendency that will become a much more prominent issue in *Honglou meng*, although such gender fluidity does not automatically guarantee a more advantageous gender status for women.[40]

The novel's conclusion, in which the male and female protagonists are finally reunited, is supposed to meet the generic requirements of scholar-beauty fiction. However, there is a more important reason for Miss Jiang to be miraculously rescued: the reunion enables the novelist to avoid the dilemma created by Shuang Xing's pledge of "chastity" in refusing to consummate his marriage with Caiyun. Otherwise, this pledge would conflict with other, more solemn duties of a man, such as the need to carry on his family line by having sons. Consequently, there are limits on a man's ability to insist on his chastity or "stabilizing" his *qing*.

Chastity receives a much stricter interpretation in *Dingqing ren* than it does in *Jin Yun Qiao zhuan*. One reason is that the female protagonist of *Jin Yun Qiao zhuan* has been "the wife of ten thousand men," and therefore its author has to propose a more subtle concept of chastity that emphasizes the "spiritual dimension." Consequently, the novel shows more tolerance for physical contact between the sexes; such behavior would be considered unchaste in novels such as *Dingqing ren* and *Haoqiu zhuan*. For example, despite her repeated refusal to yield her body to Jin Zhong, Wang Cuiqiao does allow other forms of physical contact between herself and her lover. When Jin Zhong first tries to embrace her, Wang Cuiqiao reprimands him for being too wild (*qingkuang* 輕狂; 3.18). But moments later, she jumps into his arms herself (3.21). This is certainly not an action expected of a chaste girl. The situation is dramatically different in *Dingqing ren*; not only is there absolutely no physical contact between Shuang Xing and Miss Jiang during their courtship, but they almost never see each other alone. Most of their communications are relayed through Miss Jiang's maids. After much deliberation with her maid Caiyun about the appropriateness of her plan to help Shuang Xing regain his health, Miss Jiang finally decides to see Shuang Xing from a distance; she stands on an artificial hill in her compound that allows her to see into a neighboring house where Shuang Xing is (6.51). Miss Jiang consents to such an arrangement only because she is persuaded that Shuang Xing will not be able to recover fully from his illness without re-

40. For a discussion of what I have termed "gender fluidity" in *Honglou meng*, see my *Literati and Self-Re/Presentation*, pp. 88–97.

ceiving a verbal pledge of love from her in person. This kind of scrupulous insistence on physical chastity determines that Miss Jiang will try to commit suicide before anything can happen to her body when she is forced to become a palace lady for the prince. Consequently, in the novel, all bodies in the end are virginal, including the two that have been married for quite some time. In fact, Wang Cuiqiao also faces a similar problem in *Jin Yun Qiao zhuan*, but she chooses not to commit suicide initially, because she believes, the reader is specifically told, that the person who purchased her would create problems for her parents if she commits suicide, since he has paid for her body (7.58). This insistence on physical chastity will become even more scrupulous in *Haoqiu zhuan*, the last work to be explored in this chapter.

Qing and Tests of Virtue in *Haoqiu zhuan*

Haoqiu zhuan tells the story of the resistance of the male and female protagonists Tie Zhongyu and Shui Bingxin to attempts by their enemies to undermine their moral integrity and their eventual triumph. In the end, they are blessed with a happy marriage, after successfully insisting on behaving according to the strictest moral codes despite extremely compromising circumstances. Tie Zhongyu and Shui Bingxin have to pass a series of tests to prove their impeccable chastity. In the first test, for example, Tie Zhongyu falls seriously ill after being tricked into eating poisoned food prepared by a monk. To save him, Shui Bingxin, who, like Yan Mengqing in *Lin Lan Xiang*, is a *nü daoxue* 女道學 (a female puritan or female Confucian moralist; 7.96), has him brought to her own home so that she can care for him, despite the possible appearance of improprieties since she is an unmarried maiden from a respected family. During Tie's entire stay, the two young people behave irreproachably. When they talk to each other, there is a screen between them. Although their talk sometimes can be very friendly and even affectionate (*xiangqin xiang'ai* 相親相愛), there is absolutely no word touching on even hinting at private passion between man and woman (*siqing* 私情; 7.94).[41]

Many pages are devoted to the pair's determined efforts to resist the pressures (some from their own parents) to marry each other, simply because

41. Cf. the repeated references to the concept of *siqing* in *Lin Lan Xiang*, discussed in Chapter 7. All references to the novel are from *Haoqiu zhuan* published by Zhongzhou juji; chapter and page numbers are given in parentheses.

this will compromise the moral integrity of their previous actions (Tie's rescuing of Shui and Shui's nursing of the sick Tie) by giving people an excuse to impute ulterior motives to them. To quote Tie Zhongyu: "How could we even talk about becoming husband and wife if we have already been true friends in need" (既在患難中已爲良友, 安可复言夫妻; 8.107). Their reasoning may be a bit puzzling. Tie Zhongyu and Miss Shui seem to be trapped in a quandary created by their own insistence that their helping of each other was motivated by pure and honorable intentions. The purity of their intentions would be tarnished if they marry. Tie Zhongyu's confession to his father captures the essence of this dilemma:

> I dare not withhold anything from you, my parents: Miss Shui is so graceful and pretty that she is certainly the kind of girl I would like to marry. If I could indeed marry her, how dare I pretend to be so high-minded (*jiaoqing* 矯情)? Now, however, I can only deplore that fate does not want us two to become a couple. We met in special circumstances, and normal protocols could not be followed fully. Under constant suspicion of impropriety, we have tried our best to prove our chastity. If we were to marry despite all this, people would have reason to suspect that our previous chivalric actions were indeed the result of some ulterior motives. I would rather lose this opportunity of a great marriage than be viewed as someone who has behaved against the teachings of the sages (*mingjiao zuiren* 名教罪人). (14.193–94).

For both Tie Zhongyun and Miss Shui, proving their chaste intentions is more important than anything else, even their happiness together (they do occasionally admit to themselves that they admire and even love each other). Here reputation is everything. They agree to be nominal husband and wife only after being convinced that someone is plotting to force both of them into disastrous marriages with other partners. However, their marriage is not consummated until Shui Bingxin's virginity is attested under imperial supervision (proof that nothing improper occurred between the two). The conversation between the emperor and Miss Shui is interesting:

> The emperor asked: "If you really wanted no trouble, why didn't you try to avoid taking any action that would arouse suspicions and gossip (*bixian* 避嫌)? Instead you had Tien Zhongyu move into your house to recuperate."
>
> "To reciprocate his favor," Shui Bingxin answered, "I had to act in disregard of the possible appearance of improprieties."
>
> The emperor asked with smile: "You decided to disregard the possible appearance of improprieties when he was still a stranger. Now why, with the blessing of

your parents to get married, are you two still sleeping in different rooms, and why are you taking such an extreme measure to avoid suspicions?"

Shui Bingxin replied: "The suspicion caused then was only the suspicion of the moment; if there were gossip, it could be cleared were I to get married. However, the suspicion today is the kind of suspicion that will follow me all my life. If I didn't have my original body (*yuanti* 原體) to prove my chastity, then my husband of today would be no different from the stranger of yesterday." (20.247–48)

The emperor's verdict is the ultimate authentication of Shui Bingxin's chastity, and he summarizes the remarkable nature of the protagonists' morally impeccable behavior:

Throughout history, there have indeed been examples of a woman maintaining her body's chastity when she is not married. However, I have never heard of [another case in which] a couple of virtuous young people refused to consummate their marriage in a hurry in order to avoid gossip, even though they were already formally married and they did admire each other. (20.250)

The novel is designed to show that this couple is rewarded because of their insistence on keeping their *qing* in perfect accord with the strict moral codes prescribed by orthodox Confucianism. The novel's central message is captured in one sentence: "Morality and the principles of the sages' teachings can be maintained only when *qing* is kept in harmony with one's moral nature [*xing*]" (調乎情與性, 名與教方成; 14.196). In other words, *qing* can only be vindicated through desexualization by proving that sexual passion is irrelevant to true *qing*.

Although *Haoqiu zhuan* is traditionally viewed as a work of scholar-beauty fiction, many elements in the novel are anything but typical of this genre, and some of them even amount to a deliberate critique of certain major traditional scholar-beauty motifs.[42] Tie Zhongyu, although as handsome as a pretty girl (*meiren* 美人) and well-versed in Confucian learning, is first presented as a knight-errant who is physically strong and who even excels at martial arts. This contrasts with the usual image of a hero in a scholar-beauty novel, such as that of Shuang Xing, who is a scholar known for his femininity. There is no conventional love-at-first-sight meeting between Tie Zhongyu and Shui Bingxin, in which one picks up something dropped by the other. Tie Zhongyu comes to know Miss Shui when he saves her from

42. Cf. Cao Yibing, "*Haoqiu zhuan* fei caizi jiaren xiaoshuo lun."

being kidnapped and forced into marriage. Nor do the two engage in an exchange of poems, although Miss Shui does think about writing some poems. As soon as he recovers from his illness, Tie Zhongyu decides to leave town to avoid any possible appearance of impropriety as quickly as possible. Miss Shui tries to give him some gifts as tokens of her gratitude. But he declines. This only increases her respect for him. As a last resort, she thinks about writing him a poem to show her gratitude, but she soon dismisses this idea because this, she is convinced, would demean their relationship by making it into an affair of *siqing* between a man and a woman (6.74).

Tie Zhongyu is always careful to distinguish *en* 恩 (gratitude or indebtedness) from *qing*. He insists that one could speak of *en* in relation to Miss Shui and himself but not of *qing* (8.109). It is their impeccable moral integrity and their refusal to follow the model of *caizi jiaren* that enables them to thwart their enemies' repeated attempts to embarrass them. For example, Kuo Qizu and others try to trick Tie Zhongyu into a rendezvous with Miss Shui in the rear garden (*hou huayuan* 後花園) of her residence so that they can ambush and humiliate him. However, they never succeed because Tie Zhongyu, by virtue of his high moral discipline, would never consent to a rendezvous with a girl. Moreover, Tie Zhongyu knows that the invitation did not originate from Miss Shui. She, with her moral integrity, would never *lower* herself and issue such an invitation (11.150–51). Secret pledges of love in a rear garden (私訂終生後花園) are a staple of scholar-beauty fiction; both *Jin Yun Qiao zhuan* and *Dingqing ren*, for example, have such scenes. In *Haoqiu zhuan* such behavior is viewed as an act of *siqing* that should be avoided.

In the explorations of desire in these three novels, *siqing*, although having different implications, is often contrasted with the concept of *gong* 公. In *Jin Yun Qiao zhuan*, instead of dramatizing the tension between the private and the public in Wang Cuiqiao's role in the demise of Xu Hai and the pirates he leads (the conflict between her public obligations to the nation to see that he surrenders to the government and her private love for him) as one would expect, the author chose to emphasize the conflict between the public nature of her decision not to consummate the marriage with Jin Zhong and the private nature of marriage:

Jin Zhong asked: "I really admire you for your insistence on chastity (*mingjie*). However, I believe there is nothing more private than the relationship between a husband and a wife. Can the secrets of the boudoir be more private [than what happens between a husband and a wife]? Why should you dwell on the most public in the realm of the most private?"

Cuiqiao replied: "It is true that marriage is the most private relationship. When certain things become common knowledge between husband and wife, however, then that husband-wife relationship also acquires public implications. I am insisting on the public instead of the private (*yukong buuyu sizhe* 欲公不欲私者) for the sake of no one other than you and me. If I have certain secrets and you have complete knowledge of them, then you will have to pretend that you don't have any knowledge of them. This will result not only in my causing you to feel ashamed but also in your causing me to feel ashamed. If you really love me and allow me have certain secrets [*si*] of my own and do not insist on being intimate [*si*] with me, this will enable my chastity to remain intact although the jade is already shattered. The chastity of my defiled body depends on this." (20.209)

By virtue of this tortuous play with the intricate meanings of *si* and *gong*, Wang Cuiqiao insists that Jin Zhong allow her to keep her body (which is already defiled) private by not consummating the marriage and that he should not do anything private with her already defiled body.

The contrast between *si* and *gong* receives much more attention in *Dingqing ren* and *Haoqiu zhuan*. This growing attention parallels the increasingly rigid interpretations of chastity in these two works. In chapter 15 of *Dingqing ren*, the maid Caiyun is said to marry Shuang Xing for the sake of *gong* (she does this at the request of her mistress), but, the reader is told, her private wishes (*yipian sixin* 一片私心) are that Shuang Xing treat her as a "real" wife (15.139). When Shuang Xing tries to commit suicide, his father-in-law appeals to his sense of public duty to prevent him from attempting such an act because as a public official serving the imperial government, he should not take his own life merely for the sake of *siqing* (怎敢忘公義而徇私情; 14.127).[43]

In *Dingqing ren*, the reader is told that *qing* becomes acceptable only when the private is completely identified with the public.[44] In true *qing*, the private is in perfect accord with the public—romantic love between two young people should make them even more virtuous:

If *qing* is not greedy, even being excessive won't damage *yi* [righteousness],	情不貪淫何損義

43. See also the references to *si* 私 in the titles of chaps. 6 and 7.

44. See also my discussions in Chapter 2 of late Ming and early Qing thinkers' efforts to justify private desires in terms of public interests.

While *yi* won't hurt *qing* if it can be tactfully executed.	義能婉轉豈傷情
Don't you say there is no perfect thing in the world,	漫言世事難周到
Because sages' teachings will prevail when *qing* and *yi* are in harmony. (15.140)	情義相安名教成

Here *qing* is a powerful force that leads to feelings of loyalty and commitment, not because it is associated with the individual and the different as claimed by some radical writers during the late Ming, but because it is harmonized with *xing* or public morality, which, according to Neo-Confucian teachings, is inherent in one's heaven-endowed nature.[45]

In *Haoqiu zhuan* this contrast between *si* and *gong* receives even more emphasis. The perception of being *si* is considered the most serious threat to one's reputation of being chaste. Tie Zhongyu declines the gifts Miss Shui offers because to do so would tarnish his chivalric action of helping her and make it into an act of *si* in the eyes of others (6.73). Tie refers to the concept of *jiagong jisi* 假公濟私 (doing selfish things in the name of public good) to caution himself against visiting Miss Shui when he learns she has successfully avoided the prefect's attempt to force her to marry Kuo Qizu (11.149); indeed, this is what Kuo Qizu suspects Tie is doing with regard to Miss Shui (7.87). Miss Shui gives up the idea of writing poems and sending them to Tie Zhongyu because this would be an act of *siqing*. Miss Shui often praises Tie Zhongyu's exercise of his *qing* for the sake of *gong* (*qing yongyugong* 情用於公; 9.122). This dichotomy between *si* and *gong* provides the basic moral structure within which Shui Bingxin frames her argument about the *qing* between herself and Tie Zhongyu:

When I arranged for you to recuperate in my house, the matter became personal, although my motivation was honorable [literally, "not selfish at all"] (心雖出于公,而事涉于私). That is why I did not dare to invite you to stay longer although I indeed wished so, and I did not dare to be close to you even though I wanted to. Today, under the order of our parents and with the words of the matchmakers, our relationship has been blessed with public sanction (事既公矣), but we have yet to be vindicated in terms of our private intentions (心之私猶未白). This is reason why we cannot consummate our marriage, although we are already married. (15.210)

45. Here we may recall Feng Menglong's famous dictum "transforming private *qing* into what is worthy of public sanction," discussed in Chapter 2. Feng Menglong was, of course, an important figure in promoting the cause of *qing* during the late Ming, but some of his views also anticipated the early Qing conservative trend of trying to "tame" the radical implications of *qing*.

A dominant theme in *Dingqing ren* and *Haoqiu zhuan* is the importance of being able to resist physical temptation. The ultimate *qing* is nonsexual or even nonphysical, and must remain so until it has been proved by an elaborate series of tests to be in harmony with the "public" and has received the blessings of one's parents and of society. In an analogy to the civil-service examinations, which test one's ability to comprehend the moral teachings of the sages, Shuang Xing brilliantly composes an "essay" on the topic of finding an ideal mate (好逑的題目; 1.7)[46] and demonstrates that the *qing* in his "essay" is morally impeccable. In moving from *Jin Yun Qiao zhuan* to *Dingqing ren* to *Haoqiu zhuan*, we witness an increasing emphasis on chastity as well as an increasingly rigid view of *qing*. As we shall see in the next chapter, this conservative concept of *qing* would have a profound influence on the eighteenth-century novel *Yesou puyan*.

46. The similarities between the two novels are substantial, although we would need more evidence to conclude that *Dingqing ren* was directly influenced by *Haoqiu zhuan* or vice versa. Here the reference in *Dingqing ren* to *haoqiu* 好逑 (seeking an ideal mate; an obvious allusion to the famous line from the first poem in the *Book of Poetry*; see Hao Zhida et al., *Guofeng shizhi zuanjie*, p. 1) becomes an intriguing comment on the same allusion in the title of *Haoqiu zhuan*.

CHAPTER NINE

Qing *Versus* Yu: *The Polarization of Desire in* Yesou puyan *and* Guwangyan

Confucian *Qing* in *Yesou puyan*

Unlike the three early Qing novels discussed in preceding chapter, the two eighteenth-century full-length novels discussed in this chapter, *Yesou puyan* 野叟曝言 (The humble words of an old rustic) and *Guwangyan* 姑妄言 (Preposterous words), contain extensive and explicit descriptions of sex. Although continuing to define *qing* in contrast to *yu* as in the three seventeenth-century works, the authors of the two eighteenth-century novels deliberately juxtaposed *qing* and *yu* and gave both full attention. The undeclared purport (whose fulfillment is facilitated by the enormous length of these novels) is to provide a comprehensive picture of all forms of desire, both good and bad. Apparently bothered much less by the eroticism of the "distant" late Ming than the authors of the three early Qing novels had been, these two writers never shied away from erotic details in describing *yu*, especially the author of *Guwangyan*.

Xia Jingqu 夏敬渠 (1705–87), the author of *Yesou puyan*, took upon himself the task of testing the limits of *qing* established by the "purists" of the early Qing (such as the author of *Haoqiu zhuan*). He redefined *qing* as containing almost all kinds of physical intimacy except sexual intercourse, provided that the specific situation demands such "expedient intimacy" and that one's intention is honorable or nonsexual.

The story of *Yesou puyan* centers around the career and life of the male protagonist, Wen Suchen, and his eradication in China, as well as Japan and Europe, of heterodox ideologies such as Buddhism and Taoism and his restoration of peace and order in the Ming empire by adhering to orthodox Confucian beliefs (mainly, the Cheng-Zhu version of Neo-Confucianism). Wen Suchen's spectacular achievements in his public career are matched by his successes in private life—his ability to win the hearts of many beautiful women and, with the help of his mother, the sagely Madame Shui, to create a harmonious polygamous family that produces and raises many male descendents.

Wen Suchen is not only a great Confucian hero but also a handsome, virtuous, and extremely talented man. Furthermore, as the narrator takes great pains to point out, Wen Suchen is also rich in emotions (*duoqing* 多情; 9.136),[1] despite his image as a *daoxue xiansheng* 道學先生 (a puritan or

1. All future references to the novel will be to the edition published by Jilin wenshi chubanshe, with chapter and page numbers given in parentheses. According to the editor's "Houji" 後記, or postscript (p. 2483), this edition was based on the Piling huizhenlou 毗陵匯珍樓 and the Shenbao guan 申報館 editions. This is also the only modern typeset edition, as far as I know, that reprints all the commentaries contained in the two late Qing editions. The version in the Guben xiaoshuo jicheng series, which is a facsimile reprint of the Piling huizhenlou edition, will be cited whenever the explicit descriptions of sex expurgated from the modern typeset edition or specific differences in wording become significant to my discussions. Chapter and page numbers are given in parentheses, with the references to the modern typeset edition given first when both editions are cited.

There are two main late Qing printed editions still extant: the Piling huizhenlou edition, dated 1881, and the Shenbao guan edition, dated 1882. The Piling huizhenlou edition has 152 chapters with interlinear and chapter-end commentaries, but contains various lacunae. The Shenbao guan edition has 154 chapters with only chapter-end commentaries similar to those of the Piling huizhenlou edition. However, the novel was also serialized in the Shanghai newspaper *Hubao* 滬報 (the newspaper changed its name to *Zilin Hubao* 字林滬報 on Aug. 10, 1882) beginning on May 18, 1882; the serialization of the entire novel was finished on Dec. 15, 1884. The serialized version also contains 154 chapters and is probably identical to the Shenbao guan edition (I am grateful to Patrick Hanan for bringing my attention to the existence of this serialized version of the novel). This certainly testifies to the popularity of the novel during the late Qing. Many scholars believe that the Piling huizhenlou edition is closer to Xia Jingju's original manuscript, and the Shenbao guan edition, despite (or because of) its completeness, was re-edited by someone else. See, e.g., Sun Kaidi, "Xia Erming yu *Yesou puyan*," pp. 238–40. Ouyang Jian ("*Yesou puyan* banben bianxi") was probably the first scholar to argue that both editions are incomplete but equally authentic versions of Xia's manuscript. Ouyang Jian's argument seems to be supported by the existence of a holograph version of the novel dated 1878 that is identical to the Shenbao guan edition. For descriptions of this manu-

straight-laced Confucian).[2] The reader is told at the very beginning of the novel that "although he does not appear to be capable of being romantic, he is actually a person rich in emotions, just like Song Yu (說他不會風流，卻多情如宋玉; 1.3); he is said to be a man full of feelings (*qingzhong zhi ren* 情重之人; 6.94). A set phrase used by both the narrator and the commentator to describe his response in several emotion-laden scenes is: "The valor of a great hero is turned into the tender feelings of a young lover" (英雄氣短，兒女情長; 7.107; see also 6.87 and the interlineal comment at 20.331). In the novel, especially in the early chapters, Suchen is repeatedly involved in emotional entanglements with various beautiful and talented women, and in each case, he demonstrates abundant *qing* without overstepping the bounds of Confucian propriety, or *li* 禮. Almost at the end of the novel, some of the women who have been saved or helped by Wen Suchen and have wanted but failed to marry him as concubines confess the difficulty they have in addressing Wen Suchen properly, presumably because of their past experiences. He should be respected as a "father figure" (*enfu* 恩父) according to *qing*, but Madame Shui believes this is improper according to *li*. This makes these women quite uneasy. Their anxiety prompts Madame Shui to launch a Neo-Confucian lecture on the relationship between *qing* and *li*:

[Suchen's] declining to marry you himself and acting as matchmaker instead for others are both actions designed to avoid overstepping the limits of propriety (*beili* 悖禮) and to avoid being indifferent to your feelings (*jiaqing* 恝情) at the same time. There is nothing to be sad about. The ancient kings established rites and codes of behavior according to specific human situations (因人情而制禮). *Li* is actually *qing* (*li ji qing ye* 禮即情也), and the only difference is that *li* functions to keep *qing* on the right track when it becomes excessive or improper. Now your feeling uneasy is the result of excessive *qing*. This is why you need *li* to keep your *qing* in good measure (*yili jiezhi* 以禮節之) so that you can distinguish what is inherently natural (*bensheng* 本生) from what is artificial (*jiahe* 假合) and feel at ease. Even if you still have thoughts of gratitude, you can keep them within yourself (*mocun yu zhong* 默存於中). This [*qing*] does not contradict [*li*] at all.[3] (145.2339)

---

script version of the novel, see the brief entry on *Yesou puyan* in Liu Shide et al., *Zhongguo gudai xiaoshuo baike quanshu*, p. 669; and Wang Qiongling, *Qingdai sida caixue xiaoshuo*, pp. 81–115.

2. In the interlineal comments on Suchen's treatment of Su'e in chapter 20, the commentator praises his Neo-Confucian integrity (*daoxue qijie* 道學氣節) as well as his romantic sentiments (*ernü qingchang* 兒女情長) (20.331).

3. Here Madame Shui's choice of words such as *jie* and *zhong* is meant to remind readers of *Zhongyong*; see further discussion below. The commentator praises her point that *li* is actu-

To the extent that Wen Suchen is often presented in the novel as a model of perfect balance of *li* and *qing*, he embodies Madame Shui's sagely advice. In a word, the novel tries to create a romantic image of a larger-than-life Confucian (*fengliu daoxue* 風流道學), to use the term of the seventeenth-century writer Li Yu (cf. Wang Cuiqiao's characterization of her actions as *mingjiao fengliu*, or romance Confucian-style, in *Jin Yun Qiao zhuan*; 3.19).

In the novel *qing* as exemplified in Suchen is meant to be understood first of all in opposition to *yu*. A conversation between Suchen and Xuangu 璇姑, his future concubine, illustrates how the distinctions between *qing* and *yu* are supposed to be maintained. According to Suchen:

> The pleasure between a man and a woman originates from *qing*. If they love each other, they will naturally feel the spring-like bliss throughout their bodies. When a vulgar country bumpkin is married to a beauty or a stupid woman fails to win over her husband's heart, even if they have sex every night, they will experience only momentary excitement, which will soon fade away. . . . In addition, the real pleasure between a man and a woman lies in the experience before sexual intercourse when they are full of tender feelings; this is the time of endless pleasure. Once they have sex, [the tender feelings] soon die away. (8.126)

This observation provokes an even more interesting remark from Xuangu:

> I believe that pleasure has its roots in one's heart; if one derives pleasure from *qing*, then one would not feel so much physical yearning (*yunian* 慾念); if one derives pleasure from physical lust (*yu* 慾), then one would not have tender feelings (*qingnian* 情念). That day, once my desire was aroused (*yuxin shaodong* 慾心稍動), it became difficult to suppress, and soon I forgot all about *qing*. . . . Therefore, sex is indeed something superfluous, just like insisting on adding legs to a snake when drawing its picture (*huashe tianzu* 畫蛇添足). (8.126; 6.11b [p. 150])[4]

The commentator, in his chapter-end comments, elaborates on this view:

> Like staging a play, scores of scenes concentrate on the sorrows of separation and the happiness of reunion, and they are often very moving. But the grand finale is inconsequential (*keyou kewu* 可有可無), although a theater troupe usually insists on performing the conclusion. This is like a rendezvous in which the couple insist on

---

ally *qing* as insightful enough to serve as a "gloss" on the relevant passages in the Confucian classics (*keru zhushu* 可入注疏; 145.2339).

4. Here and elsewhere I also refer to the 1881 edition because the modern typeset edition is printed in simplified Chinese characters, and it does not distinguish between the two characters *yu*, one with the heart radical and the other without.

consummating their relationship with sex. In fact, just like the grand finale, sex is not always a must. This is a fact only those deep in *qing* are aware of. Although works such as *Xixiang ji* insist on describing the pleasures of sex in graphic detail, this only applies to those possessed by lust (*yugui* 慾鬼) rather than people of true love (*qingzhong* 情種). (8.128; 6.13b [p. 154])

The commentator's rhetoric is reminiscent of that of Miss Cao in Li Yu's *Lianxiang ban*, as well as that of the commentator of *Lin Lan Xiang*. Both of them try to claim that physical desire is irrelevant to *qing* (see Chapter 7). The *Yesou puyan* commentator believes what has transpired is a battle in which "heavenly principles" (*tianli*) are victorious over "human desire" (*renyu*) (7.103). This conversation between Suchen and Xuangu suggests that *qing* is mostly sentiments experienced in the heart and *yu* is pure physical desire and, what is more interesting, that sex is irrelevant or even unnecessary as far as the fulfillment of genuine *qing* is concerned. Ultimately *qing* and *yu* are mutually exclusive in the sense that the more *qing* one feels, the less room there is for *yu*, or vice versa.

This dichotomy between the two is reinforced by the fact that throughout the novel the Confucian world of *qing* represented by Wen Suchen is repeatedly contrasted with the heterodox world of *yu*, which is dominated by people deluded by Taoism and Buddhism as well as by evil officials. The imperial decadence is in large part attributed to Emperor Xianzong's (r. 1465–88) failure to control his own sexual desire and his susceptibility to the evil influence of various Buddhist and Taoist teachings. In the novel, therefore, *yu* is identified with heterodox ideologies, which are in direct conflict with values of the Confucian world of *qing*. *Yu* is presented as being as dangerous as any ideological heresy, an evil force that needs to be eliminated completely. Almost all the negative characters in the novel become evil because of their failure to control their *yu*, especially their sexual desire, and they tend to have uncontrollable desires or *yu* because they are under the sway of evil forces such as Buddhism and Taoism.

Furthermore, *yu* renders one vulnerable. In fact, some of Suchen's spectacular successes in defending the imperial throne are due to his knowledge of how to take advantage of this vulnerability to *yu* on the part of his enemies. Furthermore, assuming an appearance of such vulnerability sometimes becomes a necessary tactic on Wen Suchen's part to avoid suspicion or to divert the attention of his enemies by creating the false impression that he is interested only in the sensual life and has withdrawn from politics. In chapter 132 of the novel, Wen Suchen, after hearing the roaring of a lion, suddenly falls ill and begins to indulge in carnal pleasures. He continues in this state of debauchery for seven years. The reader is not told the reason for this mysterious illness until chapter 149 when Madame Shui offers an interesting explanation: When Suchen submits a memorial to Emperor Xiaozong detailing the need to eradicate Buddhism and Taoism, the former sovereign (*taishang huang* 太上皇), Xianzong, becomes very upset. To save Suchen from harm, Xiaozong suggests that he pretend to be sick. Suchen miraculously recovers from his illness as soon as Emperor Xianzong passes away and a new reign period is formally declared. Here indulgence in *yu* is a form of camouflage. Because Suchen is not really interested in sensual pleasures (he is only pretending to be sick, or *tuobing* 托病), he is never made vulnerable by his debauchery, physically or mentally.

However, even for the morally impeccable, *yu* in the form of sexual desire can present problems. Ideally, in a harmonious marriage, a couple has sex only for the purpose of procreation. That is why, we are told, Suchen subscribes to the ingenious theory that "having less desire brings more male offspring" (*guayu duonan* 寡慾多男), and he sleeps with each of his wives only once a month, timing his visits according to their menstrual cycles (88. 1380; 86.2b [p. 2362]). The commentator characterizes this as "preserving pure *yang* essence by abstinence" (*chunyang guayu* 純陽寡慾; chapter-end comments, 38.637; 36.14a [p. 1051]). *Yu* is thus detrimental to one's ability to fulfill one's ultimate filial obligation—to have male offspring to carry on the family line. Despite his many marriages, we are told, Wen Suchen has never seen a woman's private parts (卻並未目擊其形; 69.1082)—further testimony to Suchen's capacity for *qing* untainted by *yu*. This, however, does not necessarily mean that Suchen is immune to the temptations of *yu*, and there are moments when he has to make a special effort to suppress his own *yu* (see, for example, the subtle description of his response to Xuangu's pleading; 6.112).

The commentator on *Yesou puyan* repeatedly mentions *Jin Ping Mei* as a "negative" model and praises *Yesou puyan* for surpassing it (see, for example, 4.81, 70.1105, and 71.1123). One interesting example the commentator uses to support his argument that *Yesou puyan* is a much superior work is its author's appropriation of the famous motif of the "grape arbor" from *Jin Ping Mei*, which also appears in *Xu Jin Ping Mei* and *Xingshi* (see Chapter 6). In chapter 62 of *Yesou puyan*, the grape arbor, instead of being a setting for sexual escapades as it is in *Jin Ping Mei*, becomes a setting where the maids discuss the intellectual issue of the differences between two schools of Neo-Confucianism, those of Zhu Xi and Lu Xiangshan.[5] The commentator observes:

> In *Jin Ping Mei* the man and his concubines are playing the game of *touhu* 投壺 [tossing arrows into a jug; the commentator here may also be using the game as a metaphor to refer to the sexual acts performed in the setting of grape arbor in that novel], while a servant is peeing. Here in this novel, the maids are debating learning while the mistress is peeing. One is concerned with heavenly interest, the other ghostly obsession; one is the realm of human beings, the other the realm of animals. What a difference this is! (60.975)

The commentator wants the reader to see the distance between *Jin Ping Mei* and *Yesou puyan*. A household living in perfect harmony under the enlightening leadership of the sagely Madame Shui has no place for the kind of sexual indulgence prevalent in Ximen Qing's household. In the household of Wen Suchen, people have sex only to procreate! But the commentator also takes the opportunity to point out that when it comes to explicit descriptions of sex, the author of *Yesou puyan* also outshines that of *Jin Ping Mei*, although the two authors have entirely different agendas (69.1090). He cites the example in chapter 69 in which the harem master Li Youquan wants to drink Wen Suchen's semen and orders his concubines to perform various sexual acrobatics in order to arouse Suchen.[6] In *Yesou puyan*, the concept of *yu*, the commentator emphasizes, is associated only with evil people, whereas *qing* is the province of people like Wen Suchen. Ironically, another important difference between Ximen Qing and Wen Suchen is illustrated by the implications of the incidents in which people are eager to drink their urine. As mentioned in Chapter 4, in *Jin Ping Mei*, women like Pan Jinlian and Ruyi drink Ximen Qing's urine in order to please him and show (or pretend to show) their submission to him. In *Yesou puyan*, many people are eager to drink Wen Suchen's urine largely because they consider it a tonic (68.1069 and 70.1096). And early in the novel (chap. 20), Wen Suchen mixes his urine with herbs to make a medicine for Su'e (20.335). The commentator

5. For a discussion of the significance of such differences in the novel, see my *Literati and Self-Re/Presentation*, 129–33.

6. This chapter in the Shenbao guan edition corresponds to chap. 67 in the Piling huizhenlou edition.

notes that Su'e is the first to taste his urine (20.335), implying there are many people in line to drink it later in the novel. In this contrast of *yu* and *qing*, even bodily fluids (or human wastes) assume different meanings![7]

In Chapter 8, I noted the special efforts of the authors of the three early Qing novels to desexualize *qing*. *Yesou puyan* obviously shares this agenda in its attempt to distinguish *qing* from *yu*, despite the fact that it does not lack graphic descriptions of sex. One common strategy is to appeal to the perennial idea of the *zhiji* in the literati tradition—the other person who recognizes and appreciates one's talents. Suchen's decision to marry Xuangu as a concubine is based on the following rationalization: "It is very rare to be able to find a beautiful woman who has the discerning mind to appreciate a man's talent and value (*huixin jieren* 慧心解人). The ancients had a saying that one could die without regret if one is able to have a *zhiji*" (8.121). After reading poems written by his future concubine Xiangling, Suchen concludes: "She is really my *zhiji* and a friend who can command my respect (*weiyou* 畏友)." He even compares Xiangling to Mo Ye 莫邪, the famous wife of Gan Jiang 干將, during the Chunqiu period (776–476 B.C.). This legendary couple are famous for their superb skills in making swords and their devotion to each other (21.350).[8] In fact, all four concubines Suchen eventually marries are experts in one of the four "arts," namely, mathematics, medicine, poetry, and military strategy. Suchen is a master of all four and often discusses these "intellectual" topics with them, as two like-minded male literati would do. Here *Yesou puyan* adds a new dimension to the *zhiji* relationship so conventionalized in the romantic fiction of *qing*. In a typical scholar-beauty novel, a romantic involvement often emphasizes the poetic talents of the lovers.[9] No other work goes as far as *Yesou puyan* in trying to intellectualize *qing* by insisting that it is based on the lovers' intellectual ability (that is, it is more

7. The ninth concubine of the harem master Li Youquan drinks Li's urine because she is afraid the weather is too cold for him to go to the restroom (68.1069). This is obviously modeled after Pan Jinlian's and Ruyi's drinking of Ximen Qing's urine in *Jin Ping Mei*. For a discussion of the erotic significance of urination in the nineteenth-century novel *Ernü yingxiong zhuan* 兒女英雄傳 (The tale of the heroic lovers), see McMahon, *Misers, Shrews, and Polygamists*, pp. 274–77. See also McMahon's discussions of "urination" as a narrative device in other fictional works in his *Causality and Containment*, pp. 20–21.

8. The idea of *zhiji* also looms large in Suchen's relationships with men such as Luanchui's father (20.327) and Hong Changqing (11.172–74).

9. For an interesting discussion of the relationship between scholar-beauty fiction and the poetic tradition, see Xiao Chi, "Cong caizi jiaren dao *Shitou ji*."

than just poetic ability). Perhaps the most dramatic scene demonstrating the extent to which *qing* is desexualized and intellectualized is the discussion of mathematics in which Suchen uses Xuangu's stomach and "fragrant navel" (*xiangqi* 香臍) to illustrate his points (8.115–16). Here the physical body is literally desexualized into an instrument for teaching and learning and functions only to facilitate an intellectual exchange. The novelist outdoes his predecessors in scholar-beauty fiction in purifying *qing*.

On the other hand, in exploring the romantic implications of *qing* within the limits of the Confucian prescriptions of propriety, *Yesou puyan*, like so many works in the scholar-beauty genre, constantly appeals to the Confucian idea of *jingquan* 經權 (standards and expediency). In works such as *Haoqiu zhuan* and *Dingqing ren*, circumstances often compel the protagonists to be creative in adhering to the Confucian sense of propriety while laying claim to being a gentleman or lady of *qing*. Wen Suchen is certainly a master in exploiting situations of expediency. He often resorts to such ingenious tactics as stripping a woman naked or using his own naked body to warm a sick women in order to save her (Su'e also uses her naked body to warm him when he is sick). These episodes are meant to demonstrate, among other things, the importance of expediency in keeping the proper balance between *qing* and Confucian *li*, especially when the circumstances become "existential" and there is no perfect choice.[10]

Yesou puyan has a rather complicated relationship to the romantic conventions of scholar-beauty fiction. Although apparently indebted to the latter for the general strategy of desexualizing *qing*, it takes every opportunity to differentiate itself from those works by means of parody or other critiquing tactics. *Haoqiu chuan* was probably one of the first works in the genre of scholar-beauty fiction to use the Confucian concept of expediency to justify various acts of *qing* by its protagonists. In response to an uncle's accusation that she has violated the Confucian code of sex segregation by taking care of the sick Tie Zhongyu in her own home, Shui Bingxin launches into an eloquent defense in which she appeals to the *locus classicus* of the Confucian theory of expediency in *Mencius*[11] (6.82–83). She compares her nursing of the

10. Here *qing* becomes very close to *li* in referring to "specific situations" as suggested by the expression *qingli* 情理. See the discussions of the idea of expediency in the novel in my *Literati and Self-Re/Presentation*, pp. 120, 193–94*nn*25–28; and McMahon, "Case of Confucian Sexuality," pp. 11–17.

11. Jiao Xun, *Mengzi zhengyi*, pp. 306–7; Lau, *Mencius*, 4a, p. 124.

sick Tie Zhongyu to a man's extending his hand to save a drowning sister-in-law, an action justified by Mencius in terms of the idea of *quan*, or expediency, in contrast to the rites, which prescribe that a man may not touch a woman who is not his wife. In *Dingqing ren*, when Shuang Xing is seriously ill, Miss Jiang and her maid Caiyun debate whether she, knowing that the cause of his illness is his mistaken belief that she opposes their marriage, should send him a message clarifying her true feelings. Their discussions of the alternatives are framed in terms of the concept of expediency.

In *Haoqiu zhuan* Shui Bingxin's chastity is vindicated after her virginity is verified by the empress. This must have inspired the author of *Yesou puyan* to present a similar story about Su'e. When Su'e and Wen Suchen become seriously ill, they are able to cure each other's illness because both are extremely knowledgeable in medicine. But their treatment is anything but conventional. Here Xia Jingju outdoes the author of *Haoqiu zhuan* in terms of testing what is permissible under the rules of expediency. Su'e and Wen Suchen use their naked bodies to warm each other. In contrast in *Haoqiu zhuan*, Shui Bingxin has to sit on the other side of a screen while talking to Tie Zhongyu, when the latter is recuperating from his illness. However, like Shui Bingxin's purity, in chapter 18 of *Yesou puyan* Su'e's virginity is verified, this time by the wife of a magistrate rather than an empress.

Haoqiu zhuan is mentioned in *Yesou puyan*, although in a manner that makes one doubt whether Xia Jingju was willing to acknowledge his indebtedness to it. In chapter 31, Lian Cheng, acting on the suggestion of Li sisao, tries to seduce Xuangu by introducing her to "lecherous" books, such as *Huizhen ji* 會眞記, *Jiao Hong zhuan* 嬌紅傳, and *Haoqiu zhuan*. Although containing almost no explicit sexual descriptions, *Huizhen ji* (another name for *Xixiang ji*) and *Jiao Hong zhuan* (an alternative title for *Jiao Hong ji*) were considered morally questionable (presumably because both focus on love between a young man and a young woman). The inclusion of *Haoqiu zhuan* is indeed a surprise since among all the books on love, it is the most "Neo-Confucian" (*daoxue qi* 道學氣), and *Yesou puyan*, despite its obsession with the erotic, shares its moralistic pedantry. This may be an interesting example of the "anxiety of influence"—the author of *Yesou puyan* is trying to distance himself from a work that has apparently influenced his own work.

Other evidence of this distancing effort can be seen in the story of Suchen's friend Jin Chengzhi's love for Miss Min, which follows the plot pattern typical of scholar-beauty fiction. The two fall in love after they overhear each other composing poems on the road, one on the back of a donkey and the other in a cart. Their love soon deepens through the exchange of poems. In order to be close to Miss Min, Jin agrees to become her brother's tutor. However, her father wants her to marry a rich person. What turns this episode into a parody critiquing the scholar-beauty theme is Suchen's advice to his frustrated friend that he should forget the girl if her father does not approve the marriage: "You are entrapped in a crisis. You have to be resolute in guarding your mind and body against temptations (*shouding shenxin* 守定身心); you must free yourself from not only the entanglement of physical attraction (*sequan* 色圈) but also the entanglement of romantic attachment (*qingquan* 情圈)" (48.779). Of course, with a twist of fate, the lovers are finally united, and the father reluctantly gives his consent. This story critiques love without parental consent celebrated in many works of scholar-beauty romance (the most famous being the late Ming play *Mudan ting*).

Talent and beauty are usually the two most important qualifications for becoming a romantic lover in scholar-beauty fiction, and talent is defined almost exclusively as poetic talent. In *Yesou puyan*, these two qualities, although still important, are by no means enough to make a romance of *qing*. Upset by the relentless pursuit of Lian Cheng, Xuangu, who is already engaged to Suchen, declares: "How can this guy be compared with Master Wen when the latter is so learned, handsome, and talented in everything; even if the person I am already engaged to were a fool or extremely ugly, I would remain faithful to him no matter how handsome the other guy is" (27.456). Shishi concurs: "In these writings, a girl gives herself up as soon as she meets someone who is talented and handsome; on the other hand, she hates the man who may not be that appealing in appearance but who is chosen by her parents. She insists on following that handsome and talented guy [of her own choice]; otherwise she will commit suicide. I get really upset whenever I come across this kind of evil book" (27.457). Obviously this is meant to critique the practice of choosing one's own mate so celebrated in many works of scholar-beauty fiction (for example, in *Dingqing ren*). But what about Wen Suchen? He does not seem blameless in this regard, although the author constantly relates how successfully he resists the pressures to consummate a relationship until his mother approves. Another key redeeming factor is that he is often thrown into a romantic situation due to circumstances beyond his own control or, even better, due to his chivalric rescue of a beautiful woman in danger.

As defined in *Yesou puyan, qing* is more than just pure sentiment, however. In fact, except for sexual intercourse, many acts of physical intimacy are tolerated or even admired as expressions of genuine *qing*. The author seems obsessed with the body, especially naked bodies. This is probably due to the fact that the physical body is usually associated with *yu* and sexual desire. By underscoring the body's potential as a site for authentic expressions of morally upright *qing* devoid of *yu* elements, the novel is aiming at the maximum desexualization of *qing*. The body is the crucial battlefield where good (*qing*) and evil (*yu*) contest for supremacy. Touching and even caressing are often highlighted as expressions of tender *qing*; whether one can exercise self-control and avoid slipping into *yu* (namely, having sexual intercourse) becomes the ultimate test of one's *qing*. This can be seen in the graphic accounts of Suchen's "emotional" encounters with Xuangu and Su'e. Both involve numerous and very intimate acts of touching and embracing. The author of *Yesou puyan* obviously believed that intimate contact is an appropriate expression of *qing* and will not necessarily degenerate into *yu* as long as the contact is justified by the situation (i.e., expediency is required) and the lovers are able to shun sexual intercourse. The essential point is that the Confucian sense of propriety prescribes that a couple not consummate their relationship without parental approval. Therefore, whether an act is judged to be appropriate *qing* or unethical *yu* ultimately depends on whether it is sanctioned by Confucian *li*, although the need to be expedient is always duly recognized.

Often, however, the concept of expediency is stretched so far and the physical contact between two lovers becomes so intimate that *qing* and *yu* become indistinguishable, despite the novel's insistence on their incompatibility. For example, when the otherwise extremely virtuous Su'e mistakenly takes the aphrodisiac *butian wan* 補天丸 she finds herself overwhelmed with sexual desire. This gives rise to one of the most dramatic clashes between *qing* and *yu* in the novel. Su'e embraces Suchen and begs him to have sex with her. Suchen resists, interestingly enough, by covering her mouth with his own and caressing her all over her body, even her private parts (17.268); by the usual standards, the intimacy here is "sexual." However, the novel insists Suchen's actions are acts of *qing* precisely because his intention is anything but sexual and has nothing to do with *yu*. He is working to cure her illness; therefore it is an act of *qing*. It is *qing* because his caresses are desexualized. Ironically, these "desexualized" acts of *qing* prove to be most efficacious in quenching Su'e's seemingly uncontrollable sexual desire or *yu*. When Suchen learns that Su'e's fits of sexual passion are due to the pills, he rids her of it by giving her cold water to drink. However, in this graphic passage, the implications of *qing* become rather ambiguous: in one instance, the word *qing* is used in the sense of physical *yu* to describe Su'e's state as "sexual desire fully aroused" (*qingxing borang* 情興勃然; 17.267); elsewhere we encounter the expression "loving feelings deep as the sea" (*qingshen sihai* 情深似海;17.269). The character *qing* can refer to both sexual desire and lofty romantic sentiments in different character combinations, and the narrator takes great pains to underscore the differences. Of course, this is related to the ambiguities of *qing* in various discourses in pre-twentieth-century China.

In fact, the reader is repeatedly reminded that *qing* always has to be held in line with *li*; otherwise there is a serious danger it will deteriorate into *yu*. Learning that Suchen is about to be executed for reprimanding Emperor Xianzong, his wife and concubines are overwhelmed by sadness, although Suchen's mother, Madame Shui, remains rather calm. This puzzles her daughters-in-law and provokes a lengthy Neo-Confucian lecture on *qing* from the always wise and sagely Madame Shui: "How can there ever be a mother who does not love her own son? Happiness, anger, sorrow, and delight (*xinu aile* 喜怒哀樂) are what we call *qing*. But due measure and proper degree (*zhongjie* 中節) are the key to controlling *qing*; if one forgets about the heavenly principle (*tianli* 天理) for the sake of selfish feelings (*siqing* 私情), then the due measure and proper degree can never be attained." This is certainly a fairly standard Neo-Confucian view of *qing*. Then she cites various historical figures whose expressions of *qing* are either "appropriate" (*qing zhi zheng* 情之正) or "inappropriate" (*qing zhi bai* 情之敗; 40. 661–62). Awed by this learned discourse on *qing*, the daughters-in-law realize that the "differences between the *qing* of common people (*ernü zhi qing* 兒女之情) and what is being taught in the sagely learning (*shengxian xuewen* 聖賢學問) are as big as that between heaven and earth" (40.662). Phrases such as "keep *qing* appropriate with the help of principle" (*yili jieqing* 以理節情; 20.331) or " be loving but stick to the rules of propriety" (*duoqing shouli* 多情守禮; 50.807) are often used to describe a particular character's behavior. This is why Suchen urges his friend Chengzhi to free himself from not only the physical temptations (*sequan* 色圈) but also the entanglements of *qing* (*qingquan* 情

圈) if his love for Miss Min does not have the blessing of her father. *Qing* can literally become a trap or even a pit of passion (*qingkeng* 情坑; 50.803). Ultimately *qing* is as dangerous as, if not more dangerous than, *yu*, partly because it is more subtle and therefore sometimes more problematic. All this is meant to underscore the need to contain *qing* within the proper limits of *li*.

Yesou puyan's attitude toward *qing*, however, is not always consistent. There are occasions when the reader is made to wonder whether *li* is suffocating *qing*. What Suchen witnesses on his trip to the homeland of the aboriginal Miao people presents a rather different perspective on the issue of *qing* versus *li*. Among these people, who are not influenced by Confucianism, men and women are not segregated from each other, and premarital sex is considered necessary for a harmonious marriage. The reader is introduced to the teachings of the native sage of the Miao people (*tu shengren* 土聖人):

> The Dao of Heaven and Earth is nothing but the principle of *yin* and *yang*; the descending of the heavenly ether and ascending of earthly ether result in what is called the interaction of Heaven and Earth. There will be congestion if there is no such interaction. The women in the grottoes hold hands, pat shoulders, hug, and hold faces with men, thus facilitating the flow of the heavenly and earthly ether, and this is the principle of the interactions of *yin* and *yang*. Chinese custom prescribes that men and women be segregated and that women must hide their faces when going out. This blocks the intercourse of *yin* and *yang* and results in congestion. When the *qing* between men and women is not allowed proper outlet, it will try to destroy the constraints and overflow. Consequently, people will have affairs (*zuanxue yuqiang* 鑽穴逾牆) and commit many acts of indecency; some will even resort to elopement or abductions, jealous fighting, murdering husbands, and other kinds of crime that cannot be stopped. All this is due to the apparently too strict constraints that have deprived people of the outlet for sexual love (*nannü muyue zhi qing* 男女慕悅之情). (94.1475)

The native sage's critique of the Confucian view of marriage is even more specific:

> As for the custom of marriage in China, all depends on parental direction and the words of the matchmakers; the man and woman involved are not allowed to make their own decisions. How could the two love each other as a result? But the custom in the grottoes is quite different: a man and a woman sing to each other, and they consent to marriage only after they fall in love with each other; thus nothing is forced and everything is done according to *qing* (feeling and specific situation); when a girl meets a man, she is allowed to pat his shoulders and hold his hands so that she

could communicate her feelings to him; if she loves him, she can hug him and hold his face to express her love fully (*yizhi qiqing* 以至其情); if the ether has free flow, there should be no congestion and no scandals of adulteries. Human heart/mind is something that cannot be oppressed, and the kingly principles originate from human *qing* (*renqing* 人情). (94.1475–76)

This is a fairly eloquent and commonsensical discussion of sexual love. What is especially interesting is that Wen Suchen, who, under normal circumstances, seldom forgoes an opportunity to critique ideologies in conflict with orthodox Confucianism, remains rather conspicuously quiet.[12] Wen Suchen's silence may be understood as a result of his wish to avoid offending the Miao people, who have not been exposed to the benign influence of Han culture. However, the presence of this heretical view of *qing* in the novel is significant in itself. What is even more interesting is how the native sage bases his defense of the Miao marriage custom on the concept of *qing* by playing on its ambiguities (*qing* as feeling, truth/reality, and even human nature). The fact that this alternative view of *qing* can be permitted only in the context of a supposedly uncultured race also tells the reader that the orthodox Confucian view of *qing* is still the only viable one despite this interesting though rather unexpected exception.

What further complicates the representation of desire in *Yesou puyan* is the insistence on presenting Wen Suchen as a man of tremendous sexual potency, despite the fact that he, unlike the male protagonist in a typical erotic fiction, never takes advantage of his unusual endowment to engage in illegitimate sex and despite his belief that sex is superfluous. Suchen's male potency, the reader is repeatedly told, is used solely for the purpose of procreation. However, Suchen, because of his handsome appearance as well as his unusually impressive sexual endowment, often attracts unwelcome attention. Once Wen Suchen unwittingly attracts the attention of a peeping maid when he urinates. The reader is told that the size of Suchen's member is extremely impressive and that it takes a long half-hour for him to finish urinating, presumably because of its size (67.1050; this is a common plot device in erotic fiction, as we will see in the discussion of *Guwangyan*). Then we are told the harem master Li Youquan is able to suck a large quantity of semen from Wen Suchen when the latter is drugged. Suchen's semen turns

12. For a discussion of "Miao sexuality" in the novel, see Kuriyama, "Confucianism in Fiction," pp. 174–85.

out to be more potent than anything Li Youquan has ever taken (it is certainly much more potent than an aphrodisiac). The magical effect of Suchen's semen enables Li Youquan to wage "battles" with fourteen of his concubines during one night and achieve unconditional victory. Suchen is repeatedly admired as *chunyang* 純陽 (pure essence of the *yang* energy) by others in the novel (see, e.g., 67.1057). Almost all the women in Li Youquan's harem go crazy over his urine and semen because of their tonic or aphrodisiac benefits. One woman claims that his urine is sweet and fragrant, better than any tea (68.1068). These women become so crazy about Suchen that the maid Xingxiao kills herself by smashing her head against the ground when that "treasure" (Suchen) is snatched away from her care at the order of Li Youquan, presumably because she is so despondent at the loss of access to this wonder of "supreme male sexuality" (67.1057). Wen Suchen is the ultimate symbol of male sexual potency, even though he never intentionally allows his endowment to be misused. Consequently, despite the novel's repeated insistence that sex is superfluous except for the solemn purpose of procreation, sex does matter in the case of Wen Suchen, even when the sole concern is sometimes sexual pleasure rather than the duty of procreation. To complete his image as a super-literatus and all-around talent (including sexual "talent"), Wen Suchen has to be presented as someone with a tremendous sexual endowment, just like a male protagonist in a typical erotic fiction, despite, or precisely because of, the fact that sex is superfluous and physical desire is condemned in the novel. To authenticate this condemnation, Wen Suchen has to be blessed with an enormous capacity for sex, and that capacity has to be celebrated.

Qing and *Yu* in *Guwangyan*

It is a generally accepted among scholars of Chinese fiction that the late sixteenth and early seventeenth centuries represent the heyday of Chinese erotic fiction and that it underwent a significant decline after the seventeenth century. However, the rediscovery of *Guwangyan* may compel us to revise this view, not the least because this full-length eighteenth-century erotic novel shows an impressive creativity and a determination to outdo all previous works in this genre. Almost all the important bibliographies of traditional Chinese fiction either list *Guwangyan* as "not seen" or fail to mention it at all. Part of the novel (about two chapters) was published separately, in a very limited edition in the 1930s. It was not until 1997 that a complete modern typeset edition of the novel was published; this edition is based on a nineteenth-century hand-copied manuscript held in the National Library of Russia in Moscow.[13] This lengthy novel of almost one million characters is divided into only twenty-four chapters (*juan* 卷). Each chapter has a couplet-title and a subtitle in the form of another couplet. This is a rather unique feature for a traditional Chinese novel.

Guwangyan consists mainly of the stories of Tong Zida (a wealthy landowner and merchant), Huan E (a rich relative of a high official), Jia Wenwu (a *jinshi* degree holder), Zhong Qing (a poor student who later succeeds in the civil-service examinations), and Qian Gui (a talented and beautiful courtesan), with lengthy digressions that relate the stories of many other, less significant characters. One character trait shared by a majority of the characters is that they are consumed by lust, and many of them suffer a tragic end or undergo a terrible retribution as a result of their inability to control their desires, a common fate for the libertine characters in many works of erotic fiction. Some well-known late Ming, early Qing historical figures, such as the notorious official Ruan Dacheng 阮大成 (1587–1646) and the leader of the peasant rebellion Li Zicheng 李自成 (ca. 1605–45), also make an appearance and receive ample attention in the novel. The "evil deeds" of these historical figures are now, however, attributed to their sexual lust, and we are told in detail how their excessive sexual desire contributed to their moral degeneration or, vice versa, how their corrupt morality led them to seek maximum gratification of their sexual lusts at any cost. Despite his generous hand with all the titillating details of the sexual (mis)adventures of various characters, the narrator, like the typical narrator in erotic fiction, repeatedly reminds us that uncontrollable sexual desires are the ultimate cause of disaster (in fact, the fall of the Ming monarchy is in large part blamed on the uncontrollable craving for sex of many high officials and crooks). The

13. For a brief discussion of the textual history of the novel and the manuscript copy in Russia, see "*Guwangyan* chuban shuoming" 姑妄言出版說明, in *Guwangyan*, Siwuxie huibao series, pp. 15–27. All references to the novel, unless otherwise noted, are to this edition with chapter and page numbers given in parentheses. A new typeset edition of the novel published by Zhongguo wenlian chuban in Beijing (1999) came to my attention after the draft of this chapter had been completed. I suspect, however, that this edition is probably a pirated version of the Siwuxie huibao edition, with all the explicit passages expurgated.

general picture of society presented in this long novel is that of a sea of lusts (*yuhai* 欲海).

The wives of Tong Zida, Huan E, and Jia Wenwu are shrews who terrorize their husbands, presumably because the husbands cannot satisfy their wives' sexual needs. In the second half of the novel, however, these husbands regain control of their households and the respect of their wives after they receive help from Buddhist monks and Taoist priests who are experts on the arts of the bedchamber. In fact, this instruction is in large part a retributive reward the husbands receive for reforming themselves morally. The novel's message is the "common wisdom," preached repeatedly in erotic fiction, that a sexual encounter is a "battle"—a battle of the sexes. The partner who "outlasts" his or her partner in sex (a question of sexual endurance) is the one who achieves control and dominance. The men use the arts of the bedchamber to tame their shrewish wives (the wives torture their husbands because of their frustrations in bed, but more symbolically, they are the agents of retribution and punish their husbands for their moral incompetence, which is in turn symbolized by their sexual inadequacy). Thus, the importance of sex is indirectly acknowledged in the novel in spite of the concerns over the potential of sex to become excessive or lead to evil, as demonstrated by the majority of its characters, who are ruined because of their failure to control their sexual desires. It is probably accurate to say that the narrator does not see sexual desire per se as evil, although he focuses on the dangers and consequences once it becomes uncontrollable.

Of course, telling cautionary stories about the dangers of excessive sex is a well-established convention of Chinese erotic fiction, and *Guwangyan*'s indebtedness to several well-known erotic novels is obvious. On the one hand, there are explicit references to works such as *Ruyijun zhuan* (24.2952) and *Dengcao heshang* (5.645), and the commentator constantly reminds the reader of the differences or similarities between this novel and works such as *Jing Ping Mei*. There are also direct borrowings. One classic erotic fiction that *Guwangyan* consciously emulates, for example, is the seventeenth-century *Rou putuan* attributed to Li Yu. In chapter 8, the character Jiashi tries to seduce her servant Ainu by purposely yelling that no one should come into the room because she is taking a bath. Of course, her real intent is to catch the servant's attention and invite him in (8.990). This scene of a mistress trying to seduce her servant by exhibiting herself in a bathtub more than likely was inspired by the similar scene in *Rou putuan*.[14] Obviously impressed by the witty discourse on the pros and cons of sex at the beginning of *Roupu tuan*, at one point in the novel the narrator of *Guwangyan* delivers a similar message:

> Only then did he realize that *The Great Pharmacopoeia* (*Bengcao gangmu* 本草綱目) had failed to mention the potential harm of this thing [the female sexual organ]. . . . Therefore I would like to add the following passage to *The Great Pharmacopoeia* so that people of later generations can be warned. . . . It is just like the tonic ginseng; it will improve your health if you take it occasionally; however, it will be fatal if you take it as daily food. This is not the fault of ginseng, but the result of the ignorance on the part of the person who takes it this way. (6.730–31)[15]

Guwangyan outdoes its models, however. To the best of my knowledge, no other full-length Chinese novel has ever devoted so many pages to explicit descriptions of sex; even the famous *Jin Ping Mei* pales in comparison. *Guwangyan* boasts the whole repertoire of sexual encounters found in traditional Chinese erotic fiction: adultery, orgies, sexual vampirism (*caizhan* 採戰), the sexual awakening of precocious youngsters, sex between fox-spirits and humans, sex between animals and humans, and the uses of various aphrodisiacs. In fact, the novel has been described as a grand "compendium" (*jidacheng* 集大成) of all the major erotic motifs in traditional Chinese literature.[16] By virtue of its sheer length and its comprehensiveness, *Guwangyan* outdoes all other previous works in the genre of erotic fiction by presenting lengthier and more outrageous descriptions of all kinds of sexual encounters (most works of erotic fiction are of medium length; *Jin Ping Mei* is one of the few exceptions).

Another important difference, of greater interest to the present discussion, is that, unlike many other erotic novels such as *Rou putuan*, the author of this eighteenth-century novel included a few oases of ardent love, or *qing*, in the novel's vast desert of promiscuous lusts, or *yu*. Indeed, in a world in

14. In chapter 14 of *Rou putuan*, Yuxiang uses the same trick to seduce the servant Quan Laoshi; see Li Yu, *Rou putuan*, 14.376–77; and Hanan, trans., The *Carnal Prayer Mat*, p. 210.

15. Cf. Li Yu, *Rou putuan*, 1.136–37; and Hanan, trans., *The Carnal Prayer Mat*, pp. 5–6. The influence of Li Yu can be found elsewhere in *Guwangyan*. For example, the passage in chap. 19 that describes how Zhenshi is tricked into losing her chastity by a monk with the help of her maids and how she commits suicide may have been inspired by the prologue story in "Fuyun lou" 拂雲樓 in Li Yu's *Shi'er lou*, pp. 152–53; see also Hanan, trans., *A Tower for the Summer Heat*, pp. 118–20.

16. "*Guwangyan* chuban shuoming," in *Guwangyan*, p. 19.

which most people seek maximum gratification for their animal lust, the story of Zhong Qing's love for the courtesan Qian Gui stands out. In deliberate contrast to almost all other characters in the novel, Zhong Qing and Qian Gui are romantic lovers, and their commitment to each other never wavers. With this pair of "exceptional" lovers, the novel polarizes sexual relationships into the two distinct categories of faithful love (*qing*) and promiscuous lust (*yu*). In contrast to the detailing depictions of the bedroom activities of the other characters, the narrator always carefully refrains from explicit description in the scenes of intimacy between Zhong Qing and Qian Gui, as if he fears that direct reference to the physical aspects of their relationship might seriously compromise the sanctity of their saintly love as well as the sacredness of the enterprise of *qing* they are meant to symbolize. Of course, all this is made even more remarkable by the contrast with the graphic and detailed accounts of sheer animal lust in the rest of the novel.[17]

As is immediately apparent from the name Zhong Qing 鍾情 (literally, "faithful and loving"), this character is a symbol of the essence of *qing*. The story of Zhong Qing and Qian Gui—how a poor student falls in love with a beautiful courtesan and eventually achieves success in the examination and in his career with her help and encouragement—is a conventional plot in Chinese romantic literature, and *Guwangyan* adds nothing to this trope. What complicates this story and thus makes it more significant, however, is its juxtaposition with various stories of sheer lust. Here, the concept of *qing* is renegotiated within the context of overwhelming *yu*, or lust and promiscuity. The desexualized *qing* typical of many early Qing scholar-beauty novels is carefully *re*framed within the context of an oversexualized erotic narrative.

A closer look at specific strategies of desexualization in this peculiar erotic novel will make this clear. Early in the novel, Qian Gui is said to have been forced into prostitution by her mother, who is an extremely lustful and

17. Of course, it is not unusual for the narrator of a work of traditional fiction to refrain from being specific when it comes to the description of the intimate moments involving a "positive" character. As pointed out by David Rolston ("*Lin Lan Xiang* yu *Jin Ping Mei*," p. 117), both Zhang Zhupo and Jilü sanren in their respective comments on *Jin Ping Mei* and *Lin Lan Xiang* observed that the authors tended to be more sexually explicit in the cases of insignificant or negative characters. See Zhang Zhupo, "Dufa," no. 51, *Zhang Zhupo*, pp. 41–42; and *Lin Lan Xiang*, 13.103.30, 21.167.10, and the chapter-end comment, 28.221. However, the contrast in *Guwangyan* is so deliberate that the effect is much more striking.

promiscuous prostitute. Beautiful and talented, Qian Gui possesses all the attributes of a romantic courtesan (*mingqi* 名妓). She is able to endure the life of a prostitute only because she harbors the hope that one day she will marry a promising and loving young man (*congliang* 從良). She declines a marriage proposal from the handsome and rich Mr. Qi because she is convinced that he is interested only in *se* (a woman's physical beauty) and not in *qing* (3.376). Meeting Zhong Qing for the first time, she immediately spots in him talent and a heart for deep *qing*. Once Qian Gui pledges her love for Zhong Qing, she decides to resort to suicide without hesitation to protect her "chastity" (*shoujie* 守節) despite, or because of, the fact that she has been a prostitute for many years (4.466–67).[18] As a symbol of female chaste *qing*, Qian Gui, we are told, likes to quote from the poems of the legendary Xiaoqing (12.1375), whose name was synonymous with a talented woman of great *qing* during the late Ming and early Qing (see Chapters 7 and 8). At one point in the novel, Qian Gui is referred to as a *shizhen ji* 矢貞妓 (a chaste prostitute or a prostitute who has sworn to be chaste; the title of chapter 14, p. 1623).

For his part, Zhong Qing is no less faithful a lover. After Qian Gui and Zhong Qing become engaged, Qian Gui expresses her fear that Zhong Qing will forget her once he passes the civil-service examinations. Zhong Qing goes out of his way to remind her (as well as the reader) of the symbolic meaning of his own name—"faithful in love" (4.467). His name may also be associated with that of the male protagonist Qin Zhong 秦重 (a pun on *qingzhong* 情種) of the third story, "The Oil Peddler Marries the Most Beautiful Girl," in Feng Menglong's *Xingshi hengyan* 醒世恒言 (Constant words to awaken the world). In fact, Qian Gui mentions that she wants to follow the example set by the female protagonist (a courtesan who marries an oil peddler) in the drama *Zhan huakui* 占花魁 by Li Yu 李玉 (ca. 1591–ca. 1671), which has the same plot and was probably influenced by Feng's story. Furthermore, Zhong Qing repeatedly declines the advances of several beautiful women (*quese* 卻色). For instance, when a woman offers herself to him after he has rescued her, Zhong Qing says: "Given that men are naturally attracted toward beautiful women, I would have loved to marry a beautiful woman like you, had I not been engaged already. It would be a lie if

18. Later Qian Gui indeed tries to commit suicide when forced by her mother to receive a guest (5.655–56).

I insisted that I were not tempted at all. Despite my tender sentiment toward you, there are things one cannot do because of one's sense of propriety" (9.1136). This is certainly a diplomatic way of saying no to a woman, something Wen Suchen also has to do repeatedly.

Zhong Qing is admired for his great *qing* by many in the novel because he insists on fulfilling his pledge to marry Qian Gui despite the fact that she is a prostitute, even though he has already achieved success in the civil-service examinations. The greatness of his *qing* in large part hinges on the fact that Qian Gui is a prostitute, a woman who has been taken by ten thousand men (to use a phrase from *Jin Yun Qiao zhuan*). However, this fact does become a source of anxiety and uneasiness for the novelist. The narrator pointedly emphasizes that Qian Gui's maid, Daimu, has managed to keep her virginity intact (保住了女身; 14.1683), although she is eighteen years old. The commentator is quick to alert the reader to the significance of this crucial fact: Daimu is later to be married to Zhong Qing as a concubine at the encouragement of her mistress. It would have been a great pity if none of Zhong Qing's wives was a virgin (14.1683). Later in this chapter, the narrator even relaxes his reluctance to describe physical passion in relation to Zhong Qing in the description of Zhong Qing and Daimu's wedding night (he is always quite reticent when it comes to intimate scenes between Zhong Qing and Qian Gui) so that he can emphasize how much Zhong Qing relishes the "taste of a virgin" that night (14.1742). This is obviously meant to be a compensating experience for Zhong Qing since Qian Gui as a prostitute cannot provide him the "pleasure" to which every husband is entitled. Daimu's 代目 name "Substitute Eyes," is given her by Qian Gui, who is blind and has to rely on her eyesight to see things. Here the maid not only provides "eyesight" for her mistress (*daimu*) but also offers her own virginal body as a substitute for her mistress's defiled body (*daishen* 代身) in order to compensate Zhong Qing. Wang Cuiqiao in *Jin Yun Qiao zhuan* also resorts to *daishen* when she asks her sister Yunqiao to replace her as the wife of Jin Zhong; a virginal body becomes especially significant when one of the women is no longer a virgin. Although Zhong Qing does consummate his marriage with Qian Gui, a prostitute, Jin Zhong's marriage with Wang Cuiqiao is never consummated precisely because she used to be a prostitute, despite the fact that a substitute (a virginal body) has already been provided. Zhong Qing's love for Qian Gui, no matter how perfect, has to be authenticated in the patriarchal value system by a virginal body (even in the form of a substitute). The desexualization of *qing* never means that bodily concerns (especially the concern about a female virginal body) are no longer important. In fact, the body becomes even more important, although often by default.

The beautiful woman who happens to be a prostitute or a singsong girl but is able to spot a talented man and pledges herself to him even before he has achieved any career success has been a familiar theme in the Chinese romantic tradition ever since the Sui dynasty love story of Hongfu 紅拂 became popular. Again, the idea of *zhiji* or, in the words of the novel, *zhixin* 知心 (soul mate; literally, "understanding one's heart"; 4.451–52), looms very large in Zhong Qing and Qian Gui's relationship. In fact, Zhong consents to visit Qian for the first time only after he is persuaded that she has a knack for spotting the talented but poor young scholar: "I don't believe there will ever be such a woman in the pleasure quarters. Given the fact that nowadays very few people are able to tell a talented man when they encounter one, how can a blind girl have such insight and such a romantic heart?" (4.451). The commentator is quick to remind the reader that Zhong Qing's bitter lament that "very few people are able to tell a talented man" is the *guzi* 骨子 (literally, "the bone"; by implication, the central theme) of the whole novel. To further emphasize the importance of the concept of a frustrated literatus finding appreciation in a beautiful woman, the novelist, the commentator tells the reader, has purposely created this blind female beauty to shame those who lack insight into others, because, unlike them, even a blind courtesan (*guqi* 瞽妓) can tell a talented man when she meets one (meaning these men are the ones who are "blind"; see the pre-chapter comment, 2.192). If we accept the commentator's interpretation, then we have to read Qian Gui as a character with the rhetorical function of shaming those who are "blind" to others' talents. It is indeed remarkable that this erotic novel contains such a carefully told story about "faithful love" or *qing*. It is even more remarkable that the author chose the medium of erotic fiction to vent his frustrations over the lack of appreciation for his talents, if we are persuaded by clues provided in the novel and by the commentator, who claimed a close personal relationship with the author of the novel.[19]

19. For the commentator's claim that he and the author are close friends, see "Zongping" 總評 (General comment; p. 75). For the author's complaint that he has been a loner and his frustrations over being unappreciated by others, see his "Zixu" 自序 (Self-preface; p. 65). In his "Ziba" 自跋 (Self-postscript) to the early Qing erotic romance *Taohua ying*, the author, Yanshui shanren 煙水山人 (*Taohua ying*, p. 221), claims that writers often write this kind of

Qing as it is conceived in the novel is closely associated with what has been called the "recognition motif" in literati writings (see Chapter 3). In other words, here *qing* is in large part defined as the ability to spot and the willingness to appreciate an unrecognized talent as well as the yearning to find such an appreciating mind and the determination to show appropriate gratitude after such appreciation is demonstrated. Zhong Qing, even before meeting Qian Gui in person, has already fallen in love with her because his friend is able to convince him that she possesses the rare ability to recognize a talented man before he achieves any success (*huiyan shi yingxiong* 慧眼識英雄). For her part, Qian Gui as a woman of *qing* can love only a handsome young man with great talent (才郎) such as Zhong Qing, a rather familiar theme in scholar-beauty fiction. However, what is unique about *Guwangyan* is its deliberate placement of a chaste romance amid the sordid world of the high erotic without blending the two worlds into a coherent whole (in the novel the two worlds are separate realms). In the erotic romances of the early Qing, erotic details and the scholar-beauty motifs are usually carefully integrated, but this is definitely not the case in *Guwangyan*. This awkward juxtaposition of the high erotic and the chaste compels the reader to take another look at the familiar scholar-beauty theme, which has became a cliché of many fictional works during the seventeenth century.

Another conventional aspect of *qing* that receives much emphasis in this erotic novel is the familiar idea of faithfulness in love (or "chastity" in the case of a woman). For example, the reader learns that Qian Gui begins to entertain the idea of quitting prostitution by marrying a talented young man after her maid reads her the story of Du Xiaoying in a collection titled *Lienü zhuan* 烈女傳 (Stories of heroic women of chastity). Du Xiaoying was probably a historical figure, and her story was recorded in many literati writings.[20] When still very young, Du Xiaoying already had a low opinion of

---

erotic novel (such as *Taohua ying*) to vent their frustrations and that they should be read as allegories.

20. In the recent article "*Guwangyan* sucai laiyuan chukao" (pp. 306–7), Chen Yiyuan points out that the passage on Du Xiaoying in the novel is copied almost verbatim from Chen Ding's 陳鼎 (b. 1650) *Liuxi waizhuan* 留溪外傳. The only change is Du's eloquent speech to the general (thus, she is presented not only as a chaste woman but also someone with political insight), which was added by the novelist. Du's story can be found in other literati writings of the time. For a brief discussion of Chen Ding's *Liuxi waizhuang*, see Xie Gouzhen, *Zengding WanMing shiji kao*, pp. 739–41. For a discussion of Du Xiaoying's writings, see Fong, "Signifying Bodies."

the famous Mulan 木蘭, who joined the army by masquerading as a man. According to Du, Mulan had compromised her chastity by living among the men, even though technically she remained a virgin. This testifies to Du's unusually strong sense of chastity. Later Du was kidnapped by Ming government troops dispatched to suppress a peasant rebellion. Brought before the commanding general of the government troops, Du's eloquent accusation that the troops who had been sent to fight for the country by crushing the peasant rebellion were instead oppressing the common people fell onto deaf ears. To protect her chastity, she committed suicide by jumping into Dongting Lake before the general could sexually assault her. Before her death, however, she composed ten poems declaring her intention to keep her chastity at any cost ("suicide poems" or *jueming shi* 絕命詩). After listening to the story of Du, Qian Gui pledges in tears:

> This is how a woman should conduct herself. Unfortunately I was born into a family in the profession of prostitution. My body is already soiled, and even death cannot change this fact. Although it is too late for me to change the beginning of my life but there is still time to shape the end. If one day I can find a talented man (*cailang* 才郎) I shall chasten my body to offer it to him. I will not allow myself to follow the route many others have already taken and thus become a laughingstock. (3.367)

An interesting fact in this story of Du Xiaoying is that she sealed the poems into the clothes she was wearing before she committed suicide with a note for those who found her body. The note said that since Nanchang was the capital of the province and a gathering place for many scholar-officials (*shidafu* 士大夫) and since that year was the year of the provincial exams (thus many examination candidates would be in the capital), she believed that these morally upright scholars would deliver her poems to her parents if they discovered her body in the lake (3.363–64). Du Xiaoying seemed convinced that the literati were the people who could appreciate her heroic act of chastity and were sure to spread her good name. By implication, her heroic act of suicide was performed in part for the sake of being appreciated by these literati. And she was right: her story and her poems, due to the efforts of literati, indeed were widely circulated later. No wonder Qian Gui, after listening to her story, vows to discipline her body if she can spot a talented young scholar (of course, the fact that Qian Gui is a courtesan to start with makes such an act of heroic chastity even more remarkable). Consequently, female chastity is here presented as an important quality of *qing* that is somehow related to the moral makeup of a literatus—only an upright literatus will appreciate such a virtuous act on the part of a chaste girl. The image of *lienü* or women determined to keep their chastity at any cost appears many times in *Guwangyan* (7.814, 19.2408, and 21.2581), a fact that gains added significance given the stories of promiscuity that fill the rest of this novel.

Such acts of female chastity, in turn, parallel the equally heroic acts of political loyalty on the part of some male characters. The novel's ultimate "loyal" minister happens to be none other than Zhong Qing. There is a close correspondence, the novel seems to insist, between a man's private moral integrity and his political virtue in public arenas. A faithful lover is a loyal official, as demonstrated by the story of Zhong Qing. Not only is he a great lover in terms of his commitment to Qian Gui, but he is also an upright and loyal subject/official to the imperial throne. Just as Qian Gui is willing to vindicate her chastity with her own life, Zhong Qing, out of his strong sense of loyalty, risks his own life to remonstrate with the Chongzhen emperor. He is saved from being flogged to death, ironically, only because the emperor is reminded of the unpleasant possibility that a martyred Zhong Qing is sure to win a reputation as a loyal minister (16.1955–59). This is reminiscent of similar acts of political loyalty on the part of Wen Suchen.[21] The novel seems to suggest that loyal ministers must be men of great *qing* (dedicated lovers or husbands) as well, and that disloyal, evil ministers such as Ruan Dacheng are lustful, promiscuous men (the novel devotes many pages to horror stories of Ruan Dacheng and his family members, who seek to gratify their endless sexual desires in total disregard of all social or ethical rules).

In *Guwangyan*, *qing* means loyalty in both private relationships and imperial politics. Sometimes the two areas are almost interchangeable. However, political loyalty has priority over personal commitments, if one is forced to choose between the two. At the end of the novel, disillusioned with politics (at a time when China is already under the firm control of the Manchus), Zhong Qing chooses to become a hermit living in a remote area, an ultimate gesture of loyalty to a toppled monarchy that almost amounts to a renouncement of private *qing* (he leaves Qian Gui and his family), an end reminiscent of the ending of *Taohua shan* (the author of *Guwangyan* might have read *Taohua shan* or seen it performed if the dating of the novel to

21. For discussions of Wen Suchen, see my *Literati and Self-Re/Presentation*, pp. 132ff, 138ff.

around 1730 is accurate). Here we may understand better why the author of this erotic fiction is so obsessed with the image of *lienü*, which can certainly have political implications. The narrator deplores that no official is ready to die (*sijie* 死節) for the Hongguang emperor of the short-lived Southern Ming monarchy (24.3027). Zhong Qing's renouncing of the world should therefore be read as an act of chastity (*jie* 節) for the fallen Ming monarchy, just as *lienü* sacrifice their bodies or lives to preserve their chastity.[22] Both are, of course, acts of *qing*.

Well aware of the possibility of being blamed for following the conventions of erotic fiction in which the libertine male protagonist often becomes a Taoist and enjoys sexual bliss with his lovers (now wives) at an even higher level, the novel's narrator proclaims that he is not sure whether Zhong Qing became a Taoist. Of course, Zhong Qing is not a promiscuous libertine but a faithful lover and later an official of high moral standards. It is probably this keen "political" consciousness that sets *Guwangyan* apart from many other erotic novels and that conditions its conceptualization of *qing*. Qian Gui and Zhong Qing mirror each other in their chastity and loyalty. Their story reminds people of the scholar-beauty fiction, in which the "relationship of the beauty and scholar takes on the characteristics of the friendship between two literati men" and "the couple replaces sex with words: poems, letters, and engaging conversation. Resembling two literati friends, they become *zhiji*."[23] This story of *qing* is obviously meant to serve as an antidote in the erotic world of the novel. It is almost deliberately anti-erotic. By juxtaposing stories of the contrasting aspects of desire—both the erotic and the "anti-erotic"—the novelist drives home the message that *qing*, understood as lofty sentiments, has to be desexualized and that *yu* is naturally a result of oversexuality. *Guwangyan* demonstrates that in the purifying process of *qing*, romantic love has to be desexualized into a relationship between two like-minded literati. Thus, it highlights a more general phenomenon in the tra-

22. For a general discussion of the late Ming fascination with *lienü*, see Carlitz, "The Social Uses of Virtue in Late Ming Editions of *Lienü zhuan*." For a discussion of the ambivalence exhibited by the literati toward *jie* during the turbulent years of the Ming-Qing transition, see Zhao Yuan, *Ming Qing zhiji shidafu yanjiu*, pp. 23–57.

23. McMahon, *Misers, Shrews, and Polygamists*, p. 103. See also his observation (p. 99): "The woman achieves her superiority only by becoming like a man, that is, by cross-dressing and literally acting and writing like him. The relationship of the beauty and scholar thus takes on the characteristics of the friendship between two literati men."

ditional discourse on love—the perceived presence of *qing* elements in a particular relationship is often in proportion to the degree to which the relationship is desexualized. In other words, sexuality in a relationship of *qing* has to be displaced by or allegorized into a male-male "homosocial" friendship—the story of how one literatus finds appreciation in another.[24]

Given the discussion so far, it may appear that there are only two distinct groups of characters in *Guwangyan*: a few saintly lovers, and a much larger number of characters under the total sway of uncontrollable lust. The author must also have felt the need to provide some "in-between cases." There are indeed moments in the novel when the distinctions between the two groups are problematized. The story of Yinshi is a good example.

As a teenager, Yinshi has already had many affairs with different boys. Her notoriety makes it unlikely her family can find her a decent husband. Finally, her father has to marry her to the actor Ying Yang (acting being one of the lowliest professions in traditional Chinese society). Ying Yang, who was violently raped by the vicious hooligan Nie Bianbao, cannot satisfy Yinshi's needs. They are also plagued by poverty. But their love for each other seems to be able to survive all this adversity. One day Yinshi meets a rich young man named Jin Kuang 金礦 (literally, "gold mine"), who takes a fancy to her. This provokes the following reasoning in Yinshi's mind: "We would not have to worry about our livelihood if I could capture him. . . . But my husband might be upset." However, on second thought, she reasons: "Now he is poor and exhausted by his work. Why can't he rest himself if there is money readily available. Poor in health, he must feel guilty when I, as young as I am, feel frustrated in bed. . . . It would be wrong of me to have a secret affair behind his back. Why don't I discuss this with him directly and see what he says?" (6.763). This plan can kill two birds with one stone—her husband can regain his health without having to work hard, and she can satisfy her physical needs, although she does not explicitly refer to the second benefit when she talks to her husband. According to her, this is a matter of "sacrificing her body to seek a living" (*sheshen yanghuo* 捨身養活) or, even better, "sacrificing her body to nurture her sick husband" (*sheshen yangfu* 捨身養夫; 6.744). This is indeed a plan that takes into account both *qing* and

24. Cf. Richard Hessney's ("Beautiful, Talented, and Brave," p. 95) observation on the gender relationship in a typical scholar-beauty fiction: "If the scholar and the beauty share their most vital characteristics, then they are essentially interchangeable."

yu. Yinshi's plea to her husband is full of tender *qing*: clasping the hands of her husband and with tears in her eyes, Yinshi begs:

> Take good care of your health. From now on you don't have to work. Dearest brother, I am doing this really for your sake. Do not think that I'm making up this sweet story in order to have a lover for myself. With your being absent from home all day working, I could have easily done something behind your back if I were really after my own pleasure. (6.745)

This earnest expression of *qing* finally persuades her husband to accept her arrangement, which brings lots of money into the family and takes care of her sexual needs. Yinshi's trading of her body for money may remind the reader of the notorious Wang Liu'er in *Jin Ping Mei*. With the approval and encouragement of her husband, Wang has sex with Ximen Qing to earn money. Like Ying Yang, Wang's husband, Han Daoguo, conveniently disappears whenever Ximen Qing comes to visit. However, in *Guwangyan* Yinshi's action is described as an act of *qing* (her concern for her husband's health) although it is also motivated by her own sexual needs, which Ying Yang, as her husband, has failed to satisfy. In contrast, Wang Liu'er's action in *Jin Ping Mei* is attributed to sheer avarice. Whereas there is indeed tenderness between Yinshi and Jin Kuang despite the "commercial" nature of their relationship, Wang Liu'er never has such feelings toward Ximen Qing. The commentator of *Guwangyan* is probably right when he observes that "Yinshi is a character made of seventy percent *qing* and thirty percent lust" (7.793).

The episode of Yinshi seems to suggest that the distinction between *qing* and *yu* is not always categorical. To a degree, Yinshi's story is more persuasive than that of Zhong Qing and Qian Gui, partly because theirs is overburdened with the conventional literati values associated with *qing*, which tend to desexualize a relationship between a man and a woman into abstract political clichés. Despite ambiguous moments like this, the general pattern of meaning in *Guwangyan* is predicated largely on the polarity of *qing* and *yu*.

Another message of the story of Yinshi is that a woman has the right to seek sexual fulfillment, even if this means affairs with someone other than her own husband, a message repeatedly articulated in the novel. After finding his wife has had an affair with a monk, Wu He 鄔合 (the name puns on *wuhe* 烏合, something put together improperly or, by extension, incompetence), who is sexually dysfunctional, demonstrates remarkable understanding: "A blooming young woman such as yourself is wasted on a man like me" (7.757).

This leads us to the interesting question about the relationship between *Guwangyan* and *Xingshi yinyuan zhuan*. Like that novel, *Guwangyan*, especially the first half, is full of stories of henpecked husbands and shrewish wives. The narrator even coins a comic term, *qingpa* 情怕 (fear arising out of love), to characterize these men's fear of their wives (2.291). The violent ways in which these husbands are physically abused and tormented by their wives resemble the similar descriptions in *Xingshi*. Tong Zida, no longer able to endure the physical abuse of his wife, tries to ask for help from his relatives. Much to his surprise and dismay, he finds out that all the men he approaches are even more henpecked than he. Even the magistrate is no exception. This is reminiscent of chapter 91 of *Xingshi* in which all Di Xichen's peers are said to be henpecked and to suffer from abusive wives. Furthermore, Tong Zida learns from gossip in a teahouse that the magistrate's wife, in order to keep her husband from having affairs with other women, stamps his penis when he leaves the house and checks it when he returns. If the stamp is smudged, she has evidence that he has been unfaithful to her and thus deserves a severe punishment. That is why the magistrate is always bent over (3.355). Jijie uses the same ingenious tactic on Di Xichen in chapter 79 of *Xingshi* (of course, *Xingshi* was not the first work to mention this practice by a jealous wife).[25]

Guwangyan, however, seems to offer a different explanation why these women became shrews by transforming these women into model wives once their husbands' performance improves with the aid of potency pills and special bedroom techniques. In other words, these wives became shrewish only because they were sexually frustrated by their husbands' failure to properly perform their duties as men. The narrator defends the wives by saying: "As for their needs in bed, this is something unavoidable as far as women are concerned. We should not blame them" (17.2032). Consequently, the importance of sex is indirectly acknowledged in the novel in spite of the author's overriding concerns with its potential to lead to excess and evil, which receive so much attention in the novel.

There are other similarities between this novel and *Xingshi*. Both are steeped in the theory of karmic retribution, although this is more prominent

25. See note 28 in Chapter 6, p. 150.

in *Xingshi*. Both narrators like to quote morality books such as *Taishang ganyingpian* 太上感應篇 and like to tell jokes, or *xiaohua* 笑話. Both novels share the same satirical tone, especially when it comes to depicting the embarrassment of their henpecked husbands. The mischievous behavior of Tie Hua (a friend of Chu Sikuan, the lover of Qian Gui's mother) during his childhood (2.237) matches the description of the childhood of Di Xichen in *Xingshi*. These similarities, as well as the lament over the fall of the Ming dynasty in the second half of the novel, tend to give people the impression that *Guwangyan* is a work typical of the "mood" of the early Qing when *Xingshi* was probably written despite the fact that the author's preface to *Guwangyan* is dated 1730.

On the other hand, it is tempting to speculate about the relationship between *Guwangyan* and *Honglou meng* and the possibility that Cao Xueqin might have read this work. The author of *Guwangyan* addresses himself as "Cao Qujing from SanHan" (三韓曹去晶) in his self-preface to the novel. During the early Qing, the area of Liaodong 遼東 (now part of the Liaoning province) was often referred to as SanHan. And we know that the ancestors of Cao Xueqin were probably from the same area.[26] The question whether the two Cao families were related is an interesting one, although so far no one has found any evidence. Both Cao Qujing and Cao Xueqin were apparently familiar with Nanjing (Nanjing is an important setting in *Guwangyan*).[27]

More significant is the kind of meta-fictional self-consciousness with which *Guwangyan* starts and that shows up sporadically throughout the novel. This self-consciousness on the part of *Guwangyan*, despite the two novels' many apparent differences, may anticipate *Honglou meng* and especially its much more elaborate beginning(s). Often the narrator of *Guwangyan* interrupts his narration to poke fun at the reader or remind him or her of certain meta-fictional points. For example, when the Taoist priest from the E'mei Mountain is reintroduced after his initial appearance at the beginning of the novel, the author questions the reader's memory:

26. There are two theories regarding the "ancestral native place" *zuji* 祖籍 of Cao Xueqin: one is that his family came from Fengrun 丰潤 (now part of Hebei province); the other possibility mentioned is Liaoyang 遼陽 (now part of Liaoning province). For a survey of the history of this debate, see Zhang Qingshan, "Cao Xueqin zuji lunzheng shuping" (Zhang favors Liaoyang). It seems that both theories agree that by the mid-seventeenth century, the Cao family was already living in Liaoyang.

27. See "*Guwangyan* chuban shuoming," in *Guwangyan*, pp. 16–17.

Where has this E'mei Mountain priest come from? Isn't he a character just fabricated by the author (*zuoshuren* 做書人) for the sole purpose of bringing about this happy affair for Jia Wenwu later? A reader should always have insights and good memory, keeping himself alert throughout his reading and being able to read the novel as a whole. Only by being such a reader will he really be able to appreciate the enormous pains (*kuxin bili* 苦心筆力) that have gone into the writing of this novel on the part of its author (*zuoshuzhe* 作書者). This old priest is actually the same person who took in residence in the Chaotian gong Temple in Nanjing many years ago. (15.1838–39)

At the end of the novel, when Zhong Qing has seen through the world and run away from his family to become a hermit, the author comments on the relationship of his own novel to the conventions of popular fiction:

Although I am rather reluctant to follow the conventions (*sutao* 俗套) of those fiction writers (*xiaoshuo jia* 小說家) by saying that Zhong Qing, such a gentleman of great virtue, has also become a Taoist, he must have become a recluse (*chushi de gaoren* 出世的高人) who is to enjoy longevity. (24.3047–48)

This meta-fictional gesture on the part of *Guwangyan* becomes more significant when we consider its generic nature as an erotic novel. A libertine male protagonist becoming a Taoist recluse and enjoying even more sexual bliss after numerous sexual escapades is a common feature of many works of erotic fiction such as *Langshi*, *Taohuaying*, and *Xinghua tian* 杏花天 (The paradise of apricot blossoms).[28] Obviously, Zhong Qing, as a man of great Confucian learning and deep *qing*, is anything but a typical libertine protagonist, although *Guwangyan* is certainly a highly erotic novel. Probably this is the very point the author is trying to emphasize: *Guwangyan* is an erotic novel of an entirely different sort.

The novel's most elaborate meta-fictional play occurs at its beginning. The story proper of *Guwangyan* begins (after the "Yinwen" 引文) with a drifter (*xianhan* 閑漢), whose first name is Dao 到 and last name is Ting 聽 and whose courtesy name is Tushuo 圖說. All this apparently puns on

28. For discussions of *Taohua ying* and *Xinghua tian*, see McMahon, *Misers, Shrews, and Polygamists*, pp. 142–46. For a discussion of the Taoist elements in the Ming literary romance *Tianyuan qiyu*, which was to exert a great influence on works such as *Taohua ying* and *Xinghua tian*, and its contribution to the formation of the convention of the libertine protagonist becoming a Taoist with his wives and concubines, see Wang Gang, *Langman qinggan yu zongjiao jingshen*, pp. 135–64.

daoting tushuo 道聽塗說 (street talk), the classic definition of *xiaoshuo* offered in the "Yiwenzhi" 藝文志 of the *Hanshu* 漢書 (History of the Han dynasty) by Ban Gu 班固 (A.D. 32–92).[29] Dao Ting likes to listen to gossip and has a good memory that enables him to remember all he has heard. He is also known for his ability to gossip and to talk nonsense (*baihua* 白話). One day, loafing along the street, he meets four or five people who are gossiping (*shuo xianhua* 說閑話). These people try to stop him and ask him to tell them some rumor or trivial news (*baihua*). He escapes from their harassment by telling them he has something important to attend to. They insist on knowing what it is. He tells them that because there are many fish in the Mochou Lake, people are borrowing nets and that he is going to get some fish for food and for a good drink. They believe him and go all the way to the lake only to find out he was lying. When asked why, Dao Ting retorts that they were the ones who had asked him to talk nonsense (*baihua*).

Later after drinking some wine, Dao Ting falls asleep. He dreams of entering the underworld, where he overhears verdicts sentencing ghosts to be reborn as different people as retributive punishment for what they have done in their previous lives. Among them are five ghosts who are reborn as the main characters in the story proper of the novel: Qian Gui, Zhong Qing, Huan E, Tong Zida, and Jia Wenwu. All four men are associated with Qian Gui in their previous lives. One is the ghost of a woman named Bai Jinzhong 白金重 in her previous life. Because of her stunning beauty, she is determined to marry the richest man under heaven, but her parents want her to marry a handsome and talented young man. She falls in love with an ugly young man named Huang Jinse 黃金色 from a rich family. However, her parents oppose the marriage. Consequently, Huang dies of lovesickness. Bai Jinzhong feels that she has to die because of her belief that "a woman should adorn herself for the man who admires her." Then three young scholars die of lovesickness for Bai Jinzhong after she refuses to marry any of them. The judge sentences Bai Jinzhong to be reborn as a blind prostitute to punish her for her love for money and her "blindness" to handsome men. In her forthcoming life, she will fall for a poor and but talented young man. To refer to her love for money in her previous life, her name will be Qian Gui 錢貴 (precious money). Huang is sentenced to be reborn as a poor scholar Zhong Qing 鍾情 (a man of deep love or *qing*), and the three talented young schol-

29. Ban Gu, "Yiwen zhi" 藝文志, in idem, *Hanshu*, p. 1745.

ars will be reborn as three rich men without any talent. Furthermore, these three rich men will marry shrewish wives as a punishment for their lust for female beauty.

This hilarious karmic scheme satirizes the scholar-beauty convention. What is even more interesting is the self-conscious parody of this convention. Qian Gui and Zhong Qing, in the story proper, play the exact roles of a scholar and a beauty, which they were not allowed to play or refused to play in their previous lives. The three young men are punished by being married to shrewish wives as a karmic punishment for their desire for a beautiful girl, something every male protagonist does in a typical work of scholar-beauty fiction. This seems to follow the allegorical rationale we discussed in relation to *Xingshi* (the shrews are meant to be a symbol of their husbands' uncontrollable desire), although this karmic explanation for their shrewishness is complicated by the fact that later in the novel these jealous and abusive women become model wives once their husbands become more competent sexually (as well as "ethically").

After waking up, Dao Ting tries to tell a group of people what he has "witnessed" in his dream. One of these people is not convinced and asks:

> "Brother, were you awake or dreaming when you overheard all this?"
>
> "I was awake when I overheard this," Dao Ting replied.
>
> "Are you now awake or still sleeping when you are talking to us at this moment?" asked the young man.
>
> "This is really ridiculous. I am talking to you while standing in this broad daylight. How can you say that I am sleeping!"
>
> "Brother, don't be offended. If you are awake, then why are you talking dream talk (*menghua* 夢話) with your eyes wide open?" asked that man.
>
> . . . Another person said: "This is not what we have meant. But did you overhear all this alone or with someone being together with you?"
>
> "This happened during the middle of the night. How could there be anyone else?"
>
> "Here you are wrong. You just said there were other junior judges and small ghosts. Just grab one of them to be your witness. Then you don't have to be afraid of others trying to refute your nonsense talk (*guihua* 鬼話). You haven't thought about this. That is why you are wrong."
>
> All the people began to clap and laugh. . . .
>
> At that moment, a Taoist priest walked up and said with a smile: "There are many strange things under Heaven. What this gentleman has just said may not necessarily be something totally fabricated. There might be some truth in it. Who

knows? Don't take it too seriously. If you believe what he has said, just treat it as something newsworthy. If you suspect what he has said is nonsense, then don't believe it." (1.145–48)

Dao Ting reappears in the last chapter of the novel. By now the novel's story has come to an end, and Dao Ting's dream has been confirmed by what the reader has read so far in the novel. This is why, the narrator/author tells us, he bothered to write this novel. Here the argument gets a bit tautological since Dao Ting's words are confirmed by what is narrated in the novel and the validity of the novel is in turn confirmed by Dao Ting's words. However, this nevertheless is an interesting meta-fictional ploy. In the author's self-preface to the novel, in which he tries to explain the meaning of *wang* 妄 (literally, "preposterous and false") in the title of the novel, he considers himself the only person who is awake (he calls his residence Duxing yuan 獨醒園 [Garden of the awakened loner]). As an awakened person who observes the deluded (*hun* 昏), he, the author argues, naturally finds all of them preposterous (*wang*). And these people would find him absurd in return. Therefore it is indeed difficult to tell who is false or preposterous (p. 65). The idea of being awake and drunken (*zui* 醉) is again referred to at the end of the novel. The author/narrator explains that he has titled the novel *Guwangyan* because he expects few readers to believe what has been said in the novel and that most will instead consider it preposterous (*wang*). Therefore, he has no choice but to entitle it "preposterous words," and consequently, the complete title is *Guwangyan* (literally, "preposterous words for the moment" or "stories told just for the sake of telling stories"). The self-mockery here betrays a deep frustration and bitterness, which are shared by the author of *Honglou meng*.

Here *wangyan* is reminiscent of *huangtang yan* 荒唐言 (absurd words), the phrase Cao Xueqin used to characterize the *Honglou meng*. Overhearing in a dream a prediction of what will happen to the major characters, the questioning of the authenticity of dream experience, and the joke about finding a witness to authenticate the dream experience all point to a meta-fictional self-consciousness that also characterizes *Honglou meng*. However, one thing that distinguishes *Honglou meng* from *Guwangyan* and probably many other novels is that this meta-fictional reflexivity is never sustained or integrated into the plot development of these works as it is in *Honglou meng*. There are many moments of brilliance in *Guwangyan*, but as a whole it never reaches the level of sophistication witnessed in *Honglou meng*.

CHAPTER TEN

Qing and the Reluctance to Grow up in Honglou meng

Despite moments of ambiguity, the insistence on the dichotomy between *qing* and *yu* remains fairly consistent in *Yesou puyan* and *Guwangyan*. The much more famous eighteenth-century novel *Honglou meng* obviously shares this obsession, although the concept of *qing* becomes much more subtle as well as more complex in this novel.

From the conversation between the Buddhist monk and the Taoist priest overheard by Zhen Shiyin in his dream in chapter 1, the reader learns that the story about to unfold is not the usual erotic romance (*fengyue gushi* 風月故事) but a novel about "genuine *qing* between young men and young women" (*ernü zhi zhenqing* 兒女之眞情; H, 1.8–9),[1] a message the author/narrator wants to establish in his reader's mind right at the outset. Indeed, the familiar polar concept of *qing* and *yu* occupies an important position in *Honglou meng*, but it is reconceived as the opposition between the "promiscuous lust of the flesh" (*pifu lanyin* 皮膚濫淫) and the "lust of intent" (*yiyin* 意淫) proposed by the Goddess of Disenchantment in her lecture to Baoyu in

1. All references to the novel, unless otherwise noted, are to the *Honglou meng* published by Renmin wenxue chubanshe in 1982, the first 80 chapters of which are based on the Gengchen 庚辰 manuscript edition. It is referred to as "H." In referring to the different manuscript versions of the novel, I follow the "naming" conventions adopted by Feng Qiyong et al., *Zhiyanzhi chongping "Shitou ji" huijiao.*

his dream journey in chapter 5. The "lust of the flesh" and the "lust of intent" may, at first glance, seem to correspond roughly to the usual senses of *yu* and *qing*: physical lust and romantic sentiment. Since the lust of intent is presented in contrast to the lust of the flesh, the former might be understood as "spiritual love" and as having little to do with physical desire. However, its implications are much more complicated, since in Baoyu's dream, the Goddess of Disenchantment asks him to sleep with her cousin Jianmei. Later, upon awakening, Baoyu insists on practicing with his maid Xiren what he has just learned in his dream, as if his dream experience had to be authenticated in real life. Consequently, physical desire is not completely excluded from the lust of intent (more on this point below). The specific implications of the concept of the lust of intent are nevertheless far from clear. Its ambiguities are underscored by the Goddess's caution that it "can be grasped by the mind but not expressed, apprehended intuitively but not described in words" (H, 5.90).[2] The concept defies verbal articulation, a fact not unrelated to the ambiguities associated with the concept of *qing* in Chinese cultural history.[3]

The Goddess's caution, however, did not discourage many readers from attempting to determine the meaning of this new concept. As soon as hand-copied manuscripts of the novel began to circulate in the mid-eighteenth century, the commentator Zhiyanzhai embarked on an effort to espouse this concept in terms of one's capacity to empathize with other people's wishes or feelings (*titie* 體貼), almost a kind of sentimental altruism.[4] Furthermore,

2. The English translation here follows Hsien-yi Yang and Gladys Yang, *The Dream of Red Mansions*, 1.80.

3. One of the related concerns of the novel is the inadequacy of the language of *qing*, as demonstrated in the tortuous love relationship between Baoyu and Daiyu. I will return to this point below.

4. I believe that the emphasis in vernacular fiction on "being considerate to others" as an important aspect of *qing* can probably be traced to the concept of *bangchen* 幫襯 celebrated in "The Oil Peddler Courts the Courtesan," the third story in Feng Menglong's *Xingshi hengyan*. See also Zhiyanzhai's interlineal comments in the Jiaxu 甲戌 manuscript version, in Zhu Yixuan, *"Honglou meng" Zhiping jiaolu*, p. 102. Hereafter, all citations of Zhiyanzhai's comments will refer to this convenient collection, with information on the manuscript version and page numbers given in parentheses. For the sake of convenience, I treat the Zhiyanzhai commentaries as a "collective term" referring to comments in the so-called Zhiyanzhai-commented manuscripts. These comments, however, are sometimes signed with other names, such as Qihusou 畸笏叟. For a discussion of the complicated issue of the identity of Zhiyanzhai, see Sun Xun, *"Honglou meng" Zhiping chutan*, 43–77.

Zhiyanzhai tried to associate *titie* with what he called *qing buqing* 情不情 (to have feeling for the unfeeling), which, according to him, is the category to which Baoyu will be assigned when he is entered in the Goddess of Disenchantment's register of love (*qingbang* 情榜) at the end of the novel, the part of the "original" manuscript supposed to have been lost (marginal comment in the Jiaxu manuscript; see Zhu Yixuan, p. 152). Throughout his commentaries on the novel, Zhiyanzhai repeatedly used the term *qing buqing* to account for some seemingly strange behavior on Baoyu's part. For example, in chapter 19, Baoyu pays a visit to a scroll hung on the wall of a study because he imagines that the lady portrayed in the painting might feel lonely. This, according to Zhiyanzhai, is an act of *qing buqing*—to love someone or something that is not necessarily able to reciprocate such love (comment in the Mengfu 蒙府 manuscript; Zhu Yixuan, p. 267). Obviously, the lady painted in the portrait has no "feelings" (*buqing*) but Baoyu feels for her. Indeed, there are only too many examples in the novel in which Baoyu is shown to be a person of tremendous empathy; sometimes he appears to be almost completely selfless in his devotion to all the beautiful and talented girls in his life. In chapter 30, when it suddenly starts to rain, Baoyu's immediate concern is that the actress Lingguan (Charmante) might catch cold and he urges her to go inside to avoid getting wet, oblivious to the fact that he himself is also standing in the rain. Again in chapter 35, when hot soup is spilled over his own hand, Baoyu, instead of feeling his own pain, first inquires if the maid Yuchuan has been hurt. This provokes ridicule from the two elderly women visitors from the family of Fu Qiufang; they are convinced that Baoyu "must be a simpleton" (*daizi* 呆子; H, 35.482; S, 2: 189).[5]

However, there is a more subtle aspect of *qing buqing* on Baoyu's part that bespeaks a very different implication for the lust of intent. Recently critics have called attention to the importance of "subjectivity" in understanding Baoyu's desires. In fact, the character *yi* 意 in the word *yiyin*, which I have chosen to translate as "intent" rather than "mind" as David Hawkes and others have done in their English rendering of this term (the lust of the mind), carries an implicit emphasis on "subjective will." In traditional philosophical discourse, the "private" nature of *yi* is sometimes contrasted with the "public"

5. See Wai-yee Li, *Enchantment and Disenchantment*, pp. 202–10, for a detailed discussion of Baoyu's *yiyin* in terms of Zhiyanzhai's concept of *qing buqing*. Unless otherwise noted, all English translations of passages in the novel are from Hawkes and Minford, *The Story of the Stone*, with volume and page numbers given in parentheses. Their translation will cited as "S."

implications of *zhi* 志 (which can also be translated as "intent"). Zhu Xi distinguished the two by observing that "*zhi* refers to what one intends to do publicly (*gongran zhuzhang* 公然主張), whereas *yi* refers to what one intends to do in private (*sidi qianxing* 私地潛行)."[6] By translating *yi* as "intent," I also wish to emphasize that as a form of desire *yiyin* is concerned more often with the act of "intending" itself rather than with the actualization of any specific intent or the object of that "intent" (more on this point below).

In a recent study of the novel, Anthony Yu points out that the kind of desire Baoyu is experiencing is "determined more by his own subjectivity than by its object. Intellectually and emotionally far more capacious than those worldly profligates who respond to immediate physical stimuli, he is someone who also feels the grip of desire through vicarious participation in memory or imagination."[7] Yu then goes on to interpret Baoyu's visit to the lady in the portrait in chapter 19 as an illustration of this intensively subjective nature of his desire. We may go one step further by observing that it is precisely this indifference to the object of his desires that compels us to see a more subtle and very different aspect of Baoyu's "lust of intent," namely, his excessive self-indulgence or even narcissistic inclination.[8] In Baoyu's encounter with Lingguan in chapter 30, for example, Baoyu's seemingly selfless concern for Lingguan may turn out to be less selfless when it is carefully scrutinized and properly contextualized:

> . . . he saw a tearful girl crouching down on the other side of the trellis, scratching at the ground with a hair pin.
>
> "Can this be some silly maid coming here to bury flowers like Ping'er [Daiyu]?" he wondered. "If this is true, this is really a case of 'the ugly neighbor trying to ape the frowning of the beautiful Xishi.' This is not only far from refreshing (*xinte* 新特) but even disgusting." (H, 30.425; S, 2: 102; trans. modified)

As long as Baoyu mistakenly believes that Lingguan is trying to ape Daiyu's burying of fallen flower petals, his response is disgust apparently because he assumes that only someone as graceful as Daiyu is entitled to perform this

6. Zhu Xi, *Zhuzi yulei, juan* 5, p. 96.

7. Anthony Yu, *Rereading the Stone*, pp. 202–3.

8. Cf. Wai-yee Li's observation (*Enchantment and Disenchantment*, p. 207): "The obverse side of this selfless devotion is extreme self-indulgence, the desire that the universal order of things should conform to one's wishes." Li, however, does not elaborate on this point. For a discussion of Baoyu's narcissism in terms of his "*ziai zilian*" 自哀自憐, see Chen Weizhao, *Lunhui yu guizhen*, pp. 143–45.

aesthetic ritual. He changes his mind, however, when he finds out that the girl is one of the twelve actresses rather than a maid (in his mind, an actress probably enjoys a higher status than a maid). Baoyu is touched when he sees her writing the character *qiang* 薔 on the ground; he thinks she must have something burdensome on her mind and wishes he could share this burden with her. Then the rain starts. Here the deep concern for others attributed to Baoyu (an act of *qing buqing*) is problematized by his initial mistaken assumption that he is witnessing a maid's blaspheming of the sacred pose of a beauty burying fallen flower petals.

Baoyu views everything *aesthetically*, as if he were a completely disinterested observer. However, this aesthetic observation is complicated by Baoyu's sense that an actress is somehow more qualified than a maid to mimic Daiyu. Is this because acting is itself a profession of imitation? Later, in chapter 36, however, this aesthetic distance disappears quickly; Baoyu's status as a disinterested observer cannot be sustained after he witnesses what is going on between Jia Qiang and Lingguan, which, strangely enough, is reminiscent of the tortuous relationship between Baoyu and Lin Daiyu (Lingguan resembles Lin Daiyu in appearance). Much to his dismay, Baoyu is forced to the painful conclusion that his assumption that he has every right to share with Lingguan what is on her mind is seriously mistaken! Not only are there many things that a girl definitely does not want to share with him, but also, even more shockingly (to him), not every girl finds his attentions welcome. This revelation is shocking to him precisely because it never occurred to him that any girl as pretty as Lingguan could be interested in a man other than himself (a fairly egoistic expectation).

Baoyu here is obviously as conceited as his father Jia Zheng has alleged. In Baoyu's own words, he now realizes that he will not be able to claim "the tears of all the girls" (*buke quande* 不可全得):

> "What I told you the other night was wrong. No wonder father tells me that I am too self-conceited (*guankui lice* 管窺蠡測). I now realize that I was wrong to say that all of you will shed tears exclusively for me when I die. Obviously I cannot claim the tears of all the girls." (H, 36.495; S, 2: 210; trans. modified)

Soon after this painful realization, Baoyu begins to wonder who will shed tears for him when he dies. That all the pretty girls should do so obviously obsesses Baoyu. It is no coincidence that in his dream in chapter 5, one of the drinks that the Goddess of Disenchantment offers him is called *qianhung yiku* 千紅一窟, a homophonic pun on "the tears of all the maidens" (千紅一哭) and that another is called *wanyan tongbei* 萬艷同杯, a homophonic pun on "the sorrows shared by all the beauties" (萬艷同悲; H, 5.82–83).[9] The most direct reference to this obsession is his expressed wish to die while all the girls are still there to cry for him (ironically, the very next day he meets Lingguan and is forced to face the simple facts that not every pretty girl is interested in him and that many of them would not care at all if he were to die):

> Now *my* idea of a glorious death would be to die now, while you are all around me; then your tears could combine to make a great river that my corpse would float on, far, far away to some remote place that no bird has ever flown to, and gently decompose there until the wind had picked my bones clean, and after that never, never to be reborn as a human being—that would be a really *good* death. (H, 36.486; S, 2: 206)

Earlier Baoyu was moved when he found out that Baochai and others shed tears after he received a severe beating from his father:

> What have I undergone but a few whacks of the bamboo?" he thought, "—yet already they are so sad and concerned about me! What dear, adorable, sweet, noble girls they are! Heaven knows how they would grieve for me if I were actually to die! It would be almost worth dying, just to find out. The loss of a life's ambitions would be a small price to pay, and I should be a peevish, ungrateful ghost if I did not feel proud and happy when such darling creatures were grieving for me." (H, 34.462; S, 2: 116)

What stands out in this self reflection is Baoyu's desire to relish the thought that all the girls will "grieve for me." This explains why Baoyu is so disturbed that he cannot please both Daiyu and Xiangyun at the same time: "If I can't even take care of these two girls, how am I going to manage later on?" (H, 22.306). The underlying assumption is that he will win admiration from many more girls. By the same token, this can also account for Baoyu's excitement when he has an opportunity to ingratiate himself with Ping'er (Patience) and Xiangling (Caltrop), the cherished concubines of two of his male cousins. For him, this is "an unlooked-for happiness he might otherwise have waited a lifetime for in vain" (H, 44.611; S, 2: 44). His lifelong wish is to

9. See Zhiyanzhai's interlineal comments in the Jiaxu manuscript version, in Zhu Yixuan, pp. 96–97.

please and win admiration from every beautiful girl he encounters. Consequently, the reader has to read more into the allegorical explanation provided early in the novel—Daiyu cries so much because she has to repay Baoyu's previous incarnation, the Divine Stone-in-Waiting, for watering her previous incarnation as Crimson Pearl Flower. Baoyu's attention to a girl is not completely altruistic: his favor needs to be returned in the form of "tears." In other words, Baoyu's compensation for his devotion is these girls' feeling of loss when they can no longer have his company.

Baoyu's initial shock when he overhears Daiyu reciting her poem on fallen flowers is also interesting in this regard. Daiyu is one of the most overtly narcissistic characters in the novel,[10] and her poem on fallen flower petals is the most articulate expression of this. And yet her narcissistic expression provokes an equally narcissistic response from Baoyu:

> Lin Daiyu dead! A world from which that delicate, flower-like countenance had irrevocably departed! It was unutterable anguish to think of it. Yet his sensitized imagination *did* now consider it—went on, indeed, to consider a world from which the others, too—Baochai, Caltrop [Xiangling], Aroma [Xiren] and the rest—had also irrevocably departed. Where would *he* be then? If his own corporal self (*zishen* 自身) were nowhere to be found, what would become of the Garden, the rocks, the flowers, the trees? To whom would they belong? (H, 28.385; S, 2: 41–42; trans. modified)

Here the ultimate point of reference is his own self, or *zishen*. Daiyu's lament over her own fate saddens him because the prospect that all the girls might depart from the world before he does would deny him the opportunity to relish the thought that they will mourn his death. This obsession with claiming the tears of all the girls is the essence of Baoyu's lust of intent. For Baoyu, probably nothing is more effective in terms of enhancing his sense of self-importance than to imagine the impact of the loss of his self on all these pretty girls—the ultimate significance of his self can be measured only in proportion to the amount of grief its loss will inflict on all these female others. To be grieved for is to be appreciated, or vice versa, to be appreciated is

10. Daiyu's main poetic theme is self-pity, as characterized by one of her own poetic lines: "The pages are filled with self-pity and sorrows" (滿紙自憐題素怨; H, 38.525). Daiyu as a narcissistic character may remind the reader of Yan Mengqing in *Lin Lan Xiang* and, to a lesser degree, Wang Cuiqiao in *Jin Yun Qiao zhuan*. All these characters seem to enjoy their image as an ill-fated girl. Of course, in the novel, Daiyu is frequently associated with Du Liniang, the narcissistic heroine of *Mudan ting*.

to cause others to grieve for oneself. To be grieved for not just by one girl but by all the beautiful girls is the ultimate appreciation Baoyu could hope to attain.

As discussed in preceding chapters, a frustrated literatus finding appreciation in a beautiful woman is a familiar theme of *qing* in literati literature. The motif of appreciation of unrecognized talent, when introduced into a romance about the love between a man and a woman, often turns *qing* into a narcissistic gesture—a male literatus's unrecognized worth is vindicated by the grace of a beautiful and loving woman. What is more significant, the female lover's beauty has to be matched by her wisdom, which enables her to spot male talent. Therefore, it is the male literatus's self-love (his sense of self-importance) that ultimately legitimizes sexual love in the name of *qing*, which is, to a large degree, homosocialized—the woman's appreciation functions as a token in male–male relations. In fact, as we have seen, many early Qing writers of scholar-beauty fiction emphasized the role of "appreciation" or "recognition" in *qing* as a tactic to distinguish their romances of *qing* from erotic novels that focus on the immediate gratification of physical lust. Baoyu's narcissism is in this tradition of homosocial *qing*. His implicitly or potentially homosexual relationships with several male characters such as Qin Zhong (the name itself is reminiscent of a series of characters of *qing* with similarly allegorical names in the romantic literary works discussed in Chapter 9) vaguely remind the reader of the perennial concept of *zhiji* so much celebrated in literati literature. When Qin Zhong first meets Baoyu, he insists on having one or two like-minded friends (*zhiji*) as study companions (H, 7.117). Incidentally, Daiyu also uses the word *zhiji* to gauge her relationship with Baoyu in chapter 32 (H, 32.446). However, despite this inescapable association with the motif of recognition in literati literature, Baoyu's *qing*, or lust of intent, seems concerned with securing a different kind of recognition from his appreciative audience of females. In fact, the stereotypic plot of the beautiful talent scout who sees the hidden promise in a male literatus who has yet to achieve career success is parodied at the beginning of the novel—Jia Yucun's rather anti-romantic encounter with Zhen Shiyin's maid Jiaoxing 嬌杏, whose name puns on *jiaoxing* 僥幸 (fluke), and their subsequent marriage, which results from Jia Yucun's mistaken assumption that the maid's casual glance is a sign of her ability to spot in him an unrecognized talent. At least on the surface, the appreciation Baoyu seeks from the girls whom he worships so much has little to do with a male literatus's self-pitying complaint that his talent has not received enough recognition. What Baoyu seeks from these girls is an appreciation of his ability to appreciate their "femininity." One's ability to appreciate an other needs to be validated by that other's reciprocal appreciation.

One factor that makes Baoyu different and thus seemingly able to postpone the public judgment (which almost every educated male had to face in traditional China) whether he is talented (i.e., whether he can achieve success in an official or literati career) seems to be his perceived youth or the claim that he is still a young child.[11] It is this claim that enables him to almost succeed in indefinitely deferring this dreadful judgment. This should account, at least in part, for his reluctance to grow up or, rather, his reluctance to be reminded that he is growing up. In other words, Baoyu's ability to indulge in his lust of intent is predicated on his youth, and the lust of intent as experienced by him is, to a certain extent, a result of this insistence on being young. Zhiyanzhai tried to associate Baoyu's peculiar behavior of *qing buqing* with his supposed youth or childishness (*xiao'er xinyi* 小兒心意) (interlineal comments in the Jiaxu, Gengcheng, and Liecang 列藏 manuscripts, in Zhi Yixuan, p. 267). Much of Baoyu's behavior in "the lust of intent" category (such as eating rouge, talking to birds, or crying for no apparent reason) is explained as typical of a whimsical, spoiled child. At the same time, this claim of youthfulness has made readers hesitant to dismiss Baoyu's narcissism as merely another case of the frustrated literatus's self-indulgence described in so many romances of *qing* (as in the case of Zhong Qing in *Guwangyan* or Wen Suchen in the early part of *Yesou puyan*). There is a tension between the novel's attempts to transcend the limits of *qing* prescribed by the traditional recognition motif and the lack of a vocabulary to describe the kind of *qing* Baoyu is determined to pursue or to invent under the claim that he is still a young child, when growing up is an inescapable fact.[12]

11. Of course, another factor might be family background—the fact that the Jias are an aristocratic family makes this judgment less imminent. For a discussion of Baoyu and the question of literati identity, see my *Literati and Self-Re/Presentation*, pp. 104–6.

12. Baoyu's insistence on being young seems also to be motivated by his wish to avoid the consequences of *yu*, a reality that concerned many late Ming literati, as we have discussed in Chapter 1. Baoyu, by pursuing his "lust of intent" or *qing*, is also trying to differentiate himself from people such as Ximen Qing in *Jin Ping Mei*, who suffer the deadliest consequences of *yu*. Despite his expressed wish to die while all the girls are still alive, Baoyu seems to suffer from a profound fear of death. Staying young is, at least in part, an effort to defy death.

To complicate the matter further, the question of Baoyu's age is far from unproblematic, given the novel's complicated textual history and its notoriously inconsistent statements about the ages of many of its main characters (including Baoyu). Baoyu does not always behave as the child his apparent age would suggest. Some of his actions could only be attributed to a mature adult. According to the most plausible internal chronology,[13] Baoyu is only eight in chapter 6 when he puts the lessons he has just learned from the Goddess of Disenchantment (the art of sex) in his dream into practice with Xiren! In chapter 13, the eleven-year-old Baoyu already has enough wisdom to suggest to Jia Zhen that Wang Xifeng should be asked to help manage the daily matters of the Ningguo Mansion; in chapter 25, the thirteen-year-old Baoyu is entertained by a prostitute; in chapter 35 this same thirteen-year-old Baoyu is said to express admiration for Fu Qiufang, a girl of twenty-three! This list could go on and on. This problem is compounded by the inconsistencies in the ages of many other important characters in the novel, especially since their ages are crucial in determining Baoyu's age because the reader is often told that one particular character is so many years younger or older than another.[14] Most scholars believe that these inconsistencies and confusions can be attributed to the complicated writing and rewriting processes the novel underwent. A brief discussion of some aspects of this process should help us appreciate better how the concepts of *qing* and *yu* or "the lust of the flesh" and "the lust of intent" were conceived and reconceived by the author.

There is strong evidence that *Honglou meng* as we have it now evolved from an early manuscript titled *Fengyue baojian* 風月寶鑒 (A mirror for the romantic). *Fengyue baojian* is explicitly mentioned in the text proper of the novel as one of several titles suggested for the novel. "Old Kong Meixi from the homeland of Confucius called the book *A Mirror for the Romantic*"[15] (H,

13. Given the complexities of the novel, no chronology can be perfectly accurate or always consistent; the reader has to choose the most plausible chronology among several possible ones. For discussions of the novel's complicated chronology, see Du Jinghua, "*Honglou meng* de xushi liunian jiqi yinyu tankao."

14. For a thorough discussion of the anachronisms and the confusions in the ages of some characters, see Dai Bufan, "Shixu cuoluan pian."

15. Zhang Ailing ("*Honglou meng*" *yan*, p. 74) suggests that by telling the reader that this title was given by someone from the homeland of Confucius, the narrator is emphasizing its didactic nature. However, some comments in the Jiaxu and Gengchen manuscript versions are signed with the name Meixi 梅溪; see the comments in chapter 13, Zhu Yixuan, p. 136.

1.6; S, 1: 51). What is even more intriguing is Zhiyanzhai's marginal comment in chapter 1 of the Jiaxu manuscript: "Cao Xueqin originally had a manuscript/book titled *Fengyue baojian* with a preface [or prefaces] written by his younger brother Tangcun. Now that Tangcun has passed away, reading this new [manuscript] reminded me of the old [the deceased?], I decided to preserve the preface(s)" (Zhu Yixuan, p. 7). This brief remark has given rise to many disputes among scholars as to whether *Fengyue baojian* was written by Cao Xueqin or by someone else or whether *Honglou meng* is a result of Cao Xueqin's rewriting of someone else's work. Barring new evidence, this will remain a question that can never be answered with complete certainty. But one thing that is certain is that a substantial portion of *Honglou meng* as we have it now was based on that earlier manuscript: parts such as those about Qinshi and her mysterious death, Jia Rui's infatuation with Wang Xifeng and his eventual death, the school scene in chapter 11, Jia Lian's affairs in chapters 21 and 44, and the several chapters devoted to the story of the You sisters. All these parts are much more melodramatic and quick-paced, and they focus on sexual transgressions.[16] This suggests that *Fengyue baojian* was probably a cautionary tale about the dire consequences of seeking immediate gratification of *yu* (the lust of the flesh) much in the fashion of those didactic works of vernacular fiction that contain erotic details, such as *Jin Ping Mei*. In fact, Zhiyanzhai's comparisons of the novel with *Jin Ping Mei* refer to passages likely to have been adopted from *Fengyue baojian*.[17]

Despite Cao Xueqin's efforts to suppress the erotic details in the parts adopted from *Fengyue baojian*, these parts constitute a fairly distinct world of *yu* within the present *Honglou meng*, in marked contrast to the other world in the novel, the world of *qing* in which Baoyu and his female cousins roam. It

16. For a discussion in English of some of the common features of these parts, see Wai-yee Li, *Enchantment and Disenchantment*, pp. 237–42.

17. See, e.g., the marginal comment on Jia Zhen's asking the price of the coffin timber in chap. 13 of the Jiaxu manuscript (Zhu Yixuan, p. 189), which suggests a possible influence of the account of Li Ping'er's burial in *Jin Ping Mei* on that of Qinshi's burial in *Honglou meng*; the marginal comment on Xue Pan's drinking game in chap. 28 of the Jiaxu manuscript (Zhu Yixuan, p. 413), which may parallel Ximen Qing's drinking game in the house of the prostitute Li Guijie; and the interlineal comment in the Jimao 己茂 manuscript version (Zhu Yixuan, p. 518) on Liu Xianglian's assertion in chap. 66 that everything in the Ningguo Mansion, except for the two stone lions, is dirty, which reminds Zhiyanzhai of a phrase in *Jin Ping Mei*.

is likely that the elaborate story of the world of *qing* is largely the result of Cao Xueqin's substantial revision or rewriting of *Fengyue baojian*. More specifically, the stories of the Daguan yuan garden and what happens within the compound most probably are Cao Xueqin's additions or expansions. This is confirmed by the fact that in the Menggao 夢稿 manuscript version, the first line of the couplet-title of chapter 17 reads "Literary Talent Is Tested in the Composition of Inscriptions in Huifang yuan" (會芳園試才題對額), whereas in all other versions the title refers to Daguan yuan.[18] This leads us to suspect that in *Fengyue baojian*, there was probably no Daguan yuan and that the Daguan yuan appeared in a later rewriting. In all extant manuscript versions of the novel, Huifang yuan is the garden within the Ningguo Mansion, which will later become part of Daguan yuan when the latter is built in preparation for the visit by the imperial concubine, Yuanchun. However, Huifang yuan still occupies an important position in the present novel because it is the place where Jia Rui has his fatal encounter with Wang Xifeng. In *Fengyue baojian* Huifang yuan must have served as a more important setting for many crucial incidents such as the incestuous affair between Qinshi and her father-in-law, Jia Zhen, which Cao Xueqin apparently took out at the suggestion of one of the commentators (see Zhiyanzhai's interlineal comment in the Jingcang 靖藏 manuscript version and the chapter-end comment in the Jiaxu manuscript version; Zhu Yixuan, pp. 184, 193).

If we accept the speculation that in *Fengyue baojian*, the Jia family was not divided into two households, the Ningguo Mansion and the Rongguo Mansion, as it is now,[19] then we have to assume that by creating the Ningguo Mansion and then confining most of the incidents of sexual transgression to that setting in his later revisions (Liu Xianglian, in chapter 66, claims that everything in the Ningguo Mansion is "dirty" except for the two stone lions outside its gate), Cao Xueqin is able to provide a relatively clean environment in the Rongguo Mansion for Baoyu and his female cousins. Of course, later in the novel they move into an even cleaner place—Daguan yuan—and Huifang yuan, the reader is told in chapter 17, is now integrated into this new garden. Consequently, Huifang yuan becomes part of the setting of the garden world of innocent *qing*, in which Baoyu is allowed to pursue his "lust

18. Feng Qiyong et al., *Zhiyanzhai chongping Shitou ji huijiao* (hereafter *Huijiao*), p. 792.
19. See Zhang Ailing, *"Honglou meng" yan*, p. 241.

of intent." This factor complicates the status of Daguan yuan as a land of pure *qing*.

The one common characteristic of the inhabitants of the garden world is their youth. Li Wan is the only exception. However, Baoyu's comment on her future residence in Daguan yuan implies that its resident is "unnatural" and "out of place" in relation to the surrounding buildings. According to the most plausible chronology of the novel, Baoyu is thirteen when he moves into the garden, and he remains thirteen until chapter 53 (he is only fifteen at the end of the first eighty chapters). Most of his female cousins are about the same age, one or two years different at the most. Just like the story of the garden world, the youthfulness of these characters was probably the result of Cao Xueqin's deliberate design in his revisions. The inconsistencies in the ages of various characters in the extant manuscript versions imply a process of revision in which the ages of several important characters were gradually reduced.

Occasionally, in one or another of the extant manuscript versions of the novel, a character's age is explicitly said to be much older than he or she should be according to the chronology of the novel: for example, in chapter 3 of the Jimao 己茂 and Menggao manuscript versions, upon her arrival at the Jia family compound, Daiyu says she is thirteen when asked by Wang Xifeng (this exchange between the two can be found only in these two manuscripts).[20] This is seven years older than she should be according to chapter 2![21] However, in chapter 45 of the Gengchen manuscript version, Daiyu states that she is now fifteen years old, and Zhiyanzhai even makes a point of this in his interlinear comment (Zhu Yixuan, p. 475).[22] However, according to the chronology of the novel, the events of chapter 45 should take place six years after those of chapter 3. Therefore, based on this clue in chapter 45 of the Gengchen manuscript, Daiyu should be nine in chapter 3. Thus when Daiyu first arrives at the Jia family compound in chapter 3, she is either six or nine or thirteen. The thirteen-year-old Daiyu probably fits the chronology of *Fengyue baojian*, and the nine-year-old Daiyu that of a manuscript written sometime before the novel achieved its present form (in which

20. *Huijiao*, p. 131.

21. Daiyu is said to be five years old in chapter 2 in all versions (*Huijiao*, pp. 73–74). She should therefore be six when she goes to the Jias the next year.

22. The wording is the same in all other manuscript versions; see *Huijiao*, p. 2415.

Daiyu should be six).[23] This would explain the apparent discrepancy between Daiyu's supposed age (six) and her precocious behavior—her perspicacity and maturity—as described in chapter 3 of the present version. The fact that Daiyu's age was reduced twice—from thirteen to nine, and then to six—suggests that a gradual reduction of the ages of some of the major characters must have been an important part of Cao Xueqin's revisions.

By the same token, those parts of the present novel in which Baoyu behaves like a mature young man were probably adopted from *Fengyue baojian*. The portrayal of this "mature" Baoyu is often inconsistent with that of the younger Baoyu in the rest of the novel. Instead of being motivated by a lust of intent, this Baoyu is closer to characters associated with the lust of the flesh, such as Xue Pan and Jia Lian, who must have enjoyed more prominence in *Fengyue baojian* (this is understandable since this early manuscript apparently focused more on physical desire).[24] For example, in chapter 26, Baoyu's conversation with Jia Yun is concerned mainly with questions such as "Which family has the best theater troupe?" or "Which family has the best garden?" or "Which family has the prettiest maids?" Here Baoyu sounds more like Xue Pan (H, 26.364). In chapter 66, when asked by Liu Xianglian about You sanjie, Baoyu's response is even more puzzling:

> "You said just now you even didn't know about her sister's marriage," said Xianglian. "How do you *know* she is so beautiful?"
>
> "I have mingled with (*hun* 混) them for a month after they were brought there by Cousin Zhen's mother-in-law," said Baoyu. "How could I fail to know? [The two sisters] are really a pair of bewitching beauties (*yidui youwu* 一對尤物). Besides, her last name happens to be *you* (尤)."
>
> Xianglian stamped impatiently.
>
> "And everyone else's, no doubt." Baoyu's execrable pun had not amused him. "It won't do. This is a thoroughly bad business. The only clean things about that Ningguo Mansion are the stone lions that stand outside the gate. The very cats and dogs there are corrupted!" (H, 66.944; S, 3: 303; trans. modified)

23. Jiang Wenqin ("*Honglou meng* chengshu de sanchong xitung"), based on the three scenarios of Daiyu's age in chap. 3, has suggested that there were three main stages in the complicated writing process of the novel. See also Zhang Ailing, "*Honglou meng*" *yan*, pp. 147–48; Chen Qinghao, "Bashihui *Shitou ji* chengshu chukao"; and idem, "Bashihui *Shitou ji* chengshu zaikao."

24. For an interesting discussion of this issue from a slightly different perspective, see Xue Ruisheng, "Da Baoyu yu *Fengyue baojian*." This article came to my attention when the draft of this chapter was already completed.

This exchange between Baoyu and Liu Xianglian is puzzling because it is not what the reader would expect from Baoyu, who elsewhere demonstrates so much respect and empathy (*titie*) for women. In fact, Baoyu's remark may inadvertently lead to You sanjie's suicide because it helps convince Liu Xianglian of her dubious past and thus to nullify their engagement. The word "hun" used by Baoyu suggests some involvement with the two sisters. What is equally shocking is Baoyu's use of *youwu* (bewitching beauties) to describe the two sisters. This phrase is usually used to describe women who are charming but dangerous, and it may reflect unfavorably on the person who employs the phrase. Here the distinctions between Baoyu and characters like Jia Lian and Xue Pan are becoming dangerously thin. Read within this context, the story of Baoyu's wet dream and his maid Xiren's coming into "contact with something cold and sticky" in chapter 6 should prepare the reader for Jia Rui's gruesome death in a pool of semen in chapter 12. Both young men have wet dreams, and both are experiencing what a young man at this age is supposed to experience (Baoyu should be around fourteen if his having a wet dream is plausible and if we accept what we can infer from the fact that Daiyu is already thirteen in chapter 3).[25] What Baoyu does with Xiren immediately after the dream was sanctioned by contemporary social norms, whereas Jia Rui's desiring of Wang Xifeng was a "transgression." Despite these differences, both incidents point to the inevitability of the lust of the flesh. All this should alert the reader to the possibility that in *Fengyue baojian*, Baoyu might have been someone deeply afflicted by the lust of the flesh, because these parts (including the account of his first sexual experience with Xiren) happen to be the parts that are likely to have been adopted from this early manuscript. Like several other characters, such as the enigmatic You sanjie, during Cao Xueqin's repeated rewritings of the novel, Baoyu must have undergone a purifying process (being *re*-presented); from someone suffering from the lust of the flesh, he became someone obsessed with the lust of intent.

The enigmatic and controversial Qinshi may have undergone a similar chastening process. Yu Pingbo was probably the first modern critic to ex-

25. In chapter 3, when Daiyu first meets Baoyu, the latter is presented as a "young master," or *nianqing de gongzi* 年輕的公子 (H, 3.49; this is quite consistent in all extant versions of the novel; see *Huijiao*, p. 153). To describe a fourteen-year-old boy as a *nianqing de gongzi* is appropriate but to say so of a seven-year-old boy is not (according to the most plausible chronology of the novel Daiyu should be only six and Baoyu seven at the time).

press a suspicion that Qingshi may have committed suicide after her incestuous affair with her father-in-law, Jia Zhen, is exposed. Yu Pingbo believes that our uncertainty is due to the author's reluctance to present too negative a picture of Qingshi.[26] With the coming into light of the Jiaxu and the Jingcang manuscripts, which contain some important comments made by Zhiyanzhai and others regarding the curious case of Qinshi (the Jingcang manuscript is no longer extant, but the commentaries were copied and thus are still available),[27] we can almost be certain that the inconsistencies in the character of Qinshi are largely the result of the author's revision(s). In the interlineal comments and chapter-end comments in chapter 13 in the Jiaxu manuscript, Zhiyanzhai mentioned that he had asked the author to remove several sections, including one in which Qinshi hangs herself (Zhu Yixuan, pp. 184, 193).

Most scholars now accept the theory that the early manuscript(s) contained a detailed account of Qinshi's incestuous affair with her father-in-law. But what about her relationship with Baoyu? First, it is significant that in the present novel Baoyu dreams of having sex with someone who has the same name as his niece (*zhixifu* 侄媳婦), while he is taking a nap in that niece's bedroom. Baoyu is dreaming of an affair that is implicitly incestuous, a repetition of Qinshi's more bluntly incestuous affair with her father-in-law. The exposure of this incestuous affair is the reason that she apparently commits suicide in *Fengyue baojian*. In chapter 7 of the Jiaxu manuscript, an unidentified commentator expresses a belief that something incestuous happened between Baoyu and Qinshi. In an interlineal comment (*cepi* 側批) beside the shocking remark by the drunk Jiao Da (Big Jiao) about "carrying on with younger brothers-in-law" (養小叔子), this commentator insists that "Brother Bao is also included" (寶兄在內). Above the passage in which Baoyu asks Xifeng what "poking in the ashes" means, the commentator in a marginal comment (*meipi* 眉批) asks a series of rhetorical questions: "Why should he himself ask this question? Does he really not understand or does he just pretend? Or is this just to deceive people or to deceive himself? But people are not easy to deceive."[28] Although these comments were obviously not made by Zhiyanzhai, they point to the likelihood that this commentator

26. Yu Pingbo, "Lun Qin Keqing zhi si."
27. See Sun Xun, "*Honglou meng*" *Zhiping chutan*, pp. 22–23.
28. *Qianlong jiaxu Zhiyanzhai chongping Shitou ji*, 7.15b (p. 111).

had read an earlier version of the novel that contained details about an incestuous affair between Baoyu and Qingshi.[29] This is especially plausible

29. Zhiyanzhai's comments are usually written in red or vermilion ink (*zhupi* 朱批). The identity of the author(s) of some of the comments (most of them are marginal comments or *meipi*) written in black ink in the Jiaxu manuscript remains a thorny problem. In a postscript to the facsimile reprint of the Jiaxu manuscript, "Ba *Qianlong jiaxu Zhiyanzhai chongping Shitou ji* yingyin ben," Hu Shi (pp. 9–10) observed that based on the similarities between the views expressed in the long marginal comment (*meipi*) in chap. 3 (3.2b; p. 35a), which is signed with the name Zuomian chidaoren 左綿痴道人, and those found in the preface to the *Miaofuxuan pi Honglou meng* (here it should be *Shitou ji* instead of *Honglou meng*), which was written by Sun Tongsheng 孫桐生 (1824–1904), Sun was the author of this marginal comment. Hu Shi's belief seems to be supported by Sun's mention in the same preface that he had borrowed a copy of a collection of comments on the novel from Liu Quanfu 劉銓福 (ca. 1818–80), the book collector who once owned the Jiaxu manuscript (see "*Miaofuxuan pi Shitou ji* xu" 妙復軒評石頭記敘, in Yisu, *Honglou meng juan*, pp. 39–40). Liu Quanfu mentioned in his colophon at the end of the Jiaxu manuscript that he had read a copy of the Miaofuxuan edition of the novel (p. 246a). This at least establishes the possibility that Liu might have loaned the Jiaxu manuscript to Sun and that Sun might have indeed commented on it. However, Hu Shi takes this a step further by observing that based on the "similar handwriting," the comments written in black ink (*mopi* 墨批) in the Jiaxu manuscript copy were written by Sun Tongsheng. It seems to me, however, that the comments are in different hands and were authored at least by two different people. The marginal comment in chap. 7 that I cite was apparently written by someone other than the person who wrote the comment in chap. 3, which is signed with the name "Zuomian chidaoren" (believed to be one of Sun Tongsheng's *hao*). Hu Shi's identification of the author of the comments written in black ink in the Jiaxu manuscript seems to have been accepted by other scholars. See, e.g., Pan Zhonggui, "Jiaxu ben *Shitou ji* helun"; and Deng Qingyou, "Sun Tongsheng yu *Honglou meng*" (Deng Qingyou is also the author of the entry on Sun in Feng Qiyong and Li Xifan, "*Honglou meng*" *da cician*). I have yet to find anyone who disputes Hu Shi's view that all these comments were authored by the same person; however, although I am not a handwriting expert, the differences, at least to me, are quite obvious. More recently, Ouyang Jian ("Cong Zuomian chidaoren meipi ziji jianding kan Jiaxu ben de zhenwei wenti") has raised serious doubt about Hu Shi's attribution of these comments to Sun Tongsheng by comparing the comment signed with the name Zuomian chidaoren with verified examples of Sun's handwriting. However, Ouyang Jian does not touch on the issue whether Sun or Zuomian chidaoren was the author of other marginal comments in the Jiaxu manuscript of the novel. Ouyang Jian's main purpose in that essay is to question the authenticity of the Jiaxu manuscript, part of his controversial effort to prove that all the manuscripts with comments by Zhiyanzhai were fabrications by people of the late Qing (such as Liu Quanfu) and even of the Republican period and that Hu Shi was also a participant (whether willing or unwilling) in this conspiracy of "forgery" that continued into the twentieth century (for Ouyang Jian's arguments, see the essays collected in his *Honglou xinbian*). Personally, I believe that to prove this hypothesis Ouyang Jian needs to produce far more evidence than he has so far, although his findings do alert us to many problems in the manuscript copies associated with Zhiyanzhai.

since the extant version of the Jiaxu manuscript contains only sixteen chapters. Furthermore, the erotic images that abound in the description of Qinshi's bedroom (H, 5.71–72) reinforce the possibility that she is a character associated with the lust of the flesh.[30]

It is even more significant that in Baoyu's dream the Goddess of Disenchantment introduces Qinshi as the ideal mate or Jianmei 兼美 (i.e., combining [*jian*] the different charms [*mei*] of both Daiyu and Baochai). This leads to the prophetic verse on Qinshi in the register that Baoyu reads in his dream:

> Body of *qing* is but an illusion caused by boundless love; 情天情海幻情身
> When two people of *qing* meet, excessive must they be. 兩情相逢必主淫
> Say not our troubles all from Rong's side came; 漫言不肖皆榮出
> For their beginning Ning must take the blame. 造釁開端實在寧
> (H, 5.81; S, 1.135; trans. modified)

Here the body of *qing* or *qingshen* must be Qinshi, who appears in Baoyu's dream to have sex with him. When two people of *qing* (Baoyu or Jia Zhen and Qinshi) meet each other, transgression is unavoidable. This is why people from the Ningguo Mansion (such as Qingshi) are to be blamed for leading astray the people of the Rongguo Mansion (such as Baoyu).[31] What is particularly interesting is the word *qingshen* or "body of *qing*." Here *qing* must be conceived in the bodily form of a seductive woman, something that shares the meaning of both the lust of intent and the lust of flesh. All these subtle pieces of evidence point to the fact that the author's purification of both Qinshi and Baoyu was, deliberately or not, left incomplete (more about the case of Baoyu below).

You sanjie is another character whose inconsistencies are caused in large part by an incomplete process of revision. Some readers have noted that the

30. See Yu Pingbo, "Zhaji shize" 箚記十則, in idem, *"Honglou meng" bian*, pp. 313–15. Chen Zhao ("Yetan Qin Keqing de chushen wenti," esp. p. 734) suggests that the "erotic" description of Qinshi's bedroom must have been inspired by the similar description of Jinshi's bedroom in the late Ming erotic novel *Xiuta yeshi* (see the modern typeset edition collated from the *Zuimian ge* ed., 2.157–58). My impression is that the similarities between the two works are too general for us to reach a definitive conclusion about such an intertextual relationship, although I agree with Chen's main argument that Qinshi in the present version of the novel is a result of several revisions and that the Qinshi in *Fengyue baojian* must have borne a much closer resemblance to Li Ping'er in *Jin Ping Mei*.

31. Cf. Cai Yijiang's comments in idem, *"Honglou meng" shici qufu pingzhu*, p. 54.

characterization of You sanjie must have been much more negative in the *Fengyue baojian*. This is supported by the fact that in the title of chapter 65 in the Mengfu, Qixu 戚序, and Qi'ning 戚寧 manuscripts, she is referred to as a "loose woman" (*yinben nü* 淫奔女).[32] By comparing subtle differences in wording with regard to the presentation of You sanjie in different extant manuscript versions, Zhang Ailing has been able to demonstrate that Cao Xueqin exonerated her by removing her from the flirting scenes involving Jia Rong and You erjie.[33] Although Cao Xueqin's purifying revisions succeed in alleviating the abruptness of You sanjie's radical transformation from slut to faithful lover, most readers still find it difficult to place this problematic character in the category of either the lust of intent or the lust of the flesh. In other words, You sanjie as a character tends to question the appropriateness of these two categories (a point explored further below).

An examination of Baoyu's relationship with Xiangling will show how he, too, was purified as the novel was revised and rewritten. The central story of their relationship happens at the end of chapter 62: Xiangling's new skirt is soiled in a puddle during a tussle with the other girls who are laughing at her for her saying she got the "husband and wife" orchid in a game of "match-my-flower." Baoyu arrives at this moment and suggests to Xiangling that she exchange her skirt for a similar one belonging to Xiren so that Aunt Xue and the others will not find out what has happened. After Xiren brings her skirt, Xiangling asks Baoyu to turn his back while she changes. This is already significant—it demonstrates the degree of intimacy she is allowing between herself and Baoyu by undressing in his presence, although he is asked to turn his back. This action is even more significant since Xiangling, unlike the other, unmarried girls in the garden, is the concubine of another man, as the novel reminds us:

Baoyu got up and began to go. Caltrop [Xiangling] started walking off, too, in the opposite direction. She had gone no more than a few steps, however, when she turned and called to him to stop. Baoyu, supposing that she had something more to say to him, turned smilingly towards her, holding up his muddy hands.

But Caltrop merely stood there, smiling and saying nothing.

32. *Huijiao*, p. 3678.

33. Zhang Ailing, "*Honglou meng*" *yan*, pp. 192–96. Zhang (pp. 196, 241) concludes that the purifying of You sanjie starts in several manuscript versions, contrary to her own views in earlier writings and those of others who believe that it starts only in the Cheng-Gao printed versions.

Just then her little maid Advent came up to tell her that Baoqin wanted to talk to her. After that, finally, she spoke.

"You won't ever tell your Cousin Pan [her husband] about this, will you?"

"What, put my head inside the mouth of a tiger?" said Baoyu, laughing. "You must think I'm crazy!" (H, 62.884; S, 3: 215–16)

One late Qing commentator characterized this scene as typical of the lust of intent.[34] However, "lust of intent" may not be the most appropriate term to describe their relationship. Xiangling is obviously aware that something significant has transpired between herself and Baoyu, and, interestingly, she takes the step of deliberately reminding Baoyu of its implications.[35] Baoyu is, of course, fully aware of this from the very beginning. This episode is reminiscent of the earlier scene in which Baoyu takes advantage of a rare chance to come to the rescue of Jia Lian's concubine Ping'er after Wang Xifeng and Jia Lian have abused her. On both occasions, Baoyu invites Ping'er and Xiangling to wear Xiren's clothes, presumably because their own clothes are soiled (the exchange of clothes may carry added symbolic implications since Xiren is Baoyu's "unofficial" concubine). However, a key difference is that this time both Xiangling and Baoyu are explicitly said to be fully aware that what has transpired between them is somehow inappropriate and should be kept a secret. Yu Pingbo, for one, believes that the drastic change in Xiangling's fortune at the hands of Xue Pan later in the novel has a lot to do with Xue Pan's furious jealousy after what has taken place between Xiangling and Baoyu is revealed.[36] Of course, Xue Pan can be very jealous. In chapter 25 of several manuscript versions, right after the description of Baoyu's and Wang Xifeng's possession because of the schemes of Auntie Zhao, is the following peculiar passage:

Most remarkable, perhaps, was the spectacle of Xue Pan fussing over his womenfolk, one moment afraid that his mother would be jostled in the crush, the next that Baochai might be ogled or Caltrop [Xiangling] glad-eyed by some wanton male.

34. See Huhua zhuren's 護花主人 (Wang Xilian 王希廉, fl. 1832–75) chapter-comment, in Feng Qiyong et al., *Bajia pingpi "Honglou meng,"* p. 1535.

35. There are some textual variations in different versions of the novel: in the Mengfu and Chengjia 程甲 versions, Xiangling is twice said to be blushing (*lianhong* 臉紅) and "she tries to say something but holds herself back" (see *Huijiao*, p. 3486). Obviously, in these two versions, the impression that something untoward is going on between them is even stronger.

36. Yu Pingbo, "Xiangling diwei de gaibian."

Cousin Zhen and others, he knew for a fact, all were good womanizers. Then he caught sight of Daiyu and forgot his anxiety in gawping admiration of that ethereal beauty. (H, 25.345; S, 1: 471; trans. modified)

This passage is peculiar first of all because it disrupts the flow of the narrative; presumably, this is the reason it was deleted from the other manuscript versions, as well as later printed editions.[37] Nothing else in all the extant editions of the novel suggests that more is going on between Xiangling and Baoyu, although we are left with the impression that there may have been much more in some early versions. In interlineal comments in the Gengchen manuscript, Zhiyanzhai calls the reader's attention to the enormous pains the author took to create the episode in which Xue Pan is beaten by Liu Xianglian and then decides to go on a business trip in order to avoid seeing his friends and relatives because he feels so ashamed. All this fuss, Zhiyanzhai believes, is designed to create an excuse to justify Xiangling's move into the garden (Zhu Yixuan, p. 482). But nothing particularly eventful happens to her after she moves into the garden. It is possible that the author later decided to tone down the significance of what happens between Baoyu and Xiangling and eliminate other corroborative incidents involving the two (some of these incidents probably could not be excused as manifestations of the lust of intent). This change of mind on the author's part is plausible. After all, many episodes surrounding Xue Pan in *Fengyue baojian* are likely to have been deleted in later revisions.[38]

This incident of "a touched Xiangling unfastens her pomegranate skirt" (*qingjie shiliuqun* 情解石榴裙) is also interesting in that it problematizes the boundaries between the lust of intent and the lust of the flesh and complicates the relevance of the factor of age to the implications of this bipolar concept. The girls' game of "match-my-flower" seems to be harmless and innocent, typical of young children, until the "husband-and-wife" flower is mentioned by Xiangling. Even Xiangling's unfastening of her skirt in Baoyu's presence may be understood as the innocent act of a child until she is shown to be self-conscious enough to deliberately remind Baoyu that she

37. See *Huijiao*, pp. 1329–30.

38. One such omitted episode is that of "Xue Pan harassing Qin Zhong" 薛潘戲秦鍾. After the turmoil in the clan school in which Jin Rong is humiliated, he takes revenge on Qin Zhong by encouraging Xue Pan to harass the latter sexually. For a more detailed discussion, see Liu Shide, "Jiepo le *Honglou meng* de yige mi"; see also Zhang Ailing, "*Honglou meng*" *yan*, p. 109.

is an "adult" woman married to another man by asking him not to tell her husband, Xue Pan. Of course, the last thing Baoyu would do is to tell Xue Pan, and Xiangling knows this. Xiangling's request is thus redundant and unnecessary, and the intention behind this calculated redundancy is something Baoyu will not fail to appreciate. The reference to the adult world of the lust of the flesh represented by Xue Pan introduces some rather unexpected implications, as if to remind Baoyu that he can no longer indulge in his lusts of intent under the pretext of his youth. Early in the novel, when Baoyu's nanny objects to "Uncle" Baoyu's sleeping in his niece Qinshi's bedroom, Qinshi brushes aside the objection by insisting on Baoyu's youth (H, 5.71). Because of his ambiguous age identity, Baoyu's involvement with the girls, regardless of his own intention, has sexual undertones. What is being questioned in this episode of Xiangling's skirt is the purity of Baoyu's "lust of intent" as well as the legitimacy of Baoyu's frequent claim that he is still a young child.

Thus far we have examined the close relationship between the age of a character and that character's possible association with the two categories of lust. This close relationship should explain why the ages of many characters were such a crucial issue in Cao Xueqin's revisions. The author's decision to make many characters *younger* is consistent with a shift from a focus on *yu* to a fascination with *qing* that becomes discernible when we compare the parts likely to have been adopted from the earlier *Fengyue baojian* with the rest of the novel. Cao Xueqin's decision to concentrate more on *qing* in his revision or, to use the Monk's words in chapter 1, to focus more on *ernü zhenqing* (the genuine *qing* between young men and young women), must have necessitated reducing the age of many of his characters. The adult world of *yu*, or lust of the flesh, in *Fengyue baojian* is replaced in the revised novel with the seemingly innocent world of *qing*, in which teenagers can involve themselves in various emotional entanglements without being threatened by anything menacingly sexual, which, of course, an adult would find difficult to avoid. Youth seems to mean carefree innocence or lowered vulnerability to the corrupting influences of the lust of the flesh. No wonder that the most dreadful thing for Baoyu is a marriage of one of his female cousins—marriage is the ultimate reminder that a girl has come of age. Indeed, Baoyu's many strange acts of *qing*, such as talking to birds or thinking that the lady in the painting might feel lonely, make sense only when they are admired as childlike or ridiculed as childish.

From a different perspective, being young is also a necessary condition for Baoyu's pursuit of the lust of intent; his youth frees him from the suspicion that his involvements with the girls are necessarily sexual and thus need to be censured. For example, in chapter 19 Baoyu and Daiyu play in bed; neither their elders nor readers find this activity particularly scandalous thanks to the impression that they are still two young children. Therefore the legitimacy and purity of Baoyu's lust of intent are somehow contingent on people's impression that he is still a young child. A major function of the garden world of Daguan yuan for Baoyu and his female cousins is that it is a safe environment where they can still (pretend to) act like young children. In fact, people are quick to point out that Baoyu is growing up to explain their feeling that his continued association with his female cousins is improper. Baoyu's reluctance to grow up is obviously related to his desperate attempt to cling to his ideal of *qing* and his freedom to pursue his "lust of intent." However, since growing up is an unavoidable part of life, the logical conclusion is that Baoyu must outgrow his lust of intent. Throughout the novel, *qing* or the lust of intent is often associated with attempts to resist or defy the passage of time. The lyrical world of the garden seems to enable its inhabitants (especially Baoyu) to turn away from or forget, at least temporarily, the fact that they are growing up and that they will eventually be forced to confront the adult world lurking beyond the garden. Often the adult world intrudes into the garden not because the garden world does not have a wall strong enough to function as a defense but because its inhabitants have a problematic age identity—Baoyu behaves like a child at one moment and like an adult the next. Even more poignantly, as happens between Xiangling and Baoyu, an incident that starts as innocent play between children ends up as something that must remain an *adult* secret.

As long as Baoyu is able to maintain that he is still a young boy and as long as others are willing to accept this claim, Baoyu can continue to pursue the lust of intent, but his adventures are often disrupted or stopped by a sudden and often unexpected reminder that he is an adult. Cao Xueqin's "failure" to keep his characters *consistently* young after deciding to reduce their ages in his rewriting may paradoxically have the effect of highlighting the ultimate futility of any attempt to stay young or to maintain the purity of one's lust of intent. Baoyu's behavioral inconsistencies (his acting like Xue Pan on a few occasions) point to the pains of growing up and the inevitable lusts of the flesh that accompany growing up. The fact that in all extant manuscript versions of the novel, Baoyu is presented as an "adult" in chapter 6, almost at the beginning of the novel, when he undergoes a sexual rite of initiation with his maid Xiren, despite or because of the author's rewriting, should emphasize that "he is still young" can be nothing more than a claim. No wonder Baoyu is so captivated by Baochai's snow-white arms. Sensuality does appeal to him. The distinctions between two varieties of lust are sometimes difficult to maintain, and these polar concepts become inadequate to explain certain cases of love in the novel, especially the "sacrificing love" (*lieqing* 烈情) stories that often end up in suicide (such as those of the maid Siqi or Chess, You sanjie, Fengyuan, and Jin'ge).[39] These semi-independent episodes of violent passions are, to judge from their melodramatic nature, likely to have been incorporated from *Fengyue baojian*. It is crucial that traces of the world of *Fengyue baojian* are not completely suppressed in the revised novel, not least because they complicate and even problematize Baoyu's version of the lust of intent and question its validity as a viable alternative to the lust of the flesh.

The insistence on the lust of intent and the simultaneous problem of how to behave in accordance with his supposed age play an interesting role in Baoyu's difficult and sometimes even tortuous relationship with Daiyu. They can be intimate with each other only when they believe and when others believe that they are still children. However, the more intimate they become, the more conscious of their adult status they become: Daiyu worries who will help arrange her marriage to Baoyu since both of her parents are dead, and Baoyu tries harder to alleviate Daiyu's anxieties and suspicions by pledging his devotion via many *indirect* means, which often makes her even more suspicious. Daiyu's reluctance to acknowledge the adult nature of her own feelings predetermines that such feelings can be communicated only indirectly. They are caught in a paradox—they have to express their "adult feelings" to each other in a language that convinces themselves as well as others that they are not yet adults, and that language must allow them to continue to maintain their ambiguous age identities.

39. Cf. Zhiyanzhai's pre-chapter comment on chapter 66 (Zhu Yixuan, p. 517), in which he praises You sanjie's suicide as an expression of *zhengqing* 正情 (a similar term used by the contemporary dramatist Jiang Shiquan, as discussed in Chapter 2), something to be distinguished from *yin* or debauchery. However, the ambiguities associated with You sanjie problematize such praise.

All the miscommunications between Daiyu and Baoyu seem to result from the lack of a language that can resolve this paradox. Consequently, they are forced to rely heavily on the words of others, such as passages from famous romantic plays of the past like *Xixiang ji* and *Mudan ting*, to communicate their feelings, but the end result is equally frustrating. Daiyu likes to read books about the desires of adults, but she does not want Baoyu or anyone else to apply these adult languages to herself so that she and others would be reminded of the possible adult nature of her own feelings toward Baoyu. That would deprive her of the opportunity to associate with Baoyu since their intimate association is possible only because others believe that they are still young.

There is an additional danger associated with these borrowed words and with the impulse to imitate what one has read:

> Now Daiyu had observed that in the romances of scholars and beauties which Baoyu smuggled in to her and of which she was nowadays an avid consumer, it was always some trinket or small object of clothing or jewelry—a pair of lovebirds, a male and female phoenix, a jade ring, a gold buckle, a silken handkerchief, an embroidered belt or what not—that brought the heroes and heroines together. (H, 32.445; S, 2: 131; trans. modified)

Indeed, Daiyu sometimes appears weary of others' "languages," especially when they tend to justify her rivals' cause in part because her relationship with Baoyu contains elements that transcend the formulas of scholar-beauty romances. What distinguishes their love from the stereotyped affairs in these romances, ironically, is the fact that theirs is being cultivated while Baoyu and she are still *growing up* together (the maturing of their unique love, paradoxically, is contingent on the fact that they are already at the end of this process—they are grown up now).

To overcome the inadequacy of the available languages, Daiyu has to learn to read ingeniously. Daiyu is able to secure confirmation of Baoyu's reciprocal feelings toward herself only when she *unexpectedly* overhears Baoyu praise her in front of Xiangyun and Xiren for never urging him to seek examination successes (chapter 32). Baoyu's later explicit confession of love to Daiyu, however, finds the wrong audience when, in his excitement, he mistakes Xiren for Daiyu after Daiyu suddenly departs precisely because of her fear of such direct confession of adult feelings. For Daiyu, the feelings expressed in Baoyu's confession should never be articulated verbally. They can be mentioned only *accidentally* when one does not mean to make such a reference (as in Baoyu's praise of her in front of others). The successful conveying of these tabooed adult feelings depends on the listener's ability to find the "supposed" intention behind such unintended references. It is dangerous to verbalize adult feelings. Verbalization eventually makes such feelings impossible. Daiyu's fear is at least partially justified. Xiren immediately senses from Baoyu's misdirected confession that Baoyu is engaging in something improper, and this has something to do with his no longer being a young child and his growing capacity for adult feelings. Of course, in a way Xiren must have been aware of this for a long time since she is supposed to have slept with him several years earlier in chapter 6, if we accept the somewhat confusing chronology suggested in the novel as we have it now.[40] She soon advises Lady Wang that Baoyu should move out of the garden and away from his female cousins since "Master Bao is already grown up" (如今二爺也大了; H, 34.467). Here Daiyu's eavesdropping is unintentionally repeated by Xiren in the sense that Xiren is not supposed to be the audience for Baoyu's confession just as Daiyu is not supposed to be the audience for Baoyu's praise of her.

Both acts of eavesdropping produce a moment of truth, although they have entirely different ramifications: Daiyu acquires unexpected confirmation from Baoyu about his true feelings toward herself, and Xiren learns of the true dangers of their feelings toward each other. Later, Baochai learns that Baoyu prefers Daiyu over herself when she unexpectedly hears Baoyu talking in his sleep, another case of eavesdropping (chapter 36), although Baochai does not anticipate overhearing anything when she sits beside the sleeping Baoyu (more about this point below). All these twisted communi-

40. It is very likely that in some earlier manuscript versions, Baoyu's first sexual experience with Xiren takes place much later in the novel. This was confirmed by Ming Yi 明義 (ca. 1740–1805), who may have known Cao Xueqin personally. In the sixth poem in his "Ti *Honglou meng*" 題紅樓夢 poems (collected in his *Lüyan suochuang ji* 綠煙瑣窗集), which are believed to be chronologically arranged summaries of the main plot of the version of the novel Ming Yi happened to be reading at that time, Baoyu's dream journey is mentioned together with his writing of his "Four Seasons Poems," an incident that takes place in chap. 23 of all extant versions of the novel; see the poem by Ming Yi reprinted in Yisu, "*Honglou meng*" *juan*, p. 11. For an informative discussion of the possible clues provided in Ming Yi's poems regarding the particular version of the novel he was reading, see Zhu Danwen, "*Honglou meng*" *lunyuan*, pp. 201–59. See Wu Enyu, "Ming Yi de *Lüyan suochuang ji shixuan*," for more information on Ming Yi.

cations—"speaking to the wrong person" or "listening to a speech one is not supposed to listen to"—can, at least in part, be attributed to the lack of an adequate language for communication among these young children, who have something unspeakable (something about their being no longer children) to speak about.[41]

Daiyu's grandest attempt to find a language to express her own adult feelings is perhaps her daring verbalizations in the poems she writes down on the handkerchiefs sent by Baoyu, but such poems are not meant to be read by anyone else but herself. They are not written for communication and have to be burned before anyone else can have access to them (if we are ready to accept the rendering of the author of the last forty chapters, Gao E, as a valid reading of the first eighty chapters).

On the other hand, reading about other adults' desires becomes an extension of Baoyu's and Daiyu's own desires, even though they do not have much success in appropriating the languages of these others.[42] Baoyu often turns to reading about the desires of others when he is in a state of complete contentment—when he seems to have everything he wants. Part of Baoyu's lust of intent seems to be the desire for desire itself—he needs to be in a state of continual desiring. This predetermines that once he is satisfied, he immediately has to invent a new object of desire in order to sustain his act of desiring. (Compare Ximen Qing's attempt to invent a new object of desire after he seemingly has everything he wants, as discussed in Chapter 4. Although a character of the lust of the flesh, Ximen Qing is not as different from Baoyu as he may first appear.) In chapter 23, Baoyu starts reading books about romantic love brought by his page Mingyan (Tealeaf), just when he is feeling out of sorts after he has moved into the garden and everything seems so perfect:

> A day arrived when Baoyu seemed to have exhausted the Garden's possibilities, and its charms were beginning to weary him. *The Return of the Soul* was very much on his mind at this time. He had read it through twice without in any way abating his appetite for more. Having recently been told that the best singer among the twelve little actresses of Pear Tree Court was the soubrette called Charmante [Lingguang],

41. As discussed in Chapter 4, eavesdropping also plays an important role in *Jin Ping Mei*. However, in *Honglou meng* its significance is somehow tied with the important question of communications, especially the communicating of *qing*.

42. See Anthony Yu, *Rereading the Stone*, pp. 210–18, for a discussion of how reading about desire also generates desire on the part of Baoyu and Daiyu.

he resolved, for a change of scene, to go over there and look her up, so that he could ask her to sing him some of the arias from it. (H, 36.493–94; S, 2: 206–7)

Reading about others' desires is not enough. Baoyu has to see their desires being performed by yet another other. Being completely bored by his own life, Baoyu needs to witness the re-enactment of others' desire at a double distance—the desires of an other being mimicked by yet another other. But Lingguan refuses his request that she sing a few arias from this play—she refuses to imitate for his sake. Instead, she chooses to perform something very different—her real love with Jia Qiang. Consequently, instead of a re-enactment of the desires of some textualized other, Baoyu witnesses how the real people around him come to terms with their own desires. He is forced to see Lingguan for the first time as someone with her own desires rather than just an actress capable only of mimicking others' desires, as he mistakenly assumes when he believes that she is aping Daiyu's act of burying fallen flower petals. The simple fact confronting Baoyu is that quite a few girls are reluctant to imitate (Lingguan does not imitate Daiyu); that he does not have the right to claim the tears of every girl just because Lin Daiyu is willing to make such a commitment to him. Paradoxically, the desire to see another's desire imitated leads Baoyu to realize that others' desires can be something more than just imitations. This compels him to face the narcissistic nature of his own desire, which thus far has always had an "altruistic" appearance (*qing buqing*). On the other hand, imitation (choosing to play a role in those romantic plays and quoting lines from them) is important for Baoyu in the sense that he needs imitation to sustain his own desires. However, imitation has its perils. Perfect imitation is impossible, as Daiyu sometimes makes him realize when she is upset by his frequent references to these plays, because repetition also highlights differences at the same time.

This fear of adult language is shared by another important female character in the sense that it is equally, if not more, important for Baochai to deny that she is capable of improper adult desires with regard to Baoyu. For Baochai, to verbalize these feelings, even to herself, is absolutely unthinkable. She has to be on constant guard to suppress these desires. But this proves extremely difficult. After all, in this segregated society, Baoyu is the only young man Baochai associates with on a daily basis. Baochai is a controversial character in *Honglou meng*, not only because of her apparently conservative views and her sometimes manipulative personality but also because of the way she is presented.[43] Throughout the novel, the narrator is often reluctant to enter Baochai's mind to allow the reader a clear view of her psyche at a particular moment. Compared with the ample information we have about Daiyu's inner world (the most representative case is the detailed and lengthy description of Daiyu's inner thoughts after she overhears Baoyu's praise of her in chapter 32), we are left in the dark about Baochai's psychological state at an otherwise equally revealing moment:

Baochai meanwhile continued her sewing undisturbed. She had just completed her second, or maybe it was her third petal, when Baoyu, who appeared to be dreaming, cried out angrily in his sleep,

"Why should I believe what those old monks and Taoists say? I don't believe in the marriage of gold and jade. I believe in the marriage of stone and flower."

The words astounded her. She had still not recovered from the shock of hearing them when Aroma returned. (H, 36.492; S, 2: 203)

Here at this moment of another crucial case of eavesdropping, the narrator chooses to keep silent. The timely return of Xiren saves him from the need to detail Baochai's response because her reflection is conveniently cut short. What the reader is given is the unusually cryptic description that she is shocked (*bujue zhengle* 不覺怔了; H, 36.492). This is certainly a deliberate ploy on the part of the author. The narrator's silence is in sharp contrast to his lengthy description of Daiyu's feelings (both are truth-revealing cases of eavesdropping).[44] It is this deliberate *qubi* 曲筆 (indirect approach) on the part of the author that alerts the reader to the need to adopt a different reading strategy in understanding Baochai, whose complex character requires the reader to go beneath the surface in deciphering all the hidden meanings and hidden motives. This is a point underscored in the subtle description of her future residence in the garden—the Allspice Court (Hengwu yuan):

"This building seems rather out of place here," said Jia Zheng.

But as he entered the gate, the source of his annoyance disappeared; for a miniature mountain of rock, whose many holes and fissures, worn through it by

43. For a discussion of some late Qing commentators' views on Xue Baochai as a "duplicitous character" and possible "historical" precedents in other novels, see Rolston, *Traditional Chinese Fiction and Fiction Commentary*, pp. 216–23.

44. For a discussion of the novel's masterful description of Daiyu's psychological state after she overhears what Baoyu has said about her in front of Xiangyun and Xiren, see my "Notes Towards a Poetics of Characterization in the Traditional Chinese Novel," pp. 18–20.

weathering or the wash of waters, bestowed on it a misleading appearance of fragile delicacy, towered up in front of him and combined with the many smaller rocks of various shapes and sizes which surrounded it to efface from their view every vestige of the building they had just been looking at. (H, 17–18.234; S, 1.339)

To appreciate the full beauty of Baochai's future residence, one has to walk behind the misleading "miniature mountain of rock."

In fact, this need to get behind the appearance or beneath the surface to appreciate Baochai is referred to in chapter 5 in the picture and the accompanying verse from the main register that Baoyu reads but cannot comprehend in his dream journey:

In this album the picture on the first page represented two dead trees with a jade belt hanging in their branches and on the ground beneath them a pile of snow in which a golden hairpin lay half-buried. This was followed by a quatrain:

> One was a pattern of female virtue
> One a wit who made other wits seem slow
> Jade belt in the greenwood hangs
> The gold pin is buried beneath the snow (H, 5.77–78; S, 1:133)

Obviously, the picture and verse refer to both Lin Daiyu and Xue Baochai. The first three characters (*yu dai lin* 玉帶林) of the line "Jade belt in the greenwood hangs" (玉帶林中掛), when read in reverse, become "lin dai yu" and thus homophonic with Daiyu's full name as it is pronounced in Chinese. Relying on the suggestions provided by the last line in the poem and the picture in which the gold pin lies half-buried in the snow, the reader would read Xue Baochai's (薛寶釵) name as "the snow completely wraps up [covers] the pin" (*xue bao chai* 雪包釵, which is also a homophonic pun on her name). In other words, the golden nature of the hairpin cannot easily be appreciated because the pin is "wrapped up" or covered in the snow. Of course, throughout the novel Baochai is often associated homophonically with "snow" (*xue* 雪) by virtue of her last name xue 薛 and thus with "coldness." As early as chapter 4, the Xue family is referred to with the character *xue* (snow) in a couplet in the *Mandarin's Life Preserver* (*Huguan hu* 護官符): "Good harvest depends on frequent snow / The Xue family are so rich that they spend money like dirt" (丰年好大雪, 珍珠如土金如鐵; H, 4.59–60). There are few decorations in Baochai's residence, Allspice Court, and it looks so stark and bare that it is compared to a "snow cave" (*xuedong yiban* 雪洞一般; H, 40.555). It is true that Baochai, unlike Daiyu, seldom shows her emotion and almost never loses her cool. She can certainly be called a "cold beauty," or *leng meiren* 冷美人.

Interestingly enough, the reader is also told that this cold beauty, who is often associated with coldness and snow, suffers from a mysterious illness called *redu* 熱毒, or "a congenital tendency toward overheatedness" (H, 7.108; S, 1: 168). However, what is even more intriguing is that this overheating can be controlled only by a medicine called *lengxiangwan* 冷香丸, or Cold Fragrance Pills (H, 7.109; S, 1: 169). That is to say, despite her cold appearance, which might be the result of a deliberate controlling mechanism (the Cold Fragrance Pills), Baochai can be very warm or even hot inside, as symbolically suggested by a homophonic reading of her name as *xue bao chai* 雪包釵. This seems to be confirmed by lines in her own "self-referential" poems such as: "Guard the sweet scent behind closed courtyard door" (珍重芳姿晨掩門) and "For beauty in plain whiteness best appears" (淡極始知花更艷; H, 37.505; S, 2: 223). All this testifies to the complexity of Baochai as a character—she may be much more emotional than she appears to others not the least because she suffers from a congenital "overheating" (some repressed desire that even she herself is probably unconscious of).

A close look at the fascinating account of Baoyu's visit to Baochai in chapter 8 should help us see this aspect of Baochai more clearly. During that visit, it is Baochai who first mentions to Baoyu that she would like to have a close look at his famous jade. Obviously her interest in Baoyu's jade is not unrelated to the fact that a monk has predicted that she will marry someone with a piece of jade, which is to match her own golden locket. After studying the jade and its inscriptions for a while, Baochai turns to her maid:

"Why aren't you pouring the tea?" she asked Oriole. "What are you standing there gawping for?"

Oriole [Ying'er] laughed.

"Because those words sounded like a perfect match to the ones on your necklace."

"So you have an inscription, too?" said Baoyu pricking up his ears. "I must have a look."

"Don't take any notice of her!" said Baochai. "There is no inscription."

"Cousin, cousin," said Baoyu entreatingly, "*you*'ve had a look at mine. Be fair!"

Baochai could not escape the logic of this entreaty. . . .

He recited them a couple of times and then recited the words of his own inscription a couple of times.

"Why, yes!" he cried delightedly. "The two inscriptions are a perfect match!"

"A scabby-headed old monk gave Miss Baochai the words," said Oriole. "He said they must be engraved on something made of gold. . . ."

Baochai angrily cut her short, telling her to mind her business and pour the tea. (H, 8.125–126; S, 1: 189–90)

Although this may not be a planned "operation," Baochai's maid is certainly aware of her mistress's unexpressed wishes. When Baochai asks her maid why she is standing there doing nothing, she is probably reminding her maid that it is the time to mention her locket and the story associated with it.[45] The ultimate purpose of this ingenious joint effort is to make Baoyu aware of the "marriage of gold and jade." Even Baochai's cutting her maid short underscores the importance of what remains unsaid but can easily be inferred (Baoyu's knowledge is confirmed by the words he utters in his sleep in chapter 36). Everything is done so naturally that no one could blame Baochai for broaching this sensitive subject. After all, who could suspect this girl of perfect Confucian virtue of reminding a man that they are destined to marry each other? Immediately after this, very appropriately, the narrator tells the reader that Baoyu smells the Cold Fragrance Pills as if to remind everyone (including the reader) that Baochai's hesitations or "ingenious ruse" is the inevitable result of an uneasy compromise between her tendency to overheat and the medicine she is taking. This reference to the Cold Fragrance Pills is immediately followed by the statement that it is *snowing* outside and thus very *cold* because the newly arrived Daiyu is wearing a greatcoat (throughout the triangular relationship, Baochai and Daiyu always manage to interrupt each other's rendezvous with Baoyu). Then Baochai explains to Baoyu why he must not drink wine cold:

I'm surprised at you, Cousin Bao!" said Baochai with a smile. "With all your enthusiasm for out-of-the-way learning, fancy not knowing a thing like that! Wine has an exceptionally fiery nature, and therefore must be drunk warm in order to be quickly digested. If it is drunk cold, it congeals inside the body and harms it by absorbing heat from the internal organs. From this day on you must reform! No more cold wine!" (H, 8.127; S, 1: 193)

45. Our impression of her maid Ying'er's "complicity" in this "operation" is to be reinforced in chapter 35 when she is unexpectedly cut short by the sudden arrival of Baochai before she can tell Baoyu what are her mistress's other "good qualities" besides her good looks (H, 35.181). She is certainly eager to point out to Baoyu her mistress's attractive qualities whenever she gets a chance.

Even though Baochai herself is suffering from overheating and needs Cold Fragrance Pills to control this condition, she advises Baoyu that cold wine will absorb "heat from the internal organs." For similar reasons, the Cold Fragrance Pills, Baochai has told Zhou Rui's wife, are also supposed to be taken in hot soup (*jiantang* 煎湯; H, 7.169). Some degree of "heat" needs to be maintained inside one's body. Symbolically, one can read this incident as suggesting that Baochai still feels the heat inside herself, and that desire such as that for sexual fulfillment is as important to one's health as heat is to one's internal organs. After all, Baochai's "overheatedness" is "congenital" (從娘胎里帶來的; H, 7.108). In other words, one's inborn desires, though suppressed (or repressed) with the help of cold pills, are nevertheless difficult to eradicate. Complete eradication may even be harmful to one's health.

All this talk about cold and heat makes Daiyu uncomfortable and even jealous. She soon airs her displeasure:

> Daiyu, who sat cracking melon-seeds between her teeth throughout this homily, smiled ironically. Just at that moment her maid Snowgoose [Xueyan] came hurrying in with a little hand-warmer for her.
>
> "Who told you to bring this?" Daiyu asked her. "Very kind of them, I am sure. But I was not actually freezing to death here."
>
> "Nightingale [Zijuan] told me to bring it, Miss. She was afraid you might be cold." (H, 8.128; S, 1: 193)

Daiyu apparently does not mind the cold or the fact that Baoyu feels the coldness on Baochai's part. This is probably the densest focus in the novel on images of cold and heat and the subtle interplay between the two.[46] Here even the otherwise innocent name of Daiyu's maid Snowgoose (Xueyan 雪雁) takes on an unexpected symbolic meaning. The atmosphere inside the house is certainly very hot despite the repeated references to the *cold* weather and *snow* outside the house. All this becomes symbolically significant in understanding Baochai, who often appears cold *outside* and yet suffers from overheating *inside* and needs medical help to sustain her cold appearance.

46. Of course, the fascination with the symbolic implications of the images of cold and heat is a long-standing tradition in Chinese fiction. Well-known examples can be found in both *Suihu zhuan* and *Jin Ping Mei*. For a discussion of cold and heat in *Jin Ping Mei* and the commentator Zhang Zhupo's insights, see Plaks, *Four Masterworks*, pp. 82–85. See also Zhang Zhupo's short essay "Lengre jinzheng" 冷熱金針, in *Zhang Zhupo*, p. 11.

Often, however, her personality and the pills to the contrary, the heat within her radiates out.

Of course, there are other overheated moments in the novel. After Baoyu is severely beaten by his father, Baochai's show of emotion is anything but cold:

> Baochai was relieved to see him with his eyes open and talking again. She shook her head sadly.
>
> "If you had listened to what one said, this would never have happened. Everyone is so upset now. It isn't only Grandmother and Lady Wang, you know. Even—"
>
> She checked herself abruptly, regretting that she had allowed her feelings to run away with her, and lowered her head, blushing. Baoyu had sensed hidden depths of feeling in the passionate earnestness of her tone, and when she suddenly faltered and turned red, there was something so touching about the pretty air of confusion with which she dropped her head and played with the ends of her girdle, that his spirits soared and his pain was momentarily forgotten. (H, 34.461–62; S, 2: 156)

This is apparently one of the several moments in the novel when Baochai's Cold Fragrance Pills fail to work. No wonder Baoyu detects the heat and begins to think that this kind of show of emotion is worth dying for. Another such moment is her unexpected show of deep concern with Baoyu's well-being:

> "Where was Cousin Bao rushing off to just now, all dressed up for going out?" said Baochai. "I was going to call out and ask him, but he is getting so crotchety lately that I thought I had better not."
>
> "The Master sent for him," said Aroma.
>
> "Oh dear!" said Baochai. "I wonder why he should send for him in *heat* like this? I hope he hasn't thought of something to be angry about and called him over to be punished."
>
> "No, it isn't that," said Aroma. "I think it's to receive a visitor."
>
> "It must be a very tiresome visitor," said Baochai, "to go around bothering people on a *boiling* day like this instead of staying at home and trying to keep *cool*." (H, 32.448; S, 2: 135–36; italics added)

Here Baochai is saying something quite out of character. She is obviously siding with Baoyu in his argument with Xiangyun and Xiren as to whether he should receive these visitors whom his father has asked him to associate with (so that he can "learn about the way the empire is governed" from these officials). It is ironical that it is the hot weather that prompts Baochai to show a bit too much of her own "overheatedness" or deep feelings for Baoyu.

The seemingly innocent and intimate scene between Baochai and Baoyu that initially so alarms Daiyu may be capable of a more subtle interpretation if read in the context of Baochai's sometimes uncontrollable tendency to overheat.

Aroma [Xiren] sat at his bedside sewing, a white horse-hair fly-whisk with a handle of white rhinoceros-horn (*yibin baixizhu* 一柄白犀麈) at her side. Baochai entered the "cabinet" and laughed softly at Aroma.

"Aren't you being rather over-cautious?" she whispered. "What's the fly-whisk for? Surely no flies or mosquitoes can get in *here?*"

"Oh, it's Miss Bao! I wasn't expecting you," she whispered. "You gave me a shock—no, we don't get any flies or mosquitoes in here, but there's a little tiny insect that finds its way through the holes in the netting. They're so small, you don't notice them; but when you're asleep they can give you a nasty bite—a bite like an ant-bite."

"That's not surprising," said Baochai. "You've got water behind you here, you see; you've also got a lot of sweet-smelling flowers outside; and indoors is perfumed as well. This kind of insect breeds in the insides of flowers and is attracted towards anything fragrant. That's why you get them inside the house."

While she was speaking, her eye fell on the sewing that Aroma had just put down. It was a pinafore of the kind children wear, with bib and apron in one (*doudu* 兜肚). It was of white satin lined with red silk, and the pattern Aroma was embroidering on it was mandarin ducks disporting themselves in a background of lotuses....

"I've done such a lot of work on it today," said Aroma, "my neck is quite stiff from bending over." She smiled at Baochai entreatingly: "Do us a favor, Miss: sit here a bit in my place, will you, while I go off and stretch my legs? I'll be back directly."

Saying this, she slipped quietly out, not waiting for a reply.

So intent was Baochai on the embroidery that she sank down almost without realizing what she was doing into the place Aroma had just vacated. It really *was* a most beautiful piece of work; in fact, she found it irresistible, and taking up the needle, began sewing it where Aroma left off.

Daiyu just happens to witness this scene:

... She saw Baoyu, clothed in little else but a thin, rose-colored shirt, sprawled out asleep on the bed and Baochai sitting beside him sewing, with a fly-whisk in readiness at her side.

For some moments she goggled incredulously at this touching domestic scene, then, fearful of disturbing it, she tore herself away to stifle her mounting giggles. (H, 36.490–91; S, 2:201–3)

It is obviously improper for Baochai to sit beside the thinly-clothed, sleeping Baoyu. Moreover, Baochai sits in the place just vacated by Xiren, who is Baoyu's concubine and personal maid (a fact known to almost everyone), as if Baochai were also acknowledging, or even insisting on, her special relationship with Baoyu. The late Qing commentator Hong Qiufan 洪秋蕃 (fl. 1862) saw this as a revealing moment:

Baochai has been a very thoughtful and careful person all her life. She usually leaves a scene whenever there is the possibility of causing gossip or suspicion. Why should she behave so carelessly in such an intimate situation this time? This must be due to her secret wishes to be close to Baoyu. Being alone with him is exactly what she has been waiting for, just as a honeybee is always attracted to fragrant flowers. The author wants to test the reader's attentiveness by taking advantage of Baochai's moment of carelessness (*bu liuxin* 不留心). Just recall Baochai's deliberate attempt to keep a distance from Baoyu in chapter 33 to see whether she is really being "careless" here.[47]

Interpreted in the context of this unexpected "carelessness" on Baochai's part, the late Qing commentator Zhang Xinzhi's 張新之 (fl. 1828–50) seemingly more outrageous reading of this scene may turn out to be not so outrageous after all. Zhang saw the "white horse-hair fly-whisk with a handle of white rhinoceros-horn" as a phallic reference since rhinoceros horn (*zhubing* 麈柄) is a common euphemism for the male sexual organ in traditional erotic literature. He further reminds the reader that Baochai's remark that "this kind of insect breeds in the insides of flowers" (這些蟲子都是花心裏長的) echoes the line "the honeybee pushed and squeezed trying to get inside" (一個蟲兒往裏蹭; H, 28.396) in the erotic song sung by the prostitute Yun'er, who entertains Baoyu and his friends in chapter 28. Commenting on the pinafore and its embroidered patterns and colors, Zhang asks a series of rhetorical questions: "What kind of bird is the mandarin duck? What kind of game is taking place among the lotuses (*xilian* 戲蓮)? Where is the part of body that is below the abdomen and is supposed to be covered by the pinafore? What kind of thing is white outside and red inside?

47. Feng Qiyong et al., *Bajia pingpi "Honglou meng,"* p. 881.

All these are extremely significant."[48] Of course, what adds to the irony of this scene is that it is here that Baochai overhears, much to her astonishment, the sleeping Baoyu's revelation that he prefers the marriage of wood and stone to that of gold and jade.

To reinforce the reader's impression that Baochai is indeed a character whose internal heat often radiates out despite her cold appearance, this conservative girl, who is always regarded by others as a model of Confucian female virtue, sometimes becomes a quite sensuous woman.

But now here was Baoyu smiling at her with sudden interest.

"Cousin Bao, may I have a look at your medicine-beads?"

She happened to be wearing one of the little chaplets on her left wrist and began to pull it off now in obedience to his request. But Baochai was inclined to plumpness and perspired easily, and for a moment or two it would not come off. While she was struggling with it, Baoyu had ample opportunity to observe her snow-white arm, and a feeling rather warmer than admiration was kindled inside him.

"If that arm were growing on Cousin Lin's body," he speculated, " I might hope one day to touch it. What a pity it's hers! Now I shall never have the good fortune."

Suddenly he thought of the curious coincidence of the gold and jade talismans and their matching inscriptions, which Daiyu's remark had reminded him of. He looked again at Baochai—

that face like the full moon's argent bowl;
those eyes like sloes;
those lips whose carmine hue no Art contrived;
and brows by none but Nature's pencil lined.

This was beauty of quite a different order from Daiyu's. Fascinated by it, he continued to stare at her with a somewhat dazed expression, so that when she handed him the chaplet, which she had now succeeded in getting off her wrist, he failed to take it from her. (H, 28.401–2; S, 2: 66–67)

A more elaborate and even more daring reference to Baochai's sensuality can be found in chapter 27:

48. See Zhang Xinzhi's interlineal comments, in ibid. p. 866. Andrew Plaks (*"Honglou meng" piyuan pianquan*, pp. 656–57) also calls attention to these comments by Zhang Xinzhi. In many manuscript versions of the novel, the character *zhu* is written as *chen* 塵, probably a result of miswriting. See note 5 of the "Jiaoji" 校記 (Collating notes) at the end of chapter 37 (H, 37.497).

But just at that moment she noticed two enormous turquoise-colored butterflies a little way ahead of her, each as large as a fan, fluttering and dancing on breeze. She watched them fascinated and thought she would like to play a game with them. Taking a fan from inside her sleeve and holding it outspread in front of her, she followed them off the path and into the grass.

To and fro fluttered the pair of butterflies, sometimes alighting for a moment, but always flying off again before she could reach them. Once they seemed on the point of flying across the little river that flowed through the midst of the garden and Baochai had to stalk them with bated breath for fear of startling them out on to the water. By the time she had reached Raindrop Pavilion she was perspiring freely and she was almost out of breath, and her interest in the butterflies was beginning to evaporate. (H, 27.374; S, 2: 25–26; trans. modified)

Euphemistic phrases such as "perspiring freely" (*xianghan linlin* 香汗淋淋), "out of breath" (*jiaochuan xixi* 嬌喘細細), and "to and fro fluttered the pair of butterflies" (*yishuang hudie yiqiyiluo* 一雙蝴蝶一起一落) immediately conjure up an amorous picture in the mind of readers familiar with the narrative conventions of traditional erotic literature.[49] Indeed, Pan Jinlian in *Jin Ping Mei* is twice said to be chasing butterflies during her repeated flirtation with Chen Jingji (19.192, 56.6). Furthermore, the image of a pair of butterflies fluttering to and fro may also remind the reader of the sexual images associated with Ping Caiyun in *Lin Lan Xiang* discussed in Chapter 7. In his interlineal comment on the phrases "perspiring freely" and "out of breath" in the Gengchen manuscript version, Zhiyanzhai wrote: "If our Brother Yu were here, he would have a lot to busy himself with" (若玉兄在, 必有許多張羅; in Zhu Yixuan, p. 392).[50] However, right after this scene, Baochai is

49. In his chapter-comments, Hong Qiufan saw the pair of fluttering butterflies as symbolizing Baochai's desire to marry Baoyu, whereas Zhang Xinzhi, in his interlineal comments, urged the reader to associate the erotic image here with what happens in chapter 36 when Baochai sits beside the napping Baoyu (see Feng Qiyong et al., *Bajia pingpi "Honglou meng,"* pp. 633, 618).

50. Based on what is suggested in the fourth poem in "Ti *Honglou meng*" poems by Ming Yi (see Yisu, *"Honglou meng" juan*, p. 11), we may infer that the account of Baochai's chase of butterflies was presented in more detail in an earlier version of the manuscript. The description should be substantial enough to conjure up an impressive picture that neatly parallels the now much more famous image of Daiyu burying fallen flower petals, as suggested by the couplet/title of chap. 27, "Beauty Perspiring Sports with Butterflies by the Raindrop Pavilion / And Beauty Suspiring Weeps for Fallen Blossoms by the Flowers' Grave" (滴翠亭楊妃戲彩蝶, 埋香冢飛燕泣殘紅). The balance between the two beauties in terms of the attention each receives seems to have been more consistently maintained in the early ver-

alarmed when she overhears a secretive conversation between two maids about an ongoing love affair. As if shocked into reality by the illicit nature of their affair—however reminiscent of her own momentary lapse just a moment before—Baochai is once again under the control of the Cold Fragrance Pills. She immediately decides that she should get away as far as possible. Once again, Baochai is torn between her conscious effort to control herself and the almost irrepressible heat deep inside her, which, we are told, is something congenital and therefore difficult to eradicate.

Baochai's internal heat even appears in her otherwise frigid, censorious advice to Daiyu against reading literature that advocates an individual's right to seek sexual fulfillment. This renders her lecture much more problematic than it may have otherwise sounded. After catching Daiyu reciting lines from romantic plays, Baochai launches into a long homily that begins with a halfhearted self-criticism:

"What do you take me for? I'm just as bad. At seven or eight I used to be a real little terror. Ours was reckoned to be rather a literary family. My grandfather was a bibliophile, so the house we lived in was full of books. We were a big family in those days. All my boy cousins and girl cousins on my father's side lived with us in the same house. All of us younger people hated serious books but liked reading poetry and plays. The boys had got lots and lots of plays: *The Western Chamber, The Lute-player, A Hundred Yuan Plays*—just about everything you could think of. *They* used to read them behind *our* backs, and we girls used to read them behind theirs. Eventually the grown-ups got to know about it and then there were beatings and lectures and burning of books—and that was the end of that.

"So, you see, in the case of us girls it would probably be better for us if we never learned to read in the first place. Even boys, if they gain no understanding from their readings, would do better not to read at all; and if that is true of boys, it certainly holds true for girls like you and me. The little poetry-writing and calligraphy we indulge in is not really our proper business. Come to that, it isn't a boy's proper business either. A boy's proper business is to read books in order to gain an understanding of things, so that when he grows up he can play his part in governing the country.

"Not that one hears of that happening much nowadays. Nowadays their reading seems to make them even worse than they were to start with. And unfortunately it isn't merely a case of their being led astray by what they read. The books, too, are

---

sion. See Zhang Ailing, "*Honglou meng*" *yan*, p. 187; and Zhu Danwen, "*Honglou meng*" *lunyuan*, p. 203.

spoiled, by the false interpretations they put upon them. They would do better to leave books and take up business or agriculture. At least they wouldn't do so much damage.

"As for girls like you and me: spinning and sewing are *our* proper business. What do we need to be able to read for? But since we *can* read, let us confine ourselves to good, improving books; let us avoid like the plague those pernicious works of fiction, which so undermine the character that in the end it is past reclaiming." (H, 42.582–83; *S*, 2:333–34)

This lengthy lecture on proper reading is so full of contradictions that it tends to make us suspect the speaker's real intention may be more than what Baochai is explicitly claiming—what a girl should not read. In the guise of self-criticism, Baochai is actually bragging about her wider and earlier acquaintance with the works Daiyu is quoting. Obviously, her memory of these "pernicious books" is strong enough that Baochai can identify the sources of Daiyu's casual quotations. So far the lecture almost amounts to a deliberate flaunting of her knowledge. Then Baochai shifts her focus to the importance of proper reading and argues that one should not ruin the books (*ba shu zaota le* 把書糟蹋了) by failing to read them properly. One unexpected message of her homily is that the question of how one reads is more important than the question of the moral worth of the book one is reading (Baochai apparently studied the essays of the fiction commentator Zhang Zhupo). This logic, pushed further, has some dangerous implications. Is it permissible to read a "bad" book so long as the reader knows how to read it? Does the moral worth of a book ultimately depend on how one reads it? Baochai's complaint that nowadays very few men know how to read is even more shocking, especially considering the fact that her ostensible message is that reading is not a proper activity for women. Here she oversteps the limits of what a well-bred girl can do (as she seems to insist at the end of her lecture) by offering a scathing and very political comment on men's failures not only to read books properly but also to carry out their duties as men! Her concluding salvo that a girl should behave as prescribed by the Confucian moral codes for women is advice she herself has failed to observe just a moment before.

These occasional radiations of unexpected warmth often captivate Baoyu, despite Baochai's conscious attempt to make herself appear cold and distant. The inscription on the card Baochai draws in a drinking game is that she can still be very charming even though she appears passionless (任是無情也動

人), and Baoyu must have been busy pondering the line's implications when he is subsequently lost in deep thought (H, 63.891–92). Of course, Baochai is a very complex character. She can be manipulative and cunning. However, she is apparently bothered by her own heat, which may be read as referring symbolically to her innermost desires. They can be sexual as well as political in the sense that her attraction to Baoyu may be related to the fact that Baoyu is the most important male heir in his generation of the Jia family.

Baochai's complexities as a novelistic character also reside in the fact that she does not fit comfortably in the paradigm of the lust of intent versus the lust of the flesh as proposed by the Goddess of Disenchantment. The three female characters who symbolically share Baoyu's bed are said to resemble one another in appearance as well as in temperament. Daiyu shares a bed with Baoyu in chapter 19 when he joins her when she is taking a nap (H, 19.273); Qingwen (Skybright) warms herself in Baoyu's bed after she tries to scare another maid during a cold night (H, 51.715); and Fangguan (Parfumee) sleeps next to Baoyu after they get drunk during Baoyu's birthday party (H, 63.895). The novel emphasizes that Daiyu's relationship with Baoyu is "clean." And although Lady Wang accuses both Qingwen and Fangguan of trying to seduce Baoyu, it is clear that neither of them has a physical relationship with him (of course, Qingwen's dying regret is that she might as well have had a physical relationship with Baoyu now that she has been falsely accused of having such a relationship).

Baochai and Xiren, who also resemble each other in appearance and temperament, are the ones who have a physical relationship with him (of course, Baochai eventually marries him). Although we may feel justified in classifying Daiyu, Qingwen, and Fangguan as characters representing the lust of intent, it is difficult to classify Baochai and Xiren as characters in either category of lust. These two do have desires, but they seem to try, with considerable success, to channel these desires into something sanctioned by the existing familial and social order as "acceptable" and appropriate "aspirations" (here *qing* can be identified as *zhi*). Baochai is an excellent example of a character who tries to comply with the wishes of the elders of the family and the prescriptions of Confucian moral codes by virtue of her good use of the Cold Fragrance Pills, although, as we have seen, not all her attempts at self-control are equally successful. Here we may recall the strange prescription for the Cold Fragrance Pills in chapter 7 (H, 7.108–9). The process of making this medicine is so complicated and contains such a fastidious insistence on the number twelve (every ingredient has to weigh twelve ounces or drams) that it cries out to be interpreted symbolically. The significance of the repeated references to the number twelve did not escape the notice of the commentator Zhiyanzhai. In his interlineal comments in the Gengchen manuscript, he pointed out: "All the references to the number twelve should be read as symbolic of the twelve beauties [of Jinling]" (凡用十二字樣,皆照應十二釵; Zhu Yixuan, p. 121). That is to say, the pursuit of the symbolic implications of the Cold Fragrance Pills cannot be confined to the reading of the character of Baochai, who is the only person taking this medicine. The need to control one's desires or "overheatedness" with "cold pills" is common to the many female characters in the novel whose desires will eventually have tragic results. Daiyu may be an example by default: her tragedy lies partly in her failure to take enough cold pills. Even Baoyu will learn that he has to take cold pills too (albeit a different kind of pill)—escape into the Buddhist world of no desire. The commentator Zhiyanzhai saw the Cold Fragrance Pills as relevant not only to the twelve beauties of Jingling but also to all those suffering from desires (世皆同有者; interlineal comment in the Jiaxu manuscript, in Zhu Yixuan, pp. 121–22).

The complicated textual history of *Honglou meng* (not to mention the fact that the last forty chapters as we have them now are most likely another author's "conclusion") and the numerous revisions it underwent determine that its meanings (including that of the concept of the lust of intent) cannot be finalized. As the Goddess of Disenchantment insists early in the novel, Baoyu's *qing* "can be grasped by the mind but not expressed, apprehended intuitively but not described in words." It can be experienced but not described verbally. Desire understood as *qing* or the lust of intent has to be an act, a performance, and a process that is self-generating as well as narcissistic, whose existence is predicated on the constant reinventing of the object by itself. Baoyu is reluctant to admit that he has grown up so that he can constantly reinvent the object that will sustain his desiring and allow him to continue to pursue the lust of intent, much like as the author of the novel, who could not bring himself to conclude his story by offering a definitive concept of *qing*.[51] There can never be a "final" version of *Honglou meng* despite the efforts of so many sequel writers (including the very competent Gao E).

51. Although his approach is quite different from mine, Ho Yongkang also touches on this issue of "unfinalizability" of the novel in "Yige yinren zhumu de shenglüehao shishuo."

The novel is a "process" in the further sense that it is a work in which we are able to witness different stages in a gradual shifting of focus from *yu* to *qing*. And yet it is much more than that. It is a novelistic re-enactment of a complicated movement in the history of the traditional Chinese novel from the sixteenth-century *Jin Ping Mei*, which concentrates on *yu*, to those seventeenth-century works such as *Jin Yun Qiao zhuan*, *Haoqiu zhuan*, and *Dingqing ren* that focus exclusively on *qing*, and finally to several eighteenth-century works dominated by a trend culminating in *Honglou meng* that explores the subtle differences between *yu* and *qing* as well as their ultimate inseparability.[52] This trajectory from *yu* to *qing* re-enacted in *Honglou meng* parallels the seemingly never-ending writing and rewriting process the novel itself has undergone. It is this sense of an almost infinite process in *Honglou meng* that, among other things, compels us to set it apart from novels such as *Yesou puyan*, *Guwangyan*, and, to a lesser degree, *Lin Lan Xiang*, in which *yu* and *qing* are deliberately juxtaposed and contrasted. Precisely because *Honglou meng* presents desire as a process, it does not provide a means of determining whether a particular form of desire can be judged to be *qing* or *yu*. Although acknowledging the differences between *qing* and *yu*, *Honglou meng* also masterfully explores their inseparability and *qing*'s foredoomed attempt to transcend *yu*. The "process" from *yu* to *qing* is not a forward movement along a straight line in the sense that *qing* could exist without *yu* (after all, *yu* is one of the seven *qing* according to the definition in the *Book of Rites*), a fact poignantly underscored by the *unfinished* purifications of many characters in the revising and rewriting of the novel.

Jia Baoyu cannot be completely different from Ximen Qing. Both like women: one wants to possess the "bodies" of as many women as possible, whereas the other, though not completely immune to such physical temptations, wants to possess the "tears" (the hearts) of as many girls as possible. Both are the center of attention for many women, and both are troubled by the intense rivalry among these women, which is almost inevitable in polygamous relationships. Both repeatedly feel bored with what they already have and constantly have to invent new objects of desire. In many ways, Jia Baoyu is Ximen Qing; in even more ways, he is not Ximen Qing. The

52. The most thoroughgoing study of the relationship between *Jin Ping Mei* and *Honglou meng* to date is Mary Scott's Ph.D. dissertation, "Azure from Indigo: *Hongloumeng*'s Debt to *Jin Ping Mei*."

"change" from Ximen Qing to Jia Baoyu illustrates the distance the Chinese novel traveled in two hundred years. One important achievement of *Honglou meng* is its persuasive demonstration of how difficult it is to invent a *qing* that can transcend *yu* without completely excluding the latter, as attested by the persistent presence of *Fengyue baojian* in the novel.

Reference Matter

Bibliography

The following abbreviations are used in the Bibliography:

BCJ	Baibu congshu jicheng 百部叢書集成
CLEAR	*Chinese Literature: Essays, Articles, Reviews*
GXJ	Guben xiaoshuo jicheng 古本小說集成
HJAS	*Harvard Journal of Asiatic Studies*
HXK	*"Honglou meng" xuekan* 紅樓夢學刊
MQXL	*Ming Qing xiaoshuo luncong* 明清小說論叢
MQXY	*Ming Qing xiaoshuo yanjiu* 明清小說研究
MXJ	Mingdai xiaoshuo jikan 明代小說輯刊
SH	Siwuxie huibao 思無邪匯寶
SKQS	Siku quanshu 四庫全書
ZZJC	Zhuzi jicheng 諸子集成

An Pingqiu 安平秋 and Zhang Beiheng 章培恒. *Zhongguo jinshu daguan* 中國禁書大觀. Shanghai: Shanghai wenhua chubanshe, 1990.

Armstrong, Nancy. *Desire and Domestic Fiction*. New York: Oxford University Press, 1987.

———. "Postface: Chinese Women in a Comparative Perspective: A Response." In Ellen Widmer and Kang-I Sun Chang, eds., *Writing Women in Late Imperial China*, pp. 397–422. Stanford: Stanford University Press, 1997.

Atwell, William. "Ming China and the Emerging World Economy, c. 1470–1650." In Denis Twichett and Frederick W. Mote, eds., *The Cambridge History of China*, vol. 8, pt. 2, pp. 376–416. Cambridge, Eng.: Cambridge University Press, 1998.

Bakhtin, Mikhail. *The Dialogic Imagination*, ed. Michael Holquist, trans. Caryl Emerson and Michael Holquist. Austin: University of Texas Press, 1981.

Ban Gu 班固. *Hanshu* 漢書. Beijing: Zhonghua shuju, 1962.

Barrett, T. H. *Li Ao: Buddhist, Taoist, or Neo-Confucian?* Oxford: Oxford University Press, 1992.

Bian er chai 弁而釵. MXJ series 2, vol. 2. Chengdu: Bashu shushe, 1995.

Bian er chai 弁而釵. SH series. Taiwan: Taiwan daying baike, 1995.

Birch, Cyril, trans. *The Peony Pavilion*. Bloomington: Indiana University Press, 1980.

Birdwhistell, Ann. *Transition to Neo-Confucianism: Shao Yung on Knowledge and Symbols of Reality*. Stanford: Stanford University Press, 1989.

Bloom, Irene, trans. and ed. *Knowledge Painfully Acquired: The "K'un-chih chi" by Lo Ch'in-shun*. New York: Columbia University Press, 1987.

Brandauer, Frederick. *Tung Yüeh*. Boston: Twayne, 1978.

Brokaw, Cynthia. *The Ledgers of Merit and Demerit: Social Change and Moral Order in Late Imperial China*. Princeton: Princeton University Press, 1991.

Brook, Timothy. *The Confusions of Pleasure: Commerce and Culture in Ming China*. Berkeley: University of California Press.

———. *Praying for Power: Buddhism and the Formation of Gentry Society in Late Ming China*. Cambridge, Mass.: Harvard University, Council on East Asian Studies, 1993.

Bu Jian 卜鍵. *"Jin Ping Mei" zuozhe Li Kaixian kao* 金瓶梅作者李開先考. Lanzhou: Gansu renmin chubanshe, 1988.

———. *Li Kaixian zhuanlüe* 李開先傳略. Beijing: Zhongguo xiju chubanshe, 1989.

Butler, Judith. "Desire." In Frank Lentricchia and Thomas McLaughlin, eds., *Critical Terms for Literary Study*, pp. 369–86. Chicago: Chicago University Press, 1995.

———. *Subjects of Desire: Hegelian Reflections in Twentieth-Century France*. New York: Columbia University Press, 1987.

Cai Yi 蔡毅, comp. *Zhongguo gudian xiqu xuba huibian* 中國古典戲曲序跋彙編. Ji'nan: QiLu shushe, 1989.

Cai Yijiang 蔡義江. *"Honglou meng" shici qufu pingzhu* 紅樓夢詩詞曲賦評注. Beijing: Beijing chubanshe, 1979.

Cao Dawei 曹大爲. "*Xingshi yinyuan zhuan* de banben yuanliu he chengshu niandai" 醒世姻緣傳的版本源流和成書年代. *Wenshi* 文史 23 (1984): 217–38.

Cao Xueqin 曹雪芹 and Gao E 高鄂. *Honglou meng* 紅樓夢. Ed. Zhongguo yishu yanjiu yuan, *Honglou meng* yanjiu suo 中國藝術研究院紅樓夢研究所. Beijing: Renmin wenxue, 1982.

Cao Yibing 曹亦冰. "*Haoqiu zhuan* fei caizi jiaren xiaoshuo lun" 好逑傳非才子佳人小說論. *MQXY* 3 (1997, no. 1): 190–97.

Carlitz, Katherine. "Puns and Puzzles in the *Chin P'ing Mei*." *T'oung Pao*, 67, no. 3–5 (1981): 216–39.

———. Review of *The Late-Ming Poet Ch'en Tzu-lung* by Kang-i Sun Chang. *HJAS* 35, no. 1 (1995): 225–37.

———. *The Rhetoric of "Chin P'ing Mei."* Bloomington: Indiana University Press, 1986.

———. "The Social Uses of Virtue in Late Ming Editions of *Lienü zhuan.*" *Late Imperial China* 12, no. 2 (1991): 117–48.

———. "Style and Suffering in Two Stories by 'Langxian.'" In Theodore Huters, R. Bin Wong, and Pauline Yu, eds., *Culture and State in Chinese History*, pp. 207–35. Stanford: Stanford University Press, 1997.

Cedzich, Ursula-Angelika. "The Cult of the Wu-t'ung/Wu-hsien in History and Fiction: The Religious Roots of *The Journey to the South.*" In David Johnson, ed., *Ritual and Scripture in Chinese Popular Religion: Five Studies*, pp. 137–218. Berkeley: University of California, Chinese Popular Culture Project, 1994.

Chan, Leo Tak-hung. "Narrative as Argument: The *Yuewei caotang biji* and the Late Eighteenth-Century Elite Discourse on the Supernatural." *HJAS* 53, no. 1 (1993): 25–62.

Chan, Wing-tsit, trans. *Instructions for Practical Living and Other Confucian Writings by Wang Yang-ming*. New York: Columbia University Press, 1963.

Chan, Wing-tsit, trans. and comp. *A Source Book in Chinese Philosophy*. Princeton: Princeton University Press, 1963.

Chang, Kang-i Sun. *The Late-Ming Poet Ch'en Tzu-lung: Crisis in Love And Loyalism*. New Haven: Yale University Press, 1991.

Chanzhen houshi 禪眞後史. MXJ, series 1. Chengdu: Bashu shushe, 1994.

Chen Cuiying 陳翠英. *Shiqing xiaoshuo zhi jiazhiguan tantao: yi hunyin wei dingwei de kaocha* 世情小說之價值觀探討：以婚姻爲定位的考察. Taipei: Guoli Taiwan daxue chuban weiyuanhui, 1997.

Chen Dakang 陳大康. "Lun Yuan Ming zhongpian chuanqi xiaoshuo" 論元明中篇傳奇小說. *Wenxue yichan* 文學遺產 1998, no. 3: 49–64.

———. *Tongsu xiaoshuo de lishi guiji* 通俗小說的歷史軌跡. Changsha: Hu'nan chubanshe, 1993.

Chen Dongyou 陳東有. *Reyu de jiefang: Ming Qing shehui jingji bianqian yu dazhong shenmei* 人欲的解放：明清社會經濟變遷與大衆審美. Nanchang: Jiangxi gaoxiao chubanshe, 1996.

Chen Hong 陳洪. "*Lin Lan Xiang* chuangzuo niandai xiaokao" 林蘭香創作年代小考. *MQXY* 9 (1988, no. 3): 151–55.

Chen Qinghao 陳慶浩. "Bashi hui *Shitouji* chengshu chukao" 八十回石頭記成書初考. *Wenxue yichan* 文學遺產 1992, no. 2: 80–92.

———. "Bashi hui *Shitou ji* chengshu zaikao" 八十回石頭記成書再考. *HXK* 1995, no. 1: 164–89.

Chen Que 陳確. *Chen Que ji* 陳確集. Beijing: Zhonghua shuju, 1979.

Chen Shou 陳壽. *Sanguo zhi* 三國志. Beijing: Zhonghua shuju, 1959.

Chen Shulu 陳書錄. *Mindai shiwen de yanbian* 明代詩文的演變. Nanjing: Jiangsu jiaoyu chubanshe, 1996.

Chen Wanyi 陳萬益. "WanMing xingling wenxue sixiang yanjiu" 晚明性靈文學思想研究. Ph.D. dissertation, National Taiwan University, 1978.

Chen Weizhao 陳維昭. *Lunhui yu guizhen: Zhongguo jingquan wenxue chuantong de shengcun tiyan yu yiyi zhuiwen* 輪回與歸眞：中國警勸文學傳統的生存體驗與意義追問. Shantou: Shantou daxue chubanshe, 1993.

Chen Yiyuan 陳益源. *Cong "Jiao Hong ji" dao "Honglou meng"* 從嬌紅記到紅樓夢. Shenyang: Liaoning guji, 1996.

———. "*Guwangyan* sucai laiyuan chukao" 姑妄言素材來源初考. In idem, *Cong "Jiao Hong ji" dao "Honglou meng"* (q.v.), pp. 304–19.

———. "*Guwangyan* sucai laiyuan erkao" 姑妄言素材來源二考. *MQXY* 46 (1997, no. 4): 127–36.

———. "Ming Qing xiaoshuo li de *Jiao Hong ji*" 明清小說里的嬌紅記. In idem, *Cong "Jiao Hong ji" dao "Honglou meng"* (q.v.), pp. 34–76.

———. *Yuan Ming Qing zhongpian chuanqi xiaoshuo yanjiu.* 元明清中篇傳奇小說研究. Hong Kong: Xuefeng wenhua shiye gongsi, 1997.

Chen Zhao 陳詔. "Yetan Qin Keqing de chushen wenti" 也談秦可卿的出身問題. In Feng Qiyong 馮其庸 et al., eds., *Jiu'er Zhongguo guoji "Honglou meng" yantaohui lunwen ji* 92 中國國際紅樓夢研討會論文集, pp. 731–39. Beijing: Wenhua yishu chubanshe, 1995.

Cheng, Chung-ying. "Reason, Substance, and Human Desires in Seventeenth-Century Neo-Confucianism." In Wm. Theodore de Bary, ed., *The Unfolding of Neo-Confucianism*, pp. 469–509. New York: Columbia University Press, 1975.

Cheng Yi 程頤. *Yichuan wenji* 遺川文集. In *Er Cheng quanshu* 二程全書. Sibu beiyao ed.

Cheng Yizhong 程毅中. *Song Yuan xiaoshuo yanjiu* 宋元小說研究. Nanjing: Jiangsu guji, 1998.

Chin, Ann-ping, and Mansfield Freeman, trans. *Tai Chen on Mencius: Explorations in Words and Meaning*. New Haven: Yale University Press, 1990.

Chipozi zhuan 痴婆子傳. SH series. Taipei: Taiwan daying baike, 1995.

Chongding Xingshi yinyuan zhuan 重訂醒世姻緣傳. Tongde tang 同德堂 printed ed. GXJ series. Shanghai: Shanghai guji, 1990.

Chou, Chih-p'ing, *Yüan Hung-tao and the Kung-an School*. Cambridge, Eng.: Cambridge University Press, 1988.

Chundeng nao 春燈鬧. SH series. Taipei: Taiwan daying baike, 1995.

Ciyuan 辭源. Rev. ed. Beijing: Shangwu yinshuguan, 1988.

Clunas, Craig. *Superfluous Things: Material Culture and Social Status in Early Modern China*. Cambridge, Eng.: Polity Press, 1990.

Cosslett, Tess. *Woman to Woman: Female Friendship in Victorian Fiction*. Sussex, Eng.: Harvester Press, 1988.

Dai Bufan 戴不凡. "Shixu cuoluan pian: qian bashi hui shixu de maodun" 時序錯亂篇：前八十回時序的矛盾. In idem, *Hongxue pingyi waipian* 紅學評議外篇, pp. 269–331. Beijing: Wenhua yishu chubanshe, 1991.

Dai Zhen 戴震. *Dai Zhen quanshu* 戴震全書. Hefei: Huangshan shushe, 1995.

de Bary, Wm. Theodore. "Individualism and Humanitarianism in Late Ming Thought." In idem, *Self and Society in Ming Thought* (q.v.), pp. 145–247.

de Bary, Wm. Theodore, ed. *Self and Society in Ming Thought*. New York: Columbia University Press, 1970.

Deng Qingyou 鄧慶佑. "Sun Tongsheng" 孫桐生. In Feng Qiyong 馮其庸 and Li Xifan 李希凡, eds., *"Honglou meng" da cidian* 紅樓夢大辭典, p. 1182. Beijing: Wenhua yishu chubanshe, 1990.

———. "Sun Tongsheng yu *Honglou meng*" 孫桐生與紅樓夢. In Feng Qiyong 馮其庸 et al., eds., *Jiu'er Zhongguo guoji "Honglou meng" yantao hui lunwen ji* 92 中國國際紅樓夢研討會論文集, pp. 522–43. Beijing: Wenhua yishu chubanshe, 1995.

Dengcao heshang 燈草和尚. SH series. Taipei: Taiwan daying baike, 1995.

Dengyue yuan 燈月緣. GXJ series. Shanghai guji, 1990.

Ding Xigen 丁錫根, comp. *Zhongguo lidai xiaoshuo xuba ji* 中國歷代小說序跋集. Beijing: Renmin wenxue chubanshe, 1996.

Ding Yaokang 丁耀亢. *Xu Jin Ping Mei* 續金瓶梅. In Lu He 陸合 and Xing Yue 星月, eds., *Jin Ping Mei xushu sanzhong* 金瓶梅續書三種. Ji'nan: QiLu shushe, 1988.

Dingqing ren 定情人. Shenyang: Chunfeng wenyi chubanshe, 1983.

Dong Wencheng 董文成. "*Jin Yun Qiao zhuan* banben kao" 金雲翹傳版本考. *MQXL* 2 (1985): 163–81.

———. "*Jin Yun Qiao zhuan* banben kao buzheng" 金雲翹傳版本考補正. *MQXL* 5 (1987): 113–17.

———. "*Jin Yun Qiao zhuan* dui *Honglou meng* yishu chuangxin de duochong yingxiang" 金雲翹傳對紅樓夢藝術創新的多重影響. 2 pts. *HXK* 1999, no. 3: 178–95; no. 4: 247–72.

———. "*Jin Yun Qiao zhuan* gushi de yanhua" 金雲翹傳故事的演化. *MQXL* 3 (1985): 27–47.

———. "*Jin Yun Qiao zhuan* renwu yuanxing kao" 金雲翹傳人物原型考. *MQXL* 4 (1986): 80–91.

Dong Xi Jin yanyi 東西晉演義. Reprint of the Dayetang ed. 大業堂本. GXJ series. Shanghai: Shanghai guji, 1990.

Du Jinghua 杜景華. "*Honglou meng* de xushi liunian jiqi yinyu tankao" 紅樓夢的敘事流年及其隱寓探考. *HXK* 1991, no. 4: 165–86.

Ebrey, Patricia Buckley. *Family and Property in Sung China: Yüan Ts'ai's Precepts for Social Life*. Princeton: Princeton University Press, 1984.

Egerton, Clement, trans. *The Golden Lotus: A Translation, from the Chinese Original, of the Novel "Chin P'ing Mei."* 4 vols. London: Routledge & Kegan Paul, 1972.

Epstein, Maram. "Beauty Is the Beast: The Dual Face of Woman in Four Ch'ing Novels." Ph. D. dissertation, Princeton University, 1992.

———. *Competing Discourses: Orthodoxy, Authenticity, and Engendered Meanings in Late Imperial Chinese Fiction*. Cambridge, Mass.: Harvard University Asia Center, 2001.

Faderman, Lillian. *Surpassing the Love of Men: Romantic Friendship and Love Between Women from the Renaissance to the Present*. New York: William Morrow, 1981.

Fan Lian 范濂. *Yunjian jumu chao* 雲間據目抄. Reprinted in *Biji xiaoshuo daguan* 筆記小說大觀, vol. 13. Yangzhou: Jiangsu Guanlin guji kanyinsuo, 1983.

Faure, Bernard. *The Red Thread: Buddhist Approaches to Sexuality*. Princeton: Princeton University Press, 1998.

Feng Congwu 馮從吾. *Feng Shaoxu ji* 馮少墟集. Ming printed ed. (1612; 2d ed., 1621). Copy in Harvard-Yenching Library.

Feng Menglong 馮夢龍. *Feng Menglong quanji* 馮夢龍全集. Shanghai: Shanghai guji, 1993.

———. *Jingshi tongyan* 警世通言. Hong Kong: Zhonghua shuju, 1986.

———. *Pingyao zhuan* 平妖傳. Taipei: Zhiyang chubanshe, 1991.

———. *Yushi mingyan* 喻世明言. Hong Kong: Zhonghua shuju, 1986.

Feng Mengzhen 馮夢禎. *Kuaixue tang ji* 快雪堂集. Wanli ed. (1616). Copy in Taiwan Guoli zhongyang tushuguan in Taipei. Microfilm in the University of Michigan East Asian Library.

Feng Qiyong 馮其庸 and Li Xifan 李希凡, eds. *"Honglou meng" da cidian* 紅樓夢大辭典. Beijing: Wenhua yishu chubanshe, 1990.

Feng Qiyong 馮其庸 et al., eds. *Bajia pingpi "Honglou meng"* 八家評批紅樓夢. Beijing: Wenhua yishu chubanshe, 1991.

———. *Jiu'er Zhongguo guoji "Honglou meng" yantaohui lunwen ji* 92 中國國際紅樓夢研討會論文集. Beijing: Wenhua yishu chubanshe, 1995.

———. *Zhiyanzhai chongping "Shitou ji" huijiao* 脂硯齊重評石頭記彙較. 5 vols. Beijing: Wenhua yishu chubanshe, 1987–89.

Fong, Grace S. "Signifying Bodies: Self-inscription and the Female Embodiment of Violence." Paper presented at the annual meeting of the Association for Asian Studies, Boston, March 11–14, 1999.

Foucault, Michel. *The History of Sexuality*, trans. Robert Hurley. Vol. 1. New York: Vintage Books, 1990.

Fuery, Patrick. *Theories of Desire*. Melbourne: Melbourne University Press, 1995.

Fung, Yulan. *A History of Chinese Philosophy*, trans. Derk Bodde. Princeton: Princeton University Press, 1953.

———. *A Short History of Chinese Philosophy*, ed. and trans. Derk Bodde. New York: Macmillan, 1948.

Geng Dingxiang 耿定相. *Geng Tiantai xiansheng wenji* 耿天臺先生文集. Facsimile reprint of the 1598 ed. Mingren wenji congkan 明人文集叢刊. Taipei: Wenhai chubanshe, 1970.

Gong Zizhen 龔自珍. *Gong Zizhen quanji* 龔自珍全集. Beijing: Zhonghua shuju, 1959.

Goodrich, L. Carrington, and Chaoying Fang, eds. *Dictionary of Ming Biography*. 2 vols. New York: Columbia University Press, 1976.

Graham, A. C. *Disputers of the Tao: Philosophical Argument in Ancient China*. La Salle, Ill.: Open Court, 1989.

———. *Later Mohist Logic, Ethics and Science*. Hong Kong: Chinese University Press, 1978.

———. "The Meaning of *Ch'ing* 情"; appendix to "The Background of the Mencian Theory of Human Nature." In idem, *Studies in Chinese Philosophy and Philosophical Literature*, pp. 59–66. Albany: State University of New York Press, 1986.

———. "What Was New in the Ch'eng-Chu Theory of Human Nature." In idem, *Studies in Chinese Philosophy and Philophical Literature*, pp. 412–35. Albany: State University of New York Press, 1986.

Gu Qiyuan 顧起元. *Kezuo zhuiyu* 客座贅語. BCJ ed.

Gu Yanwu 顧炎武. *Rizhi lu jishi* 日知錄集釋, annot. Huang Ruchen 黃汝成. Sibu beiyao ed.

Guo Shaoyu 郭紹虞. "Shilun *Wenxing tiaolong*" 試論文心雕龍. In idem, *Zhaoyushi gudian wenxue lunji* 照隅室古典文學論集, 2: 11–33. Shanghai: Shanghai guji, 1983.

Guose tianxiang 國色天香. Fascimile reprint of the 1597 Wanjuan lou 萬卷樓 ed. GXJ series. Shanghai: Shanghai guji, 1990.

Guwangyan 姑妄言. SH series. Taipei: Tawain daying baike, 1997.

Guwangyan 姑妄言. Beijing: Zhongguo wenlian, 1999.

Han Dacheng 韓大成. *Mingdai chengshi yanjiu* 明代城市研究. Beijing: Zhongguo renmin daxue chubanshe, 1991.

Hanan, Patrick. *The Chinese Vernacular Story*. Cambridge, Mass.: Harvard University Press, 1981.

———. "The Erotic Novel: Some Early Reflections." Paper presented at the conference on *Jin Ping Mei*, Indiana University, Bloomington, May 12–14, 1983.

———. "The Fiction of Moral Duty: The Vernacular Story in the 1640s." In Robert E. Hegel and Richard C. Hessney, eds., *Expressions of the Self in Chinese Literature*, pp. 189–213. New York: Columbia University Press, 1985.

———. *The Invention of Li Yu*. Cambridge, Mass.: Harvard University Press, 1988.

———. "A Landmark of the Chinese Novel." In Douglas Grant and Millar MacClure, eds., *The Far East: China and Japan*, pp. 325–36. Toronto: University of Toronto Press, 1961.

———. "Sources of the *Chin P'ing Mei*." *Asia Major*, n.s. 10, no. 1 (1963): 23–67.

———. "The Text of the *Chin P'ing Mei*." *Asia Major*, n.s. 9, no. 1 (1962): 1–57.

Hanan, Patrick, ed. and trans., *Silent Operas*. Hong Kong: Chinese University of Hong Kong, 1990.

Hanan, Patrick, trans. *The Carnal Prayer Mat*. New York: Ballantine Books, 1990.

———. *A Tower for the Summer Heat*. New York: Columbia University Press, 1998.

Hansen, Chad. "Qing (Emotions) in Pre-Buddhist Chinese Thought." In Joel Marks and Roger T. Ames, eds., *Emotions in Asian Thought: A Dialogue in Comparative Philosophy*, pp. 181–211. Albany: State University of New York Press, 1995.

Hao Zhida 郝志達 et al., eds. *Guofeng shizhi zuanjie* 國風詩旨纂解. Tianjin: Nankai daxue chubanshe, 1990.

Haoqiu zhuan 好逑傳. Zhengzhou: Zhongzhou juji, 1991.

Hawkes, David, and John Minford, trans. *The Story of the Stone*. 5 vols. Harmondsworth, Eng.: Penguin, 1973–86.

He Changjiang 何長江. "Lun Yuan Ming changpian chuanqi xiaoshuo de fazhan licheng" 論元明長篇傳奇小說的發展歷程. *MQXY* 32 (1994, no. 2): 134–44.

He Liangjun 何良俊. *He Hanlin ji* 何翰林集. A facsimile reprint of the Jiajing 嘉靖 ed. Taiwan Guoli zhongyang tushuguan, 1971.

———. *Siyou zhai congshuo* 四友齊叢說. Beijing: Zhonghua shuju, 1959.

He Qimin 何啓民. *Zhulin qixian yanjiu* 竹林七賢研究. Taipei: Zhongguo xueshu zhuzuo jiangzhu weiyuanhui, 1966.

He Xin 何心. *Shuihu yanjiu* 水滸研究. Shanghai: Shanghai guji, 1985.

He Xinyin 何心隱. *He Xinyin ji* 何心隱集. Beijing: Zhonghua shuju, 1960.

He Yongkang 何永康. "Yige yinren zhumu de shenglüehao shishuo: Cao Xueqin zhijiang qian bashihui wenzi duiqing" 一個引人注明的省略號試說：曹雪芹只將前八十回文字對清. In Feng Qiyong et al., eds., *Jiu'er Zhongguo guoji "Honglou meng" yantao hui lunwen ji* 92 中國國際紅樓夢研討會論文集, pp. 161–74. Beijing: Wenhua yishu chubanshe, 1995.

Hegel, Robert E. *The Novel in Seventeenth-Century China*. New York: Columbia University Press, 1981.

———. *Reading Illustrated Fiction in Late Imperial China*. Stanford: Stanford University Press, 1998.

———. Review of *The Four Masterworks of the Ming Novel*. *HJAS* 50, no. 1 (1990): 346–52.

Hegel, Robert E., and Richard C. Hessney, eds. *Expressions of Self in Chinese Literature*. New York: Columbia University Press, 1985.

Henricks, Robert G., trans. and annot. *Philosophy and Argumentation in Third-Century China: The Essays of Hsi Kang*. Princeton: Princeton University Press, 1983.

Henry, Eric. "The Motif of Recognition in Early China." *HJAS* 47, no. 1 (1987): 5–30.

Hessney, Richard C. "Beautiful, Talented and Brave: Seventeenth-Century Chinese Scholar-Beauty Romances." Ph. D. dissertation, Columbia University, 1978.

———. "Beyond Beauty and Talent: The Moral and Chivalric Self in *The Fortunate Union*. In Robert E. Hegel and Richard C. Hessney, eds., *Expressions of Self in Chinese Literature*, pp. 214–50. New York: Columbia University Press, 1985.

Hinsch, Bret. *Passions of the Cut Sleeve: The Male Homosexual Tradition in China*. Berkeley: University of California Press, 1990.

Hong Sheng 洪昇. *Changsheng dian* 長生殿, ed. and annot. Xu Shuofang. Beijing: Renmin wenxue chubanshe, 1997 [1958].

Hou Zhongyi 侯忠義 and Liu Shilin 劉世林. *Zhongguo wenyan xiaoshuo shigao* 中國文言小說史稿. Beijing: Beijing daxue chubanshe, 1990–93.

Hsia, C. T. "Time and the Human Condition in the Plays of T'ang Hsien-tsu." In Wm. Theodore de Bary, ed., *Self and Society in Ming Thought*, pp. 249–51. New York: Columbia University Press.

Hsia, C. T., and T. A. Hsia. "New Perspectives on Two Ming Novels: *Hsi Yu Chi* and *Hsi Yu Pu*." In Tse-tsung Chow, ed., *Wen-lin: Studies in the Chinese Humanities*, pp. 229–45. Madison: University of Wisconsin, 1968.

Hu Shi 胡適. "Ba *Qianlong jiaxu Zhiyanzhai chongping Shitou ji* yingyin ben" 跋乾隆甲戌脂硯齊重評石頭記影印本. In *Qianlong jiaxu Zhiyanzhai chongping Shitou ji*, 1a–9b. Reprinted in idem, *Hu Shi lun Zhongguo gudian xiaoshuo* 胡適論中國古典小說, pp. 155–75. Wuhan: Changjiang wenyi chubanshe, 1987.

———. "*Xingshi yinyuan* kaozheng" 醒世姻緣傳考正. In idem, *Hu Shi lun Zhongguo gudian xiaoshuo* 胡適論中國古典小說, pp. 365–415. Wuhan: Changjiang wenyi chubanshe, 1987.

Hu Shihou 胡世厚 and Deng Shaoji 鄧紹基, eds. *Zhongguo gudai xiqu jia pingzhuan* 中國古代戲曲家評傳. Zhengzhou: Zhongzhou guji, 1992.

Hu, Siao-chen. "Literary *tanci*: A Woman's Tradition of Narrative in Verse." Ph.D. dissertation, Harvard University, 1994.

Hu Wanchuan 胡萬川. "Guanyu *Xingshi yinyuan zhuan* de chengshu niandai" 關於醒世姻緣傳的成書年代. In idem, *Huaben yu caizi jiaren xiaoshuo zhi yanjiu* 話本與才子佳人小說之研究, pp. 295–308. Taipei: Da'an, 1994.

Hu Yinglin 胡應麟. *Shaoshi shanfang bicong* 少室山房筆叢. SKQS ed.

Huang Lin 黃霖. "*Jin Ping Mei* zuozhe Tu Long kao" 金瓶梅作者屠龍考. In idem, *Jin Ping Mei kaolun* 金瓶梅考論, pp. 199–217. Shenyang: Liaoning renmin chubanshe, 1989.

———. "*Jin Ping Mei zuozhe* Tu Long xukao" 金瓶梅作者屠龍續考. In idem, *Jin Ping Mei kaolun* 金瓶梅考論, pp. 218–31. Shenyang: Liaoning renmin chubanshe, 1989.

Huang Lin 黃霖, ed. "*Jin Ping Mei*" *ziliao huibian* 金瓶梅資料匯編. Beijing: Zhonghua shuju, 1987.

Huang Lin 黃霖 and Han Tongwen 韓同文, eds. *Zhongguo lidai xiaoshuo lunzhu xuan* 中國歷代小說論著選, vol. 1. Nanchang: Jiangxi renmin chubanshe, 1982.

Huang, Martin W. "Author(ity) and Reader in Traditional Chinese *Xiaoshuo* Commentary." *CLEAR*, 16 (1994): 41–67.

———. "Dehistoricization and Intertextualization: The Anxiety of Precedents in the Evolution of the Traditional Chinese Novel." *CLEAR* 12 (1990): 45–68.

———. "Karmic Retribution and the Didactic Dilemma in the *Xingshi yinyuan zhuan*." *Chinese Studies* 漢學研究 15, no. 1 (1997): 397–440.

———. *Literati and Self-Re/Presentation: Autobiographical Sensibility in the Eighteenth-Century Chinese Novel*. Stanford: Stanford University Press, 1995.

———. "Notes Towards a Poetics of Characterization in the Traditional Chinese Novel: *Honglou meng* as Paradigm." *Tamkang Review* 21, no. 1 (1990): 1–27.

———. "Sentiments of Desire: Thoughts on the Cult of *Qing* in Ming-Qing Literature." *CLEAR* 20 (1998): 153–84.

———. "Stylization and Invention: The Burden of Self-Expression in *The Scholars*." In Roger Ames et al., eds., *Self as Image in Asian Theory and Practice*, pp. 89–112. Albany: State University of New York Press, 1998.

Huang Xingqi 黃星琦. "*Chipozi zhuan* fafu"痴婆子傳發覆. *MQXY* 35 (1995. no. 1): 107–22, 231.

Huang Zongxi 黃宗羲. *Mingru xue'an* 明儒學案. In idem, *Huang Zongxi quanji* 黃宗羲全集, vols. 1 and 2. Hangzhou: Zhejiang guji, 1985.

———. *Ming wenhai* 明文海. Siku wenxue zongji xuankan 四庫文學總集選刊. Shanghai: Shanghai guji, 1994.

———. *Nanlei shiwen ji* 南雷詩文集. In idem, *Huang Zongxi quanji* 黃宗羲全集, vols. 10–11. Hangzhou: Zhejiang guji, 1993.

Huanxi yuanjia 歡喜冤家. SH series. Taipei: Taiwan daying baike, 1995.

Idema, W. L. *Chinese Vernacular Fiction: The Formative Period*. Leiden: Brill, 1974.

———. "Female Talent and Female Virtue: Xu Wei's *Nü Zhuangyuan* and Meng Chengshun's *Zenwen ji*." In Hua Wei 華瑋 and Wang Ailing 王瑷玲, eds., *MingQing xiqu guoji yanao hui lunwen ji* 明清戲曲國際研討會論文集, pp. 549–71. Taibei: Zhongyang yanjiuyuan, Zhongguo wenzhe yanjiusuo choubeichu, 1998.

Jan, Yün-hua. "The Chinese Understanding and Assimilation of Karma Doctrine." In Ronald W. Neufeldt, ed., *Karma and Rebirth: Post-Classical Developments*, pp. 145–68. Albany: State University of New York Press, 1986.

Ji Kang 嵇康. *Ji Kang ji jiaozhu* 嵇康集校注, ed. Dai Mingyang 戴明揚. Beijing: Renmin wenxue chubanshe, 1962.

Ji Yun 紀昀. *Yuewei caotang biji* 閱微草堂筆記. Shanghai: Xinwenhua shushe, 1936.

Jiang Shiquan 蔣士銓. *Jiang Shiquan xiqu ji* 蔣士銓戲曲集. Beijing: Zhonghua shuju, 1993.

Jiang Wenqin 蔣文欽. "*Honglou meng* chengshu de sanchong xitong" 紅樓夢成書的三重系統. 2 pts. *Wenzhou shizhuan xuebao* 溫州師專學報 1985, no. 2, 13–24; 1985, no. 3: 36–47.

Jiao Xun 焦循, ed. *Mengzi zhengyi* 孟子正義. ZZJC ed.

Jin Ping Mei cihua 金瓶梅詞話. Quanjiao Wanli ben 全校萬歷本, ed. Mei Jie 梅節. Hong Kong: Xinghai wenhua, 1987.

Jinshu 晉書. Beijing: Zhonghua shuju, 1974.

Jin Yun Qiao zhuan 金雲翹傳. Shenyang: Chunfeng wenyi chubanshe, 1983.

Jin Yun Qiao zhuan 金雲翹傳. GXJ series. Fascimile reprint of the Kangxi ed. held in the Asakusa Bunko 淺草文庫 in Japan. Shanghai: Shanghai guji, 1990.

Knechtges, David. *The Han Rhapsody: A Study of the Fu of Yang Hsiung*. Cambridge, Eng.: Cambridge University Press, 1976.

Knoblock, John. *Xunzi: A Translation and Study of the Complete Works*. 3 vols. Stanford: Stanford University Press, 1988, 1990, 1994.

Ko, Dorothy. *Teachers of the Inner Chambers: Women and Culture in Seventeenth-Century China*. Stanford: Stanford University Press, 1994.

Kuriyama, Joanna Ching-yüan. "Confucianism in Fiction: A Study of Hsia Ching-Ch'ü's *Yeh-sou pu-yen*." Ph.D. dissertation, Harvard University, 1993.

Langshi 浪史. SH series. Taipei: Taiwan daying baike, 1995.

Laplanche, Jean, and J.-B. Pontalis, eds. *The Language of Psycho-analysis*, trans. Donald Nicholson-Smith. New York: Norton, 1974.

Lau, D. C. "The Doctrine of Kuei Sheng 貴生 in the *Lü-shih ch'un-ch'iu* 呂氏春秋." *Bulletin of the Institute of Chinese Literature and Philosophy, Academia Sinica* 2 (1992): 51–92.

Lau, D. C., trans. *The Analects*. Harmondswoth, Eng.: Penguin, 1979.

———. *Mencius*. Harmondsworth, Eng.: Penguin, 1970.

Legge, James, trans. *Li Chi: Book of Rites*. Reprinted—New Hyde Park, N.Y.: University Books, 1967.

Lei Yong 雷勇. "Mingmo Qingchu de cainü chongbai yu caizi jiaren xiaoshuo de chuangzuo" 明末清初的才女崇拜與才子佳人小說的創作. *MQXY* 32 (1994, no. 2): 145–54.

———. "Mingmo Qingchu shiqing xiaoshuo dui cainü mingyun de guanzhao yu fansi" 明末清初世情小說對才女命運的觀照與反思. *MQXY* 50 (1998, no. 4): 74–81.

———. "Mingmo Qingchu xiaoshuo xiqu chuangzuo zhong Feng Xiaoqing re chutan." 明末清初小說戲曲創作中馮小青熱初探. *MQXY* 38 (1995, no. 4): 199–208.

Li Ao 李翺. *Li Wengong ji* 李文公集. SKQS.

Li Bai 李白. *Li Taibai quanji* 李太白全集, annot. Wang Qi 王琦. Beijing: Zhonghua shuju, 1977.

Li Kaixian 李開先. *Li Kaixian ji* 李開先集. Beijing: Zhonghua shuju, 1959.

Li Mengsheng 李夢生. *Zhongguo jinhui xiaoshuo baihua* 中國禁毀小說百話. Shanghai: Shanghai guji, 1994.

Li, Qiancheng. "Fictions of Enlightentment: An Intertexual Study of *Xiyou ji, Xiyou bu,* and *Honglou meng*." Ph. D. dissertation, Washington University, St. Louis, 1998.

Li Rihua 李日華. *Weishuixuan riji,* 味水軒日記, ed. and annot. Tu Youxiang 屠友祥. Shanghai: Shanghai Yuandong chubanshe, 1996.

Li, Wai-yee. *Enchantment and Disenchantment: Love and Illusion in Chinese Literature.* Princeton: Princeton University Press, 1993.

———. "The Late Ming Courtesan: Invention of A Cultural Ideal." In Ellen Widmer and Kang-i Sun Chang, eds., *Writing Women in Late Imperial China*, pp. 46–73. Stanford: Stanford University Press, 1997.

———. "The Rhetoric of Spontaneity in Late Ming Literature." *Ming Studies* 35 (1995): 32–52.

Li Yu 李漁. *Lianxiang ban* 憐香伴. In idem, *Li Yu quanji* 李漁全集, vol. 4. Hongzhou: Zhejiang guji, 1992.

———. *Rou putuan* 肉蒲團. SH series. Taipei: Taiwan daying baike, 1994.

———. *Shen luanjiao* 慎鸞交. In idem, *Li Yu quanji* 李漁全集, vol. 5. Hongzhou: Zhejiang guji, 1992.

———. *Shi'er lou* 十二樓. In idem, *Li Yu quanji* 李漁全集, vol. 9. Hongzhou: Zhejiang guji, 1992.

———. *Wusheng xi* 無聲戲. In idem, *Li Yu quanji* 李漁全集, vol. 8. Hongzhou: Zhejiang guji, 1992.

Li Zhenyu 李眞瑜. "Yibu dui *Honglou meng* chansheng guo yingxiang de xiaoshuo: *Dingqing ren yu Honglou meng* guanxi qianshuo" 一部對紅樓夢產生過影響的小說—定情人與紅樓夢關係淺說. *MQXL* 5 (1987): 85–92.

Li Zhi 李贄. *Fenshu, Xu Fenshu* 焚書續焚書. Beijing: Zhonghua shuju, 1975.

Li Zhi 李贄, ed. (attrib.). *Shanzhong yixi hua* 山中一夕話. Facsimile reprint (n.d.). Taipei: Tianyi chubanshe, 1985.

Li Zhongxia 李中馥. *Yuan Li erzhai* 原李耳載. In Wang Wenru 王文濡, comp. *Shuoku* 說庫. Shanghai, 1915; rpt. Hangzhou: Zhejiang guji, 1986.

Liao Kebin 廖可斌. *Mingdai wenxue fugu yundong yanjiu* 明代文學復古運動研究. Shanghai: Shanghai guji, 1994.

Song Maocheng 宋懋澄. *Jiuyue ji* 九籥集, ed. Wang Liqi 王利器. Beijing: Zhongguo shehui kexue chubanshe, 1984.

Stone, Charles. "The *Ruyijun zhuan* and the Origins of the Chinese Erotic Novel." Ph. D. dissertation, University of Chicago, 1999.

Sun Kaidi 孫楷第. "Li Liweng yu *Shi'er lou*" 李立翁與十二樓. In idem, *Cangzhou houji* 滄州後集, pp. 151–205. Beijing: Zhonghua shuju, 1985.

———. *Riben Dongjing suojian xiaoshuo shumu* 日本東京所見小說書目. Beijing: Remin wenxue chubanshe, 1958.

———. "Xia Erming yu *Yesou puyan*" 夏二銘與野叟曝言. In idem, *Cangzhou houji* 滄州後集, pp. 238–47. Beijing: Zhonghua shuju, 1985.

———. *Zhongguo tongsu xiaoshuo shumu* 中國通俗小說書目. Beijing: Renmin wenxue chubanshe, 1982.

Sun Xidan 孫希旦, ed. *Liji jijie* 禮記集解. Beijing: Zhonghua shuju, 1989.

Sun Xun 孫遜. *"Honglou meng" Zhiping chutan* 紅樓夢脂評初探. Shanghai: Shanghai guji, 1981.

Sung, Maria H. *The Narrative Art of Tsai-sheng-yüan: A Feminist Vision in Traditional Confucian Society*. Taipei: Chinese Materials Center, 1994.

Taiping guangji 太平廣記. Beijing: Zhonghua shuju, 1995.

Taishō shinshū Daizōkyō 大正新修大藏經. Tokyo: Taishō Issai-kyō kankōkai, 1924–32.

Tan Yuanchun 譚元春. *Tan Yuanchun ji* 譚元春集, ed. and collated by Chen Xingchen 陳杏珍. Shanghai: Shanghai guji, 1998.

Tang Xianzu 湯顯祖. *Mudan ting* 牡丹亭, ed. and annot. Xu Shuofang 徐朔方 and Yang Xiaomei 楊笑梅. Beijing: Renmin wenxue chubanshe, 1998 [1963].

———. *Tang Xianzu shiwenji* 湯顯祖詩文集, annot. and ed. Xu Shuofang 徐朔方. Shanghai: Shanghai guji, 1982.

Tao Wangling 陶望齡. *Xie'an ji* 歇庵集. Facsimile reprint of Wanli ed. Taipei: Weiwen tushu chubanshe, 1976.

Taohua ying 桃花影. SH series. Taipei: Taiwan daying baike, 1994.

Tu Long 屠龍. *Baiyu ji* 白榆集. Facsimile reprint of the Wanli ed. held in Taiwan guoli zhongyang tushuguan. Taipei: Weiwen tushu chubanshe, 1977.

———. *Hongbao ji* 鴻苞集. Ming printed ed. (1610). Copy in Harvard-Yenching Library.

———. *Xichen guan chi* 棲眞館集. Ming Wanli edition. Copy in the National Library of Peiping. Microfilm in University of Michigan East Asian Library.

van Gulik, R. H. *Sexual Life in Ancient China*. Leiden: E. J. Brill, 1961.

Van Zoeren, Steven. *Poetry and Personality: Reading, Exegesis, and Hermeneutics in Traditional China*. Stanford: Stanford University Press, 1991.

Vicinus, Martha. "Introduction." In idem, ed., *Lesbian Subjects: A Feminist Studies Reader*, pp. 1–22. Bloomington: Indiana University Press, 1996.

———. "'They Wonder to Which Sex I Belong': The Historical Roots of the Modern Lesbian Identity." In idem, ed., *Lesbian Subjects: A Feminist Studies Reader*, pp. 233–59. Bloomington: Indiana University Press, 1996.

Vitiello, Giovanni. "Exemplary Sodomites: Male Homosexuality in Late Ming Fiction." Ph.D. dissertation, University of California, Berkeley, 1994.

———. "The Fantastic Journey of an Ugly Boy: Homosexuality and Salvation in Late Ming Pornography." *Positions* 4, no. 2 (1996): 291–320.

Volpp, Sophie. "The Discourse on Male Marriage: Li Yu's 'A Male Mencius's Mother.'" *Positions* 2, no. 1 (1994): 113–32.

von Glahn, Richard. "The Enchantment of Wealth: The God Wutong in the Social History of Jiangnan." *HJAS* 51, no. 2 (1991): 651–714.

———. *Fountain of Fortune: Money and Monetary Policy in China, 1000–1700*. Berkeley: University of California Press, 1996.

Wang Bijiang 汪辟疆, ed. *Tangren xiaoshuo* 唐人小說. Shanghai: Shanghai guji, 1978.

Wang Chong 王充. *Lunheng* 論衡. ZZJC.

Wang Fuzhi 王夫之. *Chuanshan quanshu* 船山全書. Changsha: Yuelu shushe, 1996.

Wang Gang 王崗 (Richard G. Wang). "The Cult of *Qing*: Romanticism in the Late Ming Period and in the Novel *Jiao Hong ji*." *Ming Studies* 33 (1994): 12–55.

———. *Langman qinggan yu zongjiao jingshen: WanMing wenxue yu wenxue sichao* 浪漫情感與宗教精神—晚明文學與文學思潮. Hong Kong: Tiandi tushu, 1999.

Wang Hanmin 王漢民. "Lun Meng Chenshun xiqu de chuanqing yishi." 論孟稱舜戲曲的傳情意識. *Zhongguo wenxue yanjiu* 中國文學研究 (Changsha), 1998, no. 1: 48–52.

Wang, Jing. *The Story of Stone: Intertextuality, Ancient Chinese Stone Lore, and the Stone Symbolism of "Dream of the Red Chamber," "Water Margin," and "The Journey to the West."* Durham, N.C.: Duke University Press, 1992.

Wang Ling 王淩. *Qiren, qingzhong, qipin guan* 畸人情種七品官. Fuzhou: Haixia wenyi chubanshe, 1992.

Wang Liqi 王利器. *Yuan Ming Qing sandai jinhui xiaoshuo xiqu shiliao* 元明清三代禁毀小說戲曲史料. Shanghai: Shanghai guji, 1981.

Wang Qiongling 王瓊玲. *Qingdai sida caixue xiaoshuo* 清代四大才學小說. Taipei: Taiwan Shangwu yinshuguan, 1997.

Wang Shizhen 王世貞. *Yanyi bian* 艷異編. GXJ series. Shanghai: Shanghai guji, 1990.

Wang Xianqian 王先謙, ed. *Xunzi jijie* 荀子集解. ZZJC.

Wang Yangming 王陽明. *Chuanxi lu* 傳習錄. In idem, *Wang Yangming quan ji* 王陽明全集. Shanghai: Shanghai guji, 1992.

Wang Yuji 王育濟. *Tianli yu renyu* 天理與人欲. Ji'nan: QiLu shushe, 1992.

Wang Zhongmin 王重民. *Zhongguo shanben shu tiyao* 中國善本書提要. Shanghai: Shanghai guji, 1983.

Weber, Max. *The Sociology of Religion*, trans. Ephraim Fischoff. Boston: Beacon Press, 1963.

Wei Yong 衛泳, comp. *Bingxue xie* 冰雪攜. Guoxue zhenben wenku 國學珍本文庫. Shanghai: Zhongyan shudian, 1935.

———. *Yuerong bian* 悅容編. In *Zhaodai congshu* 昭代叢書, ed. Zhang Chao 張潮 et al. Shanghai: Shanghai guji, 1991.

Whitman, Christina. "Privacy in Confucian and Taoist Thought." In Donald J. Munro, ed., *Individualism and Holism: Studies in Confucian and Taoist Values*, pp. 85–100. Ann Arbor: University of Michigan, Center for Chinese Studies, 1985.

Widmer, Ellen. "Ming Loyalism and the Women's Voice in Ficton after *Honglou meng*." In Ellen Widmer and Kang-i Sun Chang, eds., *Writing Women in Late Imperial China*, pp. 366–96. Stanford: Stanford University Press, 1997.

———. "Xiaoqing's Literary Legacy and the Place of the Women Writers in Late Imperial China." *Late Imperial China* 10, no. 2 (1989): 1–43.

Widmer, Ellen, and Chang, Kang-i sun, eds. *Writing Women in Late Imperial China*. Stanford: Stanford University Press, 1997.

Wong, Siu-kit. "*Ch'ing* in Chinese Literary Criticism." Ph. D. dissertation, Oxford University, 1969.

Wu Chengxue 吳承學. *WanMing xiaopin yanjiu* 晚明小品研究. Nanjing: Jiangsu guji, 1998.

Wu Cuncun 吳存存. "*Bian er chai yu Yichun xiangzhi* de niandai kaozheng jiqi shehui wenhua shi yiyi fawei" 弁而釵與宜春香質的年代考證及其社會文化史意義發微. *Dongfang wenhua* 東方文化 32, no. 1 (1994): 67–72.

Wu Enyu 吳恩裕. "Ming Yi de *Lüyan suochuang ji* shixuan jiqi 'Ti *Honglou meng* ershi shou shi" 明義的綠煙瑣窗集詩選及其題紅樓夢二十首詩. In idem, *Cao Xueqin congkao* 曹雪芹叢考, pp. 203–9. Shanghai: Shanghai guji, 1980.

Wu, Fatima. "Foxes in Chinese Supernatural Tales." *Tamkang Review* 17, no. 2 (1986): 121–54.

Wu Jingzi 吳敬梓. *Rulin waishi huijiao huiping ben* 儒林外史會校會評本, ed. Li Hanqiu 李漢秋. Shanghai: Shanghai guji, 1984.

Wu, Pei-i. *The Confucian's Progress: Autobiographical Writings in Traditional China*. Princeton: Princeton University Press, 1990.

Wu Tinghan 吳廷翰. *Wu Tinghan ji* 吳廷翰集. Beijing: Zhonghua shuju, 1984.

Wu, Yenna. *The Chinese Virago: A Literary Theme*. Cambridge, Mass.: Harvard University, Council on East Asian Studies, 1995.

———. "The Inversion of Marital Hierarchy: Shrewish Wives and Henpecked Husbands in Seventeenth-Century Chinese Literature." *HJAS* 48, no. 2 (1988): 363–82.

———. "Marriage Destinies to Awaken the World: A Literary Study of *Xingshi yinyuan zhuan*." Ph.D. dissertation, Harvard University, 1986.

———. "Repetition in *Xingshi yinyuan zhuan*." *HJAS* 51, no. 1 (1991): 55–87.

Xia Jingqu 夏敬渠. *Yesou puyan* 野叟曝言. Changchun: Jilin wenshi chubanshe, 1994.

———. *Yesou puyan* 野叟曝言. Facsimile reprint of the 1881 Piling huizhenlou 毗陵匯珍樓 ed. GXJ. Shanghai: Shanghai guji, 1990.

Xia Xianchun 夏咸淳. *WanMing shifeng yu wenxue* 晚明士風與文學. Beijing: Zhongguo shehui kexue chubanshe, 1994.

Xiao Chi 蕭馳. "Cong caizi jiaren dao *Shitou ji*: wenren xiaoshuo yu shuqing chuantong de yiduan qingjie" 從才子佳人到石頭記：文人小說與抒情傳統的一段情結. *Hanxue yanjiu* 漢學研究 14, no. 1 (June 1996): 249–78; reprinted in idem, *Zhongguo shuqing chuantong* 中國抒情傳統, pp. 275–320. Taipei: Yunchen wenhua shiye, 1999.

———. *The Chinese Garden as Lyric Enclave: A Generic Study of "The Story of the Stone."* Forthcoming, University of Michigan, Center for Chinese Studies, 2001.

Xiao Xiangkai 蕭相愷. *Zhenben jinhui xiaoshuo daguan: baihai fangshu lu* 珍本禁毀小說大觀—稗海訪書錄. Zhengzhou: Zhongzhou guji, 1992.

Xie Gouzhen 謝國禎. *Zengding WanMing shiji kao* 增訂晚明史籍考. Shanghai: Shanghai guji, 1981.

Xie Zhaozhi 謝肇淛. *Wuzazu* 五雜組. Guoxue zhenbeng wenku. Shanghai: Zhongyang shudian, 1935.

Xihu erji 西湖二集. Hangzhou: Zhejiang wenyi chubanshe, 1985.

Xinke xiuxiang piping Jin Ping Mei 新刻繡像批評金瓶梅, ed. Qiyan 齊煙 et al. Ji'nan: QiLu shushe; Hong Kong: Sanlian shudian, 1990.

Xingshi yan 型世言. MXJ, series 1, vol. 2. Chengdu: Bashu shushe, 1993.

Xingshi yinyuan zhuan 醒世姻緣傳. Shanghai: Shanghai guji, 1981.

Xiong Chengyu 熊澄宇. *Jiang Shiquan juzuo yanjiu* 蔣士銓劇作研究. Beijing: Zhongguo xiju chubanshe, 1988.

Xiugu chunrong 繡谷春容. Nanjing: Jiangsu guji, 1994.

Xiuping yuan 繡屏緣. Facsimile reprint of the handcopied edition in the van Gulik collection. GXJ. Shanghai: Shanghai guji, 1990.

Xiuta yeshi 繡榻野史. Zuimian ge ben 醉眠閣本. SH series. Taipei: Taiwan daya baike, 1995.

Xiyou bu 西游補. Shanghai: Shanghai guji, 1983.

Xu Fuling 徐復嶺. *"Xingshi yinyuan zhuan" zuozhe he yuyan kaolun* 醒世姻緣傳作者和語言考論. Ji'nan: QiLu shushe, 1993.

Xu Shen 許慎. *Shuowen jiezi zhu* 說文解字注, annot. Duan Yucai 段玉裁. Shanghai: Shanghai guji, 1988.

Xu Shuofang 徐朔方. "Feng Menglong nianpu" 馮夢龍年譜. In idem, *Xu Shuofang ji* 徐朔方集, 2: 393–452. Hangzhou: Zhejiang guji, 1995.

———. "*Jin Ping Mei xifang lunwen ji* qianyan" 金瓶梅西方論文集前言. In idem, *Xiaoshuo kaoxin bian* 小說考信編, pp. 286–302. Shanghai: Shanghai guji, 1997.

———. "Lun *Xingshi yinyuan zhuan* jiqi he *Jin Ping Mei* de guanxi," 論醒世姻緣傳及其和金瓶梅的關係. In idem, *Xiaoshuo kaoxin bian* 小說考信編, pp. 186–205. Shanghai: Shanghai guji, 1997.

———. "Tang Xianzu nianpu"湯顯祖年譜. In idem, *Xu Shuofang ji* 徐朔方集, 4: 201–469. Hangzhou: Zhejiang guji, 1995.

———. "Tu Long nianpu" 屠龍年譜. In idem, *Xu Shuofang ji* 徐朔方集, 3: 309–94. Hangzhou: Zhejiang guji, 1995.

———. *Xiaoshuo kaoxin bian* 小說考信編. Shanghai: Shanghai guji, 1997.

———. *Xu Shuofang ji* 徐朔方集. Hangzhou: Zhejiang guji, 1995.

———. "*Yuming tang chuanqi* chuangzuo niandai kao" 玉茗堂傳奇創作年代考. In idem, *Xu Shuofang ji* 徐朔方集, 4: 484–88. Hangzhou: Zhejiang guji, 1995.

Xu Zhixiao 徐知嘯, ed. *Lidai fulun jiyao* 歷代賦論輯要. Shanghai: Fudan daxue chubanshe, 1991.

Xue Ruisheng 薛瑞生. "Da Baoyu yu *Fengyue baojian*" 大寶玉與風月寶鑒. In Honglou meng xuekan bianji huiyuanhui 紅樓夢學刊編輯會員會, ed., *"Honglou meng" xuekan zengkan: Jiuqi Beijing guoji "Honglou meng" xueshu yantao hui zhuanji* 紅樓夢學刊增刊：97北京國際紅樓夢學術研討會專輯, pp. 410–28. Beijing: Honglou meng xuekan zazhishe, 1997.

Yang Bojun 楊伯峻, ed. *Chunqiu Zuozhuan zhu* 春秋左傳注. Beijing: Zhonghua shuju, 1981.

———. *Lunyu yizhu* 論語譯注. Beijing: Zhonghua shuju, 1980.

———. *Mengzi yizhu* 孟子譯注. Beijing: Zhonghua shuju, 1984.

Yang, Hsien-i, and Gladys Yang, trans. *The Dream of Red Mansions*. Beijing: Foreign Languages Press, 1978.

———. *The Scholars*. Beijing: Foreign Languages Press, 1957.

Yang Shen 楊慎. *Sheng'an ji* 升庵集. SKQS.

Yang, Shuhui. *Appropriation and Representation: Feng Menglong and the Chinese Vernacular Story*. Ann Arbor: University of Michigan, Center for Chinese Studies, 1998.

Yao, Christina Shu-wha. "*Cai-zi jia-ren*: Love Drama During the Yuan, Ming and Qing Periods." Ph.D. dissertation, Stanford University, 1983.

Ye Dejun 葉德均. "Du Mingdai chuanqi wen qizhong" 讀明代傳奇文七鍾. In idem, *Xiqu xiaohsuo congkao* 戲曲小說叢考, pp. 535–41. Beijing: Zhonghua shuju, 1979.

Yichun xiangzhi 宜春香質. MXJ, series 2, vol. 2. Chengdu: Bashu shushe, 1995.

Yichun xiangzhi 宜春香質. SH series. Taipei: Taiwan daying baike, 1995.

Yisu 一粟, comp. *"Honglou meng" juan* 紅樓夢卷. Beijing: Zhonghua shuju, 1963.

Yu, Anthony C. *Rereading the Stone: Desire and the Making of Fiction in "Dream of the Red Chamber."* Princeton: Princeton University Press, 1997.

Yü, Chün-fang. *The Renewal of Buddhism in China: Chu-hung and the Late Ming Synthesis*. New York: Columbia University Press, 1981.

Yu Pingbo 俞平伯. "Lun Qin Keqing zhi si" 論秦可卿之死. In idem, *Yu Pingbo lun "Honglou meng"* 俞平伯論紅樓夢, pp. 264–72. Shanghai: Shanghai guji, 1988.

———. *"Honglou meng" bian* 紅樓夢辨. In idem, *Yu Pingbo lun "Honglou meng"* 俞平伯論紅樓夢, pp. 69–323. Shanghai: Shanghai guji, 1988.

———. "Xiangling diwei de gaibian" 香菱地位的改變. In idem, *Yu Pingbo lun "Honglou meng"* 俞平伯論紅樓夢, pp. 712–17. Shanghai: Shanghai guji, 1988.

———. *Yu Pingbo lun "Honglou meng"* 俞平伯論紅樓夢. Shanghai: Shanghai guji, 1988.

Yu Yue 俞樾. *Qunjing pingyi* 群經平議. Taipei: Heluo tushu chubanshe, 1975.

Yu Zhiyuan 于植元. "*Lin Lan Xiang* lun" 林蘭香論. *MQXL* 1 (1984): 190–213.

Yuan Cai 袁采. *Yuanshi shifan* 袁氏世范. In *Zhibuzu zhai congshu* 知不足齊叢書. BCJ.

Yuan Hongdao 袁宏道. *Yuan Hongdao ji jianjiao* 袁宏道集箋校, annot. and ed. Qian Bocheng 錢伯城. Shanghai: Shanghai guji, 1981.

Yuan Huang 袁黃. *Yuan Liaofan xiansheng Liangxing zhai ji* 袁了凡先生兩行齊集. 1624 ed. (a edition privately printed by the Yuan family from Jiaxing 嘉興袁氏家刊本). Copy in Taiwan Guoli zhongyang tushuguan. Microfilm in the library of the Chinese University of Hong Kong.

Yuan Zhongdao 袁中道. *Kexue zhai ji* 珂雪齊集, ed. Qian Bocheng 錢伯城. Shanghai: Shanghai guji, 1989.

Zeitlin, Judith. *Historian of the Strange: Pu Songling and the Chinese Classical Tale*. Stanford: Stanford University Press, 1993.

Zhang Ailing 張愛玲. *"Honglou meng" yan* 紅樓夢魘. Shanghai: Shanghai guji, 1995 [Taipei, 1977].

Zhang Chao 張潮. *Yuchu xinzhi* 虞初新志,. In *Biji xiaoshuo daguan* 筆記小說大觀, vol. 7. Yangzhou: Jiangsu Guanling guji keyinshe, 1995.

Zhang Dainian 張岱年. *Zhongguo zhexue dagang* 中國哲學大綱. Beijing: Zhongguo shehui kexue chubanshe, 1985.

Zhang Guoxing 張國星, ed. *Zhongguo gudai xiaoshuo zhong de xing miaoxie* 中國古代小說中的性描寫. Tianjin: Baihua wenyi chubanshe, 1993.

Zhang Han 張瀚. *Songchuang mengyu* 松窗夢語. Shanghai: Shanghai guji, 1986.

Zhang Jun 張俊. "Lun *Lin Lan Xiang* yu *Honglou meng* jiantan lianjie *Jin Ping Mei* yu *Honglou meng* de lianhuan" 論林蘭香與紅樓夢兼談聯接金瓶梅與紅樓夢的連環. *MQXL* 5 (1987): 63–84.

———. *Qingdai xiaoshuo shi* 清代小說史. Hangzhou: Zhejiang guji, 1997.

Zhang Liwen 張立文. *Zhongguo zhexue fanchou fazhan shi: Rendao pian* 中國哲學範疇發展史—人道篇. Beijing: Zhongguo renmin daxue chubanshe, 1995.

Zhang Qi 張琦. *Hengqu zhutan* 衡曲麈譚. In *Zhongguo gudian xiqu lunzhu jicheng* 中國古典戲曲論著集成, vol. 4. Beijing: Zhongguo xiju chubanshe, 1959.

Zhang Qingji 張清吉. *"Xingshi yinyuan zhuan" xinkao* 醒世姻緣傳新考. Zhengzhou: Zhongzhou guji, 1991.

Zhang Qingshan 張慶善. "Cao Xueqin zuji lunzheng shuping" 曹雪芹祖籍論爭述評. *HXK* 1998, no. 1, 268–94.

Zhang Yongjun 張永俊. *Er Cheng xue guanjian* 二程學管見. Taipei: Dongda tushu gongsi, 1988.

Zhang Zhupo piping "Jin Ping Mei" 張竹坡批評金瓶梅, ed. Wang Rumei 王汝梅 et al. Ji'nan: QiLu shushe, 1991.

Zhao Botao 趙伯陶. "*Honglou meng ying* de zuozhe ji qita" 紅樓夢影的作者及其他. *HXK* 1989, no. 3: 243–51.

Zhao Jianzhong 趙建忠. *"Honglou meng" xushu yanjiu* 紅樓夢續書研究. Tianjin: Tianjin guji, 1997.

Zhao Yuan 趙園. *Ming Qing zhiji shidafu yanjiu* 明清之際士大夫研究. Beijing: Beijing daxue chubanshe, 1999.

Zheng Peikai 鄭培凱, "Jiedao duoqing qingjinchu: cong Tang Xianzu dao Cao Xueqin" 解到多情情盡處：從湯顯祖到曹雪芹. In idem, *Tang Xianzu yu WanMing wenhua* 湯顯祖與晚明文化, pp. 328–33. Taipei: Yunchen wenhua shiye, 1995.

Zheng Run 鄭閏. *"Jin Ping Mei" he Tu Long* 金瓶梅和屠龍. Shanghai: Xuelin chubanshe, 1994.

Zheng Yuanxun 鄭元勳. *Meiyouge wenyu* 眉幽閣文娛. Ming printed ed. (1630). Copy in Harvard-Yenching Library.

Zhong Mingqi 鍾明奇. "Lun Li Yu daoxue yu fengliu he'er weiyi de qing'ai lixiang jiqi wenhua xuanze" 論李漁道學與風流合而爲一的情愛理想及其文化選擇. *MQXY* 48 (1998, no. 2): 155–64.

Zhong Xing 鍾惺. *Yingxiu xuan ji* 隱秀軒集, ed. Li Xian'geng 李先耕 and Cui Chongqing 崔重慶. Shanghai: Shanghai guji, 1992.

Zhongguo gudian xiqu lunzhu jicheng 中國古典戲曲論著集成. Beijing: Zhongguo xiju chubanshe, 1959.

Zhongguo tongsu xiaoshuo zongmu tiyao 中國通俗小說總目提要, ed. Jiangsu sheng shehui kexue yuan, Ming Qing xiaoshuo yanjiu zhongxin 江蘇省社會科學院明清小說研究中心. Beijing: Zhongguo wenlian chuban gongsi, 1990.

Zhou Juntao 周鈞韜. "*Jin Ping Mie* chaoyin *Shuihu zhuan* kaotan" 金瓶梅抄引水滸傳考探. In idem, *"Chin Ping Mei" xintan* 金瓶梅新探, pp. 198–244. Tianjin: Baihua wenyi chubanshe, 1987.

Zhou Ruchang 周汝昌. *"Honglou meng" yu Zhonghua wenhua* 紅樓夢與中華文化. Beijing: Gongren chubanshe, 1989.

Zhu Danwen 朱淡文. *"Honglou meng" lunyuan* 紅樓夢論源. Nanjing: Jiangsu guji, 1992.

Zhu Xi 朱熹. *Zhuzi quanshu* 朱子全書. SKQS.

———. *Zhuzi yulei* 朱子語類, ed. Li Jingde 黎靖德. Beijing: Zhonghua shuju, 1989.

Zhu Xi 朱熹, ed. and annot. *Sishu zhangju jizhu* 四書章句集注. Beijing: Zhonghua shuju, 1983.

Zhu Yanqing 朱燕靜. "*Xingshi yinyuan zhuan* yanjiu" 醒世姻緣傳研究. M.A. thesis, National Taiwan University, 1978.

Zhu Yixuan 朱一玄, ed. *"Honglou meng" Zhiping jiaolu* 紅樓夢脂評校錄. Ji'nan: QiLu shushe, 1986.

Zhu Ziqing 朱自清. *Shi yan zhi bian* 詩言志辨. Beijing: Guji chubanshe, 1956.

Zou Yuanbiao 鄒元標. *Yuanxue ji* 愿學集. SKQS.

Zuo Dongling 左東岭. *Li Zhi yu WanMing wenxue sixiang* 李贄與晚明文學思想. Tianjin: Tianjin renmin chubanshe, 1997.

Index

Harvard East Asian Monographs
(* out-of-print)

*1. Liang Fang-chung, *The Single-Whip Method of Taxation in China*
*2. Harold C. Hinton, *The Grain Tribute System of China, 1845–1911*
3. Ellsworth C. Carlson, *The Kaiping Mines, 1877–1912*
*4. Chao Kuo-chün, *Agrarian Policies of Mainland China: A Documentary Study, 1949–1956*
*5. Edgar Snow, *Random Notes on Red China, 1936–1945*
*6. Edwin George Beal, Jr., *The Origin of Likin, 1835–1864*
7. Chao Kuo-chün, *Economic Planning and Organization in Mainland China: A Documentary Study, 1949–1957*
*8. John K. Fairbank, *Ching Documents: An Introductory Syllabus*
*9. Helen Yin and Yi-chang Yin, *Economic Statistics of Mainland China, 1949–1957*
*10. Wolfgang Franke, *The Reform and Abolition of the Traditional Chinese Examination System*
11. Albert Feuerwerker and S. Cheng, *Chinese Communist Studies of Modern Chinese History*
12. C. John Stanley, *Late Ching Finance: Hu Kuang-yung as an Innovator*
13. S. M. Meng, *The Tsungli Yamen: Its Organization and Functions*
*14. Ssu-yü Teng, *Historiography of the Taiping Rebellion*
15. Chun-Jo Liu, *Controversies in Modern Chinese Intellectual History: An Analytic Bibliography of Periodical Articles, Mainly of the May Fourth and Post–May Fourth Era*
*16. Edward J. M. Rhoads, *The Chinese Red Army, 1927–1963: An Annotated Bibliography*
17. Andrew J. Nathan, *A History of the China International Famine Relief Commission*
*18. Frank H. H. King (ed.) and Prescott Clarke, *A Research Guide to China-Coast Newspapers, 1822–1911*
19. Ellis Joffe, *Party and Army: Professionalism and Political Control in the Chinese Officer Corps, 1949–1964*
*20. Toshio G. Tsukahira, *Feudal Control in Tokugawa Japan: The Sankin Kōtai System*
21. Kwang-Ching Liu, ed., *American Missionaries in China: Papers from Harvard Seminars*
22. George Moseley, *A Sino-Soviet Cultural Frontier: The Ili Kazakh Autonomous Chou*

Harvard East Asian Monographs

23. Carl F. Nathan, *Plague Prevention and Politics in Manchuria, 1910–1931*

*24. Adrian Arthur Bennett, *John Fryer: The Introduction of Western Science and Technology into Nineteenth-Century China*

25. Donald J. Friedman, *The Road from Isolation: The Campaign of the American Committee for Non-Participation in Japanese Aggression, 1938–1941*

26. Edward LeFevour, *Western Enterprise in Late Ching China: A Selective Survey of Jardine, Matheson and Company's Operations, 1842–1895*

27. Charles Neuhauser, *Third World Politics: China and the Afro-Asian People's Solidarity Organization, 1957–1967*

28. Kungtu C. Sun, assisted by Ralph W. Huenemann, *The Economic Development of Manchuria in the First Half of the Twentieth Century*

*29. Shahid Javed Burki, *A Study of Chinese Communes, 1965*

30. John Carter Vincent, *The Extraterritorial System in China: Final Phase*

31. Madeleine Chi, *China Diplomacy, 1914–1918*

*32. Clifton Jackson Phillips, *Protestant America and the Pagan World: The First Half Century of the American Board of Commissioners for Foreign Missions, 1810–1860*

33. James Pusey, *Wu Han: Attacking the Present through the Past*

34. Ying-wan Cheng, *Postal Communication in China and Its Modernization, 1860–1896*

35. Tuvia Blumenthal, *Saving in Postwar Japan*

36. Peter Frost, *The Bakumatsu Currency Crisis*

37. Stephen C. Lockwood, *Augustine Heard and Company, 1858–1862*

38. Robert R. Campbell, *James Duncan Campbell: A Memoir by His Son*

39. Jerome Alan Cohen, ed., *The Dynamics of China's Foreign Relations*

40. V. V. Vishnyakova-Akimova, *Two Years in Revolutionary China, 1925–1927*, tr. Steven L. Levine

*41. Meron Medzini, *French Policy in Japan during the Closing Years of the Tokugawa Regime*

42. Ezra Vogel, Margie Sargent, Vivienne B. Shue, Thomas Jay Mathews, and Deborah S. Davis, *The Cultural Revolution in the Provinces*

*43. Sidney A. Forsythe, *An American Missionary Community in China, 1895–1905*

*44. Benjamin I. Schwartz, ed., *Reflections on the May Fourth Movement.: A Symposium*

*45. Ching Young Choe, *The Rule of the Taewŏngun, 1864–1873: Restoration in Yi Korea*

46. W. P. J. Hall, *A Bibliographical Guide to Japanese Research on the Chinese Economy, 1958–1970*

47. Jack J. Gerson, *Horatio Nelson Lay and Sino-British Relations, 1854–1864*

48. Paul Richard Bohr, *Famine and the Missionary: Timothy Richard as Relief Administrator and Advocate of National Reform*

49. Endymion Wilkinson, *The History of Imperial China: A Research Guide*

50. Britten Dean, *China and Great Britain: The Diplomacy of Commercial Relations, 1860–1864*

51. Ellsworth C. Carlson, *The Foochow Missionaries, 1847–1880*

Harvard East Asian Monographs

52. Yeh-chien Wang, *An Estimate of the Land-Tax Collection in China, 1753 and 1908*
53. Richard M. Pfeffer, *Understanding Business Contracts in China, 1949–1963*
54. Han-sheng Chuan and Richard Kraus, *Mid-Ching Rice Markets and Trade: An Essay in Price History*
55. Ranbir Vohra, *Lao She and the Chinese Revolution*
56. Liang-lin Hsiao, *China's Foreign Trade Statistics, 1864–1949*
*57. Lee-hsia Hsu Ting, *Government Control of the Press in Modern China, 1900–1949*
58. Edward W. Wagner, *The Literati Purges: Political Conflict in Early Yi Korea*
*59. Joungwon A. Kim, *Divided Korea: The Politics of Development, 1945–1972*
*60. Noriko Kamachi, John K. Fairbank, and Chūzō Ichiko, *Japanese Studies of Modern China Since 1953: A Bibliographical Guide to Historical and Social-Science Research on the Nineteenth and Twentieth Centuries, Supplementary Volume for 1953–1969*
61. Donald A. Gibbs and Yun-chen Li, *A Bibliography of Studies and Translations of Modern Chinese Literature, 1918–1942*
62. Robert H. Silin, *Leadership and Values: The Organization of Large-Scale Taiwanese Enterprises*
63. David Pong, *A Critical Guide to the Kwangtung Provincial Archives Deposited at the Public Record Office of London*
*64. Fred W. Drake, *China Charts the World: Hsu Chi-yü and His Geography of 1848*
*65. William A. Brown and Urgrunge Onon, translators and annotators, *History of the Mongolian People's Republic*
66. Edward L. Farmer, *Early Ming Government: The Evolution of Dual Capitals*
*67. Ralph C. Croizier, *Koxinga and Chinese Nationalism: History, Myth, and the Hero*
*68. William J. Tyler, tr., *The Psychological World of Natsume Sōseki*, by Doi Takeo
69. Eric Widmer, *The Russian Ecclesiastical Mission in Peking during the Eighteenth Century*
*70. Charlton M. Lewis, *Prologue to the Chinese Revolution: The Transformation of Ideas and Institutions in Hunan Province, 1891–1907*
71. Preston Torbert, *The Ching Imperial Household Department: A Study of Its Organization and Principal Functions, 1662–1796*
72. Paul A. Cohen and John E. Schrecker, eds., *Reform in Nineteenth-Century China*
73. Jon Sigurdson, *Rural Industrialism in China*
74. Kang Chao, *The Development of Cotton Textile Production in China*
75. Valentin Rabe, *The Home Base of American China Missions, 1880–1920*
*76. Sarasin Viraphol, *Tribute and Profit: Sino-Siamese Trade, 1652–1853*
77. Ch'i-ch'ing Hsiao, *The Military Establishment of the Yuan Dynasty*
78. Meishi Tsai, *Contemporary Chinese Novels and Short Stories, 1949–1974: An Annotated Bibliography*
*79. Wellington K. K. Chan, *Merchants, Mandarins and Modern Enterprise in Late Ching China*

80. Endymion Wilkinson, *Landlord and Labor in Late Imperial China: Case Studies from Shandong by Jing Su and Luo Lun*

*81. Barry Keenan, *The Dewey Experiment in China: Educational Reform and Political Power in the Early Republic*

*82. George A. Hayden, *Crime and Punishment in Medieval Chinese Drama: Three Judge Pao Plays*

*83. Sang-Chul Suh, *Growth and Structural Changes in the Korean Economy, 1910–1940*

84. J. W. Dower, *Empire and Aftermath: Yoshida Shigeru and the Japanese Experience, 1878–1954*

85. Martin Collcutt, *Five Mountains: The Rinzai Zen Monastic Institution in Medieval Japan*

86. Kwang Suk Kim and Michael Roemer, *Growth and Structural Transformation*

87. Anne O. Krueger, *The Developmental Role of the Foreign Sector and Aid*

*88. Edwin S. Mills and Byung-Nak Song, *Urbanization and Urban Problems*

89. Sung Hwan Ban, Pal Yong Moon, and Dwight H. Perkins, *Rural Development*

*90. Noel F. McGinn, Donald R. Snodgrass, Yung Bong Kim, Shin-Bok Kim, and Quee-Young Kim, *Education and Development in Korea*

91. Leroy P. Jones and Il SaKong, *Government, Business, and Entrepreneurship in Economic Development: The Korean Case*

92. Edward S. Mason, Dwight H. Perkins, Kwang Suk Kim, David C. Cole, Mahn Je Kim et al., *The Economic and Social Modernization of the Republic of Korea*

93. Robert Repetto, Tai Hwan Kwon, Son-Ung Kim, Dae Young Kim, John E. Sloboda, and Peter J. Donaldson, *Economic Development, Population Policy, and Demographic Transition in the Republic of Korea*

94. Parks M. Coble, Jr., *The Shanghai Capitalists and the Nationalist Government, 1927–1937*

95. Noriko Kamachi, *Reform in China: Huang Tsun-hsien and the Japanese Model*

96. Richard Wich, *Sino-Soviet Crisis Politics: A Study of Political Change and Communication*

97. Lillian M. Li, *China's Silk Trade: Traditional Industry in the Modern World, 1842–1937*

98. R. David Arkush, *Fei Xiaotong and Sociology in Revolutionary China*

*99. Kenneth Alan Grossberg, *Japan's Renaissance: The Politics of the Muromachi Bakufu*

100. James Reeve Pusey, *China and Charles Darwin*

101. Hoyt Cleveland Tillman, *Utilitarian Confucianism: Chen Liang's Challenge to Chu Hsi*

102. Thomas A. Stanley, *Ōsugi Sakae, Anarchist in Taishō Japan: The Creativity of the Ego*

103. Jonathan K. Ocko, *Bureaucratic Reform in Provincial China: Ting Jih-ch'ang in Restoration Kiangsu, 1867–1870*

104. James Reed, *The Missionary Mind and American East Asia Policy, 1911–1915*

105. Neil L. Waters, *Japan's Local Pragmatists: The Transition from Bakumatsu to Meiji in the Kawasaki Region*

106. David C. Cole and Yung Chul Park, *Financial Development in Korea, 1945–1978*

Harvard East Asian Monographs

107. Roy Bahl, Chuk Kyo Kim, and Chong Kee Park, *Public Finances during the Korean Modernization Process*
108. William D. Wray, *Mitsubishi and the N.Y.K, 1870–1914: Business Strategy in the Japanese Shipping Industry*
109. Ralph William Huenemann, *The Dragon and the Iron Horse: The Economics of Railroads in China, 1876–1937*
110. Benjamin A. Elman, *From Philosophy to Philology: Intellectual and Social Aspects of Change in Late Imperial China*
111. Jane Kate Leonard, *Wei Yüan and China's Rediscovery of the Maritime World*
112. Luke S. K. Kwong, *A Mosaic of the Hundred Days:. Personalities, Politics, and Ideas of 1898*
113. John E. Wills, Jr., *Embassies and Illusions: Dutch and Portuguese Envoys to K'ang-hsi, 1666–1687*
114. Joshua A. Fogel, *Politics and Sinology: The Case of Naitō Konan (1866–1934)*
*115. Jeffrey C. Kinkley, ed., *After Mao: Chinese Literature and Society, 1978–1981*
116. C. Andrew Gerstle, *Circles of Fantasy: Convention in the Plays of Chikamatsu*
117. Andrew Gordon, *The Evolution of Labor Relations in Japan: Heavy Industry, 1853–1955*
*118. Daniel K. Gardner, *Chu Hsi and the "Ta Hsueh": Neo-Confucian Reflection on the Confucian Canon*
119. Christine Guth Kanda, *Shinzō: Hachiman Imagery and Its Development*
*120. Robert Borgen, *Sugawara no Michizane and the Early Heian Court*
121. Chang-tai Hung, *Going to the People: Chinese Intellectual and Folk Literature, 1918–1937*
*122. Michael A. Cusumano, *The Japanese Automobile Industry: Technology and Management at Nissan and Toyota*
123. Richard von Glahn, *The Country of Streams and Grottoes: Expansion, Settlement, and the Civilizing of the Sichuan Frontier in Song Times*
124. Steven D. Carter, *The Road to Komatsubara: A Classical Reading of the Renga Hyakuin*
125. Katherine F. Bruner, John K. Fairbank, and Richard T. Smith, *Entering China's Service: Robert Hart's Journals, 1854–1863*
126. Bob Tadashi Wakabayashi, *Anti-Foreignism and Western Learning in Early-Modern Japan: The "New Theses" of 1825*
127. Atsuko Hirai, *Individualism and Socialism: The Life and Thought of Kawai Eijirō (1891–1944)*
128. Ellen Widmer, *The Margins of Utopia: "Shui-hu hou-chuan" and the Literature of Ming Loyalism*
129. R. Kent Guy, *The Emperor's Four Treasuries: Scholars and the State in the Late Chien-lung Era*
130. Peter C. Perdue, *Exhausting the Earth: State and Peasant in Hunan, 1500–1850*
131. Susan Chan Egan, *A Latterday Confucian: Reminiscences of William Hung (1893–1980)*
132. James T. C. Liu, *China Turning Inward: Intellectual-Political Changes in the Early Twelfth Century*

Harvard East Asian Monographs

133. Paul A. Cohen, *Between Tradition and Modernity: Wang T'ao and Reform in Late Ching China*
134. Kate Wildman Nakai, *Shogunal Politics: Arai Hakuseki and the Premises of Tokugawa Rule*
135. Parks M. Coble, *Facing Japan: Chinese Politics and Japanese Imperialism, 1931–1937*
136. Jon L. Saari, *Legacies of Childhood: Growing Up Chinese in a Time of Crisis, 1890–1920*
137. Susan Downing Videen, *Tales of Heichū*
138. Heinz Morioka and Miyoko Sasaki, *Rakugo: The Popular Narrative Art of Japan*
139. Joshua A. Fogel, *Nakae Ushikichi in China: The Mourning of Spirit*
140. Alexander Barton Woodside, *Vietnam and the Chinese Model.: A Comparative Study of Vietnamese and Chinese Government in the First Half of the Nineteenth Century*
141. George Elision, *Deus Destroyed: The Image of Christianity in Early Modern Japan*
142. William D. Wray, ed., *Managing Industrial Enterprise: Cases from Japan's Prewar Experience*
143. T'ung-tsu Ch'ü, *Local Government in China under the Ching*
144. Marie Anchordoguy, *Computers, Inc.: Japan's Challenge to IBM*
145. Barbara Molony, *Technology and Investment: The Prewar Japanese Chemical Industry*
146. Mary Elizabeth Berry, *Hideyoshi*
147. Laura E. Hein, *Fueling Growth: The Energy Revolution and Economic Policy in Postwar Japan*
148. Wen-hsin Yeh, *The Alienated Academy: Culture and Politics in Republican China, 1919–1937*
149. Dru C. Gladney, *Muslim Chinese: Ethnic Nationalism in the People's Republic*
150. Merle Goldman and Paul A. Cohen, eds., *Ideas Across Cultures: Essays on Chinese Thought in Honor of Benjamin L Schwartz*
151. James Polachek, *The Inner Opium War*
152. Gail Lee Bernstein, *Japanese Marxist: A Portrait of Kawakami Hajime, 1879–1946*
153. Lloyd E. Eastman, *The Abortive Revolution: China under Nationalist Rule, 1927–1937*
154. Mark Mason, *American Multinationals and Japan: The Political Economy of Japanese Capital Controls, 1899–1980*
155. Richard J. Smith, John K. Fairbank, and Katherine F. Bruner, *Robert Hart and China's Early Modernization: His Journals, 1863–1866*
156. George J. Tanabe, Jr., *Myōe the Dreamkeeper: Fantasy and Knowledge in Kamakura Buddhism*
157. William Wayne Farris, *Heavenly Warriors: The Evolution of Japan's Military, 500–1300*
158. Yu-ming Shaw, *An American Missionary in China: John Leighton Stuart and Chinese-American Relations*
159. James B. Palais, *Politics and Policy in Traditional Korea*
160. Douglas Reynolds, *China, 1898–1912: The Xinzheng Revolution and Japan*
161. Roger Thompson, *China's Local Councils in the Age of Constitutional Reform*
162. William Johnston, *The Modern Epidemic: A History of Tuberculosis in Japan*

Harvard East Asian Monographs

163. Constantine Nomikos Vaporis, *Breaking Barriers: Travel and the State in Early Modern Japan*
164. Irmela Hijiya-Kirschnereit, *Rituals of Self-Revelation: Shishōsetsu as Literary Genre and Socio-Cultural Phenomenon*
165. James C. Baxter, *The Meiji Unification through the Lens of Ishikawa Prefecture*
166. Thomas R. H. Havens, *Architects of Affluence: The Tsutsumi Family and the Seibu-Saison Enterprises in Twentieth-Century Japan*
167. Anthony Hood Chambers, *The Secret Window: Ideal Worlds in Tanizaki's Fiction*
168. Steven J. Ericson, *The Sound of the Whistle: Railroads and the State in Meiji Japan*
169. Andrew Edmund Goble, *Kenmu: Go-Daigo's Revolution*
170. Denise Potrzeba Lett, *In Pursuit of Status: The Making of South Korea's "New" Urban Middle Class*
171. Mimi Hall Yiengpruksawan, *Hiraizumi: Buddhist Art and Regional Politics in Twelfth-Century Japan*
172. Charles Shirō Inouye, *The Similitude of Blossoms: A Critical Biography of Izumi Kyōka (1873–1939), Japanese Novelist and Playwright*
173. Aviad E. Raz, *Riding the Black Ship: Japan and Tokyo Disneyland*
174. Deborah J. Milly, *Poverty, Equality, and Growth: The Politics of Economic Need in Postwar Japan*
175. See Heng Teow, *Japan's Cultural Policy Toward China, 1918–1931: A Comparative Perspective*
176. Michael A. Fuller, *An Introduction to Literary Chinese*
177. Frederick R. Dickinson, *War and National Reinvention: Japan in the Great War, 1914–1919*
178. John Solt, *Shredding the Tapestry of Meaning: The Poetry and Poetics of Kitasono Katue (1902–1978)*
179. Edward Pratt, *Japan's Protoindustrial Elite: The Economic Foundations of the Gōnō*
180. Atsuko Sakaki, *Recontextualizing Texts: Narrative Performance in Modern Japanese Fiction*
181. Soon-Won Park, *Colonial Industrialization and Labor in Korea: The Onoda Cement Factory*
182. JaHyun Kim Haboush and Martina Deuchler, *Culture and the State in Late Chosŏn Korea*
183. John W. Chaffee, *Branches of Heaven: A History of the Imperial Clan of Sung China*
184. Gi-Wook Shin and Michael Robinson, eds., *Colonial Modernity in Korea*
185. Nam-lin Hur, *Prayer and Play in Late Tokugawa Japan: Asakusa Sensōji and Edo Society*
186. Kristin Stapleton, *Civilizing Chengdu: Chinese Urban Reform, 1895–1937*
187. Hyung Il Pai, *Constructing "Korean" Origins: A Critical Review of Archaeology, Historiography, and Racial Myth in Korean State-Formation Theories*
188. Brian D. Ruppert, *Jewel in the Ashes: Buddha Relics and Power in Early Medieval Japan*
189. Susan Daruvala, *Zhou Zuoren and an Alternative Chinese Response to Modernity*
190. James Z. Lee, *The Political Economy of a Frontier: Southwest China, 1250–1850*

Harvard East Asian Monographs

191. Kerry Smith, *A Time of Crisis: Japan, the Great Depression, and Rural Revitalization*
192. Michael Lewis, *Becoming Apart: National Power and Local Politics in Toyama, 1868–1945*
193. William C. Kirby, Man-houng Lin, James Chin Shih, and David A. Pietz, eds., *State and Economy in Republican China: A Handbook for Scholars*
194. Timothy S. George, *Minamata: Pollution and the Struggle for Democracy in Postwar Japan*
195. Billy K. L. So, *Prosperity, Region, and Institutions in Maritime China: The South Fukien Pattern, 946–1368*
196. Yoshihisa Tak Matsusaka, *The Making of Japanese Manchuria, 1904–1932*
197. Maram Epstein, *Competing Discourses: Orthodoxy, Authenticity, and Engendered Meanings in Late Imperial Chinese Fiction*
198. Curtis Milhaupt, J. Mark Ramseyer, and Michael K. Young, eds. and comps., *Japanese Law in Context: Readings in Society, the Economy, and Politics*
199. Haruo Iguchi, *Unfinished Business: Ayukawa Yoshisuke and U.S.-Japan Relations, 1937–1952*
200. Scott Pearce, Audrey Spiro, and Patricia Ebrey, *Culture and Power in the Reconstitution of the Chinese Realm, 200–600*
201. Terry Kawashima, *Writing Margins: The Textual Construction of Gender in Heian and Kamakura Japan*
202. Martin W. Huang, *Desire and Fictional Narrative in Late Imperial China*